The Hexagon of Heresy

The Hexagon of Heresy

A Historical and Theological Study of
Definitional Divine Simplicity

James D. Gifford Jr.

WIPF & STOCK · Eugene, Oregon

THE HEXAGON OF HERESY
A Historical and Theological Study of Definitional Divine Simplicity

Copyright © 2022 James D. Gifford Jr. All rights reserved. Except for brief quotations in critical publications or reviews, no part of this book may be reproduced in any manner without prior written permission from the publisher. Write: Permissions, Wipf and Stock Publishers, 199 W. 8th Ave., Suite 3, Eugene, OR 97401.

Wipf & Stock
An Imprint of Wipf and Stock Publishers
199 W. 8th Ave., Suite 3
Eugene, OR 97401

www.wipfandstock.com

PAPERBACK ISBN: 978-1-6667-5430-8
HARDCOVER ISBN: 978-1-6667-5431-5
EBOOK ISBN: 978-1-6667-5432-2

11/09/22

To Karen, Seth, Joshua, and Shelby

Contents

1 Introduction | 1
2 Pre-Nicene Christology: Ebionism, Docetism, and Origen | 14
3 The Historical Paradigm at 9:00: Arianism | 34
4 The Historical Paradigm at 3:00: Apollinarianism | 53
5 The Historical Paradigm at 7:00: Nestorianism | 72
6 The Historical Paradigm at 5:00: Monophysitism | 91
7 The Recapitulation of Christology and a Look Ahead | 117
8 Patristic Cosmology | 134
9 Cosmological Nestorianism and Monophysitism | 159
10 Cosmological Apollinarianism and Docetism | 182
11 Cosmological Arianism and Ebionism | 207
12 Concluding Thoughts | 233

Bibliography | 247
Index | 257

1

Introduction

I AM SURE THAT all of my readers have heard the old saying that something was "hidden in plain sight." That is how I feel about the book you are beginning to read. I have been a student of Christian theology for all of my adult life and a professor of it at the undergraduate and graduate levels for a decade and a half. I am going to present a rather complex argument that something has gone terribly wrong in Western theology, but I am amazed at how I missed it for so long. I hope this study will be as much of a benefit to you in your theological reflection as it has been to me.

Before I state my thesis, I want to trace out the way that most American Evangelical Protestants "do" systematic theology. Most of the best-selling systematics textbooks are laid out in the same general order that corresponds roughly to a chronological understanding of the events of the history of the cosmos. They begin with a prolegomena which sets forth the rules of engagement and methodology that they will use. Following closely is the study of revelation, both natural and special. Then comes the study of theology proper, or the doctrine of God. Most follow the Thomistic pattern of studying the attributes of the one God before moving to the examination of the Trinity.[1] Then comes the works of God in creation and providence, corresponding to the opening

---

1. It may be instructive to note that the general trend in Western methodology in theology proper since the time of Aquinas has begun with the essence and attributes of God before moving to a detailed examination of person. Virtually any systematic theology that falls within the self-identified bounds of "Protestant Evangelical" deals with the Trinity last, the one great exception being Barth, *Church Dogmatics*. A simple survey of Western evangelical treatments of the doctrine of God all yield the same result. Hodge, *Systematic Theology*, begins his discussion on the knowledge of God on page 1:191. Only in 1:442–82 does he discuss the Trinity. Berkhof, *Systematic Theology*, spends sixty-three pages on the existence and attributes of God, followed by eighteen pages on the Trinity. More recently, Frame, *Doctrine of God*, spends four pages early in the book discussing the personality of God, but then waits until page 619 to begin examining the Trinity, e.g., what personality means. Similarly, Feinberg, *No One Like Him*, spends five chapters on the existence and attributes of God before his chapter on the Trinity.

chapter of Genesis. Close on the heels of the works of God are anthropology and sin, which usually winds up the first semester of a year-long course in systematic theology.

The second semester dives into a study of the person and work of Christ, then to the doctrine of the Holy Spirit, then to salvation, the church, and last but not least, eschatology. The survey of these doctrines concludes the second semester of a year's work in systematics. With the prolegomena, revelation, and theology proper acting as a sort of a prologue, the rest of the *loci* (the subdivisions of systematic theology discussed above) follow a fairly straightforward chronological order. Creation of the cosmos comes first, followed by the creation of humans, then the fall into sin, then Jesus, then the Spirit, who work together to bring salvation in the creation of the church. It all winds up with last things, making a nice, neat, arm-in-arm walk through time and doctrine simultaneously. Each of the *loci* builds on what came before in the system as the cosmos chronologically unfolds.

I would submit—the thing hidden in plain sight—that such an approach for constructing Christian doctrine is, well, not explicitly *Christian*. That is, Jesus is not the beginning, middle, and end of it all within that structure. While there is a definite sequence of historical events in Scripture, this chronological layout is not a closed system. Even though Jesus finally appears near the end of the biblical chronology, he is no afterthought. Quite the contrary, the opening remarks of John, Ephesians, Colossians, and Hebrews actually identify him as the beginning of the story, rather than a character at the end of it. Because Jesus is the eternal Son in human flesh, "very God of very God and very man of very man," as the ancient creeds say, and because Jesus is the one man in whom the Father is well pleased, the study of any Christian doctrine that involves the interaction between God and creation/humanity must begin with the true union of God and man in Jesus Christ. In other words, a truly Christian understanding of the doctrines that concern how God is involved in the affairs of his creation must be inherently christological, which raises an issue because many of the theological *loci* that involve this God-creation interaction, namely the doctrines of revelation and cosmology (including creation, providence and theological anthropology), very rarely begin from a christological standpoint.[2] In traditional systematics, those doctrines chronologically and methodologically precede Christology, and therefore in such an approach are not dependent directly upon Jesus for a full understanding. Instead, they rely upon a form of natural theology for their foundation, a natural theology I hope to show is fraught with historical problems.[3] That Jesus should be the first word in the formation of the doctrines of revelation, cosmology, anthropology, and the God-human balance in salvation, but has not been the case in

---

2. A refreshing counterexample to the trend is Fairbairn, *Life in the Trinity*. Thanks to my friend Glenn Butner for this reminder.

3. That we "do" systematic theology in such an order is due to the immense shadow cast by Augustine of Hippo and his most brilliant disciple, Thomas Aquinas. Why this is the case will become apparent later.

Introduction

Protestant Evangelical thought, has been hidden in plain sight. My proposal here is to not only show *that* it is hidden, but also *why* it is hidden.

The *Ordo Theologiae*

By the third century, Christian thinkers felt more comfortable in explaining Christian reality at least loosely within the bounds of prevailing Greek metaphysics. One of the methodological issues at work throughout the first six chapters of this book is how we approach the metaphysical categories of person and nature. In the coming pages, I will contend, along with John of Damascus, that all of the great christological heresies confuse person and nature. To begin, a simple question describing person is "Who is it?" Similarly, the question describing nature is "What is it?" Even though these seem like two rather different questions to us, they wound up being confused in the first few centuries of Christianity, and afterward as well. This is in no small part due to the utterly impersonal "nature" of the various Hellenistic conceptions of "God." Both Platonism's Good and One, as well as Aristotle's Prime Mover, were fully impersonal, unlike the Yahweh of Judaism and Christianity. The clarification of the church's understanding of the categories of person and nature will be traced through the controversies discussed in the next five chapters.

One of the first arguments for the priority of person in the *ordo theologiae*[4] is the biblical witness. Encounters with God in the Old Testament or with Jesus in the New are not encounters with an essence but with a person. Here one may only recall the experiences of Moses in the Old Testament, Paul on the road to Damascus, or a host of other examples to see that God is personal. The one who met Paul did not refer to himself as the second personal instantiation of the one divine essence, but rather personally as Jesus. We do not know God as a nature, but as person. Similarly, in the life of faith, we do not encounter the Holy Spirit as an "it," but as someone. Jesus does not speak of God as an essence, but as a person—either in the person of the Father or in the person of the Spirit. Jesus did not come to reveal the essence of God but the person of the Father, while in turn the Spirit reveals the person of the Son. In the entirety of the biblical witness, God (Father, Son, or Holy Spirit) is not primarily some*thing*, but some*one*.

In the divine names revealed in the Old Testament, we see the name revealed to Moses at the burning bush, "Yahweh," or "I am who I am." The "I" indicates person.

---

4. Farrell, *Mystagogy*, 30. This is the earliest instance I can find of Farrell's use of the term he claims to have invented. He means by the term the order in which we encounter and reflect upon the "three primordial categories" of essence (nature), energy (work and attributes), and person (Father, Son, and Holy Spirit) of God. In Farrell, *God, History, and Dialectic*, he claims that most of the orthodox fathers utilized the *ordo theologiae* that began with person, moved to energy, and thence to nature. He defines the term thus: "The method by which the fathers thought through their theological problems, utilized three categories in a certain order: (1) Persons or hypostases, answering the question 'Who is doing it?' (2) Energies, answering the question 'What is it that they are doing?' (3) Essence or nature, answering the question 'What are they that they are doing these things?'"

In the compound divine names that bear Yahweh, Yahweh comes first, showing first who God is (Yahweh) and second what he is doing (providing, as in Yahweh-Jireh, shepherding as is Yahweh-Rohi, and so on).[5] The very revelation of God puts the first priority on person, and then secondarily on energy or attribute.[6] Similarly, in the "I am" statements of Jesus in the New Testament, we see the same pattern repeated. The energy (what Jesus is doing) follows who he is (the person). For instance, we see "I am the way, the truth, and the life" or "I am the good shepherd"[7] as examples of energy (attribute) following person. Jesus, as God, is the "I am" (*ego eimi*) of Yahweh, followed by the work he is doing in creation. "*Who* do you say that I am?" is the great question of faith posed to Peter.

It is only when we see the plurality of divine persons, with the linchpin being the person of Jesus Christ, who distinguishes himself from the Father but can be no less than God himself, that we then move to the discussion of the divine essence. The whole Trinitarian controversy turned on how Jesus can be God yet distinct from the Father. The essence of God comes into play in theological reflection once we see the persons (Father, Son, and Spirit, in this case) all doing the works of God.[8] The essence then addresses the unity of God with a plurality of persons and comes last in such a methodology of inquiry.

If, on the other hand, we think of God as first an essence (a "what"), we devalue the person (the "who") by subordinating the *he* to the *it*, effectively depersonalizing God himself. This is contrary to ordinary Christian experience, for our communion with God is something that is "personal," that is, person-to-person, rather than the communing of our human nature with his divine nature. As human beings are created in the image of this personal God, it is in the world of the personal that we are like God. As he is personal, so are we. The God we encounter in the pages of Scripture, as well as in history, tradition, and our own experience is personal. He is *someone*, first and foremost, which is why any *ordo theologiae* which does not follow person, moving to energy, thence to nature can run afoul of the biblical witness. As the rest of the book will show, inverting this order has serious theological implications.

The Hellenistic *Ordo* and Definitional Divine Simplicity

Several centuries before Christ, Greek philosophers were busy deconstructing the traditional pantheon of Greek gods, believing that they were far too human in their behavior to be worthy of the title "deity."[9] This philosophical process was dialectical in

---

5. Gen 22:14 and Ps 23:1, respectively. For more on the development of the concept of energy, see Bradshaw, "Divine Energies," 93–120.

6. In the next section, I will show why the term "attribute" is itself problematic.

7. John 14:6 and 10:30, respectively.

8. This is the line of reasoning used by Gregory of Nyssa in *To Ablabius*, for example.

9. See Farrell, *Free Choice*. Chapters 2 and 3 are most helpful here. The next few paragraphs follow

Introduction

nature (meaning any distinction between two things entailed their opposition[10]), as they defined the essence of their one "true" deity to be the negation of the observable cosmos, including all of the motion, collision, and multiplicity of the world of the senses. The "god" that results in such a construction is without any sort of change or composition—the two hallmarks of the world of matter. Such a state would be the highest possible good.[11] The "Good" or "One," as this deity was called by philosophers such as Plato and Plotinus, respectively, is uniquely good and utterly simple (without any possibility of composition or decomposition), whereas the cosmos (the "many") is relatively "less good" and composed in different ways. This de-construction is what will be called definitional divine simplicity, that is, the essence of the deity is dialectically defined to be without the possibility of any composition as opposed to the cosmos which is never without it.

Two immediate results obtain from such an exercise in natural theology. First, knowledge of things in the cosmos comes from our ability to see differences. In the observable world, we name ("attribute," accent on the middle syllable) the things that make one object distinct from another, and it is the fact that all things we see are composed that make them distinct. In the "Good-One," there is no differentiation whatsoever by definition; there is only the "Good-One" itself. It can have no distinct, discernible properties or predications, because that would indicate some form of differentiation, which is impossible by definition. Since there is only the "Good-One," any distinction in it would be opposition and therefore composition. It is above and beyond all distinctions and predications. The "Good-One," therefore, can be defined as the absence of all these specifics (definitional simplicity), or rather, and more importantly for our purposes, the identification of all possible specifics. In the "Good-One," to be is to will is to do.[12] This identification of everything that can be said about the "Good-One" is called the identity thesis, where essence equals will equals action equals "attribute" (accent on the first syllable).[13] Though we see distinctions among these categories in the observable world, in the "Good-One" they are all absolutely identical, thus all we can do is attribute the attributes to it.

The reason these distinctions are only "conceptual" (to borrow medieval language, that is, only distinctive from our vantage point as creatures) rather than "real" (really and truly existing distinctions in the One itself) in the thought of Plotinus is due to his employment of the methodology of dialectic in stating what can be known.

---

his line of reasoning.

10. Farrell, *Free Choice*, 40–41. Farrell, on page 41n16, notes that Plotinus himself states that distinction is opposition.

11. Bussanich, "Plotinus's Metaphysics," 42, writes, "The One must be simple because it is perfect, and being perfect it must be independent from all things, with all things dependent on it."

12. See Bussanich, "Plotinus's Metaphysics," 48, as well as many texts in Plotinus, *Enn.* 6.8.

13. For the technical term, "identity thesis," I am indebted to Radde-Gallwitz, *Transformation of Divine Simplicity*, 5. The identity thesis, where every attribute is identical to the essence and every other attribute, is also called polyonomous simplicity.

In Plotinus's dialectical process, distinction is opposition. Since the simple One cannot admit of any opposition within itself, dialectically there can be no real distinction either. Farrell notes that the One is "absolutely being, will, and activity because there can be nothing lacking, or external to it. Because the One is absolutely one, being, will, and activity are absolutely the same thing. There is a sense, then, in which being, activity, and will are names [that is, merely attributes] for that one something which cannot be named and in which those distinctions are no longer distinct, but identical to each other."[14] Plotinus regards this identity thesis to be a mark of perfection. Therefore, the One is both absolute unity of, and transcendent of, all observable categories, all the while being defined in terms of (that is, the negation of) those very same categories.[15] The One can finally be known by the categories of created being; after all, the "nothing" is still a thing.[16]

Second is the ambiguity built into the construction. The One may only be known by setting it in dialectical opposition to the "many" in the first place. Since the One is simple, and good is therefore one and simple, the many who are not-simple are not-good. Thus, a moral dialectic immediately obtains between the "Good-One" and the many; they are necessarily opposed. If being and will are truly identical, then the One cannot do other than what it does. That is, what the One does and all acts external to the One are just instances of "nature naturing" (*natura naturans*), or "what is natural is compelled."[17] And according to Plotinus, the One must produce other things.[18] Thus the production (via emanation) of all things which are not the One (the many) is a necessary act of the One—an act that could not be otherwise, because the One is what it does what it wills. Moreover, the One is by definition everything that the many are not, that is, it stands over against the very things that emanate from it. The observable world of the many is simultaneously the co-eternal and necessary result of the being-will-activity of the One, and is everything the One is not. The One necessarily produces everything that is not itself, to both stand in opposition to it and to be its ultimate source.[19] The One and the many, therefore, are both diametrically opposed and eternally co-dependent simultaneously.

From a "top-down" perspective, the One and many can never exist apart from one another because the One must produce the many (after all, the One *must* produce)

---

14. Radde-Gallwitz, *Transformation of Divine Simplicity*, 44.

15. See Bussanich, "Plotinus's Metaphysics," 50.

16. This "unknown god" Paul identified with the Father on Mars Hill (Acts 17:22–31), noting that the Greeks "ignorantly" worshiped him.

17. See the discussion in Farrell, *Free Choice*, 82–83. See also Bussanich, "Plotinus's Metaphysics," 50, who maintains that although Plotinus wishes to preserve the freedom of the One in *what* to produce, the fact that it *must* produce remains.

18. Because other things exist, they must exist. The One must do what it does, and it does what it must do—*natura naturans*.

19. Plotinus, *Enn.* 5.2.2, as quoted in Bussanich, "Plotinus's Metaphysics," 50, says it best himself, "All these things are the One and not the One."

Introduction

via emanation necessarily; and therefore, the One determines the many. In this way, everything—including both the One and the many—is a monist system with one real principle—the One, which produces and determines everything else. On the other hand, from a "bottom-up" point of view, the One and many are dialectically opposed, because the One is everything the many is not, so there is a dichotomist-dualist system with two poles (the One and the many) in place alongside the monism within Neoplatonism. I will call this simultaneous monism and dichotomist-dualism the "Plotinian ambiguity," because it is inherent in any theological or philosophical system that utilizes simplicity as the definition for the One (or, in Christian theology, the divine essence, or the Godhead, or the Father, as the case may be). Therefore, there are two key corollaries of divine simplicity: the identity thesis where to be is to will is to do, and the Plotinian ambiguity, where all that exists is simultaneously monist and dichotomist-dualist; and these two frameworks stand in dialectical opposition to each other. An immediate result of the Plotinian ambiguity, since both the One and the many (due to the process of emanation) are on the same "ontological plane," that is, co-eternal with and co-dependent upon one another, is the presence of a zero-sum game between the One and many.[20] Every emphasis of the One is the suppression of the many, and vice-versa. As the following chapters will show, wherever and whenever definitional simplicity occurs, there will always be the tension between a monistic confusion of God and the world and a dichotomist-dualist separation of them. Just as in Plotinus, thinkers under the sway of definitional simplicity exhibit the same tensions. Plenty of examples exist in the pages to follow.

Therefore the Platonic doctrine of definitional divine simplicity can be "defined" to be understanding the divine essence first and foremost as the absence of all specifics, which automatically entails first the identification of all specifics with the each other and with the essence itself (the identity thesis) and second the co-dependence between the simple One and the many it must produce, the latter of which finds both its source and opposition in the One (the Plotinian ambiguity). I will contend that the model for the Christian doctrine of God that both Origen and Augustine introduced into the faith is a modification of the very model of definitional simplicity as discussed immediately above,[21] a model in which the *ordo theologiae* cannot help be inverted.[22]

---

20. A zero-sum game is one in which the players compete for the same resources. Every gain by one player is necessarily offset by the losses of another, so that the net gain/loss is always zero. One player's gain must necessitate another player's loss in equivalent amounts.

21. The synthesis of Platonism and Christianity attempted by both Origen and Augustine is well documented. See Farrell, *Mystagogy*, 25 and 34 for a summary. Here I follow Farrell in using the term "definitional" simplicity, meaning that God's essence is defined as simple. Definitional simplicity is a theological axiom for Origen and Augustine, as they define the essence to be simple. Other Patristic writers use the term "simplicity" as a term of description, but here I am focusing on the definitional aspect.

22. Under definitional simplicity, the *ordo theologiae* begins with essence. As this occurs, we automatically begin with "What is it?" instead of "Who is he?" Any real personification, methodologically, at least, therefore must take a back seat to God as the simple, objective "other. Farrell, *God, History,*

The Hexagon of Heresy

When the pagan, definitionally-simple One becomes "Christianized," the first immediate implication is christological. Jesus cannot be one with both the Father and creation because they are diametrically opposed within the construct of definitional simplicity, so he must be oriented toward either God or humanity primarily. Other problems follow, as Joseph Farrell writes:

> In the "Christian" concept of such simplicity, essence, operation, and will "become merely different names for the same thing. What it is (its essence, or *ousia*), what it does (its operation, or *energeia*) and what it wills (its will, or *thelema*) are all absolutely identical. Thus if one functions with a Neoplatonic conception of simplicity within a Christian theological system, at some point, that system will evidence a breakdown which issues in the reduction of the various names of God to absolute identity. *Language itself becomes totally devalued, since all such names mean every other name.* In this case, "essence", "will", and "operation" are merely names which *we* attribute to the One, but they do not indicate any distinctions within it which really exist and which are not, therefore, the same.[23]

In the above quote, we see the identity thesis at work, as every divine attribute or action is really the same thing as God himself without any kind of real distinction. This confusion of person, nature, and operation had both immediate and far-reaching consequences in both Christology and cosmology.

The Purpose of This Book

What I first propose to do in this book is to briefly survey the six great christological heresies from a doctrinal and historical perspective, constructing what I will call the Hexagon of Heresy, a process of boundary-marking that delineates christological models that fall short of orthodoxy as "out of bounds." The next five chapters will be individual snapshots of the deviant Christologies. We will examine Ebionism, Docetism, and Origen (chapter 2), "Arianism"[24] (Chapter 3), Apollinarianism (Chapter 4), Nestorianism (Chapter 5), and Monophysitism and its aftermath (Chapter 6). Due to space constraints, these surveys will be brief, touching only the high points. In these chapters, I will argue that the four latter heresies are the immediate christological

---

and Dialectic, chapter 3, argues why the object must be the "other." It is the problem of the one and the many in Hellenism and beyond.

23. Farrell, *God, History, and Dialectic*, 105 (emphasis original). Since language is devalued, the divine names and operations become "attributes," or mere name-assignments.

24. I will make my disclaimer here at my first reference to "Arianism." I am aware that the word "Arianism" is no longer a universally acceptable name for the movement of the fourth century. Williams, *Arius*, 247–48, provides a good brief summary of why this is the case. However, I will retain use of it, if only because I wish to extend its use beyond its historical foundations, and describing those uses in language referring to Nicaea seems to me more distracting than using the now-archaic word "Arianism."

conclusions of the attempt to map definitional simplicity onto the divine essence. The diametrical opposition of God and the world entailed that Christ must be either primarily divine or primarily human. Therefore, those christological heresies cast their lot with only one reality, or "nature" in Jesus (either a creature, in dichotomist-dualist fashion, or God in a monist one).

Once the sub-thesis of this book (that is, definitional simplicity is the root cause of the christological controversies) has been demonstrated in the first six chapters, the remaining chapters argue the larger thesis, which is this: each of the historical heresies discussed in chapters 2–6 are but christological subsets of larger cosmological models that arise from definitional simplicity as a first principle, such that it is proper to extend those heresies into their cosmological counterparts.[25] That is, the heresies christologically reveal the God-world deficiencies inherent in those cosmological models, and it was the christological shortcomings that were first met with resistance in late antiquity. The challenge lying before us is to expand our historical thinking. We have traditionally identified the christological heresies as producing a deficient view of Christ (which they obviously do). The larger cosmological implications of definitional simplicity—the first principle of the deficient cosmological models that produced the christological heresies—were ignored in the Latin West, which has been under the sway of that same first principle without interruption since the days of Augustine.[26] To argue this thesis, I will first demonstrate the existence of a corresponding view of cosmology for each of the six historic christological heresies, and second that lurking behind this view of God and the world is the concept of definitional simplicity and its attendant identity thesis and Plotinian ambiguity. Sometimes, deficient cosmologies are paired alongside the corresponding heretical Christology; sometimes not.

Therefore, the christological controversies themselves were a subset of a larger issue, one that crystallized in the person of Jesus: how does the creator relate to the creature? In my opinion, the Nicene and Chalcedonian fathers, even up to the time of Maximus the Confessor in the seventh century, answered the christological question decisively and in the best way possible. What has not yet occurred, however, is to apply this Chalcedonian christological logic to the larger question of the relationship God has to the rest of creation. The Christian West inherited from its pagan past two general models—precisely those originating in the Plotinian ambiguity—of how this question was to be answered. There was the monist model that emphasized the emanation of creation from the One/Good/Prime Mover, and therefore tended to merge the deity and the observable world while seeing the difference between them as quantitative rather than qualitative (both God and the world are subsumed under

25. Tollefsen, *Christocentric Cosmology*, 67, states that "The divine economy, according to Maximus [the Confessor], is expressed and fulfilled by a threefold presence of the Logos: in the cosmos, in Scripture, and in the historical person of Jesus Christ. See also Maximus, *Ambigua* 33.

26. As I will argue in upcoming chapters, Origen first introduced definitional simplicity into the tradition which in turn spawned the christological controversies. Augustine's adoption of the same kind of definitional simplicity would have its greatest impact cosmologically.

the category of being). This results in the emphasis of the one over the many. The dichotomist-dualist model emphasized the opposition of the divine and the material, based on the principle of distinction as opposition, resulting in the emphasis of the many over the one. The Chalcedonian fathers had to reject these models and forge a third way that upheld both the transcendence of God and the real integrity of his creation. It seems to me that the fathers intuitively realized that the pagan definitional divine simplicity, with its attendant identity thesis and Plotinian ambiguity, was the catalyst behind both the monist and dichotomist-dualist models. To create this third way, this type of simplicity had to be rejected for a divine complexity that did not entail any form of composition. They were able to effectively accomplish such a task by the end of the Third Council of Constantinople late in the seventh century.

However, in the West, the same simplicity that was in the process of being defeated christologically was re-enthroned in the teaching of Augustine. As the social, political, and theological factors drove the West and East apart, Augustinism became the lens through which the Christian faith was viewed in the Latin-speaking West. To effectively apply the christological insights gained in the first six councils to the larger question of cosmology, the same definitional simplicity needs to be identified and rejected, whenever possible. To identify is fairly straightforward; to reject is a whole other matter.

Chapter 7 serves as a bridge between the first six chapters and what follows. After briefly discussing the Chalcedonian logic developed through the first six chapters, the chapter moves to a discussion of Augustine's doctrine of divine simplicity as stated in *On the Trinity* and how it affected his medieval disciples.[27] The chapter concludes with a discussion of Thomas Aquinas and William of Ockham, and the devastating effects of nominalism upon the psyche of Europe, though no cardinal teaching ever deviates from the game plan of definitional simplicity.

Chapter 8 discusses the development in cosmological reflection in the East, culminating in Maximus the Confessor. I survey Maximus's unique and, in my opinion, brilliant contribution to synthesize his received tradition in cosmology, utilizing his now-familiar "Chalcedonian logic." I also discuss the cosmology of Augustine, noting that his commitment to definitional simplicity allows him to separate creator and creation to avoid Origen's mistake of identifying Christ and creation on one hand, while on the other he identifies God and creation in the lives of the unconditionally elect. This is both a cosmological Nestorianism and Monophysitism (Monoenergism) simultaneously working in his thought, which sow the seeds for what I discuss in the later chapters.

---

27. Though Augustine was challenged throughout his career on multiple issues, he was able to either overcome the challenges or obfuscate the issues enough so that his ideas triumphed in time. Because Augustine was uniquely situated in multiple ways in Latin theology (the last and most influential of the Western Fathers; the extent and scope of his literary output; and his temporal situation where East and West began to divide in language, culture, and government; and so on), there was no Latin thinker who confounded him for over a thousand years.

Introduction

Chapter 9 is a continuation of how the medieval world attempted to balance the simultaneous separation and confusion of God and the world as introduced by Augustine. In this chapter, I discuss the growing separation between science and religion throughout the Medieval period, as well as the confusion of God in the world in the thought of the growing emphasis of divine predestination of occurrences in time.

Chapter 10 addresses the fallout from a fully mature cosmological Monophysitism and Monoenergism, which is the partial (cosmological Apollinarianism) and full (cosmological Docetism) denial of created integrity. Cosmological Apollinarians, exemplified by the wide swath of theological determinists from the fourteenth century onwards, give with one hand that creation has integrity in being not-God (through secondary causation), but take it back with the other in insisting that God ordains and renders certain all that occurs in creation through a single decree that is identical with God himself. Cosmological Docetists take it all one step further in their occasionalism and remove any possibility of secondary causation, effectively ending in the identification of God and the world from the side of God that we call panentheism.

Chapter 11 discusses cosmological Arianism (the partial denial of God in the world) and cosmological Ebionism (the full denial thereof). The cosmological Arians were the philosophers and physicists who insisted that God only interacts with the world through natural laws and that any other interaction, though theoretically possible, was either incredibly rare or nonexistent. The cosmological Ebionites took the prevailing cosmological Arianism to its logical conclusion and first identified God and the world from the side of creation (pantheism, as in Spinoza), and later rejected the idea of God altogether (the materialistic atheists). Finally, Chapter 12 is a summary of the argument and a brief analysis of its historical and theological implications.

I think it is instructive to note that in Christ, who is the person of the eternal Son, the christological heresies chronologically move from the more egregious (Ebionism and Docetism) to the subtler (Nestorianism and Monophysitism). The cosmological views, on the other hand, chronologically begin with the subtle in Augustine (the rational principles and the will of God) and move to the egregious (pantheism, panentheism, and atheism) in modernity. This will become clearer in the overall layout of chapters 8 through 11.

The Hexagon of Heresy

I have used the term "Hexagon of Heresy" for several years in my theology classes to designate the six great christological heresies. If the hexagon can be described thus, think of a clock. The hexagon will have its six flat sides at one, three, five, seven, nine, and eleven o'clock. These sides symbolize Ebionism (11:00), Docetism (1:00), Arianism (9:00), Apollinarianism (3:00), Nestorianism (7:00), and Monophysitism (5:00). I coined the term Hexagon of Heresy myself, or at least I think I did. If anyone else used it before me, I am unaware of it.

The Hexagon of Heresy

The Hexagon of Heresy comes in handy for two reasons. First, it is an easy way for my students to remember the six great christological heresies. Second, and more importantly for our study here, the sides of the Hexagon of Heresy form the boundaries of christological orthodoxy. Crossing the line over to Arianism, for example, is christologically out-of-bounds. The orthodox view of Jesus, if it can be reduced to a two-dimensional figure for illustrative purposes, lies inside the hexagon. Because the God-man is a profound mystery, we cannot say with precision exactly what the hypostatic union is. We can, however, confidently state what it is not. It is not Ebionite, Docetist, and so on.

The arrangement of the actual heresies in the Hexagon of Heresy is useful as well. The left half of the hexagon represents the three historical heresies that directly attack Jesus's divinity (because of their dichotomist-dualist orientation) while the right half represents the three that attack his humanity (due to their monism). The top of the hexagon represents the great historical heresies of omission, Ebionism and Docetism. These are the historical heresies that omit completely one of the natures of Jesus. Ebionism omits his divinity while Docetism omits his humanity. Moreover, the two heresies in the middle of the hexagon are the historical heresies of sufficiency, that is, they represent an insufficient view of Jesus's divinity ("Arianism") and humanity (Apollinarianism). The final two heresies, located at the bottom of the hexagon, are the historical heresies of emphasis, putting too little emphasis on either the divinity (Nestorianism) or the humanity (Monophysitism) of Christ. I think classifying the historical heresies into those of omission, sufficiency, or emphasis, will help us as we move past the historical heresies and into christologically-insufficient views of other doctrines, a large, medium, and small, respectively, variety of either dichotomist-dualism or monism.

I feel that it is important to say a few words about the ecumenical councils. Eastern Orthodoxy, Roman Catholicism, and some Anglicans see the seven ecumenical councils as authoritative and binding, adding to the growing body of tradition of the church. Most Protestants, on the other hand, accept the conclusions of at least the first four councils as long as they, in the view of Protestants, coincide with the spirit of Scripture. Christologically speaking, the findings of the councils find little objection with Protestants. That is, there are no expressly Arian, Apollinarian, Nestorian, or Monophysite bodies of Protestants who are not roundly condemned by the vast majority of other Protestants. There is less agreement on the pronouncements on Christology of the fifth and sixth councils from a Protestant standpoint, as some Protestants accept the Monothelitism (the belief that Jesus possesses only one will) that the sixth council condemns.[28]

---

28. See Wessling, "Christology and Conciliar Authority," 151–70. More will be said concerning the sixth council in chapter 6.

Introduction

I have no desire to argue the merits or lack thereof of definitional simplicity from a philosophical point of view. There are many much better equipped to do so than I.[29] Rather I seek to provide a broad historical analysis showing how definitional simplicity has been employed theologically in the history of the church. Some doctrines look good "on paper" but not so much in practice. I think that definitional simplicity, while impressive in theory from a philosophical point of view, results in disaster on the ground as it is lived out through the centuries.

I truly hope that you will enjoy this book. It presents some conclusions that may be controversial. So be it. If we do not think christologically about everything we believe, we should not call ourselves Christians. May Jesus as the incarnate God be at the center of all we say, do, and think. Now, let us move on to the christological heresies of Ebionism and Docetism.

---

29. Probably the best recent work on definitional simplicity is Dolezal, *God without Parts*.

2

Pre-Nicene Christology
Ebionism, Docetism, and Origen

THIS CHAPTER WILL DISCUSS the "top" of the Hexagon, as well as pre-Nicene christological development. At the eleven o'clock position, we have Ebionism (sometimes called Ebionitism)[1] and at the one o'clock position, there is Docetism. Each of these heresies I have classified to be heresies of omission, as each omits a crucial nature of Christ. Ebionism has historically been associated with the denial of the divine in Jesus, while Docetism denies the human. These seemingly-opposite heresies form the paradigms through which all of the later christological heresies may be appropriated. The heresies in the left half of the hexagon deny or diminish the fullness of the divinity of Christ, while those in the right half deny or diminish his humanity. We will begin this chapter with a brief discussion of Ebionism, then proceed to Docetism. After the discussions of those two systems are complete, we will take a closer look at the Christology of the first three centuries of church history in anticipation of the christological controversies that follow.

Ebionism

Ebionism began to flourish in the first days of Christianity. It was a sect dominated by Jews and there seems to be a connection between the Ebionites and the Essenes near the Dead Sea.[2] While the origin of the term "Ebionite" is somewhat obscure, scholarly opinion seems to lean toward a Hebrew derivation meaning "the poor," symbolizing

---

1. I will remain consistent in calling it "Ebionism."
2. See Gonzalez, *From the Beginnings*, 123–25. Here he summarizes the argument of Danielou, *Theology of Jewish Christianity*, 55–64. The important similarities between Essenian Judaism and Ebionism were the rejection of animal sacrifices and a metaphysical dualism which held to the existence of both a good and an evil principle that both come from God.

the original title for the Jerusalem Christians.³ Most of what we know of Ebionism comes from those in the early church who wrote against them, including Irenaeus, who is the first person to mention them by name.⁴ Irenaeus writes that the Ebionites used only the Gospel of Matthew, repudiated Paul as apostate, lived as devout Jews, and "adored Jerusalem as if it were the house of God."⁵ The other Ebionite writings still extant include the translation of the Old Testament by the Ebionite Symmachus and a portion of the pseudo-Clementine literature called "The Preaching of Peter."⁶

The core of Ebionite Christology is the denial of the inherent divinity of Jesus in any form, as well as any notion of pre-existence.⁷ To the Ebionites, Jesus was the greatest of the prophets but not the Son of God. The Ebionites denied the Virgin Birth and believed that Jesus received the power to fulfill his mission at his baptism.⁸ According to Irenaeus, at Jesus's baptism, the Ebionites believed a spirit named Christ descended onto the man Jesus and gave him knowledge of the unknown Father. The spirit flew away before his crucifixion.⁹ Thus Jesus himself was only a man who was possessed by the Christ-spirit for a time. In this way, the Ebionites are the best known representative of the adoptionist family of Christologies—those that believe that God "adopted" Jesus as his son at some point during his earthly life, but that there is no divinity intrinsic to Jesus whatsoever.¹⁰ There is also evidence of a "possession" Christology in the Ebionites, as they believed the "Christ" was a spirit who possessed the man Jesus.¹¹ For the Ebionites, the mission of Jesus was to call humanity to obedience of the Torah rather than save them. They regarded salvation as something entirely beyond the capability of a mere human.¹² They fully accepted the idea that Jesus fulfilled the

---

3. Kelly, *Early Christian Doctrines*, 139. For the differing opinions as to the source of their name, see Grillmeier, *From the Apostolic Age*, 76.

4. Justin Martyr, in his *Dialog with Trypho*, is certainly arguing against tendencies which were shared with the Ebionites, if not against Ebiontes themselves. A relevant portion of the *Dialog* can be seen in Hultgren and Haggmark, *Earliest Christian Heretics*, 117–18.

5. Irenaeus, *Haer.* 1.26.1 (in *ANF* 1:352).

6. According to Grillmeier, *From the Apostolic Age*, 76, there is scholarly debate concerning the legitimacy of Ebionite origin of "The Preaching of Peter" as well. It seems as though hard evidence for the origin of the name and actual works they produced have nearly faded from ecclesiastical recollection.

7. McCready, *He Came Down from Heaven*, 28–29.

8. Gonzalez, *From the Beginnings*, 124.

9. Irenaeus, *Haer.* 1.26.1 (*ANF* 1:352), as noted in Häkkinen, "Ebionites," 266.

10. Grillmeier, *From the Apostolic Age*, 77, notes that what the Ebionites would have meant by "adoption" would be that the "Gnostic idea of the union of a heavenly being with the man Jesus, resulting in the Christ, the Son of God."

11. Häkkinen, "Ebionites," 268. Papandrea, *Earliest Christologies*, 23–43, calls the two types of adoptionism "Spirit Adoptionism" and "Angel Adoptionism." The former rejects the virgin birth, while the latter affirms it. The former, the type mainly discussed in this chapter, sees Jesus as an anointed teacher, while the latter, the "possession" kind, sees Jesus as being possessed by a created spiritual being called "Christ." Papandrea's chart on page 129, provides an excellent summary.

12. Gonzalez, *From the Beginnings*, 124. Gonzalez notes here that the Ebionites did not believe

law, but by fulfillment they mean that he is the example that all are to follow in keeping the law.[13]

Gonzalez summarizes the seriousness of the challenge of Ebionism as follows:

> Ebionism was never a very widespread doctrine, and it seems to have disappeared as the church became more and more Gentile and less Jewish. This does not mean, however, that it did not present a challenge to the church of the early centuries. On the contrary, what was at stake here was the uniqueness of Jesus Christ, over against the possibility of adapting him in such a way that he could be juxtaposed to the ancient Jewish religion. When this was done, Jesus was no longer unique and central. He was no longer the only begotten Son of God, but a mere prophet within the sequence of prophets. He was no longer the Savior, but simply an element—sometimes secondary—of the action of God within this age.[14]

The great danger of Ebionism is its refusal to assert the divinity, and therefore the central uniqueness, of Jesus. Alister McGrath notes that Ebionism arose within the Jewish framework for understanding the relationship between God and the world. He writes, "Jesus was thus to be understood as analogous to the great prophets of Israel—human beings who were in some way given special insight or wisdom through the Holy Spirit. The suggestion that Jesus of Nazareth *was* himself divine does not really enter into the consideration, given the Jewish context into which Ebionitism [sic] arose."[15] The Ebionites were therefore correct in their assertion that a mere man cannot save, and incorrect in their assertion of Jesus as merely a man. Also, as Millard Erickson states, they believe the mission of Jesus was educational (showing us the proper way to live) rather than redemptive (saving humanity).[16] David Wilhite shows that Ebionism's "low Christology" entailed two unacceptable conclusions for early Christians. First, "If Jesus became God's son by keeping the law, then none of us can be saved because we cannot fully keep the law"; and "If Jesus is not truly divine, then our salvation is only *from sin* and not *to God*."[17] Given this analysis, it is easy to see why Ebionism needed to be rejected.

Further, it appears that Ebionism itself was not a monolithic movement, but rather a series of movements with the core tendencies of the denial of the divinity of Jesus, the necessity of keeping the law, and the rejection of animal sacrifices. Gonzalez lists

---

that the entire Torah originated with God. They believed that an evil principle added the commandments of animal sacrifice. To the Ebionites, obedience to the law consisted of Sabbath observance and circumcision.

13. See the words of Hippolytus, *Haer.* 7.22.
14. Gonzalez, *From the Beginnings*, 125.
15. McGrath, *Heresy*, 109. Italics in original.
16. Erickson, *Word Became Flesh*, 44.
17. Wilhite, *Gospel*, 57.

one of those, Elxaism, as a form of Ebionism.[18] Even though Ebionism is an ancient heresy, the adoptionist Christology never completely disappeared. As Douglas McCready notes, the Liberal Protestants of the nineteenth century had an Ebionite view of Jesus.[19] Ebionism is being revived in contemporary times via the Internet, as well in some strains of Messianic Judaism.[20] There is a website dedicated to preserving a kind of Ebionite religion that bears remarkable similarity to the ancient beliefs, so there really is nothing new under the sun.[21] The main beliefs of the contemporary version of Ebionism include the absence of the divine in Jesus, the denial of his messianic office, that he was a prophet only, and did not rise from the dead. Like the ancient heresy, they believe that the true religion of Jesus was corrupted by Paul, as if he were the only New Testament author who wrote about the divinity of Jesus.[22]

There is perhaps a cryptic reference to an early form of Ebionism in 1 John 2:22, "Who is the liar but the one who denies that Jesus is the Christ? This is the antichrist, the one who denies the Father and the Son."[23] Michael Gouder makes a compelling case that the first two chapters in the epistle to the Hebrews is a polemic against an Ebionite-type of Christology.[24] Numerous other Scriptures in the New Testament that attest to the full divinity of Jesus are by their nature anti-Ebionite, although they were likely written before any sort of unified Ebionism took shape.

C. Fitzsimmons Allison pinpoints some of the dangers an Ebionite Christology can cause when applied to other areas of the faith, some of which will be discussed at length in later chapters of this book. He notes that "Adoptionism reduces the essential significance of Jesus Christ to an 'example' for his followers to obey. Those who do so will similarly be rewarded with 'sonship' and divine acceptance. Adoptionism makes of Christianity a religion of control rather than a religion of redemption and reduces morals to moralism."[25] He concludes by perceptively stating that Ebionite Christology finds a welcome home in the self-absorbed human heart.[26] We will see as the book progresses that Ebionism dwells in the dichotomist-dualist half of the Plotinian ambiguity, as in it the created flesh of Jesus stands with us over against the divine, so that our only hope is to copy him in order to receive his reward.

---

18. Gonzalez, *From the Beginnings*, 125–26.

19. McCready, *He Came Down from Heaven*, 71n3.

20. On the latter, see the discussion in McGrath, *Heresy*, 111.

21. The website can be viewed at http://www.ebionite.org. It seems to be the efforts of one man and his followers, but they do seem to follow the core ideas of ancient Ebionism.

22. See the website http://www.ebionite.org.

23. Smalley, *1, 2, 3 John*, 110–14, notes that while some see the docetic-gnostic Cerinthus as the antichrist of 2:22, it could just as easily be a sect of people with a low Christology, of which the Ebiointes are a prime example.

24. Goulder, "Hebrews and the Ebionites," 393–406.

25. Allison, *Cruelty of Heresy*, 32.

26. Allison, *Cruelty of Heresy*, 34.

The Hexagon of Heresy

Docetism

If Ebionism is the emphasis of Jesus's humanity at the expense of his divinity, its counterpart Docetism is the emphasis of Jesus's divinity at the expense of his humanity. Ebionism has its roots in the Jewish paradigm of God and his world, while Docetism is fully Hellenistic. Docetism receives its name from the Greek word "*dokein*," which means "to seem," because it rejected the full reality of Jesus's humanity.[27] Docetists believed that Christ only "seemed" human. Kelly traces the origins of Docetism to "Graeco-Oriental assumptions about divine impassibility and the inherent impurity of matter."[28] One of these assumptions was that a metaphysical dualism existed between the spiritual and material worlds, which in the Greek mind would have prevented the divine from becoming truly material.[29] The Platonic philosophers had taught for centuries that anything material was evil, and that it would be impossible for anything truly divine to become truly material. The pagan Greeks taught that the Logos was the chief of all intermediaries between the world of pure spirit and the world of matter. From its earliest days, the Christian church identified this Logos with Jesus, although the concept would need to be profoundly reshaped in order to make it Christian. Paul Hinlicky writes, "The use of the philosophical [Greek] concept of the Logos also created several christological problems. Since the function of the philosophical Logos is to lend rational form to unorganized matter, the tendency in Christology will be for the Logos to substitute for the human soul of Jesus, as if in the incarnation the Logos appropriated a physical body as its puppet through which to communicate with mortals, displacing the natural human psyche."[30] Thus even though Jesus seemed to be human, he could not be truly so because the Christ—a resident of the world of spirit—would never condescend into the world of matter. Another assumption was that "the divine can experience neither change nor suffering."[31] MacLeod notes that such a metaphysically-dualistic worldview would entail the surrender of several key Christian beliefs. He writes, "The Son of God could not be born of a human mother, and certainly not linked to her by an umbilical cord; nor could he suffer and die; nor take an ordinary flesh-and-blood body."[32] It is easy to see why Docetism posed a challenge to the fledgling Christian faith.

Kelly further notes that Docetism, like Ebionism, is more of an attitude than a crystallized movement, and that such an attitude was present in other heresies such as Marcionism and Gnosticism.[33] Describing the effects of Docetic Christology,

---

27. Kelly, *Early Christian Doctrines*, 141.
28. Kelly, *Early Christian Doctrines*, 141. These assumptions are recognizable as first corollaries to definitional simplicity from chapter 1 above.
29. Erickson, *Word Became Flesh*, 45.
30. Hinlicky, *Divine Complexity*, 162.
31. MacLeod, *Person of Christ*, 157. Again, this is the "definitional" in definitional simplicity.
32. MacLeod, *Person of Christ*, 157.
33. Kelly, *Early Christian Doctrines*, 141.

Gonzalez writes, "If matter, and above all this matter which forms our body, is not the product of the divine will, but rather of some other principle that is opposed to that will, it follows that matter and the human body cannot serve as a vehicle for the revelation of the supreme God. Therefore Christ, who came to make that God known to us, cannot have come in the flesh. His body cannot have been a truly physical body."[34] The Marcionite version of Docetism, also called phantasmal Docetism, regarded the humanity of Christ as a phantom, as "a mere mask, an image without substance."[35] The Cerinthian version, also known as possessionistic Docetism, on the other hand, holds an adoptionistic Christology in that "the Christ" came upon the man Jesus at his baptism and left before his crucifixion."[36] Another form, "replacement Docetism," held that Simon the Cyrene was the one crucified in place of Jesus because the Christ could not possibly die.[37] Some of the Docetists had no problem with the virgin birth, as long as Mary had no part in Jesus's origins. As Erickson says, they believed that Jesus "merely passed through her as water passes through a tube."[38] The Valentinians, a Docetic-gnostic group, maintained that Jesus possessed a "spiritual flesh" that was unlike ours, even to the point that normal human bodily functions were beneath him.[39] All of the above reflect the Hellenistic denial of the possibility of the Christ becoming truly human.

Of course, the New Testament is a witness against Docetism. The humanity of Jesus is never questioned in the Gospels. Grillmeier notes that the great christological hymns in Paul—Phil 2:5–11 in particular—exclude any Docetic interpretations.[40] Such a Docetic attitude was certainly present at the time 1 John was composed, for it says, "By this you know the Spirit of God: every spirit that confesses that Jesus Christ has come in the flesh is from God; and every spirit that does not confess Jesus is not from God; this is the *spirit* of the antichrist" (1 John 4:2–3a). Alister McGrath notes that some scholars believe that all three of the Johannine letters were composed to fight the Docetic attitude.[41] Note that the same word, "antichrist," is used to describe the Docetic view as was used in 2:22 to describe the Ebionite view. While Serapion of Antioch was the first person to explicitly call the attitude "Docetism," it was attacked by virtually all of the early orthodox fathers.[42]

---

34. Gonzalez, *From the Beginnings*, 130.
35. MacLeod, *Person of Christ*, 157. See also Wilhite, *Gospel*, 78n41.
36. MacLeod, *Person of Christ*, 157. See Wilhite, *Gospel*, 78n42.
37. Wilhite, *Gospel*, 78n43. See also the idea put forth by McGrath, *Heresies*, 114–16, that plays upon the Greek concept of the *eidolon*, or the "double," who replaces a hero when death is imminent. Many Docetists believe that another person "replaced" Jesus before his death and died in his place, Simon the Cyrene the usual suspect.
38. Erickson, *Word Became Flesh*, 46
39. McGrath, *Heresy*, 113.
40. Grillmeier, *From the Apostolic Age*, 22.
41. McGrath, *Heresy*, 111.
42. See Grillmeier, *From the Apostolic Age*, 78–79, 87, 98, 115, 132, 136.

However, Docetism was not always a simple denial of anything human in Jesus. Raymond Brown defines the Docetism that he believes 1 John fights thus: "the human existence of Jesus, while real, was not salvifically significant . . . [but] only a stage in the career of the divine Word and not an intrinsic component in redemption."[43] It should not be, as in the case of the liberal tradition, "understood as an implausible depiction of the psychology of Jesus."[44] If Docetism is really a denial that the humanity of Jesus has any value for human salvation (rather than simply denying the existence of the human in him), then it is much easier to see why it took hold early on in the history of the faith, and spawned other similar heresies later like Apollinarianism and Monophysitism. Paul Hinlicky continues, "With this important clarification about what Docetism is, Antidocetism then indicates by contrast a theology in which the human dwelling with us of the incarnate Word is decisive for salvation itself."[45] And,

> The theological sense of Antidocetism is not the instrument of a revelation that is conceivable apart from it. Incarnation itself bears the content of the revelation. God does not merely use a human vehicle to speak a Word that is essentially detachable from it, but God speaks his own Word in assuming flesh and making it forever his own in all its historical particularity and apparent contingency. The particular humanity assumed by the divine Word then *is* (not "is like") the content of the message.[46]

Docetism, then, is grounded in the monist half of the Plotinian ambiguity (though Docetism, like Ebionism, chronologically preceded Plotinus himself). Jesus's flesh is not absolutely essential to salvation, for the visible world is one with the invisible. If Jesus is human in some sense, to the Docetist, then it is not essential to his mission that he is so. Hinlicky summarizes well: "Christology that is deeply, profoundly Antidocetist is not merely insisting that Jesus had a body, or that Jesus had a soul, but that the public obedience of Jesus in his body made complete by death on the cross is what accomplishes human redemption at the turn of the ages."[47] His humanity would only be an incidental occurrence, and not something necessary for human salvation if Docetism were true. We will discuss such thoughts further later in the book when we take up the issues in cosmology.

The practical side of a Docetic Christology can be extremely problematic. C. Fitzsimmons Allison notes that a Docetic version of Jesus eliminates suffering from his life, and implicitly removes suffering as something both experienced by God, and sanctifying to us.[48] He writes,

---

43. Brown, *Community*, 113, as quoted in Hinlicky, *Divine Complexity*, 93.
44. Hinlicky, *Divine Complexity*, 93.
45. Hinlicky, *Divine Complexity*, 93.
46. Hinlicky, *Divine Complexity*, 93.
47. Hinlicky, *Divine Complexity*, 162.
48. Allison, *Cruelty of Heresy*, 28.

> Christ's sufferings and ours are the means by which comes our 'comfort,' the very name of the Holy Spirit (2 Cor 1:3–7). The essential connection between the Holy Spirit and Christ's and our sufferings can be seen from the fact that *parakaleo* (Paraclete, Comforter) occurs ten times and suffering seven times in these five verses. The Docetic escape is seductive, indeed, but one that would leave us bereft of true life, peace, fellowship, endurance, character, hope, and, most of all, God's Comforter.[49]

In short, Docetism makes human suffering meaningless. Moreover, God never condescends to touch us in our misery. As we will see later, a monist conception of God means that God cannot condescend to us. It eliminates the doctrine of the priesthood of Jesus, because a priest is always selected from among humanity, as one of the group, to make intercession on their behalf.

Early Challenges to Christology

While the Ebionites and Docetists discussed above had departed from the apostolic *kerygma*, or proclamation of the faith that states the "crucified and risen one is Lord, God and Savior,"[50] the early orthodox Fathers tried to stay as faithful to it as possible. Until challenges arose that demanded the *kerygma* be refined and made more precise, it seemed best to them to continue to restate it. The previous section on Docetism has introduced some challenges to the presentation of the gospel in a largely Hellenistic world. Like the more popular pagan philosophies, Christianity affirmed the existence of one true God, who is transcendent above all. It also held to the existence of the Logos, who served in a mediating role between God and the rest of creation. Because of these two powerful similarities, it was easy for Christianity to adopt existing philosophical terminology to explain the gospel as we will soon see. But there were some serious discontinuities between Christianity and the philosophies. First is the stated "oneness" between the Logos and the Father, and how that plays out in the incarnation and death of the Logos—an idea unthinkable to the Greeks. Another is the inherent goodness of all creation over against the prevailing metaphysical and cosmological dualism of Hellenism. Third is the idea that only God is eternal and creation is temporal. As we will see, these differences are the tip of the iceberg. The early evangelists and apologists were keenly aware of the three main differences and attempted to address them as fully as they could.

That being said, the doctrine of subordinationism, or the belief that Jesus is somehow less than the Father, had been latent within Christianity since its very inception. Because the church had not yet been forced to seriously wrestle with precisely how Jesus and the Father are "one," they were equally fuzzy on how he was "less," though

---

49. Allison, *Cruelty of Heresy*, 28. The five "verses" he mentions are Phil 3:10, Rom 5:3–4, Rom 8:17, and 2 Cor 1:3–7. There are only four texts cited in the original.

50. Behr, *Way to Nicaea*, 77–80.

they were understandably cautious to tread on those waters. Subordination language is present throughout the Gospels, especially in the texts where Jesus says he has been sent by the Father and the *locus classicus* of subordination, John 14:28, where Jesus says "The Father is greater than I." Taken at face value, such texts could very well have led the young faith into believing that Jesus was a sort of "lesser God" than the Father in eternity, which would have made Christianity neither monotheistic nor part of the Jewish religious heritage.

Early Christian apologists, contending for the faith in the face of pagan opposition, struggled to account for such subordination in light of the apostolic *kerygma*, for the vocabulary that we have today to account for such reality had not yet been developed. Perhaps the best-known example of such struggle is the thought of the second-century apologist, Justin Martyr. Justin believed that Jesus was "another God," but not in the sense of there being two Gods. Rather, he saw the relationship of the Father and Son as analogous to that of the sun and its light.[51] John Behr notes that Justin held to the Platonist "common philosophical presupposition of his day that as God is so totally transcendent to created reality he needs an intermediary, his Word, to act for him and to mediate between himself and creation."[52] Behr continues, "Justin is clearly trying to find a way to explain how it is that Jesus Christ is God, yet distinct from the God and creator of all, his Father. However, his manner of explanation, in terms of the divinity of the ineffable Father being transcendent in a manner which prohibits him from being seen on earth, in fact undermines the very revelation of God in Christ. The divinity of Jesus Christ, an 'other God,' is no longer that of the Father himself, but is subordinate to it."[53] By all accounts, it was never Justin's intention to so subordinate the Son, but to actually preserve his deity. Like all the fathers, he believed Jesus to be divine, but the question of "how" divine, especially in relation to the Father's divinity, was yet to be answered.[54] They were all handicapped by the language and philosophical categories of the time. In the pre-Nicene world, a distinction implied a difference and for them there was no distinction (or difference) between person and nature.

Other early teachers struggled with how to express the gospel given the complex parameters of the Christian faith, namely the claim of Jesus's unity with the Father

---

51. Justin Martyr, *Dial.* 128.3, as discussed in Gonzalez, *From the Beginnings*, 107. A very similar line of reasoning in the thought of Marcellus of Ancyra will be judged deficient in the fourth century.

52. Behr, *Way to Nicaea*, 103. See also the discussion of Justin and his adoption of philosophical language in Hinlicky, *Divine Complexity*, 128–37.

53. Hinlicky, *Divine Complexity*, 104. See the similar discussion in Anatolios, *Athanasius*, 17–18. Speaking for Justin and the rest of the apologists, Anatolios writes, "They strenuously attempted to proclaim that God is both transcendent and immanent, even if this immanence was not well integrated into their doctrine of God."

54. Anatolios, *Athanasius*, 18, writes, "A prevailing tendency was, on the one hand, to affirm divine transcendence in terms of strictly contrasting God with the world, and, on the other hand, to affirm divine immanence by emphasizing God's providential care for the world. The problem is only highlighted to the extent this juxtaposition tends to be personified in the subordination of the Son, as a Mediator-God, to the transcendent first God, the Father."

coupled with his suffering and death. Hippolytus of Rome taught that the "generation of the Word depends on the will of the Father" while in no way believing that two (or even three) Gods exist.[55] Novatian implied a subordination between the Father and the Son by claiming "the distinction between the Father as the immutable and impassible God, and the Son as capable of establishing contact and relationship with humans, the world, and its events."[56] The motivation of these second- and third-century apologists was to present the gospel in language their Hellenistic audience could understand. Those existing thought-structures were all that was available to them, though they were conceptually insufficient to convey all the gospel had to say. As was noted in chapter 1, the Hellenistic conception of the cosmos was both monist/subordinationist and dichotomist-dualist, concepts that standing alone violated Jesus's intimate relationship to the Father that had to be maintained in the proclamation of the gospel. Irenaeus was one who tried to systematically tie it all together, but he needed a more precise vocabulary to adequately express it.[57] They all wished to proclaim, against adoptionistic Ebionism, the divinity of the Son (though precisely what that meant was still to be determined) along with the gospel distinction between he and his Father. The early church was then ready for the coming of its most influential theologian since Paul of Tarsus, Origen of Alexandria.

Origen and His Progeny

Origen, who lived from 184 to 253, was one of the greatest theologians of the school of Alexandria, and unique in that he exercised influence over all who came after him, towering "above all earlier theologians of record as the great master—or, in some cases, the persistent nemesis—of those who undertook to do serious theology for several centuries to come."[58] Like those who came before him, he saw the compatibility between Christianity and Platonism, and strove to explain the latter utilizing the former, specifically in his key theological work, *On First Principles*.[59]

Doubtlessly, Origen recognized that Platonism and Christianity shared two foundationally essential concepts: the transcendent one God and the mediating Logos

---

55. Gonzalez, *From the Beginnings*, 233.

56. Gonzalez, *From the Beginnings*, 236, citing Novatian, *Trin.* 17.

57. See the discussion in Behr, *Way to Nicaea*, 111–33 and in Kelly, *Early Christian Doctrines*, 147–49, as well as Davis, *Councils*, 39. Hinlicky, *Divine Complexity*, 179, summarizes, "Prior to Origen no one knew how to conceive of something 'derived' or begotten as truly divine."

58. Beeley, *Unity of Christ*, 5.

59. Beeley, *Unity of Christ*, 14. Here, Beeley writes, "In many ways, the overarching goal of Origen's work was to show the compatibility of the best of Greek culture with catholic Christianity—or better, to reorganize Greek culture under the chief principle of Christ." Hinlicky, *Divine Complexity*, 179–84, discusses Origen's attempt to synthesize two incompatible models of Logos: the pagan rational principle ordering the universe and the Christian person-communication of the free creator. The result proved to be inherently unstable.

(these are his first two "principles," after all). It seemed natural for him to recast Christian language in the, so to speak, pre-made thought structures with which every educated person in the Empire was already familiar for apologetics purposes. Therefore, he reasoned that the Christian God should be defined as metaphysically simple, that is, not composed of any physical or metaphysical parts whatsoever. From his own words in *On First Principles*, Origen writes,

> That simple and wholly intellectual existence can admit of no delay or hesitation in *its* movements or operations; lest the simplicity of the divine nature should appear to be circumscribed or in some degree hampered by such adjuncts, and lest that which is the beginning of all things should be found composite and differing, and that which ought to be free from all bodily intermixture, in virtue of being the one sole species of deity, so to speak, should prove, instead of being one, to consist of many things.[60]

Origen's definitional simplicity of the Christian Godhead follows almost thought-for-thought the understanding of the simplicity found in the One of Plotinus.[61] Though Origen is committed to a faith that requires a personal Father rather than an impersonal One as its ultimate source, the simplicity of Origen subtly shifts the "first principle" in the Christian faith to the simple One.[62] Consider Farrell's commentary on Origen's move,

> Here one must note carefully Origen's use of the neuter pronoun "it" to describe a God whom, when he worships, he addresses as "he". The "something else" for which we have been searching is now revealed precisely as this "simple deity". A second salient point emerges, and this is the use of the term "deity" or "godhead." Here the term is shorn of all personal references it had come to acquire in the more traditional of the fathers and other ecclesiastical writers. For them, the term denoted precisely the fact that the consubstantial divine essence, which the three persons of the Trinity have, is to be referred to a "head", or to a source and origin, namely, the Father, who is thus understood to be the personal locus of the *essential* unity of God. But in Origen, that essential unity is now capable of being torn from that personal locus, precisely because the conception of "simplicity" will allow it, nay, even *requires* it.[63]

---

60. Origen, *On First Principles* 1.1.6. Italics mine.

61. See Plotinus, *Enn.* 5.5.6 and 6.9.3, cited in Farrell, *Free Choice*, 42–44. Here there is no implication of dependence of Origen upon Plotinus, because there is no evidence that Origen knew his writings. That they both derived their ideas from Middle Platonism, though, is certain. For a discussion on the possibility that Origen and Plotinus may have had a common teacher, Ammonius Saccas, see Tregg, *Origen*, 12–14.

62. As we shall see, the gradual development of the concept of person will become very important in the next few centuries.

63. Farrell, *God, History, and Dialectic*, 99. Italics in original. The theological "it" combined with the liturgical "he" is an example of the unstable synthesis from n59 previously.

Pre-Nicene Christology

Recall that the two corollaries of definitional simplicity are the identity thesis (God's being, attributes, and will are all identical) and the Plotinian ambiguity (God and the world are simultaneously confused and separated). If Origen is following the same Middle Platonism that produced Plotinus, we should see the both corollaries present, and indeed we do.

Because Origen defines God as metaphysically simple, all predications of God are by definition identical to him and to each other. Thus, he identifies the names used to describe God, specifically stating that to be the Father is the same as to be the almighty creator, so that both names describe eternal realities in God. He writes, "As no one can be a father without having a son, nor a master without possessing a servant, so even God cannot be called omnipotent unless there exist those over whom he may exercise his power; and therefore, that God may be shown to be almighty, it is necessary that all things should exist."[64] He continues, "But if there was never a time when he was not omnipotent, of necessity those things by which he receives that title must also exist; and he must always have had those over whom he exercised power, and which were governed by him."[65] Because Origen has defined God to be absolutely simple in the same manner as the Middle Platonists and Plotinus—that all predications of God are indistinguishable from each other and from God himself—God as Father and God as almighty creator are to be treated in the same eternal way. Therefore, both creation and the generation of the Son are themselves eternal. Here we see the first instance of the fusion of the two great corollaries of definitional simplicity in what Joseph Farrell calls the "Origenist Problematic"—the inability to meaningfully differentiate between the generation of the Son and the creation of the world.[66] Farrell adds,

> Thus, because the philosophical conception of simplicity has been assumed to be an adequate definition of the theological and revealed unity of the Christian God, there is no difference between "Fatherhood" and "Creatorhood", or "Sonship" and "Creaturehood". Consequently, if one operated within the confines of this culturally-conditioned theology, yet were inclined to take a "traditional" view that Christ was God, one had to affirm the eternity of the world, for only that would allow Christ's person to be eternal. On the other hand, if one operated within the confines of this culturally conditioned theology, yet were inclined to take a "traditional" view that creation was *created*, that it really *began to be*, then perforce one also had to maintain that Christ

---

64. Origen, *On First Principles* 1.2.10.
65. Origen, *On First Principles* 1.2.10.
66. Farrell, *Free Choice*, 53. The lack of distinction between God as Father and as creator is due to the definition of simplicity that does not allow for any real difference in the names of God. If he is eternally Father, he is eternally creator as well. Beeley, *Unity of Christ*, 320, n43, notes that Origen asserted that the generation of the Son "is prior to and more fundamental than" creation. Though Origen is to be commended for trying to rectify the problem in his assertion of the priority of generation, his assumptions lead to their identification, and there is ample room for looking past such an assertion when God is defined to be simple in the Platonic sense.

was not eternal, and therefore not God even in the sense of eternity. The latter option, of course, was that pursued by the first great classic heresiarch, Arius.[67]

For Origen, since calling God "creator" is on exactly the same metaphysical plane as calling him "Father," the Son and creation are a package deal. The "Problematic" is just another way of stating the identity thesis in a monist light, in that God's work of creation is identical to God's essence.[68] Simplicity, for Origen, erases any real distinctions between what God is as Father and Son (and Spirit) and what God does in creating the world. The eternal existence of souls, the primordial fall, and the *apokatastasis* (the ultimate redemption of all creation, even the devil) follow.

On the other hand, in his worship, Origen held to the traditional Christian interpretation that Christ was God, but to do so in his system required him to relegate Christ and the Spirit to "second and third God" status,[69] or, a simple unity in the Father compared to a complex unity in the Son.[70] That is, Origen believed the Son to be a distinct *hypostasis* (defined to be a "distinctly existing thing, a concrete entity or being") from the Father,[71] eternally generated from the will of God rather than from the being of God.[72] Even he could not maintain his own definition of simplicity

---

67. Farrell, *God, History, and Dialectic*, 101. This quote demonstrates how two "traditional" Christian doctrines, the eternal Son and the temporal creation, are pitted against one another within the context of definitional simplicity. It must be this way, since neither the Son nor creation are the simple one (Father), they are of the many.

68. On Origen's monist orientation, see Meyendorff, *Christ in Eastern Christian Thought (1969)*, 35, who says that Origen's anthropology, Christology, and eschatology, especially as noted in *On First Principles*, "must be understood in the framework of a spiritualist and essentially Platonic monism." He further states on page 37 that Origen was anxious to "push aside all ontological dualism, whether Manichaean or Gnostic."

69. Farrell, *God, History, and Dialectic*, 286. Also, on page 781, Farrell writes, "Origen does not yet have a doctrine of person in the fully theological sense, for it seems that he can only understand the person as the *individual*, i.e., as the union of form and matter." Hinlicky, *Divine Complexity*, 187–90, asks the question, "What makes God God?" He continues, on page 190, that the Origenist (and eventually Arian) answer is ingeneracy, or an absolute, underived simplicity. For Origen and all who follow his structure, God *is not* the Logos.

70. Radde-Gallwitz, *Basil*, 66. This declension from the simple Father to the complex Son is very reminiscent of Plotinus's first emanation from the One. Bulgakov, *Comforter*, 18, writes, concerning Origen, "He did this . . . simply by putting the *hypostasis* of the Father in place of the Neoplatonic One, the *hypostasis* of the Son in place of the Neoplatonic Mind, and the *hypostasis* of the Holy Spirit in place of the World Soul."

71. Beeley, *Unity of Christ*, 19. Williams, *Arius*, 132, notes that for Origen, as well as the rest of the Greek-speaking world of his time, *hypostasis* and *ousia* functioned roughly as synonyms. Ayres, *Nicaea*, 22, writes, "Thus we see that while the Father is superior to the Son, Origen works to make the Son intrinsic to the being of God; subordinationism is an inappropriate word for describing this theological dynamic."

72. Origen, *On First Principles* 1.2.6. The same is also cited in Farrell, *Free Choice*, 54. Beeley, *Unity of Christ*, 25–26, notes that eternal generation from the being of God would be a form of Sabellianism according to Origen. Again, the Father is simple being while the Son is complex, which rules out being as the source of generation. Ayres, *Nicaea*, 24, writes, "Origen directly denies that the Son can come from the Father's *ousia*, as this would imply a material conception of the divine generation."

Pre-Nicene Christology

consistently, because the being and will should be the same thing.[73] C. C. Kroeger succinctly states the inherent contradiction in Origen's thought, which I believe is due to attempting to map the impersonal pagan definitional simplicity with its unbaptized identity thesis onto the tri-personal Christian God, "Origen affirmed God as creator of all things, Christ as eternal Son and Word, and the Holy Spirit—each member distinct from the others yet together forming a unity. The trinitarianism provided a basis for orthodox thinkers such as Athanasius, Jerome, and the Cappadocians. On the other hand, he sometimes spoke of the Son and Holy Spirit as subject to the Father, a view that led others into subordinationism and ultimately Arianism."[74] Here we see the dichotomist-dualist strain of the Plotinian ambiguity asserting itself. The Son is a second *hypostasis*, and therefore he is not the One. In a sense, then, he too stands over against the Father in a subordinate way. Origen is thus an influence on both strains of fourth-century theology—pro-Nicene and anti-Nicene.

Origen scholars tend to emphasize one side of the hierarchy/equality question or the other. For example, Leo Davis describes Origen's ideas of the Father, Son, and Holy Spirit as "three distinct subsistences, one subordinate to the other, yet one in harmony and concord of intellect and will,"[75] reminiscent of the One-*nous*-world soul triad of Plotinus.[76] This subordinationist view of the Father and Son would gain support from the anti-Nicene position years later. John Behr adds, "Yet, on the other hand, Origen's insistence on the eternity of the Son, related to the existence of God as Father, rather than Creator, firmly anticipates the key points of Nicaea."[77] Justo Gonzalez helpfully sorts out these two opposing legacies as left- and right-wing Origenism,

---

73. Here I believe is an important distinction between Christian versions of definitional simplicity and its pagan counterpart, which proves that even definitional simplicity underwent a form of "baptism." Although the terminology will not be precisely hammered out until Maximus in the seventh century, I believe Origen and other Christians who come after him make an implicit distinction between the will as a faculty of operation (which, in definitional simplicity, must be identical to the essence) and the effects which the will produces. If no such distinction is made, then the effects of the will are nothing more than emanations from the essence/will. Origen, as do all Christians, wishes to maintain a real ontological distinction between God and creation, and the implicit distinction between the faculty of and the effects of the will seems to be the key. Though still very monist in orientation, there is always, from Origen forward, a distinction between the will of God in itself and the effects of that will, at least until it is blurred in the thought of Jonathan Edwards, whom we will discuss in chapter 10.

74. Kroeger, "Origen," 870. Hinlicky, *Divine Complexity*, 192, notes that in the philosophical theology with definitional simplicity as its first axiom, the Holy Spirit tends to be superfluous because the "real" triad is God, the Logos (mediator), and creation. Ayres, *Nicaea*, 28, adds, "Origen's account is, then, complex. He speaks of the Son as inferior to the Father, and yet his explanation of this inferiority turns, at many points, into an account of the necessity of the Son within the divine life."

75. Davis, *Councils*, 50. It is impossible for the divine three to have a unity of being, for the Father is definitionally simple. Therefore, the only real metaphysical category left as a source of unity is will, in that the wills of the distinct beings (*hypostaseis*) merge together.

76. Farrell, *Free Choice*, 55.

77. Behr, *Way to Nicaea*, 201.

respectively.⁷⁸ The former is the dichotomist-dualist side of the Plotinian ambiguity asserting itself, which places the Son together with all other created beings, distinct from and therefore dialectically opposed to the Father; the latter is the monist side of the ambiguity, which places the Son together with the Father, yet subordinated, with a cosmology that is one in principle with God. Both "wings" will survive in Alexandrian theology, with Arius and Apollinarius becoming the fourth century's most famous expositors of each side's extremes.

The diametrically opposed views of the relationship between the Son and the Father that entail from Origen's thought might seem puzzling at first, until one sees that Origen's definitional understanding of divine simplicity when describing the Christian God runs into problems when the Platonic "One" is really "three." The square peg of the Christian Trinity cannot be forced into the round hole of Platonic simplicity without collateral damage to both Christology and cosmology, and the "Problematic" is but the tip of the iceberg. On the one hand, Origen's Christian sensibilities force him to take the humanity of Jesus seriously, thus Christ himself is composed of two "very different realities," the divine Son and the humanity of Jesus, the only human soul to survive the primordial fall.⁷⁹ The two realities/natures cannot interpenetrate one another, and any idea of a communication of properties between the divine and human is only predication, not real.⁸⁰ Origen describes the union between the Son and Jesus as that of the "one-flesh" union between husband and wife, that is, two distinct substances joined by will.⁸¹ Christopher Beeley notes that Origen sees the active agent in the union as the man Jesus, rather than the eternal Son, as Origen writes, "the perfect man cleaves to the Word itself by his virtue and so is united with him."⁸² Thus the real agent in Origen's version of the incarnation is human. This will be nearly the exact line of thinking displayed by Theodore and Nestorius as we will see in chapter 5.⁸³ On the other hand, Origen believes that the Logos "dominates, if not replaces" the human soul of Jesus in a way that anticipates both Apollinarianism (chapter 4) and Monophysitism (chapter 6).⁸⁴ The unstable synthesis of Origen is the father all subsequent defective Christologies. It is also readily apparent at this point that those defective Christologies are the product of defective cosmologies (how God and the world must relate) that result from Origen's first principle.

---

78. Gonzalez, *From the Beginnings*, 254–60. The origin of the two wings concept belongs to Friedrich Loofs. Because of the attendant Plotinian ambiguity present in his doctrine of definitional simplicity, there will unfortunately always and inevitably be two ways to read Origen.

79. Beeley, *Unity of Christ*, 32–34.

80. Beeley, *Unity of Christ*, 36–37.

81. Origen, *Cels.* 6.47.

82. Origen, *Cels.* 6.47–48, as quoted in Beeley, *Unity of Christ*, 41.

83. See Wellum, *God the Son Incarnate*, 278.

84. Hinlicky, *Divine Complexity*, 187.

Pre-Nicene Christology

In the end, Origen's attempt to synthesize Christianity and Platonism likely provided more problems than solutions. The positives include the doctrine of eternal generation, which in Origen made the Son *almost* as divine as the Father, as well as providing much of the ammunition for the pro-Nicene movement a few generations later. The negatives include the Origenist Problematic, along with what Khaled Anatolios calls the "break" in the flow of Christian experience, "agitations" to which Origen contributed through his teachings on eternal creation, the human soul of Jesus, and the drive toward systematization that made ignoring inconsistencies even more difficult.[85] As Anatolios argues, the Nicene controversy that follows in chapter 3 (and, quite possibly, the rest of the christological controversies covered in chapters 4 through 6 are so as well) is an attempt to reintegrate Christian experience given the "agitations" Origen introduced.[86] I am largely in agreement with Anatolios, but I see the first two agitations as a direct result of his doctrine of definitional simplicity.

To recap Origen's contributions, we start with his commitment to definitional simplicity in identifying the Father as the simple One. It immediately follows that all predications of the Father, including "Father," "creator," and "eternal" are all identical realities in God. Therefore, both the Son (of the Father) and creation (of the creator) are equally eternal (the Origenist Problematic) and this directly implies (1) the eternal preexistence of all human souls as well as (2) the *apokatastasis*. Because the Father is simple and the Son is complex, (3) the Son is a second *hypostasis* and something less than the Father. Because the Son and creation exist on the same ontological plane, there is a very real sense in which (4) how the Son is eternally "for us," a phenomenon Anatolios calls (5) a "Christology of continuity,"[87] as well as a (6) real lack of created integrity. Because of the pre-existence of human souls, which includes Jesus, there is (7) a "two sons" problem between Jesus and the Logos. The perceptive reader who is already familiar with the christological controversies discussed in the next four chapters will recognize the roots of all of them in this paragraph. All seven entailments from definitional simplicity would need to be addressed in the coming centuries.

As we will see time and again throughout this book, when definitional simplicity is at work, two possible results will obtain, often existing side by side, representing the two sides of the Plotinian ambiguity which follow from it. We see such an occurrence in Origen's progeny, as he spawned not one, but two methodologies of theological reflection that would come to a head in the fourth century. The monist right-wing held to the eternal generation of the Son and the increasingly full divinity of Father, Son, and Spirit, all the while never comfortable with an eternal creation or an *apokatastasis*. Meanwhile the left wing, in denying the eternity of creation was also required, to be true to the fullness of Origen's doctrine of definitional divine simplicity, to deny the

---

85. Anatolios, *Retrieving Nicaea*, 38–41.
86. Anatolios, *Retrieving Nicaea*, 41. The following paragraph is a recap of Anatolios's ideas.
87. Anatolios, *Retrieving Nicaea*, 93–94.

eternal generation of and therefore the equality of the Son.[88] On the monist right wing is Gregory "the Wonderworker" of Neocaesarea, one of Origen's disciples.[89] The most famous bit of theology surviving from Gregory is a creed that holds to the equality between the Father and the Son while relatively ignoring the subordinationist thinking of his teacher.[90] On the dichotomist-dualist side sits Lucian of Antioch. After detailing much of the speculation that has surrounded Lucian for more than a century, R. P. C. Hanson concludes that the only thing we can really know for sure about his Christology is that he taught that the Son at the incarnation assumed a human body without a human soul.[91] Rowan Williams adds that Lucian was a "pluralist," while "taking for granted the distinct subsistence of the Son, and perhaps also denying the presence of a human soul in Jesus."[92] Thus the Son, according to Lucian, would be changeable and much more different from the Father than the way Origen described them. That difference would be so great as to oppose the Father and Son at the point of changeability, which would set Lucian and his followers on the dichotomist-dualist side of the Plotinian ambiguity. It may be coincidence that Antioch would also be the home of the third dichotomist-dualist heresy, Nestorianism, or maybe not; we do not have enough evidence to draw a firm conclusion. At any rate, Lucian is very important because all of the followers of the various strains of anti-Nicene theology point to Lucian as their teacher and the one from whom they derived their doctrine.[93]

J. F. Bethune-Baker summarizes the difficulty Origen's students had in fully appropriating his ideas, "Origen's doctrine of the Logos and the Sonship was an attempt

---

88. Farrell, *Free Choice*, 52–56. Hinlicky, *Divine Complexity*, 181, notes Friedrich Schleiermacher critiqued Origen's doctrine of eternal generation as a way of attempting to defeat the doctrine of the Trinity. Hinlicky writes, "The point of this cunning critique by the father of liberal Protestantism is not to correct Origen's ontological subordinationism in an Athanasian way, but rather to expose the orthodox teaching of the Trinity of persons as something unseemly, unfitting, unworthy of divine simplicity."

89. Hinlicky, *Divine Complexity*, 193, notes that even those who follow Origen closely can be ambiguous too. He writes that Origen's successor at the catechetical school in Alexandria, Dionysius, defended the Christian understanding of the distinct personality of the Logos against a group of Libyan Sabellians by saying the Logos was a second *hypostasis*, that is a second concrete existence, but used creaturely metaphors to do so, that is, he likened the Father and the Logos to the creator and a creature. "Arians" would appeal to both Dionysius and Lucian for their subordinationist doctrine.

90. Gonzalez, *From the Beginnings*, 255–56. Stead, *Philosophy in Christian Antiquity*, 131, states that Gregory developed a view of the divine nature that was simple but capable of exercising a "variety of powers." This means that there is a direct link on the "right wing" of Origenism that is capable of anticipating the move Athanasius will make in a couple of generations, to be discussed in chapter 3.

91. Hanson, *Search*, 83. He cites Epiphanus, *Anc.* 33.3.4, who writes, "Lucian and all the Lucianists deny that the Son of God took on a *psyche*, with the result that they ascribe human *pathos* directly to the Word." Thus the Son, according to Lucian, would be changeable and of a different kind than the Father. Such a Christology will loom large on both sides of the Nicene controversy.

92. Williams, *Arius*, 162.

93. Williams, *Arius*, 166–67 believes that "Lucianism" is a better name for the ensuing heresy than "Arianism." Williams describes Lucian as tapping "the rich resources of the 'anti-monist', anti-Paulinian feeling in Asia and Syria."

Pre-Nicene Christology

to recognize and give due weight to all the conditions of the problem, so far as a human mind could realize them. Origen himself might see at once the many sides and aspects of the problem and succeed in maintaining due proportion; but he was obliged to express himself in antithetical statements, and his followers were not always successful in combining them."[94] This quote is instructive because Origen really was trying to give a comprehensive solution to the relationship of Father and Son given all the scriptural parameters; he was primarily a biblical commentator, after all.[95] Thus Origen's disciples gravitated toward one side of the antithesis or the other, and formed the right- and left-wings, which would eventually polarize in the Nicene controversy. Arius would retain the Problematic, but shift the emphasis from the monist half to the dichotomist-dualist half of the Plotinian ambiguity. The Nicenes would need to discover a way to disentangle the predications of Father and creator in God to allow for the eternality of the Son while affirming the temporality of creation.

To summarize Origen, his first move in *On First Principles* is to define the nature of God as simple, intellectual being. For Origen, God is primarily an ideal nature, who acts. It is the *ordo theologiae* of nature before energy. But, because God is definitionally simple, nature, energy, and person are all really the same thing.[96] Therefore, one cannot, without bald assertion, state any real difference between the creation of the world and the generation of the Son. This will yield a difficult struggle in theology proper, as the doctrine of the Trinity hangs in the balance; but it will be disastrous for Christology, when one of the divine three assumes human flesh. In the eighth century, after the ramifications of Origenism are defeated through the first six ecumenical councils, and after Origen's own teachings are condemned in the fifth council, John of Damascus will write in *On the Orthodox Faith* that the root of all heresy is the confusion of person and nature.[97] Such confusion in the teachings of one so influential as Origen leads to the great heresies of the fourth and fifth centuries, as well as to the orthodox response. Finally, I do not wish to be guilty of casting Origen in a negative light. I am actually quite sympathetic to his project. It took great learning, intelligence, and creativity to arrive at his synthesis. In the end, it was just not sufficient to bear the load of all that was necessary.

---

94. Bethune-Baker, *History*, 151.

95. See Ayres, *Nicaea*, 29–30. Origen, like all (orthodox and heretic alike) who tried to navigate Christianity's difficult and complex parameters attempted to be primarily biblical and traditional. Both "good guys" and "bad guys" used philosophy to help with the process, but the main tools were the Scriptures and tradition. He notes on page 38, helpfully, that the fathers did not distinguish exegesis and theology.

96. For Origen, as well as for all metaphysics of his day, Christian and pagan alike, person and nature were already the same thing because of the almost synonymous meanings of *hypostasis* and *ousia*.

97. John of Damascus, *On the Orthodox Faith* 3.3. Of course, as we will see, the first step to relieving the confusion is disentangling them in the first place.

The Hexagon of Heresy

Conclusion

This has been a brief survey of the erroneous Christologies at the top of the Hexagon and the Christology of the pre-Nicene era. Ebionism is the denial of the divinity of Jesus, while Docetism is the denial of his humanity. These are the two extreme heresies, because they are so opposed to the narrative and tradition of Christianity. Any close and honest reader of the New Testament will infer that the message therein is that Jesus is both truly human and truly divine. In this way, they are quite primitive and easily refuted. As to the discussion of the *ordo theologiae* from chapter 1, the two heresies are the ultimate confusion of person and nature, in that the person of Jesus has but one true nature—the human for Ebionism, or the divine for Docetism. In this sense, the two heresies are not complete opposites, but are two poles of the Plotinian ambiguity. Person and nature were still identified, both in the church and in culture. Therefore, these two heretical "opposites" are not as opposite as we might think. Within definitional simplicity there exists both the singularity of, and the dialectical opposition of, the One and many. The monist singularity and the dichotomist-dualist opposition seem themselves to be at differing poles, but they are really not, as both derive from within the system. It is not surprising that the early unorthodox reactions to the message of Jesus would fall into two camps: those that generally denied either his humanity or his divinity. What is surprising, at least to us, is that these two camps do not stand in complete opposition to one another, but rather emerge from the same set of general assumptions. In other words, the tendency for dialectical opposition is built within the system of definitional divine simplicity, something we see played out on the stage of Western history—a history replete with dialectical opposition in almost every generation. We will see remarkable similarities later on when we discuss the cosmological counterparts to Ebionism and Docetism.

These two basic heresies will morph into much more nuanced forms in the fourth century, as "Arianism" becomes the great attack on Jesus's divinity and Apollinarianism takes aim at Jesus's humanity. In the fifth century, the divine and human natures are separated to the detriment of divinity in Nestorianism and confused to that of his humanity in Monophysitism. Such a classification is not novel. Allison notes that even Adolf von Harnack divided all heresy up into two classifications, "Pneumatic" (essentially Docetist) and "Adoptionist" (essentially Ebionite). We do the same placing the Ebionite-leaning heresies at the left half of the Hexagon of Heresy, while the Docetist-leaning heresies are at the right. He further notes that Docetism "grows out of the tendency of fallen human nature to flee risky and vulnerable implications that belong inevitably to the very nature of love,"[98] while "Adoptionism is the glove that fits the hand of self-centeredness."[99] Hopefully, the arguments made later in this book will reveal the clarity of Allison's statement, "As Docetism is a religion of escape and not

---

98. Allison, *Cruelty of Heresy*, 35.
99. Allison, *Cruelty of Heresy*, 40.

fulfillment, so Adoptionism is a religion of control, not of redemption."[100] We will repeatedly see Docetism and its counterparts attempting to flee the reality of the created order toward a more ideal divine world, since there is both only one monist principle and hence the desire to give all the pieces in the zero-sum game to the divine side, while Ebionism and its fellow travelers will continuously diminish divine reality in order to give a fuller expression of reality to creation, trying to obtain as much as possible for creation and thereby diminishing the divine in the same zero-sum game. Both follow in the footsteps of Hellenistic philosophy before them, as the Ebioite-family of heresy stresses the duality between the divine and the created, aiming to give a real place to creation, though in a misplaced (distinction-as-opposition) way, while the Docetist-family of heresy flees the reality of the here-and-now to its quantitatively greater counterpart (what is natural is compelled) in the monist structure that all reality is one.

Finally, to combat Ebionism, the church confesses *Jesus* is Lord, meaning that the man is indeed the great "I Am"; and to combat Docetism, the church confesses Jesus is *Lord*, meaning that the great "I Am" has become this man. The historical and christological discussion of Ebionism and Docetism is complete. The difficulties posed by Origen have been discussed. Now we must turn our attention to the nine o'clock heresy, "Arianism."

---

100. Allison, *Cruelty of Heresy*, 42.

3

The Historical Paradigm at 9:00
Arianism

THIS CHAPTER WILL DISCUSS the "far left" of the Hexagon. At the nine o'clock position, we have Arianism. Arianism[1] is the denial of the full divinity of Jesus, operating in the dichotomist-dualist half of the Plotinian ambiguity, and as such it would appear at first glance a more refined version of adoptionism, of which Ebionism is the prime example. That is not the case.[2] "Arianism," though receiving its name from the historical figure of Arius, was in reality a loose collection of confederations over the course of most of the fourth century led by various bishops (Arius was but a presbyter, and no bishop would follow a mere presbyter) who opposed the Nicene definition of the unity of being of the Father and the Son, which states the divinity of the Son in the strongest possible terms.[3] Therefore, "Arianism" forms our first heresy of insufficiency. Though Arius held the Son to be "divine" in a reduced sense, the lack of fullness of divinity he

---

1. As I noted in chapter 1, contemporary patristic scholarship is moving away from the use of the term "Arianism" for a variety of reasons. See Williams, *Arius*, 247–48, for one example of such an argument. I retain the usage of the term, however, because there is no clear-cut way to describe what comes in later chapters in terms of Nicaea. In addition, I must note that many of the more dated sources I quote use the term "Arianism" freely. I will try to be judicious of my own usage of the term in this chapter, but in subsequent chapters I will return to it, frankly because I can think of no better word to describe the general idea.

2. McGrath, *Heresy*, 145, writes, for example, "Like Ebionitism [sic], Arius declined to accept that Jesus could be said to be divine in any meaningful sense of the term. Yet Ebionitism set out to interpret the significance of Jesus within the framework of existing Jewish models of divine presence within humanity, particularly the notion of a prophet or spirit-filled individual. Arius, in contrast, sought to accommodate Jesus of Nazareth within the frameworks made available by the strict Greek philosophical monotheisms of his age, which precluded any notion of the incarnation as inconsistent with the changelessness and transcendence of God. Ebionitism and Arianism may appear to say similar things; however, they begin from very different starting points and are guided by significantly different assumptions."

3. Ayres, *Nicaea*, 12n15, writes that Arius was "a catalyst for a controversy within which his particular theology rapidly becomes marginal."

and others upheld could not ultimately bear the weight of the soteriological model of the day, which was participation in God through Christ. If Khaled Anatolios's thesis is correct, as I believe it is, then Arius and those who came after him were meaningfully attempting to reintegrate Christian experience following Origen and his injection of the eternality of creation into the tradition.[4] Though Origen had many critics in the years following his death,[5] Arius was actually the first of his successors to try to comprehensively solve the problem he introduced. His solution would prove insufficient, as would the attempts of the rest of the anti-Nicenes, but all of theirs were steps in the right direction, as the most lasting solution remained far in the future. Here, I will examine the controversy from primarily its christological standpoint, rather than the more familiar trinitarian one.[6] Its purpose is to show that Arianism arises out of the challenge posed by the identity thesis and Plotinian ambiguity of definitional divine simplicity, and its ultimate defeat arrives when other possibilities rather those corollaries are shown to be viable options for the Father-Son relationship.

Arius in Alexandria

Though he likely does not deserve the title, Arius has come to be known as the archheretic of the early church.[7] Born in Libya around 256, he was entering elderly life as a priest and presbyter in Alexandria when the controversy that bears his name broke out in the late 310s.[8] As mentioned in the previous chapter, he claimed his theological heritage from Lucian of Antioch, the torch-bearer of the dichotomist-dualist expression of Origenism. In so doing, Arius perceived himself to be operating from within the stream of tradition handed down to him through Lucian.[9] Also, as we introduced last chapter, the most reliable tenet that we can reconstruct from Lucian's theology is that he attributes mutability to the Logos himself and that he does not believe Jesus

---

4. Anatolios, *Retrieving Nicaea*, 42–52.

5. Most notably for our purposes, his chief critic was Methodius of Olympus, who insisted upon the creation of the world out of nothing, over against Origen's speculation of eternal creation. Methodius and all who came after him (with the potential exception of Gregory of Nyssa) would reject the first two of the seven consequences of Origen's definitional simplicity: the pre-existence of souls and the *apokatastasis*.

6. Among the best studies of the Nicene controversy include Hanson, *Search*; Ayres, *Nicaea*; Anatolios, *Retrieving Nicaea*; Williams, *Arius*; and Behr, *Nicene Faith*.

7. As Anatolios, *Retrieving Nicaea*, 42–43, notes, Arius did not challenge the church from without. He saw himself as operating from within. He writes, "Arius himself did not create the break in Christian experience that was dramatized by the debates in which he was involved. Arius simply responded to this crisis by his own interpretive reintegration of the various elements of the Christian faith—a reintegration meant to restore the common flow of Christian experience."

8. Davis, *Councils*, 51. Here Davis discusses the possibilities for the theological pedigree of Arius.

9. Kelly, *Early Christian Doctrines*, 224. See also Ayres, *Nicaea*, 21 where he shows that Arius and his bishop, Alexander, are both indebted to Origen.

The Hexagon of Heresy

took on a human soul.[10] Arius will repeat these points in his own theological model, because he will attempt to hold together three main theological non-negotiables: the reality of creation from nothing, the suffering of God, and the immutability of God.[11]

Arius had three main theological presuppositions from which he operated. First was the absoluteness of God. Anatolios writes, "'God' is that being who is characterized by an absolute and unqualified priority, without any shadow of posteriority, and such a being by definition is absolutely unique."[12] Second was Arius's view of the transcendence of God, which in reality is a corollary of the first point, since God would have to create through an intermediary, because to come in contact with the material and created world could jeopardize his immutability and therefore singularity.[13] These two presuppositions are but a reworking of Origen's doctrine of divine simplicity, differing from Origen however on one important point: Arius stresses the freedom of God to create (beginning with his first creature, the Logos).[14] Arius is thus the first voice explicitly stating that the Father and Son are so different, even in a sense dialectically opposed.[15] Christopher Beeley summarizes the intensity of Arius's beliefs in his own words from his theological poem, the *Thalia*.

> Arius states in the *Thalia* that "God is essentially foreign to the Son" and that the Son is "unlike" the Father, does not participate in him, and has nothing that is proper (*idios*) to God (12.2/3.7). Consequently, even their glories are unique and unmixable (11), and they are not consubstantial (7). The Father and Son are therefore not only unequal but truly incomparable to one another (4). The Father exists independently of the Son: he is God apart from the Son's existence (14–15).[16]

---

10. Hanson, *Search*, 83, as cited in chapter 2, n91.

11. Hanson, *Search*, 109.

12. Anatolios, *Retrieving Nicaea*, 44. Beeley, *Unity of Christ*, 111, adds that the Father is "supremely unique (*monotatos*), yet the Son does not share this quality."

13. Erickson, *Word Became Flesh*, 51.

14. Williams, *Arius*, 97–98. The Father is so unique and simple that he cannot beget of his own nature, according to Arius. Recall that for Origen, the eternity of the world was at least entailed by his synthesis. Also, Williams, on pages 223–24, notes that Arius is indebted to the "Plotinian principle" that the One/Father can only be known by the negation of what he is not. The Son represents that which he is not, so Father and Son, in that sense, stand dialectically opposed, with the Son being creature (dichotomist-dualism). Though Arius follows along with Neoplatonism at this point, he cannot do so consistently, for he retains the freedom of God to create, an important part of the received Christian tradition. See the discussion between the will as faculty and the will as effect in chapter 2, n73.

15. This opposition of the Father and Son is something from which many later anti-Nicenes would distance themselves. This stark opposition of the Father and Son did not sit well even with those who would place the Son on the side of the creatures.

16. Beeley, *Unity of Christ*, 112. Parenthetical citations in the quote are from Arius's *Thalia Fragments*.

Thus, the Father is alone in his own nature, and begets by will and in (divine) time the Logos.[17] The result is two different beings, one eternal and one the first creature. Arius's third theological presupposition was his insistence of the analogy between the Father and Son and created fathers and sons.[18] Since created Fathers precede their sons in existence, it would follow that the Father preceded the Son in existence.[19] That is, the famous Arian dictum, "There was a time when the Son was not."[20] The elements of his theology that caused the controversy followed directly from his assumptions.

Millard Erickson, following Jaroslav Pelikan, notes that while in Arius's theology the Son was a creature, he was nonetheless different from all other creatures, so that he was not fully God, but not exactly like the rest of creation either. He was, in Erickson's words, an "intermediary, both cosmologically and soteriologically."[21] Such an intermediary is incapable of truly knowing the Father, and any knowledge he has of him is of the same quality as other creatures.[22] Arius did not believe it was possible for the Logos to be generated out of the being of God. Paul Hinlicky writes, "That notion would introduce becoming and plurality into God's simple, self-identical nature or substance, which is impossible since it contradicts the axiomatic idea of God as unoriginated source of all else that is not God. Anything that is originated, in turn, cannot be true God. Since the Logos cannot derive from God's being, the Logos must derive from an act of God's will commanding something to arise out of nothing."[23] That

---

17. Anatolios, *Retrieving Nicaea*, 42–52, notes that Arius was the prime theologian who saw the unity of Father and Son existing in the will (that is, the Son is a willed creation of the Father). The idea of generation by the will of the Father, emphasizing a difference between Father and Son, is what held all the various anti-Nicenes together (see his discussion on pages 53–79). He also states on page 45 that there is now general scholarly consensus that Arius extended Methodius's critique of Origen's cosmology to include the Son as first creature. See also the discussion in Ayres, *Nicaea*, 41–43.

18. Arius's idea of the Son as creature would imply that there would be an analogy between the created Son and all other created sons, so that he then could base the Father-Son relationship on father-son relationships. As Hanson, *Search*, 435, notes, the "Arians" who came later took the analogy so literally as to deny the eternality of the Son.

19. Beeley, *Unity of Christ*, 110. See also Bethune-Baker, *History*, 158. Here is the genesis of an Arian tendency in theological reflection seen most clearly in the contemporary debates concerning the eternal functional subordination of the Son. Arius argued from a distinct reality in the observable world (i.e. the distinction between created fathers and sons) and mapped that back onto the Father and Son. Once that mapping is complete, he then orders theology based on how the Father and Son relate (which itself is based on creation). It is a case of using both halves of the Plotinian ambiguity together: beginning, in a dichotomist-dualist fashion, in the observable world that stands over against God, he reasons, based on the monist half of the ambiguity, that creator and creation are parallel, then maps the parallel back into the observable world as the way things ought to be.

20. Hinlicky, *Divine Complexity*, 195, notes that by "time," Arius meant time in a divine sense rather than a created one. That is, Arius means in "divine time" rather than in "human time."

21. Erickson, *Word Became Flesh*, 51–52. Here he follows Pelikan, *Catholic Tradition*, 198. On the predominant soteriological model, that of the active work of the Logos transforming the world, see Ayres, *Nicaea*, 77.

22. McGrath, *Heresy*, 145, 151.

23. Hinlicky, *Divine Complexity*, 196. He continues, "Arius in any case seems to think that God the Unoriginate was always rational. When God decided to create the world, he made as his first creature

is, Jesus could not be "as divine" as the Father is.[24] Arius has failed to disentangle the Origenist Problematic. He has just changed its orientation in the Plotinian ambiguity from a monist to a dichotomist-dualist one. Whereas for Origen, the Son and creation are an eternal package deal, for Arius they are both created.[25] Since Arius holds that the Son is the one by which all other creation is mediated, a cosmological corollary to Arianism is that creation is mediated by a creation, rather than by the creator. We will see this concept becoming important in Augustine's cosmology later on.

Because Arius was fundamentally attempting to articulate a genuinely Christian position on the relationship of the Father and Son, he repeatedly appealed to the Bible for its foundation.[26] The chief texts used by Arius and the other anti-Nicenes to prove their point were texts that seemed to indicate that the Son is a creature (Prov 8:22; Acts 2:36; Col 1:15; and Heb 3:2); those that state the Father as the only true God (John 17:3, for example); texts implying the inferiority of the Son to the Father (John 14:28 and the "sending" texts); and the multitude of texts showing the true humanity, and therefore mutability of Christ.[27] It seems plausible that such a reading of the biblical texts could lead to the conclusion that the Father and Son are indeed different beings. The wide acceptance of such difference language as normative serves as a testimony that Arius was not a lone wolf leading the faithful astray, but rather one voice among many within a larger stream of Christian thought.

The Council of Nicaea

The question before the Alexandrian Christians was whether or not Arius's interpretation was indeed correct or could even stand together with the Alexandrian received tradition of the right wing of Origen's thinking. To ultimately defeat the views of Arius, his theological-philosophical presuppositions had to be shown to be false, thereby disentangling the packaging together of the Son and creation, and a hermeneutic would need to be articulated that properly explained both how Jesus was the Father's equal and Son simultaneously.

---

an image of his own rationality and gave to this being, the Logos, the actual work of calling forth the world and ordering it. The Logos is the mediator between mind and matter, being and becoming, spirit and flesh, ideal and real, the divine and the mortal. Therefore the Logos, eternal or not, is a creature. He is made, not begotten, out of nothing, not of the being of the Father. Thus Arius denied that the Son could be of the same being (*homoousios*) of the Father."

24. Hinlicky, *Divine Complexity*, 198. As Hinlicky notes, for Arius, "God" is a proper name.

25. Of Anatolios's seven entailments of Origen's definitional simplicity, Arius rejects the first two (eternal souls and the *apokatastasis*), but openly embraces the next three (the Son as less than the Father, the Son as eternally "for us," and a Christology of continuity).

26. See, for example, Anatolios, *Retrieving Nicaea*, 46.

27. Erickson, *Word Became Flesh*, 52–53, as well as Hanson, *Search*, 106–8. See also the discussion in Bethune-Baker, *History*, 161–63.

The Historical Paradigm at 9:00

By most historical accounts, it was in the year 318 when Alexander, Bishop of Alexandria formally challenged Arius concerning his teachings that the controversy exploded onto the scene.[28] Arius accused his bishop of Sabellianism and refused to recant.[29] It is easy to see why Arius responded as he did; to say that the Son is eternally generated from the being of the Father would sound like erasing any real distinction between Father and Son.[30] Two years later, in 320, Alexander called a synod of Libyan and Egyptian bishops, where 80% voted to condemn and exile Arius.[31] Arius fled Alexandria to Palestine, and thence to Asia Minor, where he rallied a group of bishops sympathetic to the tradition of Lucian of Antioch around him. They called a synod and upheld Arius while condemning Alexander. It is at this point that the importance of Arius as a historical figure in the controversy fades. The bishops Arius consulted were already sympathetic to his key point (the Son as a product of the Father's will rather than the Father's being, and the implication that the Son had a beginning) and now, as bishops, they move to the forefront. By 324, Constantine had solidified his position as the sole ruler of the Roman Empire and did not want any sort of religious controversy in his newly-unified political state. He greatly misunderstood the theological importance of the controversy, as Davis quotes Constantine as saying, "For as long as you continue to contend about these small and very insignificant questions, I believe it indeed to not be merely unbecoming, but positively evil, that so a large portion of God's people which belongs to your jurisdiction should be thus divided."[32] Small and very insignificant questions indeed! But, in the new era of the unified church and state, theological controversies become political, and this controversy was becoming too big for Constantine to allow to continue.

The following year, in 325, Constantine summoned all the Christian bishops to an ecumenical council in Nicaea (modern Iznik) in what is now Turkey.[33] The

---

28. For a summary of Alexander's theology concerning the unity of the Father and Son, see Anatolios, *Retrieving Nicaea*, 79–86, Ayres, *Nicaea*, 42–45, and Williams, *Arius*, 223–24. Alexander taught that the Son is the creator. Anatolios, *Retrieving Nicaea*, 80, writes, "If the most radical distinction in the unity-of-will theologies [Arius's for example] is between divine being and divine will, the most radical distinction in unity-of-being theologies [Alexander's, for example] is that between creator and creation." Alexander seeks to place the Son on the creator side of his divide, while Arius is convinced that the Son is the first product of the divine will. Here I would say that Anatolios means by "will" the effects of the will and not the faculty thereof.

29. See Erickson, *Word Made Flesh*, 49–50; Blaising, "Monarchianism," 784–85; Kelly, *Early Christian Doctrines*, 119–23 for an overview of Sabellianism. Sabellianism held that there was only one divine person with three different names (Father, Son, and Holy Spirit). It equated person with nature, since the one divine nature could admit only one divine person. Where Sabellius saw the unity at the metaphysical level of person/nature (only one person in the Godhead), Arius posited the unity of the Godhead as energetic (volitional).

30. Beeley, *Unity of Christ*, 25–26.

31. Davis, *Councils*, 53.

32. Davis, *Councils*, 54.

33. McGrath, *Heresy*, 148, notes that out of approximately 1,800 bishops throughout the Eastern and Western churches, only about 250 attended.

controversy was on the verge of dividing the Empire theologically, and an answer needed to be reached. It was assumed that the collective mind of the church could be ascertained quickly at the council. As J. F. Bethune-Baker writes, "But the mind of the Church was not made up. The actual form of the question at issue was new and technical—a question for experts. The Arians called Christ God, and Son of God, and offered him worship; and they professed entire allegiance to the teaching of Scripture. It might well seem to the mass of the bishops assembled in council that the Arians were sound at heart, and technical details should not be pressed against them."[34] The question, as should be clear by now, is to what degree Christ could be called God—either fully, somewhat (by action and will but not by nature), or barely. Bethune-Baker notes that such middle-ground folks rallied behind Eusebius of Caesarea, the learned historian and well-respected bishop, who at first did not think the position occupied by those bishops who held some degree of sympathy for Arius's position was a real problem.[35] The group aligned with Eusebius should be called, rather than Arians, "anti-Nicenes," since most of them were not fully on board with all of Arius's solutions. Alexander of Alexandria and his right-hand man Athanasius were staunchly opposed to the generation of the Son by will and any sort of creaturely status concerning him, and they were the main historical figures of the pro-Nicene party.[36]

As Leo Davis notes, the council's first order of business was to try to fashion a creed using scriptural terminology only, "but it proved impossible to word such a creed so as to exclude the Arian position in the strictest fashion possible. Arian-sympathizing bishops could be seen, it is said, winking and nodding, confident that they could twist a scripturally-worded creed to their advantage."[37] It was not until the word *homoousios*—meaning of the same essence or substance—was proposed, possibly by Hosius of Cordoba, that the anti-Nicene position looked doomed.[38] It was

---

34. Bethune-Baker, *History*, 165.

35. Ayres, *Nicaea*, 52–55, lumps Arius himself in with those who were aligned with Eusebius of Caesarea, calling them "Eusebians."

36. Anatolios, *Retrieving Nicaea*, 79–86.

37. Davis, *Councils*, 59.

38. Bethune-Baker, *History*, 167. As Ayres, *Nicaea*, 90, writes, *homoousios* was chosen because "Arius was known to reject it." Ayres adds on page 96, that the original meaning of *homoousios* was "from the *ousia* of the Father," as opposed to from the Father's will. The term "*homoousios*" was first used by third-century Bishop of Antioch Paul of Samosata, a man whom everyone at Nicaea believed to be heretical. Hinlicky, *Divine Complexity*, 194, quoting Leitzman, *Early Church*, 101, states that Paul, in attacking Origen, claimed that the title "Son of God" was a human title rather than a divine one. The Logos, to Paul, was not an independent person, "but as a form of God's operation, a manifestation of his being; in short, not a self-subsistent being (*ousia*) to be separated from God, but rather 'one in essence,' that is, *homoousios*." Leitzman describes the results of Paul's thought thus: "The Logos had no independent personality, but was only a term for a divine mode of activity [and] the way in which he dwelt in the man Jesus. Christ could only be conceived, on closer inspection, as a kind of exalted inspiration." Hinlicky writes on page 195, "Paul loses both the Trinity in theology and the unity of person in Christology. As a consequence of this controversy, the term *homoousios* became associated with modalism, just as *hypostasis* had been with subordinationism. Both the key terms in

an ambiguous term that needed precision, for it could mean numerical identity, a generic oneness (two men sharing human nature, for example, would be *homoousios*), or material things that share the same kind of substance (two pots both made of clay, for example, would be *homoousios*). While the second meaning became normative, the first meaning was always lurking behind the scenes.[39] Once the creed was finally composed and Constantine finished threatening exile to all who opposed it, only two bishops refused to sign.[40] Eusebius of Caesarea and all who followed him threw their weight behind the creed also, though, as Ayres states, Eusebius could still interpret the creed in a way that was favorable to his original position.[41] Thus, more work needed to be done, and the division in the church remained. Arius himself was excluded but the position he championed required further clarification. For such a task, we move on to Athanasius.

Athanasius

Athanasius was the able-bodied lieutenant of Bishop Alexander in Alexandria. He far exceeded his master in theological acumen, and after becoming bishop shortly after the council would ultimately prove to be the unifying force of the mid-fourth century. Much of his first decade as bishop was marked by trial and exile, as the anti-Nicenes, though "defeated" at the Council of Nicaea, held the political advantage throughout the remainder of Constantine's life.[42] As the political and ecclesiastical intrigue intertwined during the second quarter of the fourth century, numerous positions developed with nuanced variations on the Nicene formulation. By around 340, all the opponents of Athanasius were called "Arians," though that name is hardly historically precise.[43]

The rest of this section will be devoted to the methodology Athanasius initiates in his important work, *Against the Arians*, and then develops later in his career. He began on the foundation of the original argument between Arius and Alexander, that the Father is ingenerate. Athanasius makes a distinction between two kinds of

---

later Nicene theology thus entered the fourth century bearing the stigma of heresy." Hinlicky, *Divine Complexity*, 159.

39. Davis, *Councils*, 61. Later, Basil of Caesarea would state some of the apprehension behind the term *homoousios*. Some at Nicaea were afraid it implied a common substance that underlies the persons, a move where we see essence coming to the forefront in the *ordo theologiae* (something Augustine of Hippo would do in less than a century after the first ecumenical council in 325). Marcellus of Ancyra accepted *homoousios*, though he denied a real distinction between Father and Son. See the thoughts of Basil in the quote in Farrell, *God, History, and Dialectic*, 292. See also the discussion in Ayres, *Nicaea*, 93–95.

40. Davis, *Councils*, 63.

41. Ayres, *Nicaea*, 91.

42. See the discussion in Behr, *Nicene Faith*, 1:69–75. Constantine died in 337. "Arianism," with its inherent subordination of the Son to the Father, was more palatable to the emperors because they sought to subordinate the church to the state.

43. Behr, *Nicene Faith*, 1:76.

The Hexagon of Heresy

ingeneracy. If by ingeneracy, one means "it always existed," then the Son is ingenerate. But if one means "without generation," then such a meaning applies only to the Father.[44] Moreover, because the divine nature is simple (!), God has always dwelt with his Word and Wisdom. Therefore, the Son is eternally generated from the being of the Father and not from the will, and he is inseparable from the Father, as evidenced by the unity of action (energy) they undertake.[45] It is easy to see at this point that Athanasius's theology of Father and Son could be misread in two opposite directions: either there are two unbegottens or there is in reality only one principle.[46] That is, it could be interpreted through either side of the Plotinian ambiguity by his opponents. Asterius and the other anti-Nicenes could only see the two possible outcomes due to their strict adherence to a definitionally simple first principle.

Athanasius carefully seeks to affirm the ontological gulf between creator and creation that Origen confused. What he hopes to do, however, is place the Son on the creator side of the gulf (rejecting the anti-Nicene position) rather than on the created side.[47] He wishes to do this without falling into either of the above traps his opponents think are entailed by his position. He argues that since the Son is creator—an assertion both sides accepted—then if the Son does not share the divine essence, the Father cannot be creator.[48] Anatolios notes that Athanasius is flirting with the Origenist Problematic here, but is able to avoid it by arguing that God's ability to create does not necessitate the existence of creation.[49] And since "creator" can be properly applied to both Father and Son, then both are contained in the divine being.[50] Brilliantly, Athanasius forges a third way beyond both the monist Origen who confuses creator and creation and the dichotomist-dualist anti-Nicenes who insist the Son originates from the Father's will before going on to create the world. For Athanasius, the creation

---

44. Ayres, *Nicaea*, 112–13. Ayres notes that Athanasius's focus on ingeneracy as the key battle phrase may have caused a hardening of the lines that will spawn the theology of Eunomius of Cyzicus a generation later.

45. Ayres, *Nicaea*, 113–14. More on simplicity to follow.

46. Ayres, *Nicaea*, 115.

47. Ayres, *Nicaea*, 143. Anatolios, *Retrieving Nicaea*, 104, notes that for the moderate anti-Nicenes such as Eusebius, the Word played a crucial intermediary role between the (definitionally) simple and unreachable Father and the creation. Thus, Eusebius held to a very Platonic "chain of being."

48. Athanasius, *Apol. sec.* 2.2, as quoted in Anatolios, *Retrieving Nicaea*, 116.

49. Recall that Origen held the Father to be definitionally simple as a first principle, which entailed that every predication of the divine being was identical to the divine being and to every other predication of the divine being (the identity thesis). Therefore, the predication "creator" implied the eternal existence of creation, since "creator" is really indistinguishable from the divine being. Athanasius also believes in divine simplicity, but differs from Origen in that, for Athanasius, the predication "creator" need not imply the eternal existence of creation, so the Father can still be properly called "creator" though it does not imply the existence of creation. The methodological move here is subtle, but important. Athanasius is not reasoning from the many to the One as is done in definitional simplicity. His simplicity is of a different kind. We will see more shortly.

50. Athanasius, *Apol. sec.* 1.29, in Anatolios, *Retrieving Nicaea*, 117.

of the world is grounded in the Father-Son relationship in such a way that both the temporal original creation and the redemption are both derived from it.[51]

Athanasius ties the entire argument together by insisting that the mediating function of the Logos over creation is in his incarnate status rather than his pre-incarnate existence.[52] For the anti-Nicenes, the very existence of creation implied the necessity of a mediating being that was less than the Father but greater than the rest of creation. For Athanasius, creation did not require a created mediator to keep the Father from soiling himself in its affairs. In this way, he was able to avoid the extremes of Origen (the Problematic and the eternal mediation of the Logos), Marcellus (no eternal distinction between Father and Son), and Eustathius (a separation between Jesus and the Son, more on him in the next chapter), while avoiding emanationism, any kind of subordinationism, or what he perceived to be the polytheism in the anti-Nicenes.[53] That is, the unity of the Father and Son is one of being (*homoousios*), and not one of will, while they remain distinct. The Son is not willed by the Father, but is his natural offspring, not voluntary, just as God need not will to be or to be good.[54] Later, in the early 350s, Athanasius began to more deeply expound on *homoousios*. He insisted that it was to be a hermeneutical key through which the Scriptures could be interpreted on the basis of the Father-Son relationship. He argued, though not always without circularity, that it was more fitting to name God in relation to Christ than to name him from his relation to creatures.[55] Here he is taking on not only his opponents of the day, but also implicitly the definitional simplicity tradition of Origen and of the pagans that God is what creation is not. Christologically, the Son is never less than the Father and retains the same impassibility common to both. As Hanson states, "Even though the sufferings of the body did not affect the Logos, they were still the sufferings of the Logos and therefore redemptive."[56] Here we see Athanasius struggling to express—due to imprecise terminology that requires him to write in paradoxical verbiage—what those who came after him will affirm, that there is both three and one in God, and that Christ can suffer yet be unaffected by the sufferings,[57] though Athanasius displayed a lack of objection to the anti-Nicene position of no human soul in Jesus. Athanasius attacks his

---

51. Athanasius, *Apol. sec.* 2.82, in Anatolios, *Retrieving Nicaea*, 118. Also, Anatolios, 103–4, discusses how Athanasius maintains a clear distinction between creator and creation, but he also stresses that creation is "in" God, overcoming the either-or of the Plotinian ambiguity. Anatolios, *Athanasius*, 114, notes that Athanasius believed that the function of mediator had to be originated from the divine side rather than the created, and it was the very fact that the Son and Spirit mediated creation that was proof of their full divinity. On pages 115–16, he further argues that the anti-Nicenes had invented a "one true God" who does nothing, in contrast to the Old Testament witness.

52. Athanasius, *Apol. sec.* 2.73–74, in Hanson, *Search*, 424.

53. Hanson, *Search*, 425.

54. Athanasius, *Apol. sec.* 3.66, in Hanson, *Search*, 431.

55. Anatolios, *Retrieving Nicaea*, 131–33.

56. Hanson, *Search*, 448. As Anatolios, *Athanasius*, 144, writes, "It is the same Word who both suffers and suffers not."

57. Hanson, *Search*, 443–48, and Anatolios, *Athanasius*, 145.

opponents at every possible turn but is silent on this point until late in his life.[58] Such thinking will need to wait until the next chapter for resolution.

One of Athanasius's strongest arguments for the *homoousion* is that to say that the Father and Son are united by will would entail that the unity of Father and Son would be the same as that of the Father and the angels or saints, since they too will the same.[59] Though he does not work out the argument to the extent that exists in the pseudonymous *Fourth Discourse*,[60] Athanasius has made an important distinction in the advance of undoing the synthesis of Origen: he distinguishes between the being of God and the faculty of the will of God, because the will cannot be said to produce the Son. Athanasius argues in the *homoousion* that the faculty of will cannot generate the Son, though it is concordant with the act of the essence. Thus, a real distinction exists between energy (will) and being.[61] While it was noted above, Athanasius, like every other early theologian, upheld divine simplicity, the preceding argument proves he did not interpret simplicity in a definitional sense because of the real distinction he made between the being of God and the faculty of God's will. Though Athanasius remains hampered by existing terminology, he makes a critical distinction between the being of God and the three who possess it. Farrell summarizes, "Athanasius has, it is to be noted, not so much *refuted* the Arian presupposition of simplicity, as opposed his own very traditional presupposition against it, and *then* drawn its inevitable implication: *person and essence are not the same thing: there are ultimate and irreducible categorical distinctions in God*."[62] Before Athanasius, there was no real distinction between person and nature. As Balthasar writes, the birth of the concept of person as

---

58. Hanson, *Search*, 452. Hanson demonstrates on page 453 that the anti-Nicenes made a great deal out of Jesus's weaknesses because it further strengthened their position that the Logos was mutable. They did not need a human soul in Jesus, because he was already changeable. Anatolios, *Athanasius*, 78–79, argues that Athanasius's understanding of the human and divine in Jesus is more complex than just some form of composition. He states that, according to Athanasius, the Logos was simultaneously in and beyond Jesus's flesh, controlling it and elevating it in a way more profound than the human soul does to the body. Moreover, on page 147, he states that the composition of the divine and human in Jesus took a back seat to the overarching purpose of why God became man in his thought. Additionally, on page 152, salvation through *theosis* would require Jesus to be fully human.

59. Athanasius, *Apol. sec.* 3.11, in Leithart, *Athanasius*, 73–74.

60. Here I am following the argument of Farrell, *Free Choice*, 56–57. The author of the *Fourth Discourse* takes aim at the Arian application of the identity thesis: the confusion of the relational property of the Father (the generation of the Son) with the divine essence itself. If such a confusion were true, he argues, then to be God is to be the generator eternally of something else, and so on until there is a multiplicity of Gods (which is exactly the error of the Hellenistic emanation religions that both Christianity and Arianism wanted to avoid), and the argument reduces to absurdity.

61. Anatolios, *Athanasius*, 121, clarifies, "It is not God's will that is secondary to God's being, but what comes to be through God's will is secondary to what eternally exists as constitutive of the divine being. The priority of being over will is thus ultimately a reformulation of the priority of the Word over the world." See also Athanasius, *Apol. sec.* 2.2.

62. Farrell, *God, History, and Dialectic*, 112. Italics in original. Athanasius will remain fuzzy in his precision concerning "person," but the implications are there and ready to be drawn more clearly by Basil of Caesarea.

a distinct metaphysical category from essence is a Christian enterprise.[63] Not only is there now a distinction between the "who" (person) and the "what" (nature), there is also one between those two categories and energies (actions and attributes). The Cappadocians in the next generation would complete the task Athanasius began, as he laid the groundwork for those coming after him to state it in clearer terminology.

More than any of his contemporaries, Athanasius correctly discerned the real problem lying under the entire controversy—the overreaction of much of the fourth-century church against the Origenist problematic which caused the line between creator and creature to pass between the Father and Son. Due to the problematic, the Son and creation are on the same "ontological plane," so to speak—either they are both eternal or they are both temporal. Traditional Christian worship cannot and could not accept the Son and creation in such a package deal. The kind of simplicity that packages the two together would have to be disentangled. We have just seen how Athanasius begins to levy the critical distinction between who God is and what God does to the Father-Son relationship, which is the first "front" in his battle against those who would say that the Son is begotten of the Father's will.[64] The second front would be to come up with a hermeneutical rule that would answer his opponents' ability to back up their positions as noted above with select texts of Scripture to "prove" they were right, that is, a rule that would be able to show both truths concerning the Son—his ontological equality with the Father and his incarnational subordination to the Father.

The key to Athanasius's biblical argument is his insistence upon Christ as God becoming man; that is, his "christological turn" in hermeneutics. This leads him to see all of Scripture as speaking of Christ in one aspect or the other, either as the eternal Son or as the incarnate Son.[65] It is in Athanasius that we see the differentiation of what has always belonged to Christ (his being as God) and what he became for our sakes (his humanity in the economy).[66] Athanasius accuses his opponents of failing to see this basic double aspect of Christ throughout both testaments, as they tend to emphasize one or the other improperly. As Behr writes, "As Athanasius sees it, by failing to differentiate how or under what 'aspect' any given text of Scripture speaks of Jesus Christ, the 'Arians' have conflated theology and economy and have so ended up with an intermediary being, their Word."[67] He continues, "Athanasius, on the other hand, by distinguishing what is spoken of Christ as he is from what belongs to what he has done, the economy, can maintain that the abiding, timeless subject of theological

---

63. Balthasar, *Cosmic Liturgy*, 210–11.

64. In so doing, Athanasius rejects and, in my opinion, successfully rebuffs entailments 3 (the Son is less than the Father) and 4 (Christ is always and forever "for us") of Origen's definitional simplicity. He also disagrees with entailment 5 (a Christology of continuity), but others will be pro-Nicene and hold to it, as we will see Apollinarius do in the next chapter.

65. Hanson, *Search*, 423.

66. Behr, *Way to Nicaea*, 213.

67. Behr, *Way to Nicaea*, 213.

reflection is Jesus Christ, who has himself acted in time for us."[68] For Athanasius, there is only one Christ, God become human, and even though he partitively speaks of the two aspects, he is careful to maintain the existence of only one subject. In other words, Athanasius is able to distinguish between who Christ *is* in Scripture with what Christ "economically" *does* in the Scripture; it is the exegetical continuation of his philosophical argument.

The sheer brilliance of Athanasius can be seen in how his partitive exegesis is applied. Any biblical text that speaks of the equality of Christ and the Father, whether it is in the Old Testament or New, is a statement concerning his eternal being. On the other hand, any text that implies any sort of subordination of the Son to the Father speaks of the economy, what Christ has become in the incarnation for our sakes. When applied consistently, the biblical basis for a lesser Christ disappears. The proof-texting methodology of Athanasius's opponents, pulling individual verses out of the Bible without regarding their place in the larger christological picture, was shown to be a faulty enterprise because a cherry-picked proof-text could not, standing alone, meaningfully show whether it spoke of being (essence) or action (energy). For Athanasius, hermeneutics was a distinctly christological enterprise, as his partitive methodology required a priority of person over energy in his *ordo theologiae*. A key corollary here is that Christology precedes hermeneutics, for a right reading of Scripture presupposes an orthodox Christology.[69]

Also, in his argument against his opponents, Athanasius appeals to the salvation of humans as proof that they are wrong. Davis writes, "Unlike the Arians who were concerned primarily with the Son's place in creation, Athanasius begins with the firm conviction that the Word became flesh to redeem the human race, to make men godlike. But the Word could never divinize mankind if he were merely divine by participation in the Father's nature and not himself the essential Godhead, the very image of the Father."[70] In other words, only God can save. If Jesus saves, then Jesus must be truly and fully God. Davis continues, "At first Athanasius did not much use the Nicene *homoousios*, but gradually he saw its full implication and became its most resolute defender. The likeness and unity of the Father and Word cannot consist in just harmony and concord of mind and will, but must be in respect of essence. The divinity of the Father is identical to the divinity of the Word."[71] Thus in arguing from human salvation, Jesus cannot be savior unless he is *homoousios* with the Father. Justo Gonzalez

---

68. Behr, *Way to Nicaea*, 213–14. In such a statement, Athanasius anticipates the work of Cyril of Alexandria that we will see in chapter 5.

69. Such a move both casts serious doubt on any model that utilizes the Bible apart from tradition as a foundation for faith, and implies that there is no "christologically neutral" reading of Scripture. I believe I owe Perry Robinson for that phrasing, although I do not remember exactly where he said it.

70. Davis, *Councils*, 89. This quote illustrates how the Arians derived their Christology from their cosmology. Athanasius is arguing in the opposite direction: person before energy, not the other way around.

71. Davis, *Councils*, 90.

sums up Athanasius's thinking well as he writes, "There are two fundamental reasons why Athanasius abhors Arian doctrine: first, that Arianism approaches polytheism and, second, that it implies that salvation comes from a creature. In consequence, it is clear that Athanasius is opposed to Arianism, not because it attacks or denies some point of his theology, but because it is incompatible with the two pillars on which his faith stood, even before the controversy."[72] Athanasius is always stressing the importance of one God and one savior.

In the Council of Alexandria in 362, Athanasius called for the return of the "Arians," promising a clarification of the term *hypostasis* (which would not actually come for another decade or so). Following the council, many of the remaining "Arians" were satisfied with the development in language and returned to the orthodox fold. Athanasius did not just theologically solve a problem; he spent a lifetime applying the solution to ultimately heal the wounds it caused. Unfortunately, Athanasius would not live to see the end of the controversy. He died in 373, and the leadership of defending Nicene orthodoxy passed to the Cappadocian bishops, who came to the forefront following his death.

The Cappadocians

Much of the work of the Cappadocians—Basil of Caesarea, his brother Gregory of Nyssa, and their friend Gregory of Nazianzus—complements and completes that which was begun by Athanasius a generation earlier. In this section, I am limiting my discussion of them to their contributions to Christology and their approach to the *ordo theologiae*.[73] The christological fight faced by the Cappadocians was with the Eunomians, named after their leader Eunomius of Cyzicus. They were the last great "Arian" challenge to Nicene orthodoxy, effectively galvanizing all of the remaining opponents of Nicaea under a common banner.[74] Andrew Radde-Gallwitz notes that for Eunomius, "there is a fundamental contradiction in saying that the simple divine essence is simultaneously without beginning or 'ingenerate' (*agennetos*) and begotten or 'generate' (*gennetos*). These contradictory properties cannot both characterize a *simple* substance." So Eunomius must "relegate one of the contradictory terms to a

---

72. Gonzalez, *From the Beginnings*, 298.

73. I will omit any discussion of Gregory of Nazianzus here, though it is worth mentioning that he continued Athanasius's partitive hermeneutics in his struggle against the Eunomians. See Behr, *Nicene Faith*, 2:349. Gregory of Nazianzus will make his presence felt as the one who presided over the Council of Constantinople in 381 (more on this below) as well as his opposition to another side of the Hexagon of Heresy, Apollinarianism.

74. See Radde-Gallwitz, *Basil*, 87–88. Here he argues that Eunomius was able to unite the various kinds of "heteroousians" (those who, for one reason or another, rejected the idea that the Father and Son were *homoousios*) into his camp, effectively polarizing the debate between two clear adversaries—Eunomius himself and his opponents, the Cappadocians.

lower level of divinity.⁷⁵ Robert Letham summarizes Eunomius and his followers well, as they were:

> Rationalists, confident in the extensive capacities of human logic. By logic, they maintained, we are able to comprehend God. They assumed there to be a univocal relation between the divine mind and the human mind (a correspondence between divine and human thought, such that meaning is identical for both). For them, the Son is absolutely unlike the Father. God is absolute being, and generation cannot be attributed to him. Because of the identity between the mind of God and human reasoning, the Son's generation is to be understood in terms of human generation. Since eternal generation is inconceivable, the generation of the Son must have had a beginning. Hence, there was a time when the Son did not exist. The Son was the first created being, and was the instrument by which God created the world.⁷⁶

God was knowable, because all of his attributes were identical, and organized under the name "ingenerate."⁷⁷ All three Cappadocian fathers wrote against the Eunomians, who identified the *hypostasis* of the Father with one of his energies—the will, and as such entails that as human fathers sire children by an act of will, so does the Father beget the Son via will, and the Son is thus a creature.⁷⁸

Basil of Caesarea countered the Eunomians by making the vital and decisive distinction between *hypostasis* and *ousia*, defining the difference between the two as the relationship of the irreducible particular (the "who") to the kind it is (the "what" the "who" is).⁷⁹ Up until that time, the two terms had been confusingly used as synonyms throughout pagan and Christian history alike. Here is the first great step of Christian theology breaking new ground in rearranging existing terminology to fit its new metaphysical categorical insights. In trinitarian theology, *ousia* will become essence or being, while *hypostasis* will become person. As a result, Basil showed that it is possible, as Letham states, "to speak of three *hypostases* [sic] and be orthodox."⁸⁰ Basil completed, as far as the doctrine of the Trinity goes, the terminological "baptisms" needed to properly distinguish person and nature that Athanasius had begun a

---

75. Radde-Gallwitz, *Basil*, 8. I transliterated the Greek terms Radde-Gallwitz leaves in the original language.

76. Letham, *Holy Trinity*, 146. Here we see the same assumptions of Arius repeated in Eunomius: divine simplicity, nature before person in the *ordo theologiae*, and the assumption that God and creature are on the same ontological plane, so one can analogically reason from the latter to the former.

77. Radde-Gallwitz, *Basil*, 98, states that Eunomius believed we owe a debt to God to know him, and that knowledge is proven by calling God exactly who he is, the ingenerate. His understanding of definitional simplicity lies at the heart of his proposal. He further notes on page 88 that although Eunomius is identified as "Arian," he does not follow Arius in his understanding of the comprehensibility of God. Arius denied it, while Eunomius embraced it.

78. Farrell, *God, History, and Dialectic*, 272.

79. Farrell, *God, History, and Dialectic*, citing Basil of Caesarea, *Letter* 236.6.

80. Letham, *Holy Trinity*, 145.

generation before. Definitional simplicity in the doctrine of God had been replaced by three *hypostases* in one *ousia*. There is no "lesser God" in the Godhead.

Basil, in one of his letters, gives the proper starting point for theological reflection to be person, rather than nature. He writes, "If we have no distinct perception of the separate characteristics, namely, fatherhood, sonship, and sanctification, but form our conception of God from the general idea of existence, we cannot possibly give a sound account of our faith."[81] He continues concerning the primacy of the category of *hypostasis*, in the analysis of Farrell:

> The definition that St. Basil gives of *hypostasis* as that which has "so far as the peculiarity extends, nothing in common with what is of the same kind", that is, another *hypostasis*, should be given due weight. He is maintaining (1) that any given *hypostasis* is undefineable absolutely, since that which distinguishes it *as an hypostasis* is without analogy—it is irreducibly concrete and irrepeatable and without analogy in its differentiation—to any other given *hypostasis*; and therefore that (2) *hypostases* can only be *distinguished*. Thus, no natural faculty or operation defines the content of any given hypostasis.[82]

Thus *hypostasis*, more particularly the three divine ones that are irreducible, becomes the starting point for theology, since the "what"—the divine essence—only signifies the kind, which itself is distinguishable by common operation, thus yielding the *ordo theologiae* of person, energy, and finally nature.

Gregory of Nyssa, in his short treatise to Ablabius (*Not Three Gods*), argued that contrary to the Eunomians, God's essence is unknowable; he is known by his energies. One divine energy implies one essence of God, because each *hypostasis* acts together with the other two. In this way, God is contrasted to humans, because with us there is one human nature, but the human *hypostases* act differently, each acting "by themselves."[83] Here in Gregory we see the concept of the divine persons performing the same actions, which in turn reveals the one essence, which places the *ordo theologiae* correctly: persons, energy, then nature. This argument will figure prominently in chapter 6 in the refutation of Monothelitism.

Andrew Radde-Gallwitz has argued, persuasively in my opinion, that Basil and Gregory "transformed divine simplicity. They did so by articulating a version of the doctrine of divine simplicity that avoids the horns of total apophaticism and the identity thesis (as they encountered it in Eunomius), while still playing its by-then traditional role within the Christian tradition."[84] Like Athanasius, the Cappadocians discerned that the identity thesis was the problem in the arguments of their opponents. Athanasius asserted that there must be a distinction between God's essence and

---

81. Basil of Caesarea, *Letter* 236.6, quoted in Farrell, *God, History, and Dialectic*, 756.
82. Farrell, *God, History, and Dialectic*, 758. Italics in original. He quotes Basil, *Letter* 236 (38:2–3).
83. Meyendorff, *Christ in Eastern Christian Thought* (1975), 144.
84. Radde-Gallwitz, *Basil*, 6.

energies. The Cappadocians formulated a constructive theological response to back up Athanasius's intuitive assertion.

Eunomius had argued that in order to know God, one must know his essence and that any other knowledge of God was not true knowledge. For him, it was "either-or," either one knows God by his essence or one does not know God at all. Because God is simple (that is, essence is all there really is), essence is all that can be known.[85] Here is the identity thesis in full view. In Radde-Gallwitz's words, "In reply, Basil and Gregory seize upon a 'category' that as it were 'splits the difference' between these two kinds of knowledge. They construe the positive divine attributes, such as light, life, and goodness, as *propria*, that is properties co-extensive with and intrinsic to the divine essence, but not individually definitive of that essence."[86] These *propria* inhere in the divine essence, and serve as "identifying markers" for it. "Yet, at the same time, *propria* do not define the essence. God's *propria* of goodness, wisdom, power, justice, and truth do not tell us what it is to be God. God is simultaneously known and unknown, and part of the theological task is stating clearly where the lines are drawn between these."[87] This middle way preserves the truth of the biblical statements about God and keeps them from being reduced to ingeneracy. God's nature is not composed of the *propria* nor can it be broken down into them any more than he is composed of the union of the three persons. In the construction of the Cappadocians, God remains simple, but the simplicity is "irreducibly" complex.[88] The energies are neither identical to the essence nor to each other, but they are inseparable from it. God is truly known by these energies, but God's essence, against Eunomius, remains unknowable and undefinable. In doing so, the Cappadocian fathers cement the orthodox view by retaining divine simplicity as *descriptive* of God, but rejecting it as a *definition* of the divine essence, the latter task they deem impossible.

A corollary to this key insight begun by Athanasius and theologically worked out by the Cappadocians is put well by Joseph Farrell: "God is thus really one in essence, really manifold in operations, and really three in persons." He continues, "The three 'categories' of persons, operations, [and] essence are really distinct categories such

---

85. Radde-Gallwitz, *Basil*, 108, writes, "This is a modified version of the principle of the priority of definition: the idea that knowing *what* something is, its essence, is prior to knowing anything else about it. In the Eunomian theological version, it is not so much the *priority* of knowing what as the *exclusivity* of knowing what. This is a significant modification: it is not that one needs to know God's essence in order to know other things about God. Rather, God's essence is all there is to know. It should be noted, however, that the Eunomian position only requires the principle to hold in the case of simple objects of thought such as God; it would not need to hold for mundane realities." He continues on page 112, "For Eunomius, the doctrine of simplicity functioned to ensure the objective nature of knowledge of God. Because God has no non-essential properties, in so far as we know God, we know God's very essence."

86. Radde-Gallwitz, *Basil*, 107.

87. Radde-Gallwitz, *Basil*, 225.

88. The term "irreducible complexity" was coined by Michael Behe in formulating arguments for intelligent design. I borrow it here but attach a different meaning to it.

that there are three distinct kinds of realities in God, and in each case, the names of those terms—persons, operations, and essence—have nothing whatsoever to do with their corresponding meanings in any philosophical system. They have significance and meaning wholly peculiar to Christian theology."[89] Working out these distinctions along with how to appropriate them would take centuries of further reflection, along with the stretching of existing words into newer, more technical meanings. But the Eunomian Controversy ends with the Greek Fathers having drawn meaningful distinctions among God's persons, energies, and essence. All of the "Arian" theologies began their task with the essence of God, defined as simple with the identity thesis as a corollary. The methodology of both Athanasius and the Cappadocians began with the divine persons, and used the divine energies to reveal the content of the divine essence, which itself remained unknowable. With these advances in terminology and conceptuality, subordinationism in the economy did not entail the same in eternity, and all forms of "Arianism" suffered their intellectual death blow.

Conclusion

The "Arian" Controversy, which raged furiously for sixty-three years, was finally put to rest at the Council of Constantinople in 381.[90] The final condemnation of "Arianism" was one of two main objectives of the council, the other being the condemnation of Apollinarianism (more on this in the next chapter.) Like the previous Nicene Council, this one was called by a powerful emperor, Theodosius I. He was Nicene and was determined to put an end to his theological opposition, once and for all. He was successful, except for some people groups that had been evangelized as anti-Nicenes, and the heresy would persist with them for a couple more centuries.[91]

The "Arian" controversy was a long and difficult struggle but was only the first chapter in dealing with the fallout from Origen, as "Arianism" follows immediately from the identity thesis read through the dichotomist-dualist lens. Origen's definitional simplicity, where to be is to will is to do, cannot meaningfully differentiate between the creation of the world and the generation of the Son, for both the Son and creation are either eternal (monist) or creature (dichotomist-dualist). In the end, those who followed Origen in the belief that the Son is a product of the will of the Father gutted the Christian faith of its real, saving significance by placing the dialectically construed Christ as creature with us over against the Father. The orthodox response was simple: only God can save, and if Jesus is not God, he cannot save; but it had to be constructed in such a way as to not swing the pendulum back to the monist side and wind up asserting the eternality of creation. Origen's construction was the

---

89. Farrell, *God, History, and Dialectic*, 132.

90. Davis, *Councils*, 119 and 130, notes that the council was not truly ecumenical, as about 150 Eastern bishops attended, and it would not be recognized in the West for 200 years.

91. Schaff, *Nicene and Post-Nicene Christianity*, 640–41.

problem, and Athanasius and the Cappadocians dealt it the first two in a series of crushing blows. "Arian" Christology was but a subset of a larger cosmology that saw the Logos as a created intermediary between God and the world. The sheer absoluteness of the Father's simplicity rendered him incapable of meaningful interaction with his creation, so his "first" creation became the intermediary. We will address this further beginning in chapter 7.

Hermeneutical method played a key role in the pro-Nicene victory. The proof-texting hermeneutics of the "Arians" rested upon a faulty *ordo theologiae* that emphasized energy (Scripture) over person (Christ). Alister McGrath notes that "One of the outcomes of the Arian controversy was the recognition of the futility, even theological illegitimacy, of biblical 'proof-texting'—the simplistic practice of believing that a theological debate can be settled by quoting a few passages from the Bible."[92] He continues,

> Both sides on the Arian controversy were able to amass texts that seemed to support their cases. The real question concerned the overall picture disclosed by the New Testament. Indeed, the Arian controversy can be argued to be about how an ensemble of biblical texts is to be integrated, in that each side had no difficulty in identifying individual texts that supported their position. Identifying the overall pattern disclosed by those texts proved to be the decisive issue.[93]

Paul Hinlicky calls this proof-texting methodology "biblicism."[94] Even though the weaknesses of such an approach to hermeneutics was clearly shown in the Arian controversy, the process of biblicism, the habits of proof-texting for appeal to biblical authority, have continued throughout Christian history right up to the present day.

C. Fitzsimmons Allison recognizes another important danger inherent in Arianism. He notes that if the Father is eternal and the Son is not, it removes from the Father the ability to be eternally self-giving and other-dependent that he enjoys in relation to the Son. The idea of being other-centered without being either selfish or selfless is the aspect of love Allison claims is lost if Arianism wins the day.[95] We now turn to the companion christological model of "Arianism," Apollinarianism.

92. McGrath, *Heresy*, 143. Unfortunately, much of my own American Protestant Evangelical tradition ignores this important lesson. The question of the primacy of Christology or hermeneutics will arise again in chapter 5.

93. McGrath, *Heresy*, 143–44.

94. Hinlicky, *Divine Complexity*, 228, writes, "By biblicism, I mean the attempt to bypass logical, hermeneutical, and metaphysical questions probing the truth-value of Christian beliefs by direct appeal to arbitrarily selected texts of Scripture. In fact, the only right use of Scripture for purposes of theology is the one that passes through such questions in critical dogmatics. The attempt to short-circuit this rigorous examination is obscurantist, authoritarian, and Christianly speaking, self-defeating." He continues on page 229, "Such biblicism, whether in the hands of the theological left or right, is a sub-evangelical alternative to theological understanding and an uncritical evasion of intellectual responsibility in Christian thought. Eschewing critical thinking, it leaves the church to the self-proclaimed prophets."

95. Allison, *Cruelty of Heresy*, 91–93.

4

The Historical Paradigm at 3:00
Apollinarianism

THIS CHAPTER WILL DISCUSS the "far right" of the Hexagon. At the three o'clock position sits Apollinarianism, which is the denial of the full humanity of Jesus, and the heresy of insufficiency of humanity. As "Arianism" possesses similarities to Ebionism, Apollinarianism is quite Docetic in its lack of the full humanity of Jesus. Both "Arianism" and Apollinarianism can be traced to Origen and his unstable synthesis of defining the divine essence as absolutely simple. As has been discussed above, definitional simplicity yields the Plotinian ambiguity, which simultaneously produces two cosmologies: one monist with only one principle (the many emanate from the One), and one dichotomist-dualist with two principles (the One and the many dialectically opposed). Apollinarianism will be the monist reaction to the dichotomist-dualist "Arianism," and the swings from one side of the ambiguity to the other continue until the underlying assumption—definitional simplicity—is defeated. The borders of the Hexagon of Heresy are formed by these oscillations from one heresy to the other, and as such becomes a useful way to mark heresy as out of bounds. In this way, Ebionism and Docetism are necessary to get the ball rolling, and "Arianism" follows later. But, to echo the words of Millard Erickson, "those theories must now appear relatively crude by comparison with the more refined issues being examined."[1] Without Nicaea, there can be no Apollinarianism, because there is no need to explain how Christ is fully human unless his full deity is assumed. Probably more so than any of the three heresies we have already discussed, Apollinarianism depends on what has come before, and it anticipates everything to follow.

---

1. Erickson, *Word Became Flesh*, 58.

The Hexagon of Heresy

Background: Worrisome Tendencies

Origen, as described in Chapter 2, constructed a synthesis of Christianity and Platonic paganism that began with God the Father as the metaphysically simple, ingenerate One. He also attempted to identify the rational ordering Logos of Platonism as the Word of God who became incarnate as Jesus Christ. Origen's monist orientation to the Plotinian ambiguity inherent in his definitional simplicity forced him to posit an eternal creation to accompany the eternal generation of the Son. His successors in Alexandria attempted to hold to Origen's monism (a monism in Alexandria that extended back beyond Origen to the Hellenism of both its Jews and Greeks), while rejecting his doctrine of eternal creation and *apokatastasis*. Unfortunately for those successors, Origen's monism devalues the psychological humanity of Christ, and that tendency will remain in Alexandria until the latter half of the fourth century, becoming the soil in which Apollinarianism will later grow. On the other hand, through the influence of the dichotomist-dualist orientation of Lucian and the Antiochenes, Arius rejected the monist interpretation of both the Son and creation as eternal in favor of the dichotomist-dualist interpretation of the temporality of both. The ambiguity built into the system of definitional simplicity breeds a rational process of dialectical opposition. Origen's monism could only expect to be opposed by its dialectical opposite, the dichotomist-dualist Arius.[2] Athanasius the Alexandrian and his later contemporaries the Cappadocians succeeded (in the East, at least) in damaging Origen's model by disentangling creation and the Logos by showing the weakness in Origen's first axiom—defining the divine essence as metaphysically simple. They made a real distinction between God's being, from which the Son is generated eternally, and God's will, the source of the creation of the world. They started the decisive offensive against definitional simplicity, one that would see victory in coming centuries.

Beginning with Origen, we observe the beginning of a historical pendulum of the orientation of the Plotinian ambiguity in theological reflection, where the initial, Origenist view was on the monist side. Arius had rightly perceived the great weakness of Origen's position, and advocated a violent swing to a dichotomist-dualist orientation with his "Logos as a creature" doctrine in the fine fashion of dialectical opposition. Under the sway of definitional simplicity with its dialectical construction, the only way to oppose one side of the ambiguity is to embrace the other side; there is never a middle ground or a third way.[3] Even though Arius and his successors lost the battle,

---

2. The "Arians" themselves were well aware of the dialectical game. As noted in the previous chapter, "Arianism" was explicitly anti-Sabellian, because it maintained a real, ontological, essential difference between Jesus and the Father; and Arius, therefore, perceived he was reacting against Sabellianism, all the while absorbing a charge of polytheism. Wilhite, *Gospel*, 113, writes, putting Arius's self-defense in his own words, "If they say that Jesus is God (contra the Ebionites), and there is only one God (contra the Marcionites and gnostics), then [Sabellianism] seems to be the only plausible explanation of their position."

3. I would assert that whenever there seems to be a theological, social, or political polarization between the one and the many with no third way to be found, definitional simplicity lurks in the

the implications of Origen's synthesis remained. Thus, it was entirely predictable that the result of Arius's condemnation would necessitate a dialectical, violent swing back to a monist orientation, which we see in the teachings of Apollinarius.

It will become apparent that the christological controversies in this chapter and in succeeding ones utilize the dialectical methodology as the reaction against models previously declared to be heretical. As we shall see in this chapter, Apollinarius himself was about as dialectically opposed to Arius as could be (and so they are on completely opposite sides of the Hexagon of Heresy). So much of the theology of the period was framed in the negation of the opponent of choice, and in so doing created boundaries which persist to this day. By the time of Apollinarius, there were some boundaries that were either very clear or becoming so to emerging ideas of christological orthodoxy—Ebionism, Docetism, Sabellianism, and "Arianism" were all out of bounds, as was the heresy of Paul of Samosata. To use an analogy of driving a car, one of the most dangerous things one can do if he runs off the road is to overcorrect the steering wheel to get the car quickly back on the road. The danger is that the car will shoot across the road and into the opposite ditch. All of our heresies we are surveying were attempts at overcorrection or, rather, correction by dialectical opposition, from one heresy which led to the opposite ditch. Because the underlying assumption held in common by (almost) all was definitional simplicity, there was "simply" no alternative.

During the fourth and fifth centuries, the church was grasping to convey reality in precise terms that Scripture and tradition did not already supply, such as the metaphysical categories of energy and person used in the solution to the Nicene Controversy. Existing words and concepts were often not sufficient for the task. We saw this with the *homoousion* from chapter 3: a word that was once anathematized was nuanced and became orthodox. Precise language to say what was needed often did not exist. It needed to be borrowed from the existing philosophical vocabulary, "baptized," and then made to fit the meaning necessary. As we will see in succeeding chapters, the concepts of person, nature, will, and energy will need significant clarification as had *hypostasis* and *ousia* in the previous chapter.[4] Not only were there ambiguities of language in trying to keep on the playing field of orthodoxy, there were also two distinct methodological approaches to doing so that emanated from the two most significant theological centers of Christianity—Alexandria and Antioch.

---

background, either explicitly or implicitly. In our contemporary age, definitional simplicity has been buried under the rubble it produced, but it still exerts enormous influence.

4. See the ambiguity in the word "*hypostasis*" as discussed in Wilhite, *Gospel*, 134–36. He writes, "The Greek word has the sense of 'existence.' The question is whether it implies something's inner being (i.e. essence) or whether it refers to a specific being (i.e. individual entity)." It is this kind of ambiguity that still needed to be fully worked out.

The Hexagon of Heresy

A Tale of Two Cities

The cities of Alexandria and Antioch, at least in the works of their major thinkers in the fourth and fifth centuries, had very diverse approaches to theological reflection, approaches that tend to magnify either the divine or the human in the incarnation or, more importantly for our purposes, to exhibit a monist or dichotomist-dualist orientation to definitional simplicity. As this section describes the different approaches of the Christian schools of thought of the two cities, we must remember that these are general tendencies rather than the specific teachings. These tendencies are distilled from the approaches of centuries' worth of the best thinkers in both cities, and they describe the general thought patterns of each.

The Christian thinkers of Alexandria held to what historical theologians call a "Word-flesh" Christology. This means that they saw the divine Word taking on or assuming human flesh.[5] Often, the Word-flesh approach would use the analogy of how the human soul animates the human body as a model for how the Word assumed flesh. Though the words "nature" and "person" are not yet ready for a precise definition, the Alexandrian approach is that the divine "nature" would indwell the human, which entailed the risk that the fullness of Jesus's humanity could be compromised. J. N. D. Kelly notes that one of the earliest criticisms leveled against the "Arians"—an Alexandrian heresy, no less, but possessing Antiochene influence—was their denial of the presence of a human soul in Jesus.[6] For the Alexandrians, the question of whether or not Jesus had a full human soul and mind was a relatively minor issue. There is debate to what extent even Athanasius had a place for the human soul of Jesus in his Christology.[7] The Alexandrians, following their seminal master Origen, tended to veer towards a monist understanding of the Plotinian ambiguity anyway, and so their chief concern is the upholding of the divine power that motivated Jesus. In other words, the Alexandrian reaction to the Nicene controversy was to continue operating in the Word-flesh model of Christology which would eventually lead to Apollinarianism, due to the fact that the Alexandrians could not figure out a way—in fact, no way existed—to explain the union in Jesus as a union at the level of nature.

---

5. Erickson, *Word Became Flesh*, 59.

6. Kelly, *Early Christian Doctrines*, 281.

7. Kelly, *Early Christian Doctrines*, 284–89. See also Gonzalez, *From the Beginnings*, 300. A fuller treatment is given in Grillmeier, *From the Apostolic Age*, 308–28. See also n58 from the previous chapter.

The Historical Paradigm at 3:00

On the other hand, the "school of Antioch"[8] held to what will become known as a "Word-man" Christology, intent upon preserving the true and full humanity of Jesus.[9] Antioch had a different theological approach to the person of Christ due to a different theological tradition. Rowan Greer states that the Antiochene theological tradition traces back through Theophilus to the Shepherd of Hermas, though it developed and matured through the Nicene and Apollinarian controversies.[10] Eustathius (sometimes Eustace) of Antioch, a contemporary of Athanasius, is the main Antiochene voice opposing "Arianism."[11] Greer writes, "Eustace's fundamental objection to Arian Christology is that it attributes change to the Son. From his standpoint the Son as divine cannot be the subject of hunger, suffering, or any change. It is not the Word who is 'born of a woman', but the man."[12] Greer continues, "Rather than adopt Athanasius' point of view and draw a distinction between two times in the Word's existence and two manners in which attributes are applied to him, Eustace takes the more direct way of attacking "Arian" Christology head-on. The human attributes must be applied to the human subject. Nor does he fail to draw the conclusion that this implies. The Word and man are 'one and another.'"[13] In the heat of the battle against "Arianism," the question was not immediately how Jesus was human, but how he was divine.

Eustathius positions himself against Alexandria and ultimately the ideas of Origen as he, rightly, saw in him the roots of the Anti-Nicene heresy. Greer continues, "Eustace sees the Arian argument quite clearly. If a human soul is excluded from Christ, there can be no human principle of motion and no human subject in Christ. And if this were the case, then all attribution would have to be referred to as the divine subject; and that divine subject would have to be described as inferior to the immutable Father. This objection leads Eustace to argue for the existence of a human soul in Christ."[14] So Eustathius arrives at a position to uphold the real and full humanity of Christ at the expense of his unity at the personal or natural level. He and those who followed him asserted the reality and integrity of creation (here in Jesus) over against

---

8. It is probably incorrect to use the phrase "school of Antioch" in such a concrete fashion. In the previous chapter, we saw that Lucian founded a school of exegesis there, but it was not on the level of the Alexandrian catechetical school. Thus while there is a general Antiochene way of reading Scripture in a historical fashion, most of the Christology of Antioch that we will survey here lies in the Eustathius-Diodore-Theodore-Nestorius strain. See Louth, "Syrians," 108–10. On the Jewish influence in Antioch that makes a historical reading more palatable, see Meyendorff, *Imperial Unity*, 98.

9. Erickson, *Word Became Flesh*, 59. Tapia, *Theology of Christ*, 107, states that the Word-man Christology arose in Antioch to combat the Apollinarian heresy, though its roots go further back into the aftermath of the initial thrust of "Arianism." See also Adam, *Christ of Faith*, 29–37.

10. Greer, *Captain*, 176. We also know that Lucian of Antioch, a dichotomist-dualist on the "left wing" of Origenism, is the exegetical mentor of those who followed him in Antioch.

11. Ayres, *Nicaea*, 68–69, traces a link in the theology of Eustathius and Marcellus of Ancyra after Nicaea.

12. Greer, *Captain*, 135.

13. Greer, *Captain*, 135.

14. Greer, *Captain*, 136.

The Hexagon of Heresy

the divine, thereby following the dichotomist-dualist half of the Plotinian ambiguity, even to the point of eventually sundering his personal unity. The one and the many could not truly unite in him, at least not very deeply.

The question for such a theology would be how it is not Adoptionistic in some way, because if the eternal Word united to a full man, how can that not be a form of Ebionite Adoptionism? The Alexandrian Christology played very close to the boundary of Docetism, while the Antiochene Christology flirted with the Ebionite boundary. As Gonzalez notes, the West adopted Tertullian's idea of "two substances in one person" as its Christology, and although not as precise as what would develop in the fifth century, was good enough to keep the West on a middle path between the extremes typified of the cities of Alexandria and Antioch.[15] As we will see in chapter 6, such a construct would last until tested by Cyrillian Christology at Chalcedon and its aftermath.

C. Fitzsimmons Allison notes that Alexandria tended to think in terms of an ontological union in Christ, whereas Antioch stressed the power of moral example.[16] Hopefully, given the metaphysical categories of the *ordo theologiae* discussed in the previous chapters, we can see the union espoused in Alexandria tending toward nature, and the union explained in Antioch tending toward energy (will and morals). Allison continues, noting the way Docetism and adoptionistic Ebionism are employed respectively, "Alexandrians leaned, as a rule, toward a willingness to sacrifice the full humanity of Christ, and Antioch tended to produce an adoptionist Christ, sacrificing the unity between God and humanity in Christ."[17] Greer's argument, that the differing approaches to Christology used by Alexandria and Antioch is a result of two answers to the Nicene challenge, while a step in the right direction, does not go deep enough.[18] Alexandria and Antioch do not provide two answers to the Anti-Nicenes nearly as much as they are the outworking of the two sides of the Plotinian ambiguity in response to Origen. As we saw in chapter 2, Origen anticipated both christological responses. Alexandria will be the home of the monist christological heresies Apollinarianism and Monophysitism, while Antioch will be the seat of influence for the dichotomist-dualist ones, "Arianism" and Nestorianism. The monist Alexandrians will try to unite the divine and human in Christ by nature, while the dichotomist-dualist Antiochenes will try to unite them by energy (as the Logos is created by the will of God or as by a willful, moral union). But as we will see in the next chapter,

---

15. Gonzalez, *From the Beginnings*, 336–37.

16. Allison, *Cruelty of Heresy*, 82. Allison's recognition of the approaches requiring differing metaphysical levels of union in the two cities is an excellent insight. However, he attributes the difference to Alexandria's Hellenism and Antioch's Jewish influence. This is unlikely, since both Christian communities reflect differing mixtures of Judaism and Hellenism. The orientation to the Plotinian ambiguity, in my opinion, possesses more explanatory power.

17. Allison, *Cruelty of Heresy*, 82.

18. Greer, *Captain*, 136.

neither nature nor energy will be the proper metaphysical category that will yield the christological union.

Apollinarius and Nicaea

The heresy known today as Apollinarianism is named after Apollinarius of Laodicea. Even though he served as Bishop of Laodicea, a city of Asia Minor and one more influenced by the school of Antioch, he was a thoroughgoing Alexandrian in his thought and vigorously upheld the Nicene view of the Father and Son. As V. L. Walter notes, "As a revered teacher he was the friend of Athanasius, consultant by correspondence to Basil the Great, and numbered Jerome among his pupils."[19] He was so well respected that for a time his teachings were condemned but he was not.[20] Donald MacLeod has even written that the eventual condemnation of Apollinarius is a tragedy of church history.[21] The teaching was first condemned in Alexandria in 362, and then over the next two decades the outcry against it gained more steam. It did not take the Empire by storm as did "Arianism," and the heresy itself was contained to the East. Even after his condemnation, he continued to write as a man convinced that his views were correct. As with all heretics, his works were collected and destroyed, so very little remains of his actual writing today.[22] Much is seen through the eyes of his critics.

What has come down to us as Apollinarianism, the denial of the full humanity of Jesus, may not be exactly what he taught or thought. John Behr provides a helpful reconstruction, noting that the rather simplistic compositional approach of saying the Divine Logos took the place of Jesus's human spirit "seems implausibly Docetic, if not outright bizarre, especially for one who was considered to be staunchly Nicene and one of the greatest minds of his age. More recent work, however, has begun to show how Apollinarius's characteristic teaching regarding Christ is best understood in terms of his adherence to Nicaea, rather than as the result of particular anthropological presuppositions."[23] As Behr reconstructs Apollinarius's theology, he notes that Apollinarius's chief concern is to avoid making Jesus two persons at all costs, as he fears earlier theologians had done, being zealous to uphold a monist unity of being.[24] He wants to preserve the unity of the person of Christ from a Nicene perspective, taking into account his true and full deity as the Council of Nicaea affirmed,[25] and in so doing,

---

19. Walter, "Apollinarianism," 81.
20. Walter, "Apollinarianism," 81.
21. MacLeod, *Person of Christ*, 158. He quotes Prestige, *Fathers and Heretics*, 116.
22. Walter, "Apollinarianism," 82.
23. Behr, *Nicene Faith*, 2:389.
24. Here it is apparent that Apollinarius is reacting against extreme forms of the separation of the divine and human in Jesus usually associated with the Antiochene side of the struggle. Hints of this thought were also seen in Origen, as discussed in chapter 2 above.
25. Behr, *Nicene Faith*, 2:389.

uphold a vigorous form of monism in the face of the anti-Nicenes' dichotomist-dualism. Grillmeier writes that Apollinarius's purpose was "to interweave and join together God and man essentially [that is, via nature] and inseparably in Christ. This great aim should not be mistaken. Fear of division and the effort to make the unity in the Word made flesh as close and as deep as possible are, if we leave aside individual details, the two main features of the Apollinarian view. Apollinarius approaches his task with great linguistic dexterity and philosophical acumen."[26] Apollinarius the Alexandrian revolted against the dichotomist-dualist model of the anti-Nicenes with a strong monist rebuttal. The divine and human in Jesus would be one, and naturally so.

Apollinarius took seriously the concept of a full *communicatio idiomatum*, where the properties of humanity and divinity are both communicated to the God-man. To him, Jesus was a full and radical unity of divinity and humanity, where each one becomes the other in a permanent union, even to the point that the humanity cannot even be thought of apart from the divinity and vice-versa.[27] Apollinarius taught that the union became permanent in the womb of the virgin, for he received his flesh from her, and the only difference between Jesus's flesh and ours, in the Apollinarian system, is its union with the Logos.[28] It is the desire of Apollinarius to preserve the union of God and man in Christ, because he is reacting to theologies which make the union something less than permanent or less than eternal, that is, less than natural. As Grillmeier notes, Apollinarius saw the union as the conjoining of a heavenly *pneuma* (the Logos) with an earthly *sarx,* where the "man in Christ first becomes man through the union of these two components."[29] In such a framework, it is as if Logos + flesh = Christ, and that the Logos and the flesh are two parts of the whole. In this way, an Apollinarian Christology resembles "Arianism," for each heresy forms a *tertium quid* between God and humanity.[30] Apollinarius says in his own words, "A *physis* is made up of the two parts, as the Logos with his divine perfection contributes a *partial energy* to the whole. This is also the case with the ordinary man, who is made up of two incomplete parts which produce one *physis* and display it under one name."[31] Here we see how "Arianism" and Apollinarianism merge in their Christologies. Both have a being that is neither fully God or fully human, but something in between. While

---

26. Grillmeier, *From the Apostolic Age*, 330.

27. Behr, *Nicene Faith*, 2:390–92.

28. See Grillmeier, *From the Apostolic Age*, 331. Behr, *Nicene Faith*, 2:390–92, follows the thinking of Gregory of Nyssa, who mistakenly thought that Apollinarius taught that this union is not something that begins in the womb of the virgin, but something that has always existed, believing that Jesus's heavenly flesh is from eternity past.

29. Grillmeier, *From the Apostolic Age*, 331.

30. See Hughes, *True Image*, 288, where he quotes Apollinarius (*Syllogism*, Fragment 113), in stating, "In Christ there is a middle being of God and man, so that he is neither fully man nor God, but a mixture of God and man." Apollinarius continues that analogies of the mixture of which he speaks include breeding a donkey and a horse to produce a mule or mixing black and white to create gray.

31. Apollinarius, *De unione* 5, cited in Grillmeier, *From the Apostolic Age*, 332. Italics in original.

"Arianism" chooses to allow the "deity" of Christ to suffer, Apollinarianism reduces his full humanity.

Karl Adam describes Apollinarius's methodology as beginning with the Aristotelian principle that "Two complete perfected natures are not able to compound themselves into any such unity of nature. They cannot interpenetrate each other, but only exist side by side. If all the same a true unity of nature should be established, it could be only by diminishing, as it were, the human nature of Jesus at its highest point."[32] This Aristotelian principle is but a restatement of the Plotinian ambiguity: if there is to be unity between the one and the many, or in this case respectively the divinity and humanity of Christ, the many must bow to the one in a monist fashion rather than asserting its opposition in a dichotomist-dualist way. Thus, the concept of *physis*, as seen in the quote above from Apollinarius, is very important because for him, the *physis* is the principle of life. For the ordinary human, the *physis*, or what we could loosely translate the soul, is the combination of the flesh and the human spirit. For Jesus, the *physis* is the combination of the Logos and the human flesh. For there to be a real union in Christ of the divine and human, for Apollinarius, the Logos must retain control in the *physis*, otherwise the principle of life for Jesus would reside in the flesh and the union would be neither permanent nor full.[33] For Apollinarius, the flesh of Jesus Christ, therefore, is controlled by the Logos completely, by the "divine mind," or divine *nous*, which never alters its course. As Grillmeier continues, "Apollinarius distinguishes between a *nous autokinetos* such as a man also has, and a *nous tautokinetos*, that is, a *nous* which is always moved in the same way and so is unalterable. Self-determination and immutability together are the necessary factors for redemption, but these are realized only in the divine *pneuma* of Christ."[34] Definitional divine simplicity rules; the many naturally oppose the one, so the one conquers the many.

In Apollinarius's own words, there cannot be a created, fleshly *physis* together with the Logos as a *physis*, because that would destroy the essential unity as the two cannot be viewed apart from the other.[35] There is, then, only one *physis* in Christ according to Apollinarius, and that comes from the Logos. Grillmeier summarizes that the elements of such a Christology result from "a Stoic-Alexandrian anthropology and its application to Christ . . . *Physis* is here by no means the static, abstract '*essentia*', nor is it the 'nature-person' which unites in itself the two elements of the Chalcedonian

---

32. Adam, *Christ of Faith*, no page given, cited in Tapia, *Theology of Christ*, 106. As we shall see, this philosophical principle drives the distinction between Alexandria and Antioch. For the Alexandrian Word-flesh Christology, effecting some sort of natural union of the divine and human in Christ requires diminishing the human in favor of the divine in a zero-sum fashion. As will be surveyed in the next chapter, the main Antiochene tradition of the fourth to fifth centuries will abandon the quest for a natural union and settle for a "side-by-side" contiguity of the divine and human.

33. See Grillmeier, *From the Apostolic Age*, 333.

34. Grillmeier, *From the Apostolic Age*, 334. I have transliterated the Greek phrases in the quote into English characters which Grillmeier leaves in the original Greek font.

35. Apollinarius, *Epistle to Dionysius*, A8, quoted in Grillmeier, *From the Apostolic Age*, 334.

hypostasis and *physis*. *Physis* is the 'self-determining being.'"[36] He continues, "The God-man, then, is one *physis*, one *ousia*, because *one* life-giving power, which completely permeates the flesh, goes out from the Logos and unites the two in a living, functional unity."[37] This idea of the Logos permeating the flesh with his life to create a complete unity of God and man is perhaps the clearest way to understand Apollinarianism in its own terms, as the enfleshed Logos was truly living a human life but not subject to human limitation.[38] In terms of the concept of energy that we have been discussing in the *ordo theologiae*, the Apollinarian Christ has only one energy (and one will, therefore one nature)—that of the Logos.[39] This is a key observation to show how Apollinarianism will be later refined as Monophysitism and Monoenergism/Monothelitism.

Apollinarius is a good starting point to discuss the anthropological ideas that will be disputed in the third and fourth ecumenical councils. Grillmeier cites, in his quotation of Richard's reconstruction, how Apollinarius thought all these anthropological terms worked together thus, "Man is a *hypostasis* by virtue of his *nous*, which is the principle of life. His animal soul (*psyche*) and his body have their *hypostasis* in and through this *nous*. If then the Word as divine *nous* and divine *pneuma* has taken a human *nous*, there are two *hypostaseis* in Christ, which is impossible. If, on the other hand, he took only a body and an animal soul, then they are necessarily hypostasized in him and Christ is only a single *hypostasis*."[40] The following lengthy quote from Behr pinpoints the understanding of how Apollinarius thought of Jesus as "human," even though not the same as we are:

> It was Paul's description of Christ as the "heavenly man" and the "life-giving Spirit" in contrast to the earthly, animated being (1 Cor 15:45–47), that provided the material and terms for Apollinarius' further analysis of the special contribution of the Word to the incarnate Christ. According to Apollinarius, "Christ, having God as the spirit, that is, the mind, together with his soul and body, is properly called the man from heaven." Clearly behind this assertion is Paul's "anthropological formula" of "body, soul, and spirit" in his prayer that the whole human being may be kept sound and blameless at the coming of the Lord (1 Thess 5:23). As Christ has the same structure as every human being, then he too can be called "human": "If, then, a man is composed of three [elements] spirit, soul, and body." If, however, he were equal to terrestrial human beings in all their respective parts, even in his spirit or mind, then he would no longer be a "heavenly man," but rather a human "receptacle" of the heavenly

---

36. Grillmeier, *From the Apostolic Age*, 334–35.

37. Grillmeier, *From the Apostolic Age*, 336. Italics in original.

38. McGuckin, *Cyril of Alexandria*, 182.

39. Hovorun, *Will, Action and Freedom*, 7–8. Apollinarius would not even give the movements of the flesh the title of energy; they were called simply "movements." Energy belonged to the Logos alone; the human actions are merely passive.

40. Richard, "*L'Introduction*," 5–32, 243–70, esp. 9–12, cited in Grillmeier, *From the Apostolic Age*, 339. Greek words in the original are transliterated into English characters.

God. Thus, Apollinarius appeals to such anthropological formulae to assert that Christ is indeed to be considered as a human being but concludes that he is nevertheless different to other human beings.[41]

Here we see how Apollinarianism is the obverse of "Arianism." Anti-Nicene theology held that Jesus was "divine" in the sense of being the first of God's creatures but denied the organic link between Father and Son, which ultimately denies full divinity. Apollinarianism held that Jesus was "human" in the sense of having the requisite constitutional properties that define humanity but denied the organic link between him and us, which ultimately denies full humanity. In a very similar fashion later on, we will see cosmologies that deny the organic link between God and creation that follow an "Arian" Christology. Meanwhile, the cosmological ramifications of Apollinarius's Christology are immense. The only way God and the world can "get along," so to speak, is for God to enter into the world and conquer it, forcing it to conform to his will. From a fully monist perspective, the only way harmony can be achieved is for God to meticulously determine everything in creation, for there is no room for the creation to do anything apart from the controlling will of God. A "natural union" between creator and creation demands this sort of monist, "one principle" thinking, both cosmologically and soteriologically.

Apollinarius's theology also is rife with the Hellenistic dualism between changeable matter and unchangeable deity. That the *nous* of Jesus is the unchangeable Logos which is what actually saves the rest of us, because a changeable human mind would eventually "collide" with God.[42] As Demetrios Bathrellos writes, "It seems that for Apollinarianism, human person, nature, mind, will, energy, mutability, and sinfulness belong together."[43] Moreover, all of his sufferings are not as ours are, as Behr writes, "As the heavenly man, Christ's flesh conforms itself to our state but is never subject to the sufferings that subject us, so patterning a mode of life for us by which we can also live in a divine manner."[44] Allison adds, "If Christ's mind and will were immutable, it would render [his] temptations meaningless. How could he have been tempted if his will were unchangeable?[45] The inherent dual-

---

41. Behr, *Nicene Faith*, 2:395. All quotes contained in this block quotes are from fragments of Apollinarius, *Apodeixis*, and are cited in Behr.

42. Behr, *Nicene Faith*, 2:397. Apollinarius here displays the fear of what might occur if the dichotomist-dualist side of the Plotinian ambiguity holds sway, so he pitches his tent firmly in the monist camp. Also, here is clearly the "distinction is opposition" principle rooted in definitional simplicity at work.

43. Bathrellos, *Byzantine Christ*, 14. Here is the Plotinian principle discussed from Chapter 1 that distinction is opposition. Sinfulness cannot possibly be disentangled from true humanity, because if the absolutely-simple One is deemed good, then "good" is both one and simple, and thus everything not the one is not (as) good. Therefore, the many must be less than "simply" good. More will be said on this in the last section of this chapter.

44. Behr, *Nicene Faith*, 2:398.

45. Allison, *Cruelty of Heresy*, 109.

ism between the one and the many in Apollinarianism entails that humanity and divinity cannot be fully and hypostatically united,[46] therefore the union is one in which the person is a new nature which, like "Arianism," is a confusion of the two metaphysical categories.[47] This leads Apollinarius to a completely different conception of human salvation—that the human struggle is not with sin but with the old creation. "Redemption, then, represents an overcoming and transcending of the created order."[48] As Behr summarizes concerning Apollinarianism, "The focus has shifted from the crucified and exalted Christ, whose image we strive to put on and will only do so through our own death and resurrection, to a new creation effected by the descent of the heavenly man and birth of an invincible divine mind in this world, the manifestation of a new being who remains unmoved by the flesh and is unconquerable even in death and whose flesh imparts to us a new point of origin."[49] Compare the Anti-Nicene version of Christ, who is fundamentally creature though not exactly like us, and as such stands dialectically opposed to the Father as do we, and who saves by giving the rest of us an example to follow.[50] As with "Arianism," the Apollinarian "Christ" is a new kind of being, one who is fundamentally unlike us and who effects a kind of salvation that is different from the *theosis* model which the received tradition has held. The "Arian" and Apollinarian Christologies form the foundation of the soteriological paradigms which, respectively, depend on the exertion of human effort to imitate Jesus in dichotomist-dualist fashion and those which are monistically fully dependent on conquering grace from above because of human inability.[51]

Against Apollinarius and Gregory's Maxim

Once Apollinarius's teaching began to be noticed, condemnations came swiftly. As Gonzalez notes, this is unfortunate because Apollinarius was the first person in Christian history to become acutely aware of the problem of how the divine and human were joined in the incarnation. Like Origen, he plowed new ground; and like Origen again, his solution was inadequate for the immensity of the question.[52] His two ablest

---

46. Bathrellos, *Byzantine Christ*, 15.

47. Farrell, *God, History, and Dialectic*, 273, writes, "Apollinarianism identified *hypostasis* with a natural operation, since it maintained that the eternal person of the Logos took the place of the human soul and mind of Christ (the latter "not being needed" if the Logos was present)."

48. Behr, *Nicene Faith*, 2:399. This is part of a quote from Greer, "Man from Heaven," 174.

49. Behr, *Nicene Faith*, 2:401.

50. Hinlicky, *Divine Complexity*, 199.

51. Additionally, the "Arian" and Apollinarian soteriological paradigms form the basis of their eschatological counterparts that bring heaven to earth due to our efforts (postmillennialism) and our escape of the flawed earth for heaven before things get too bad (dispensational premillennialism), respectively.

52. Gonzalez, *From the Beginnings*, 345. See also Raven, *Apollinarianism*, 150.

critics, the Cappadocian Gregories (Nazianzen and Nyssen), ably pointed out his flaws but were unable to advance a positive solution.[53] As Gonzalez notes, the Christology of most Greek theologians at the time was very close to that of Apollinarius, which is why Basil first accused him of schism, rather than of heresy.[54] Even though the person and nature distinction has been worked out at the trinitarian level by these same Cappadocians, they did not yet articulate with metaphysical precision that the union of the divine and human was a union of a different metaphysical order than the union of being in the Godhead. That work remained for the next century.

The argument of the Cappadocians against Apollinarius proceeded from the same source as Athanasius's successful defense of orthodoxy against Arianism: the doctrine of salvation. The Cappadocians understood that the capstone of salvation—*theosis*, or real human participation in the divine nature via the divine energies—was not possible if Jesus was not completely human. Gregory of Nazianzus writes, "If he has a soul, and yet is without a mind, how is he man, for man is not a mindless animal? . . . But, says such a one, the Godhead took the place of the human intellect. How does this touch me? For Godhead joined to flesh alone is not man, nor to soul alone, nor to both apart from intellect, which is the most essential part of man."[55] MacLeod also quotes Gregory of Nyssa, speaking of Jesus's parable of the lost sheep, saying that Jesus laid the whole sheep on his shoulders, not just the skin.[56] Gregory of Nazianzus has given us the most devastating critique of the heart of Apollinarius's Christology, as he writes, "If anyone has put his trust in him as a man without a human mind, he is really bereft of mind, and quite unworthy of salvation. For that which he has not assumed he has not healed; but that which is united to his Godhead is also saved. If only half Adam fell, then that which Christ assumes and saves may be half also; but if the whole of his nature fell, it must be united to the whole nature of him that was begotten, and so be saved as a whole."[57] It is this maxim of Gregory's, "The unassumed is the unhealed," that has come down to us to solidly refute the Christology of Apollinarius. Allison adds, "Unless the incarnation involves the whole person, that which is replaced or left out does not become part of the salvation package. The neatness gained in the face of a real problem—how can the divine and the human be united in Christ—was purchased at too great a price. Apollinarius excluded from salvation that whole aspect of fallen human nature which involves pride, self-will, and those dangerous sins that Dante set in purgatory closest to hell."[58] Without the redeemed mind and

---

53. Grillmeier, *From the Apostolic Age*, 368–69.

54. Gonzalez, *From the Beginnings*, 350. That most existing Christologies were very close to that of Apollinarius stands to reason, since, as it has been asserted earlier, all followed Origen.

55. Gregory of Nazianzus, *Ep.* 101, cited in MacLeod, *Person of Christ*, 160.

56. Gregory of Nyssa, *Eun.* 2.13.

57. Gregory of Nazianzus, *Ep.* 101, cited in Gonzalez, *From the Beginnings*, 350.

58. Allison, *Cruelty of Heresy*, 109.

soul, the human is not saved, and without Jesus's assumption of a real human mind, there can be no redemption for it.

Finally, as Gonzalez states, there has been a great deal of criticism leveled against the Cappadocians for chastising Apollinarius so harshly when they were not far from him christologically. To their credit, the Cappadocians realized that Apollinarius's theories were the logical conclusion of the Alexandrian Word-flesh Christology and tried to make some modifications.[59] Unfortunately, they were not ultimately successful in coming up with a christological model that was noticeably better, as that would need to wait for a few more decades. This Word-flesh model had inherent weaknesses, the greatest two of which were its inability to give sufficient expression to the concrete humanity of Jesus and its eclectic nature that, while it may get the details correct, is always susceptible to a distortion of the complete picture of Jesus to the detriment of Christian worship.[60] Grillmeier notes that the Cappadocian lack of precision will come back to haunt the next great heretic, Nestorius, when he tries to apply some of their solutions and finds them wanting.[61] Ralph Tapia quotes Karl Adam as saying, "The two heretical forms of the [Word-flesh] Christology, Arianism and Apollinarianism, were probably the most dangerous invasion of Hellenistic ideas into the traditional conception of Christ."[62] Indeed they were, as they were the two sides of the Plotinian ambiguity unleashed by Origen when he tried to fuse Platonic and Christian conceptions of deity and Logos. Tapia continues, "Apollinarianism bears the first seeds of the later heresy of Monophysitism, which laid the gilding of divinity onto the picture of Christ so thickly that the Lord's human traits disappeared completely and Christ reverted to the ranks of pagan mythologies."[63] The real issue with Apollinarianism and the Word-flesh Christology in general is its continued embrace of the pagan, philosophical concept of the Logos, which is always a guest in, but never a true resident of, the material world. When John wrote "The word became flesh," he was not speaking of some abstract piece of human matter; he was speaking of Jesus of Nazareth.[64] The received interpretation of John 1:14 followed a pagan philosophical gloss on the concept of flesh and had done so for the centuries leading up to Apollinarius. It could last no longer. A new way forward had to be found theologically, and that is the subject of the next two chapters.

---

59. Gonzalez, *From the Beginnings*, 351–52. Kelly, *Early Christian Doctrines*, 298, notes that while Gregory of Nazianzus was successful in refuting Apollinarius, what he offered in its place was not sufficient to explain how Jesus grew in knowledge and wisdom, etc.

60. Grillmeier, *From the Apostolic Age*, 342.

61. Grillmeier, *From the Apostolic Age*, 375.

62. Tapia, *Theology of Christ*, 107, quoting Adam, *Christ of Faith*, n.p.

63. Tapia, *Theology of Christ*, 107.

64. See Hughes, *True Image*, 288, as he notes that the traditional interpretation of the word "flesh" is John 1:14 is that of a synecdoche, where "flesh" stands for the full humanity of Christ.

The Historical Paradigm at 3:00

The Council of Constantinople Revisited

Apollinarianism (but not Apollinarius himself!) was formally condemned at the Council of Constantinople in 381.[65] Although Constantinople was discussed in the last chapter concerning the post-Nicene controversies, it served a dual role in marking two permanent boundaries in the Hexagon of Heresy. The absence of both full humanity and full deity were marked off as being beyond the bounds of orthodox Christology. Leo Davis writes concerning the two heresies, "There is in all this a strange crossing of the positions of Arius and Apollinarius. For Arius, since the Son is the soul of Christ, the Son is not divine because open to change. But Apollinarius denied a rational soul, a human mind, in Christ precisely so that the Son would not be reduced to the state of a creature, open to change."[66] Definitional divine simplicity is still at work, due to the intense fear of introducing change into God, and a new can of worms, so to speak has been opened. Apollinarius probed new territory, but his answers to the problems he articulated were insufficient and ultimately heretical. As Allison writes, "Apollinarianism attempts to solve a real problem, yet in effect it is but a less obvious and more subtle version of earlier Docetism. Apollinarianism carries with it the whole baggage of Docetic implications for all who would 'bow the knee' in worship of the Apollinarian Christ. His insistence that Christ had only a divine nature led him to deny explicitly that Christ was a man."[67] Allison continues with insight that will be developed in later chapters, "Any teaching that asserts salvation as divinely imposed on the human predicament is like a teacher who gives answers without allowing the students to become agents in their own learning."[68] We will see when an Apollinarian-leaning view of cosmology appears in chapter 10 just how far Apollinarius's answers to the questions he posed can lead.

Grillmeier adds to Apollinarius's contribution, even if ultimately in error, "He must be credited with having introduced into Christology, or having brought to bear on the discussion, the three most important concepts which occur in the Chalcedonian definition, *physis*, *hypostasis*, and *prosopon*. These concepts were eventually taken over by the opposition as well, and finally by the Council of Chalcedon itself, but they were canonized in a refined and clarified sense."[69] For example, as Apollinarius was critiqued by his contemporaries, Grillmeier notes, the concept of *physis* underwent a change of meaning, from an active idea to a static one, becoming "almost identical with 'abstract nature' or '*essentia*.'"[70] Meanwhile, the issues between Alexandria and Antioch will continue, and in another half-century, a new controversy will arise that

---

65. Wilhite, *Gospel*, 141.
66. Davis, *Councils*, 105.
67. Allison, *Cruelty of Heresy*, 112.
68. Allison, *Cruelty of Heresy*, 113.
69. Grillmeier, *From the Apostolic Age*, 347.
70. Grillmeier, *From the Apostolic Age*, 339.

will even more precisely define the field and narrow the possibilities for a permanent solution. Before turning to those issues, we want to examine the Christology of the greatest Western father, Augustine of Hippo.

The Christology of Augustine

It is not normal to insert a discussion of Augustinian Christology into a survey of the great controversies of the fourth and fifth centuries. Up until the time of Leo I (whom we shall address in chapter 6), the West largely avoided the christological extremes so prevalent in the East. Augustine was actively writing during most of the time period between the ecumenical councils in Constantinople and Ephesus, but he wrote little that was expressly and directly christological in nature.[71] He was a vigorous opponent of both "Arianism" and Apollinarianism, but did not figure in to the next controversy, Nestorianism, at all. Since he did not presumably have a dog in the fight, so to speak, why include him here, in the chapter concerning a theology he publicly repudiated?

It was the Pelagian Julian of Eclanum who accused Augustine of harboring an Apollinarian Christology in his doctrine of original sin.[72] As stated immediately above, Augustine was a vocal opponent of Apollinarius's teachings, even though he may not have known them firsthand. It is the implications, the good and necessary consequences, of his doctrine of original sin that may belie an unwitting Apollinarianism in his view of Christ. The reason for this possibility is quite simple: Augustine forms his anthropology as a first theological principle in his dispute against the Pelagians concerning the doctrine of original sin.[73] Though Augustine did not participate in the Eastern controversies, methodologically he was identical to his Eastern counterparts, in that he formed his theological insights in direct reaction against his opponents (a notorious symptom of having definitional simplicity as a first principle, as discussed earlier). We have seen, with Arius against monist Origen and Apollinarius against dichotomist-dualist Arius, heresies tend to form in the violent pendulum swings within the framework of definitional simplicity. Augustine, as we will see both here and later, is no exception.

For Augustine, the fall extended to human nature itself, making human beings slaves to sin and mortality due to the fact that each human is conceived in sexual desire, which itself has become part of the fallen nature. As Joseph Farrell writes, "Adam, by his *personal* choice fixes the guilt, the moral responsibility, of all human nature for

---

71. Keech, *Christology of Augustine*, 5–6. Here, Keech writes, "The first problem facing any student of Augustine in search of his Christology is finding it. Throughout the Augustinian corpus, Christ is the wood among the trees, everywhere and nowhere in particular."

72. Keech, *Christology of Augustine*, 144.

73. Probably a better way to say this is that Augustine's anthropology is a "first corollary" to his real first principle, divine simplicity. More on Augustine's definitional simplicity will follow.

his sin."[74] Once the fall occurred, the natural state of humanity is to be in opposition to God. Here we see Augustine committing himself to an approach of beginning with opposing natures. The divine nature is good, while human nature is now opposed to the divine, and is therefore evil. The wills, as operations of the natures, become dialectically opposed as well. It is the dichotomist-dualist half of the Plotinian ambiguity at work, and more will be said concerning Augustine's ideas here in chapters 7 and 8. In his view, humans are no longer the creation of God gone awry; they are evil at the core, so much so that even newborns carry the liability of punishment on themselves as part of the "sinful" and "damnable mass," having done neither good nor evil.[75]

Augustine makes a second christological move that violates the *ordo theologiae* that we have been exploring. In a famous statement from his *On the Predestination of the Saints*, he writes, "The most illustrious light of predestination and grace is the Savior himself—the mediator between God and man, the man Christ Jesus."[76] Farrell insightfully notes, "It is apparent that Christ is conceived to be the same relationship to God as regards his humanity as any individual elect. He is the most 'illustrative example' amongst many other possible; he is the best particular example of a general phenomenon. Christology would thus appear to be subsumed under the greater heading of predestination."[77] In Augustine's construction of anthropology, nature—that is, fallen human nature—takes the primary position. In his construction of soteriology, we see the elevation of divine energy to the front in Augustine's particular construction of predestination. His theology proper is likewise problematic, as we will discuss more fully in chapter 7. For Augustine, Christology does not influence anthropology or soteriology nearly as much as it is influenced by them, and likewise, in our common contemporary approach to studying systematic theology, we address anthropology before Christology. Additionally, there is a tendency in Augustine to downplay material reality, as seen in his views on the theophanies in the Old Testament as well as the triumph of his psychological analogy of the Trinity.[78] With Jesus and the created world playing second fiddle to original sin, predestination, the single divine essence,[79] and the immaterial world, we have reason to be suspicious. Let us continue.

---

74. Farrell, *Free Choice*, 203.

75. The terms *massa peccatorum* and *massa damnata* are common descriptors of humanity throughout Augustine's works.

76. Augustine, *On the Predestination of the Saints*, 30.

77. Farrell, *Free Choice*, 203.

78. Gunton, "Augustine," 35, 45–47.

79. We have every reason to believe that Augustine follows Origen in defining the divine essence as metaphysically simple. Augustine, *Trin.* 7.1.2, writes, "in God, to be, is the same as to be wise. For what to be wise is to wisdom, and to be able is to power, and to be eternal is to eternity, and to be just to justice, and to be great to greatness, that being itself is to essence. And since in the Divine simplicity, to be wise is nothing else than to be, therefore wisdom there is the same as essence." As Joseph P. Farrell, *God, History, and Dialectic*, 289, says, "Augustine's Neoplatonic understanding and use of the term 'simplicity' is finally manifest. And with it is manifest another disturbing implication that will have its own long-term effects, for the attributes of God have been reduced to conventions of human language;

Augustine clearly believed that Christ had a human soul, because he experienced the suffering and agony of the crucifixion, as well as other human emotions.[80] However, Augustine's Jesus "does not experience ignorance of weakness of reason. Rather, from his infancy he enjoys both an unlimited knowledge of temporal things, including future events, and possesses the full beatific vision promised to the saints." Any hint of weakness or ignorance in Jesus is attributed to "voluntary participation in the present human condition [or] pedagogic exemplarism."[81] That is, Augustine believes that Jesus willed to feel the passions he felt.[82] Since Christ, as Augustine claims, willed his passions in the way they should be displayed, it cannot be the human will that wills them, because, as stated above, Augustine believed the human will to be in opposition to the divine will. Here is the Apollinarian moment: that in Christ which wills the right use of the passions is the divine will, i.e. the Logos, and not the human will. Keech summarizes, "Precisely where is the [highest power] in Christ? It is difficult not to situate it solely in his divine nature. In spite of Augustine's assurance that Christ is one person in two natures, that personality appears to be predominately characterized by the nature of the Word who assumes it."[83] That is, for Augustine, the Word is the real *physis* of Jesus, just as it had been for Apollinarius a generation earlier. Augustine has just switched to the monist half of the Plotinian ambiguity, as we will see him do again in chapters 7 and 8.

Even within his own construct of anthropology via original sin, Augustine's Christology remains Apollinarian. Again, we revisit Gregory's maxim that "the unassumed is the unhealed." For Augustine, Adam's sin radically altered human nature, to the point where humans are dialectically opposed to God. Does Jesus assume the original, as-created human nature, or the postlapsarian, radically altered one? Augustine tends to be ambiguous on this point. If Jesus assumes the as-created human nature or some mixture of the two, then Gregory's maxim is violated and salvation cannot occur. If he assumes postlapsarian nature, then perhaps a greater problem arises. Dominic Keech writes, "If, as Augustine himself conceded, Christ has truly human flesh, in what sense can his humanity have evaded the double punishment of mortality and concupiscence, as much one in the other as body and soul?"[84] In conceiving the psychology of Christ, Augustine denies that Christ inherited sinful concupiscence due to his virginal conception. But the problem goes deeper. Julian, along with the rest of

---

each distinct attribute's 'name' no longer stands for a distinct reality or operation in God, but now all names stand the same underlying reality." It would seem that Augustine's understanding of the divine essence is fundamentally the same as Origen's, which will entail the same range of cosmological and christological problems as Origen's as well.

80. Keech, *Christology of Augustine*, 155, cites several original sources showing Augustine's beliefs about the human soul of Jesus.

81. Keech, *Christology of Augustine*, 163.

82. Keech, *Christology of Augustine*, 177. See also Augustine, *Civ.* 14.9.

83. Keech, *Christology of Augustine*, 179.

84. Keech, *Christology of Augustine*, 148.

Christian tradition, believes that sexual desire is a gift from God to humanity and is therefore not intrinsically evil. To remove the ability to have such desire from Jesus is to make him less than authentically human. Keech insightfully writes,

> In order to isolate Christ from sin, Augustine (in company with Apollinarius) has had to sever the reproductive capacity of the flesh from Christ's human affections. In effect, this denies him a full human soul by separating his appetitive and affective capabilities. Consequently, Christ's exemplary character collapses so that Julian questions what would be the salvific power of his resisting temptation. This extends not only to his chastity but also to his fasting, as the desire to nourish oneself and to satisfy the sexual impulse are both, from Julian's perspective, integrated for the good in human nature. In addition, Augustine's Christ is in no sense passive as a human would usually be, where passivity is the corollary of both the affections and physical appetite. Julian therefore draws Augustine's understanding of the crucifixion (and thus also the resurrection) into question.[85]

We are now able to see that Augustine's Christology is Apollinarian on two counts. His doctrines of predestination and original sin both force Jesus to have the Logos as his *physis* on one hand, while assuming a nature that is not ours on the other. Both moves deny the real, full humanity of Christ and fall prey to the Apollinarian heresy, but in a flavor unlike that of the Alexandrian heresiarch. Augustine's is a kind of "cosmological Apollinarianism" into which Jesus fits.[86] In this he continues the trend of Origen (divine simplicity), Arius (absolute transcendence), and Apollinarius (divine immutability) as allowing philosophical assumptions rather than revelation be the engine driving the train of theology. The ramifications of Augustine's move are immense, and we will consider them beginning in chapter 7; we've just given a foretaste here. Now we move on to the Nestorian heresy.

---

85. Keech, *Christology of Augustine*, 148–49.
86. This idea will be drawn out further in chapters 8–10.

5

The Historical Paradigm at 7:00
Nestorianism

THIS CHAPTER WILL DISCUSS the "bottom left" of the Hexagon. At the seven o'clock position, we have Nestorianism, which is the division and separation of the divine and human natures in Jesus, which for us is a heresy of emphasis. Though it does not seem to be so, Nestorianism tends toward Ebionism in that it diminishes the divinity of Christ by so dividing the natures that two persons are the result. At the end of the last chapter, with the demise of Apollinarianism, the concepts of nature and person were not yet clearly defined. In this chapter, we will trace the continued development of these terms and the way their usage becomes more universal. As Apollinarianism was a violent monist reaction against the dichotomist-dualist "Arianism," so, helplessly trapped within the confines of definitional simplicity, dichotomist-dualist Nestorianism will rise up to condemn Apollinarianism.

Background: From One Christological Model to Another

In the last chapter, we saw the failures of the Word-flesh model of Christology and the larger worldview in which it resided. The failures were so devastating that, at the defeat of Apollinarianism, even the non-heretical forms of Word-flesh had likewise disappeared.[1] The union-of-nature-model exemplified in both "Arianism" and Apollinarianism ultimately failed due to ultimately creating a new, hybrid *tertium quid*. The category of nature cannot take the lead in the *ordo theologiae*, as the two preceding heresies have shown. The new model arising to oppose Word-flesh is the Word-man model. The difficulties in the initial stages of the Word-man model, as will be shown in this chapter, is how to arrive at "as deep and inward a conception of the unity of Christ as was possessed by the other side [Word-flesh]."[2] The Word-flesh model has

1. Tapia, *Theology of Christ*, 98.
2. Grillmeier, *From the Apostolic Age*, 347.

clear biblical warrant from John 1:14, "the Word became flesh," but as we have seen in the aberrant thought of the "Arians" and Apollinarians, it is not enough to say that Jesus was merely "flesh." He is *a man*, and that fullness of humanity cannot be sacrificed based upon Gregory's maxim, "the unassumed is the unhealed." The basic Word-flesh presuppositions remained alive and well in their native Alexandria, while the Word-man understanding comes from the tradition most generally identified with Antioch.

The Antiochene approach to Christology, as was discussed in the last chapter, emphasized the historical roots of the faith as a starting point for theological reflection.[3] The Word-man Christology had been developing in Antioch throughout the fourth century at the same time the Word-flesh ideas from Alexandria were garnering more attention. The main thinkers in the Antiochene tradition include Eustathius of Antioch, Diodore of Tarsus, and Theodore of Mopsuestia. Eustathius, as we saw in the previous chapter, in his desire to preserve the true humanity in Jesus, rejected a natural union of the divine and human. It became nothing more than a volitional union (union of wills).[4] According to Eustathius, the personality of Jesus is human, and in him the Logos dwelt like he might in a temple.[5] He believed that the "I" of Jesus was the human, and not the divine, as when Jesus said "I have not yet ascended to my Father." In Eustathius's thinking, the man spoke those words and not the eternal Son.[6] His attempt to explain the union was on the metaphysical order of energy, since it was volitional. For him, the operative energy in Jesus is human, whereas in Apollinarianism, the energy is divine. Eustathius, like his forerunner Lucian, has cemented himself squarely on the dichotomist-dualist side of the Plotinian ambiguity, and those coming after him will follow.

Diodore of Tarsus (d. 395) was a slight improvement over Eustathius as he stressed the permanence and personal nature of the Logos dwelling in the man Jesus, yet he reacted against his monist Alexandrian counterparts whom he thought destroyed Christ's true humanity due to their Word-flesh assumptions.[7] More precisely, the Apollinarian concept of a single *hypostasis* in Christ led him to believe that it would be the divinity of Christ that would be compromised in the process.[8] Therefore Diodore affirmed the existence of two Sons, one human and one divine, which separates the distinction between person and nature into two persons, and continues the dichotomist-dualist understanding of Eustathius. As we saw in chapter 2, such

---

3. Again, when we say "Antioch" or "Antiochene," we mean the teaching tradition of Eustathius, Diodore, Theodore, and Nestorius. See chapter 4, n8.

4. Gonzalez, *From the Beginnings*, 339.

5. Gonzalez, *From the Beginnings*, 339.

6. Kelly, *Early Christian Doctrines*, 283. Such a Christology is reminiscent of that of Origen as developed in chapter 2.

7. Gonzalez, *From the Beginnings*, 340.

8. Kelly, *Early Christian Doctrines*, 303.

a Christology was anticipated by Origen, who saw the Logos and the man Jesus as distinct things joined by will.

Theodore of Mopsuestia followed Diodore, and was perhaps the crowning theologian of the tradition of Antioch.[9] He followed in the tradition of Eustathius and Diodore by emphasizing that God dwells in Jesus as in the prophets, except in Jesus's case, "it is as a Son."[10] He rejects Diodore's idea that there are "two sons" in Christ, looking instead to preserve the unity therein.[11] One of his deepest convictions is that "there can be no substantial relationship between God and his creation, the relationship between the two is defined solely in terms of God's loving providence."[12] This is reminiscent of the prevailing Plotinian ambiguity, where the one is apathetic toward the many, yet cannot exist without them. Here we see Theodore's model extending beyond Christology to cosmology, as well as the strengthening of the Antiochene conviction that the union of the human and divine in Christ is on the level of energy (providence).

Theodore understood the "person" (*prosopon*) of Jesus to be the resulting "conjunction" of the human and the divine, rather than the person of the pre-existent Logos.[13] Grillmeier adds that Theodore's understanding of *prosopon* is consistent with the Antiochene understanding of the term as "the form in which a *physis* or *hypostasis* appears. Every nature and every *hypostasis* has its own proper *prosopon*. It gives expression to the reality of the nature with its powers and characteristics."[14] Theodore's understanding of the technical terms is thus: each *physis* (nature) has its own *hypostasis* (concrete reality), which is revealed by its *prosopon* (observable manifestation or expression).[15] McLeod writes, "Theodore then reasoned that, if each of Christ's two natures has its own existing nature, then there must also be present in Christ two *prosopa* as well as two *hypostaseis*."[16] The union of the divine and human in Jesus was achieved because "each of Christ's natures possessed its own *prosopon* and that the union of the two took place in 'one common *prosopon*.'"[17] Thus Jesus, according to

---

9. Davis, *Councils*, 144–45.

10. Gonzalez, *From the Beginnings*, 342.

11. Kelly, *Early Christian Doctrines*, 308.

12. Greer, *Captain*, 220. Meyendorff, *Christ in Eastern Christian Thought* (1969), 163, writes that Theodore "seemed to have had a concept of God that identified the divine essence with the philosophical concept of immutability and yet excluded any instance of divine ('uncreated') life *ad extra*. It is this concept of God that made impossible, in Theodore's thought, any form of real union between divinity and humanity, allowing only a juxtaposition of the two natures." Again, if Meyendorff is correct, we see the identity thesis of definitional simplicity at work in the identification of the divine essence and energies (here immutability), very reminiscent of the methodology of Eunomius of Cyzicus from Chapter 3.

13. Gonzalez, *From the Beginnings*, 342.

14. Grillmeier, *From the Apostolic Age*, 431.

15. See McGuckin, *Cyril*, 138–39, as well as McLeod, "Significance," 366–67.

16. McLeod, "Significance," 367.

17. McLeod, "Significance," 367.

Theodore, has this one common *prosopon*, "achieved by the Logos giving himself to the human nature which he unites to himself."[18]

Theodore's "two *prosopa* uniting in one common *prosopon*" formula suffers from both the aforementioned union at the metaphysical level of energy (a union of good pleasure) as well as the lack of a technical term not already coopted that could explain how two realities become one.[19] Moreover, here is the clearest example of the Antiochene theological methodology at work, starting with the historical, observed reality (that is, in the world of the many) that Jesus is both divine and human, and therefore *physis* receives priority of place in the discussion of who Jesus is, which leads to John Meyendorff's accusation that the Antiochenes tried to "describe the history of our salvation rather than to explain it."[20] The problem to be solved, then, in the confines of such a method, is to explain how the two natures can possibly come together to form one person (*prosopon*). This single *prosopon* was the seat of the one energy and will of Christ, so that, in an ironic twist, Theodore's Christology was "Monoenergist" (more on this in chapter 6), just like that of his arch-enemy, Apollinarius.[21]

Theodore was perhaps the strongest critic yet of the heretical, Arian-Apollinarian strain of the Word-flesh schema. Grillmeier gives an excellent summary of Theodore's argument against it, as he writes,

> Had the eternal Godhead in fact taken the place of the soul, he says, then the body could have lacked nothing, for all inadequacies result from the natural weakness of the human life principle. If, then, Christ was hungry, thirsty, and suffered in other ways, this can only have been possible because the functions of life are performed by a human soul and thus come from a finite source. If this soul is to help the body to "subsist" at all, it needs the help of a "perfect" body. If anything is lacking, it can no longer fulfill its part of the task and will itself be drawn into a community of suffering. Eventually it will even be compelled to separate from the body. But if the Godhead had taken over the place of the soul, it would have been so powerful that it would of necessity also have taken over the role of the body, and those who denied the reality of Christ's bodily nature would be right. Both body and soul, however, had to be assumed because it was necessary to make good the death of the body and the sins of the soul. The sins (as the cause of death) had to be taken away so that death itself might finally be conquered. Now the sins themselves happened in the soul. "Therefore Christ had to assume not only a body but also a soul; or rather vice-versa, first the soul had to be assumed and then the body because of the soul." It was only possible to save the body through the spiritual soul. "Now this was only possible if [Christ] made the soul immutable and delivered it

---

18. Grillmeier, *From the Apostolic Age*, 434.

19. See McLeod, "Significance," 368–70, concerning Theodore's discussion of how the human ego plays both a physical and spiritual role as an analogy of how the two *prosopa* become one *prosopon*.

20. Meyendorff, *Christ in Eastern Christian Thought* (1969), 5.

21. Hovorun, *Will, Action and Freedom*, 13.

from the movements of sin, since we will only be freed from sin when we have acquired immutability." . . . Redemption was won by the grace of God gaining dominion over a man with whom God has clothed himself.[22]

Grillmeier continues, summarizing the key results of the Word-man model, "The difference between this picture of Christ and the other, that of the [Word-flesh] Christology, is quite apparent. The human nature of Christ regains its real physical-human inner life and its capacity for action."[23] In other words, to affirm the integrity of Jesus's humanity (or of creation in general) one would have to reject any kind of monist conception of unity. Unity could not be natural, but could only be willful.[24] The separation of the two principles (the One and many) is a given; and an organic (natural) connection between them could not exist. Kelly summarizes the three great weaknesses in Theodore's thinking, which were his continuous distinction between the human and divine, even to the point of separation; his emphasis on "conjunction" rather than union of the two natures; and an incomplete understanding of "person" that would need to be worked out later.[25] Also, Theodore would not allow for a full *communicatio idiomatum* in Jesus, believing that "the attributes of the Word are extended to the human; but not vice-versa."[26] Despite these obvious flaws, the Antiochene Word-man Christology forms an important corrective to the Alexandrian Word-flesh concept in that it takes the historical reality of the humanity of Jesus seriously. Alexandria's two heretical Word-flesh adherents, Arius and Apollinarius, had failed to do justice to Jesus's humanity in taking the framework to its logical extremes. We have surveyed in this section those who take Word-man to the other extreme, thereby sacrificing the unity of Jesus in so doing. Such an unbalanced theology is the first element that contributes to Nestorianism.

Preliminary Developments for Conflict

The Word-man and non-heretical Word-flesh Christologies were on a collision course for supremacy in the East, though the roots of their quests were not completely theological, as the un-Christian rivalry between the two theological centers stemmed directly from the tie between church and state. There was an incredible amount of religious and political jealousy over which city would supply the imperial capital, Constantinople, with its religious policy, since the third canon of the Council of Constantinople gave the capital supremacy over every other see with the exception

22. Grillmeier, *From the Apostolic Age*, 427.

23. Grillmeier, *From the Apostolic Age*, 427. Quotations are cited from Theodore's *Fifth Catechetical Homily*.

24. The third metaphysical level, that of person, had not yet been fully disentangled from nature. The identity thesis, in practice if not in principle, was still strong in Antioch.

25. Kelly, *Early Christian Doctrines*, 308.

26. Gonzalez, *From the Beginnings*, 343.

of Rome itself.[27] This jealousy extended to the actions of the patriarchs of Alexandria primarily because they saw themselves as the guardians of the "city of the orthodox" and resented the usurpation they perceived coming from the upstarts in Constantinople.[28] Such a jealous rivalry meat that the two sides would be far less willing to give the other a fair hearing. It all came to a head with the appointment of the Antiochene Nestorius to the patriarchy of Constantinople.

Nestorius became bishop in 428, very near the time of the death of his teacher Theodore. In his first address to the emperor, he asked that he would be granted the power to root out heretics from the entire empire. It is ironic that in three years, he would be deposed as a heretic himself. His ability to speak in public belied a couple of faults in his own character. The first was his personal ambition and bravado which was clearly on display. He wanted his Antiochene tradition to rule the day in the imperial court. The second was his real lack of theological ability. The church historian Socrates writes concerning Nestorius,

> Having myself perused the writings of Nestorius, I have found him an unlearned man and shall candidly express the conviction of my mind concerning him. . . . I cannot concede that he was either a follower of Paul of Samosata or of Photinus, or that he denied the divinity of Christ; but he seemed scared at the term *theotokos* as though it were some terrible "bugbear." The fact is, the causeless alarm he manifested on this subject just exposed his extreme ignorance; for being a man of natural fluency as a speaker, he was considered well-educated, but in reality he was disgracefully illiterate.[29]

Such a combination of ambition and lack of real preparation in a man in his position could only set him up for trouble. His adversary Cyril of Alexandria did not embrace the heretical extremes of the Word-flesh schema that Arius and Apollinarius had done. As Grillmeier notes, Cyril's Christology was very reminiscent of that of his predecessor, Athanasius, following the great Alexandrian's interpretation of the Word-flesh model in his earlier years.[30] He was a brilliant theologian in his own right, with far more training and ability than Nestorius. Cyril's character flaws are well-documented as being contentious, malicious, and jealous.[31] Cyril was more than able to expose Nestorius's substandard Chrisology.

There is one more point of disagreement between Alexandria and Antioch, which came to light during the Nestorian controversy—the understanding of salvation. We saw salvation as the interpretive key used by both Athanasius and Gregory in their opposition to "Arianism" and Apollinarianism, respectively. Donald Fairbairn explains

27. Frend, *Saints and Sinners*, 148.
28. Frend, *Saints and Sinners*, 149.
29. Socrates, *Hist. eccl.* 7.32, quoted in Young and Teal, *From Nicaea to Chalcedon*, 292.
30. Grillmeier, *From the Apostolic Age*, 417–19.
31. Frend, *Saints and Sinners*, 150, notes that Cyril may have contributed to the murder of Alexandria's last great Neoplatonic philosopher.

how the Antiochenes and Alexandrians saw salvation differently; both Theodore and his pupil Nestorius saw salvation as a "two-part" process of human condition and human improvement, as he writes, "They see humanity's natural condition as one of mortality and imperfection and view salvation as an advance to a higher, perfect state. Furthermore, they see salvation not so much as an elevation to *divine* life but rather as progress towards perfect *human* life, and this allows them to adopt a Christology that distinguishes sharply between the Logos and the assumed man."[32] Therefore christologically, as well as soteriologically, the school of Eustathius through Nestorius followed the dichotomist-dualist side of the Plotinian ambiguity to the letter. On the other hand, Cyril and the Alexandrians adopt a "three-part" salvation process that includes creation, the fall, and finally restoration, which is deification and a share in the divine life through the Son.[33] Both sides will appeal to salvation in their arguments, but they mean different things by their appeal.

Nestorius and *Theotokos*

One of the first serious blunders Nestorius made was to criticize the term *theotokos*, which held a long-standing place in the tradition to refer to Mary as the bearer of God. Justo Gonzalez writes, "In so doing, he was not actually taking the initiative, but was rather attempting to settle a controversy that had been going on in Constantinople for some time. When Anastasius, his chaplain, attacked the use of *theotokos*, Nestorius refused to excommunicate him. Later, Nestorius himself preached his famous sermons against the title of *theotokos*."[34] For Nestorius, *theotokos* implied either "Arianism" (Jesus as a mere creature) or Apollinarianism (Jesus's manhood completed by the Logos).[35] As Bethune-Baker quotes Nestorius, "All that could be properly said of Mary was that she was the receptacle of God and gave birth to Christ."[36] Davis explains further,

> Nestorius held that in Christ there are two natures. By nature he meant the concrete character of being. Each of these two natures was a *prosopon*, a term expressing its external aspect as an individual; each was an *hypostasis* or concrete subsistent being. These metaphysical distinctions meant in the end not that each nature was an actually subsistent entity but that each nature was objectively real. These two natures remained unaltered and distinct in the union, the Godhead existing in the man; the man, in the Godhead without mixture or confusion. Divinity and humanity remained objectively real, each retaining its own characteristics and operations. The humanity was not swallowed up in the divinity, for Christ must have lived a genuinely human life if mankind

---

32. Fairbairn, *Grace and Christology*, 28. Italics in original.
33. Fairbairn, *Grace and Christology*, 63.
34. Gonzalez, *From the Beginnings*, 354.
35. Davis, *Councils*, 145.
36. Bethune-Baker, *History*, 261.

is truly to be redeemed. Yet he said, 'Christ is indivisible in his being Christ, but he is twofold in his being God and man. We know not two Christs or two Sons or Only-begottens or Lords, not one and another Son, not a first and a second Christ, but one and the same, who is perceived in his created and his incarnate natures.'[37]

Here is the clearly visible thought pattern of Antioch in full view. Nestorius started with the metaphysical level of nature, and there were, for him, two natures, practically mutually impenetrable and side-by-side in Jesus, so the union had to be one of energy.

Instead of *theotokos*, Nestorius preferred *christotokos* to describe Mary. She did not bear God, but instead bore Christ, a violation of the tradition as Erickson summarizes Nestorius to say that "God cannot have a mother; no woman can give birth to God."[38] Bethune-Baker helpfully notes that, "To refuse to the Mother of the Lord the title *theotokos* was doubtless to deny her a title of honor that was rightly hers; but it was much more than this. The English translation 'Mother of God' brings into undue prominence the thought of the glory of her motherhood; the Greek term fixes attention rather on the Godhead of him who was born. To deny that she was *theotokos* was really to deny that he who was born of her was God as well as man."[39] In such statements do the ignorance and imprudence of Nestorius meet.

In his thought, Nestorius faithfully follows those who came before him in the Antiochene tradition, such as Diodore and Theodore. Nestorius was simply able to exaggerate their shortcomings to the point of revealing what had been a concealed christological weakness. Bethune-Baker acutely summarized the problem lying dormant in Nestorius and Antioch, "The divine and human natures were distinctly separated. There was only a 'conjunction' of them—an 'indwelling' of the Godhead in the man, resulting in a moral and sympathetic union. 'I separate the natures, but the reverence I pay them is joint', are the words in which Nestorius defended his teaching."[40] From his received Antiochene methodology, the historical, observed reality of the Gospels was that there were two natures (divine and human) operative in Jesus. The metaphysical level of nature then was the starting point, and those two natures could not be joined. Two natures could not become one (that would bring change into the Godhead); two *hypostaseis* could not become one (that would be Apollinarianism). The only metaphysical level left on which to build the union in Christ would be at the level of energy—a union of will and morals. The clearest biblical passage that shows how Nestorius viewed the conjunction of God and man in Jesus is his self-reference in John 2:19, "Destroy this temple and in three days I will raise it up." As Pelikan quotes Nestorius, "Am I, then, the only one who calls Christ 'double?' Does he not designate himself both as a temple that can be destroyed and as a God that raises up? If, however,

---

37. Davis, *Councils*, 146. The quotation is from Nestorius but not cited by Davis.
38. Erickson, *Word Became Flesh*, 62. He cites Nestorius, *Sermons against* Theotokos 1.
39. Bethune-Baker, *History*, 262.
40. Bethune-Baker, *History*, 261–62.

it was God who was destroyed... the Lord would have said: 'Destroy this God and in three days he will be raised up.'"[41] Again, Nestorius writes, "The temple created by the Holy Spirit is one, and the God who hallows the temple is another."[42] It is easy to see why such language would arouse suspicion in the politically- and doctrinally-charged environment in which he lived.

Another part of the struggle was the ever-evolving terminology used in the controversies. We were introduced to some of those key technical terms in the last chapter, and then observed Theodore's use of them above. Nestorius tended to see *physis* and *hypostasis* as synonyms.[43] Neither of these terms, nor *ousia*, could be the basis of the union, since "All three terms have a direct relationship to the entity itself, there is no way that God and man can be united in *hypostasis*, essence, or nature without the loss of one or the other."[44] Nestorius, following Theodore, tended to address the common *prosopon* in Christ rather than the natures, which made the concept of *Christotokos* sensible to him.[45] In the term *prosopon*, he sees a metaphysical term that is furthest from *hypostasis/physis/ousia*, as "the concatenation of individuating characteristics which give expression to the nature."[46] John McGuckin writes, "He found it made much more sense to apply a different word altogether to *signify the distinct individualness of a thing*, and this was to be *prosopon*. For Nestorius the meaning of *hypostasis* should be restricted to connoting the concretization of a thing, and *physis* to signify the stuff of which it was made."[47] He continues,

> The *prosopon* is the external aspect or form of a *physis* as it can be manifested to external observation and scrutiny. It is a very concrete, empirical word, connoting what appears to outside observation. Each essence (*ousia*) is characterized by its proper nature (*physis*), everything that is, which makes it up, *and in turn every nature that is hypostatically real presents itself to the scrutiny of the senses in its own prosopon*—that list of detailed characteristics or "*propria*" that constitute this thing individually and signal to the observer what nature (*physis*) it has and thus to what genus (*ousia*) it belongs. In the system Nestorius is following, every nature has its own *prosopon*, that such of proper characteristics (*idiomata*) by which it is characterized in its unique individuality and made known to others as such. The word carried with it an intrinsic sense of "making known" and appeared to Nestorius particularly apt in the revelatory context of discussing the incarnation.[48]

---

41. Pelikan, *Christian Tradition*, 1:252. The citation is Nestorius, *Sermons on Theotokos* 1.
42. Nestorius, *Fragment 256*, in Pelikan, *Christian Tradition*, 1:252.
43. See McGuckin, *Cyril*, 138–39. In other words, person and nature are confused by Nestorius.
44. Greer, *Captain*, 314. See also McGuckin, *Cyril*, 142, where he notes that Nestorius used *ousia*, *physis*, and *hypostasis* largely as synonyms.
45. Young and Teal, *From Nicaea to Chalcedon*, 295.
46. Greer, *Captain*, 314.
47. McGuckin, *Cyril*, 143. Emphasis in original.
48. McGuckin, *Cyril*, 144. Emphasis in original.

The technical term *prosopon*, which is at the metaphysical level of energy, allowed Nestorius to make the union into a voluntary one.[49] As Frances Young and Andrew Teal write, "The Logos could not be the *prosopon* of union; the two natures were not two states of the Logos' being, but the two 'grounds of being' for the one Christ." They continue, "Nestorius was anxious to present an account of one concrete individual with two distinguishable metaphysical bases,"[50] and further, "He found it impossible to reserve the term *prosopon* for the union; he could not avoid talk of a human *prosopon* and a divine *prosopon*. Thus each nature had its own *prosopon* and the two natures remained personalized to the extent that his opponents were not altogether unfair in accusing him of teaching a 'double Christ,' two persons acting independently."[51] John McGuckin summarizes well,

> In so far as a *prosopon* signifies "observable aspect" or "communicable external appearance" then perhaps we can sum up Nestorius; position so far as follows: the eyes of faith recognize in Christ two clearly observed aspects of his reality, which signify to the beholder divinity as well as humanity. Christ, therefore, has two *prosopa*. At the same time the eyes of faith recognize that *this Christ who has two prosopa is not the same as those prosopa themselves. In other words Christ is not the Logos as such. It would be bad theology, for Nestorius, to speak of the pre-existent Christ, since he is not eternal as the Logos is.* Nor would it be right to make unqualified statements about the impassibility of Christ since the radical qualification of human limitations and sufferings is an integral part of what the mind understands by the word "Christ." *But in just the same way as the Logos is not synonymous with Christ, neither is the man Jesus of Nazareth.* Christ, for Nestorius, was no mere man. The word connotes far more than the term "the man Jesus"; in fact it connotes the whole mystery of the intimate relationship of *this man* with the divine Logos, and the union of the Logos with him. *Christ is not only a word for the union of these two prosopic realities*, it is also the concrete experience, in some way, of how that union has taken place, how it is to be conceived, and how it ought to be articulated by the church. The term Christ signifies the experience of the encounter with this unique composite figure of the Son of God. In light of this it is not enough merely to insist that there are two *prosopa* in Christ, because the experience of the unique revelation of Christ calls for the confession that *there this is also the "prosopon of union"* the one Christ who manifests in a single *prosopon* (observable reality) the differentiated *prosopa* of the divine Logos and the human Jesus. There are two *prosopa*, and there is one *prosopon*. This is why the starting point of one's consideration is all-important. If one begins always with the concrete experience of the incarnate Christ, the paradox is solved: the one is revealed as two-fold. The awareness of the double nature, however, is secondary to the

---

49. Greer, *Captain*, 315.
50. Young and Teal, *From Nicaea to Chalcedon*, 295.
51. Young and Teal, *From Nicaea to Chalcedon*, 295.

experience of the actual oneness of the incarnate Christ, and is only arrived at by deduction from that oneness.[52]

The meanings attached to these technical terms was becoming familiar to both sides of the struggle, and now the language would soon be used to accurately diagnose problems. Moreover, because the union was at the level of energy (moral union) for Nestorius, it allowed him to so separate the natures so that nature and person became identified.[53] In Nestorianism, all three metaphysical categories are in operation, but his starting point is nature, resulting in an energetic union, rather than following Athanasius's trinitarian example and starting from person to arrive at a union of being.

What was a real attempt to preserve the true humanity of Jesus was bought with the sacrifice of his unity. Leo Davis writes,

> Nestorius' theory is a laudable attempt to preserve intact and complete the two natures, godhead and manhood, of Christ. To his credit, Christ's humanity remains complete and objectively real. The problem which defeated Nestorius was how to unite these two real natures into a single person, a single metaphysical subject. Nestorius would not recognize the Word as that subject for fear that this would involve the Deity in suffering or imperil the complete reality of the human in Christ. So he had recourse to a third element, the result of the conjunction of natures, the common *prosopon* which could not adequately explain to the satisfaction of the Church the union of the two complete and objectively real natures which he sought so sincerely.[54]

Davis continues the analysis by quoting G. L. Prestige, who writes, "The unorthodoxy of Nestorius was not a positive fact but a negative impotence; like his master Theodore, he could not bring within the framework of a single, clearly conceived personality the two natures of Christ which he distinguished with so admirable a realism."[55] Rowan Greer summarizes the "school of Antioch" here:

> The fundamental unity of the Antiochene position can be best seen when one regards it as a platform opposing Arianism and, later, Apollinarianism. . . . The Antiochenes refuse to accept either the Arian denial of a human soul in Christ or the assertion that his human attributes must be referred to as the Word. They do agree that all predication must be predication by nature, but they create a human subject to take care of the human attributes. The Alexandrian view is totally contrary to this approach. . . . The Alexandrians are prepared to retain the main lines of the Word-flesh Christology, and insist that the Word

---

52. McGuckin, *Cyril*, 157–58. Italics in original. As Hovorun, *Will, Action and Freedom*, 13, notes, as for Theodore, Nestorius locates the will and energy of Christ in the single *prosopon*.

53. Balthasar, *Cosmic Liturgy*, 261, writes, "Nestorius attempted to find the unity in the object of [Christ's] two ways of willing. He rightly saw that their unity of object did not at all presuppose a unity of will."

54. Davis, *Councils*, 147.

55. Davis, *Councils*, 147–48. Davis does not cite where Prestige wrote this.

remains the single subject of all Christ's activities. Their opposition to Arianism takes the form of distinguishing two times and two modes of attribution. And even though they do finally agree that Christ must have a human soul, that soul never becomes a full theological factor, since it remains controlled in every way by the Word. From a strictly theological point of view, it is evident that we have witnessed the development of two opposing schools of thought. On the one side stand Eustace, Diodore, and Theodore; on the other Origenism, if not Origen himself, Malchion, Lucian, Athanasius, and Cyril.[56]

Here we can see the full expression of Antiochene Christology reacting against its dialectical opposites in Apollinarianism. Because Nestorius, like his theological forefathers before him, remained trapped in their presuppositions, both the confusion of person and nature inherited from Origen and the union at the level of will from the first Antiochene heretic, Paul of Samosata. Nestorius had succeeded in bringing the weaknesses of the Word-man Christology to light, its starting point in the metaphysical category of energy, and in doing so he aroused the patriarch of Alexandria against him.

Cyril Goes to War

Cyril of Alexandria is one of the most famous and most infamous figures of early church history. Cyril was a formidable interpreter of Scripture, and would likely have been remembered as only so if it were not for the christological controversies.[57] His ability to uphold the received orthodoxy rivaled that of his predecessor Athanasius.[58] The jealousy and rivalry between Alexandria and Constantinople was briefly mentioned above, and Cyril was fully capable at stopping at nothing to demean the rival see. Cyril attempted to get Nestorius anathematized any way he could, attempting to involve other clergy and even the emperor.[59] It is beyond the scope of this chapter to fully recount Cyril's methods. Instead, the focus will be on his theological reasoning in his battle with Nestorius.

Cyril was the senior patriarch of the four great sees, and the heir of the proud Alexandrian tradition. While he acknowledged that Apollinarius had gone too far, he still held to the Alexandrian teaching of the "single subject in the incarnate Lord" to which Apollinarius held, but did not depend on Apollinarius for it.[60] For Cyril, the incarnation occurs in order to save humans, that is, to bring humans into the life of

---

56. Greer, *Captain*, 222.

57. Young and Teal, *From Nicaea to Chalcedon*, 304.

58. McGuckin, *Cyril*, 175, notes that Cyril imposed upon himself a "major programme of patristic reading" throughout the controversy to make sure he was on solid footing with the tradition of the church.

59. Davis, *Councils*, 148–49. Gonzalez, *From the Beginnings*, 354–55, notes that Cyril used gold to buy influence and appealed to Rome as well. His appeal to Rome played off the jealously between the old imperial capitol and the new, using the motif of the enemy of my enemy is my friend.

60. McGuckin, *Cyril*, 183.

God, following in the footsteps of Irenaeus and Athanasius. The humanity is as real as the divinity, just as for Nestorius, but there is but one subject in Christ, because that is how salvation occurs. For Cyril, his Christology undergirds his soteriology. The soteriological and subject-of-Christ differences have been treated at length above.

Once word reached Cyril of Nestorius's teaching and actions, he wrote a letter, to which Nestorius responded. Cyril began his public attacks on Nestorius in his *Easter Letter* of 429, though he does not mention Nestorius by name. He continued writing polemical attacks against his position to both his monks and to members of the imperial court over the next year.[61] Cyril wrote a second letter, and again Nestorius responded seemingly ignoring Cyril's points. In Cyril's second letter, he emphasizes that the union of God and man in Christ is hypostatic, following in the Alexandrian tradition of Athanasius in making the primary metaphysical level in the *ordo theologiae* that of person, "because the Logos united humanity to himself 'in his own *hypostasis*.'"[62] Even though Cyril's attitude and actions often left much to be desired, he concluded the second letter in what appeared to be a genuine call for doctrinal unity and peace. He seemed to be more interested in getting the incarnation right than getting one over on the upstart see in Constantinople.[63]

Cyril's third letter was not a reply to Nestorius's replies to the second letter, but rather a demand for submission to the Alexandrian position, citing collaboration between Alexandria and Rome, along with twelve statements of Nestorius that Cyril demand he anathematize.[64] On the first anathema, Cyril "maintains that "Emmanuel (the incarnate Son) is truly God, and that therefore the Holy Virgin is *theotokos*—for she has generated (in fleshly wise) the Word of God who has become flesh." Nestorius's reply to Cyril states that "He who is Emmanuel is not to be called God the Word, but rather 'God with us', in the sense that, by the fact of his union with our constituents received from the Virgin, he dwelt in the nature which is like ours."[65] Here we can clearly see how Nestorius breaks the union of the natures in Christ into two separate subjects—God the Word and Jesus the man.

On the second anathema, "Cyril maintains that the Word of God the Father was hypostatically united with flesh, and with his own flesh is one Christ—one and the same God and man together." Nestorius, on the other hand, anathematizes anyone who says that the flesh was able to contain the divine nature.[66] At least part of the difficulty here lies in the use of the technical terminology. As noted above, Nestorius uses *hypostasis* and *physis* synonymously, ignoring the development the term

---

61. Young and Teal, *From Nicaea to Chalcedon*, 313–14.
62. Young and Teal, *From Nicaea to Chalcedon*, 277.
63. Young and Teal, *From Nicaea to Chalcedon*, 278.
64. Young and Teal, *From Nicaea to Chalcedon*, 279–80.
65. Both are quoted in Bethune-Baker, *History*, 263.
66. Again, both are quoted in Bethune-Baker, *History*, 264. The famous extra-Calvinisticum "the finite cannot contain the infinite" follows the same train of thought more than a millennium later.

hypostasis underwent in the Eunomian controversy in the late fourth century.[67] Cyril, on the other hand, sees a distinction in the two terms, understanding *hypostasis* to be the reality that lies beneath the *physis*. For Nestorius then, given his understanding of *physis* and *hypostasis*, a hypostatic union would involve blending the two natures into something entirely different, losing the fullness of divinity, humanity, or both.[68] Moreover, Cyril's Alexandrian methodology, with its Word-flesh model still fresh in his memory, would only allow one real subject in Jesus, the Logos. Any talk of a union at the energetic level of *prosopon* was far too external for him.

This is the decisive move for Cyril. Instead of locating the union in the nature that subsumes the person as Apollinarius had, or in the willful union of the *prosopa* forming two subjects as did Nestorius, Cyril placed the union in the person, or *hypostasis*, of the Son. The answers to the Apollinarian dilemma raised the need for clarification of the concepts of person and nature. It became apparent that the union of the divine and human in Christ was at the level of person, and not of nature. If it were of nature, then the humanity would be swallowed up by the divinity. Ralph Tapia writes,

> Where the Alexandrians from their point of departure were disposed to overstrain the unity of person in Christ into a unity of nature, the school of Antioch was inclined to extend the duality of natures to a duality of persons. It is only natural that even Cyril should, at the beginning of his speculation, base it on the traditional [Word-flesh] scheme and even go on undisturbed to use Apollinarian formulations Only in the course of the disputes with Nestorius did he come to recognize that for its part Alexandrian theory did not do justice to the peculiar importance of Christ's human soul and its deeds. It was the particular achievement of his speculation to unite the insights of both schools, and thereby to furnish a sufficiently clear basis for further correct development of the truths of Christology.[69]

Here Cyril corrects the methodology that both the Alexandrians and the Antiochenes had followed—he started with person rather than nature. The starting point for a correct Christology focused on the divine person becoming human, not how the natures coalesced together in Jesus. Once the person of the savior became the point of departure, the rest flowed easily. Unlike Apollinarius, Cyril refused to identify the Logos as the *nous* of Christ. Instead, the person of the Logos himself is the single subject,

---

67. See McGuckin, *Cyril*, 138–42.

68. McGuckin, *Cyril*, 140. McGuckin notes that Cyril sometimes equivocates on the meaning of *physis*: sometimes it means the "constituent elements of a thing" while at other times it means the "individual subject." During his dispute with Nestorius, he utilized the second meaning of the term, as had all the Alexandrians before him, but afterwards realized that, for the sake of clarity, the first definition would work best. He also states on page 175, that, for Cyril as well as for Athanasius, terminology is not as important as the central idea. Both allowed for flexible terminology in order to best illustrate the point.

69. Tapia, *Theology of Christ*, 98

thereby he did not reduce person to some aspect of the nature.[70] Nestorius may well have been saying almost the same things as Cyril, but his methodology began in the world of natures and proceeded to how the natures could be one person. Origen's definition of the essence of God as simple, which defined the person of the Father by his nature—a "turn to the nature"—which had suffered its first serious attack in the doctrine of the God *ad intra* by Athanasius and the Cappadocians, had been dealt a jarring blow by Cyril in the doctrine of the person of Christ. It remained to be worked out further, but Cyril's "turn to the person" became the blueprint for the final defeat of Origen's "turn to the nature" two centuries later in the sixth ecumenical council.[71]

Young and Teal write concerning the third anathema, "The third anathema was directed against those who divide the natures after the union, and describe the union as an association in dignity, authority, or power, rather than a conjunction by natural union (that is, by nature)."[72] Here we see the use of "nature" by Cyril to mean "person," an idea to be clarified in a few years as stated above.[73] The anathemas continue, though the first three are the most important for our discussion here. The controversy had heated to beyond any point of reconciliation. There was no way Nestorius would agree to anathematize himself in this way. He responded with twelve anathemas against Cyril.

Following R. L. Norris, Young and Teal note that Cyril's thought cannot be simplified into a Word-flesh or Word-man model. Instead, Norris opts for more of a narrative model, built upon both the servant passage of Phil 2 and the Nicene Creed, emphasizing that it was "the pre-existent Logos who was incarnate."[74] Here we see an *ordo theologiae* beginning to develop that starts, as Athanasius before him, with the person of Jesus as revealed in the biblical narrative. Unfortunately, Cyril also drew from a questionable source, as he claimed the Apollinarian phrase "one nature of God the Word incarnate," mistakenly believing it was from Athanasius, and shaped his Christology to fit the framework that phrase condenses.[75] Although the Apollinarian formula will cause serious problems after Cyril's death, he was able to use it toward further doctrinal clarity. Young and Teal write, "The Logos for Cyril is the only *hypostasis*, and that was what he intended to convey by his formula 'hypostatic union.' That

---

70. McGuckin, *Cyril*, 206.

71. Although it is popular to frame the Nestorian controversy, theologically at least, in terms of Antioch vs. Alexandria, Andrew Louth, "Syrians," 111 notes that the "Alexandrian" ideas held universal appeal. He writes, "The christological controversy was not the clash of two more-or-less equipollent 'schools', but rather a response to the dangers represented by an eccentric, and rather scholarly approach to Christology, associated with Antioch, by the broad consensus of Christian confession, of which Cyril projected himself as the spokesman."

72. Young and Teal, *From Nicaea to Chalcedon*, 283.

73. See n70 above.

74. Young and Teal, *From Nicaea to Chalcedon*, 317. Young and Teal here follow R. L. Norris, "Christological Models," 255–68.

75. Gonzalez, *From the Beginnings*, 367. This slogan will remain popular in Alexandria for decades and lead to the Monophysite heresy to be discussed in the next chapter.

is also what he meant by 'one nature', not the result of a compounding of two independent natures, though his use of the phrase 'out of two natures' came near to suggesting that it did."[76] They continue, "So what happened to Cyril's Christology was that he adopted 'monophysite' formulae to counter the 'dyophysite' position he thought he faced."[77] Terminological clarifications were progressing, but not yet complete.

Leo Donald Davis adds some helpful explanation to Cyril's position. He writes,

> The Word, having in an ineffable and inconceivable manner personally united to himself flesh animated with living soul, became man and was called Son of Man, yet not of mere will or favor, nor again by simple assumption to himself of a human person, and that while the natures which were brought together into this true unity were diverse there was of both one Christ and Son; not as though the diverseness of the natures were done away with by this union, but rather Godhead and Manhood completed for us one Lord and Christ and Son by their unutterable and unspeakable concurrence into unity.[78]

Cyril's main point is to reject such a volitional (energetic) union that creates two Sons. Davis continues, "Scripture does not say that the Word united himself to the person of man but that He became flesh, that is, he became partaker of flesh and blood like us. So the virgin is called *theotokos*, not as if the nature of the Word or his godhead had its beginning from the Virgin, but inasmuch as his holy body, endued with a rational soul, was born of her, to which body the Word was personally united."[79] Summarizing Cyril, Davis writes, "the human and divine in the one Christ cannot be divided nor connected merely by common dignity, authority, or rule. One cannot attribute the expressions of Scripture now to the man apart from the Word, now exclusively to the Word. Christ is not just man carrying God within him." In other words, the Word and Jesus are the exact same person.[80] He continues, "There was no confusion or mingling of the divine and the human, for humanity and divinity are different in essence. Union excludes division, but does not eliminate difference. Difference however, involves no separation and can be apprehended only by intellectual analysis."[81] Davis further summarizes Cyril, "All expressions found in the Scriptures are predicated of the Word, for the Word is the single metaphysical subject, the single "I" in Jesus Christ." And, "Still Cyril rejected the formula "in two natures," for this, he thought, involved separation. Nature was for him the equivalent of *hypostasis*, a concrete, objective existence. He preferred to talk of two natural properties or qualities."[82] It is easy to see why Cyril

---

76. Young and Teal, *From Nicaea to Chalcedon*, 317–18.
77. Young and Teal, *From Nicaea to Chalcedon*, 318.
78. Davis, *Councils*, 149.
79. Davis, *Councils*, 150.
80. Davis, *Councils*, 151.
81. Davis, *Councils*, 151–52.
82. Davis, *Councils*, 152–53.

would be so opposed to the teachings of Nestorius. There were real differences of both methodology and vocabulary: Nestorius was dichotomist-dualist, and Cyril was still clinging to some vestiges of monism. The two sides could not be reconciled, and the emperor called a council in Ephesus for the summer of 431.

The Council of Ephesus

Nestorius, on the advice of his friend John of Antioch, accepted the term *theotokos* before the council convened.[83] Such a gesture was of little use, however, because the fate of Nestorius was sealed. At the council, Cyril was both accuser and judge, and Nestorius would not attend.[84] The council was conceived in haste and Cyril would not await the Antiochene delegation to arrive before starting. Once the Antiochenes arrived, they had their own council, deposing Cyril. The emperor intervened, and decided in favor of Cyril.[85] Allison notes the terminology advancement to come out of the council, "The Council of Ephesus resolved the problem by using the word 'nature' (*physis*) for the divine and human aspects in Christ and 'person' (*prosopon*) for the single unity of divinity and humanity. Thus we have in Christ two natures (as against the Apollinarian one nature) and one person (as over against the Nestorian two persons)."[86] Nestorius was deposed and exiled, but lived out his life and even wrote a defense of his views under a pseudonym, *The Bazaar of Heraclides*.[87] Nestorius suffered unjustly probably due to his belligerence and lack of intellectual rigor more than anything else. It is certain that his own position was misunderstood and that he was likely not "Nestorian" in the fullest sense.[88] Unlike the "Arians" and Apollinarians, who died off in the east, Nestorianism lived on, especially in the churches of Persia. They sent missionaries to China, and church leadership was transferred to Baghdad. They later moved on to Kurdestan, and are called Assyrian Christians today. Davis estimates that over 100,000 still exist, continuing to reject Mary as *theotokos* and revering St. Nestorius.[89] This is currently the longest-running schism in the Christian church.

The immediate impact of the council itself was failure. The peace and unanimity that the participants in the council had desired never manifested. A doctrinal position had been reached, but the party from Antioch refused to accept it. Two more years

---

83. Davis, *Councils*, 153.

84. See Russell, *Cyril of Alexandria*, 47. Even though it sounds harsh that Cyril was accuser and judge, he was the senior patriarch and was the right person to lead the proceedings under church and imperial law.

85. Davis, *Councils*, 154–60.

86. Allison, *Cruelty of Heresy*, 123–24.

87. Davis, *Councils*, 163.

88. Young and Teal, *From Nicaea to Chalcedon*, 297.

89. Davis, *Councils*, 167.

would pass before a peace was finally hammered out between the two bishops, John and Cyril, and only then with the accompanying pressure from the emperor.[90]

Summary

The Nestorian controversy was yet another step in the process of refining an orthodox Christology. The Nestorian position stands on the same side of the Hexagon of Heresy as Ebionism and Arianism, and, as Pelikan notes, Nestorius and Theodore tried hard to emphasize that their position was not a form of Adoptionism, but it could easily be identified as such.[91] Like Ebionism and Arianism, Nestorianism creates an unbridgeable gulf that separates the two principles of the one and the many, as by now can be expected of all dichotomist-dualist theologies. Ebionism sets a gulf between Jesus and the Father, placing Jesus over against the Father as a creation. "Arianism" does the same, but adds another gulf between Jesus and us, since for Arius Jesus was fully creature, but not exactly creature like us. As Allison summarizes, "Nestorianism has improved on Arianism in that it asserts the full divinity and full humanity of Jesus Christ. The two fatal Arian gaps between God and Christ and between Christ and humanity are now reduced to one, and that in Christ himself. Thus, Nestorianism denies not divinity but rather the soteriological unity by which God and humanity are one in Christ."[92] Nestorianism places the fatal gap inside Jesus himself—between his divinity and his humanity. Instead of being the bridge that unites creator and creation, in Nestorianism he becomes the canyon that ensures they are never truly united, cosmologically and christologically. Additionally, Bethune-Baker puts his finger on the issue with clarity:

> The real strength of Nestorianism lay in its clear perception of the reality of the human nature of the Lord. . . . But what it gave with one hand it took away with the other. Its theory failed to cover the deepest conviction of the Christian consciousness that in Jesus God and man had really been brought together in a vital and permanent union, never henceforward to be dissolved; that the chasm between God and man had been bridged over, so that all who were united with Jesus were united with God himself. The Nestorian theory only provided for an external union, which was understood to be an alliance of two distinct beings. And so the incarnation was as much emptied of its meaning as it was by any theory which failed to provide recognition either for the complete manhood or for the complete Godhead of the Savior.[93]

He adds,

90. Russell, *Cyril of Alexandria*, 52–53.
91. Pelikan, *Christian Tradition*, 1:253.
92. Allison, *Cruelty of Heresy*, 124.
93. Bethune-Baker, *History*, 274–75.

The Hexagon of Heresy

> The Catholic interpretation of the Gospel is based on the idea of God condescending to be born as man; a divine person stoops to assume human nature and live a human life, without ceasing to be divine. About this conception there is a unity which never for a moment is in danger of dissolution. But the very starting point of Nestorian thought excluded the possibility of unity. Indeed, Nestorians started not from one point, but from two, and the lines of their thought ran always parallel, side by side. There was man, and there was God. Both were persons, and the conjunction in which the two were brought together was only one of relation. And so they never reached a clear conception of a person living in two spheres of consciousness and experience. To this conception Cyril seems really to have attained, though there were some difficulties of terminology which he did not altogether overcome.[94]

Like the contiguous steel ribbons of a railroad track, the two principles traveled side by side but never touched. Of course, the true damage done by heresy is usually clearly visible in what happens to the Christian message of salvation. Allison, with his knack for pinpointing the soteriological difficulties, writes concerning the soteriological implications of Nestorianism, "It is like going to the station to board a train, but finding that the Apollinarian train carries only freight and not people, while the Nestorian train comes through the station but does not stop. Nestorian insistence on the humanity tells us that it is the right station and the train does come through but only at full speed. Its one connection with us is the example that the human Jesus ran fast enough to catch the divine Logos and so should we."[95] He continues, "As long as this union of divine and human natures is cemented by the will alone, It may seem to work well in theory but in the real world of sinful human beings, unable to make our wills one with Christ's will, our unity with him becomes unglued. Nestorianism is 'sin soluble.'"[96] A Jesus who is not united in his divinity and humanity cannot save. That is the problem Cyril saw so clearly. As we will see in the next chapter, the pendulum will swing again in favor of monism as Nestorianism—the last dichotomist-dualist christological heresy—is defeated.

---

94. Bethune-Baker, *History*, 275.
95. Allison, *Cruelty of Heresy*, 128.
96. Allison, *Cruelty of Heresy*, 128.

6

The Historical Paradigm at 5:00
Monophysitism

THIS CHAPTER WILL DISCUSS the "bottom right" of the Hexagon. At the five o'clock position, we have the last of the six great heresies, Monophysitism, the heresy of over-emphasis on Jesus's divinity. Monophysitism, a compound word from Greek meaning "one nature," did not get its name for a few years after its inception. It is known to history as the view that states there is only one nature in Jesus, a confused and combined hybrid nature where the divine swallows up the human. Only twenty years passed between the Council of Ephesus that condemned Nestorianism and the Council of Chalcedon that would condemn the early manifestation of Monophysitism, Eutychianism. As we shall soon see, Chalcedon was not the end of the struggle, but the beginning. But first, the church had to clean up the mess caused by the poor handling of events at Ephesus.

The Reunion Formula of 433 and Its Aftermath

As stated in the last chapter, the Council of Ephesus did not bring the peace the church so desperately needed. The imperial decision to uphold Cyril's theology and maneuvers did not sit well in Antioch. Meanwhile, Cyril returned home to Alexandria to a hero's welcome. His supporters, especially those who held firmly to the "one nature of the Word incarnate" formula, felt that their theology had been decisively vindicated. The period immediately after Ephesus was indeed bleak for a united Christianity, as Alexandria celebrated her victory while Antioch fumed in defeat. The emperor understood the necessity of a united church for the health of his Empire, so he began plans to restore peace—or else—by appointing Aristolaus to go to Antioch to begin the process in 432.[1]

---

1. Russell, *Cyril of Alexandria*, 52–53.

The Hexagon of Heresy

Aristolaus proved very able for the task. He helped John of Antioch compose a letter to Cyril asking for the removal of the twelve anathemas. Cyril, who wanted peace himself, said he would not remove them only because of the heat of battle against Nestorius, but offered to help elucidate them further for anyone who truly desired peace and understanding. This was a first step of concession in both directions.[2] Negotiations then began. The Antiochene party had drawn up a creed while they were in Ephesus, which was not adopted by the Council. When it was presented to Cyril, he accepted it with only some minor changes.[3] Without reproducing the text of the creed here, it contained a clause stating Jesus was *homoousios* with God and with man (against "Arianism"), had a rational soul and body (against Apollinarianism); a union of two natures and *theotokos* (against Nestorianism), and a union that is unconfused (anticipating the future perhaps).[4] Cyril would be happy to sign the Antiochene creed if John would consent to the anathematization of Nestorius. Eventually, in 433, both parties agreed. This creed was known as the Reunion Formula, which put an end to the official schism between the two patriarchs and the two great Christian sees. Each side had to pay a little; as Alexandria agreed to an Antiochene creed, and Antioch had to depose one of its own. In the end, peace came—almost.

The Alexandrian extremists, those who held to the "one nature" statement from Apollinarius and Cyril, were not happy with the Reunion Formula. They wanted total victory over Antioch, not a peace treaty. They were unable to challenge the peace wrought by their powerful bishop, but their unhappiness continued to seethe over the next decade. Because he had accepted and signed a creed produced by Antioch, the extremist Alexandrians saw their patriarch as selling them out. During the remainder of his life, Cyril continued to clarify his position, using the phrase "*henosis physike*" to say that "the Logos has assumed human nature to such an extent that it possesses human nature 'physically' in its being, and not through some moral act of faith and love on the part of human nature."[5] Tapia clarifies the meaning of Cyril's phrase:

> The union is not accidental and dependent upon will, brought into being through a voluntary act of human nature, but is permanent, unique, brought into being by the fact of the incarnation. The self of the Logos is thus not the result but the permanent principle of the union, which already existed before any moral act that Christ was capable of, and is so close that the divine and the human in Christ can be separate only theoretically in idea. In reality it is one and the same divine self that performs not only the divine but also the

---

2. Russell, *Cyril of Alexandria*, 53. Cyril also agreed to use the term *physis* as the Antiochenes did in order to help clarify terminology as part of the process as well.

3. Russell, *Cyril of Alexandria*, 54.

4. For the important language of the Reunion formula, see Grillmeier, *From the Apostolic Age*, 498–99.

5. Tapia, *Theology of Christ*, 108.

human deeds, so that both divine and human actions are equally expressions of Christ.[6]

Standing in the way of the ultimate solution to the problem, as Tapia summarizes,

> It is true, the liberating word had not yet been uttered, that the union was not a union according to nature but only according to person. Cyril had not yet attempted to draw a clear distinction between nature and person, or to establish that existence as person can rather be distinguished from existence as nature, and that it is hence conceivable, and indeed really the case, that in Christ a human nature can certainly exist, but not a human person. Since Cyril had not gone as far as this, the suspicion could still arise that at root the Alexandrians taught the assumption of human nature into divine nature in such a way that the divine nature could absorb and assume even human qualities and powers. This possibility was first grasped at a later date by Monophysitism.[7]

This continual process of clarification was best seen in the shift in terminology and language of the Antiochene Theodoret of Cyrus. He used much more abstract language for the humanity of Jesus in his later years (mid-fifth century) than he did earlier on.[8] The more concrete early language sounds more "Nestorian" than the later terminology. Young and Teal write, "Cyril had convinced him there were dangers in treating the humanity as a concrete individual alongside the God-Word, that such expression could lead to unacceptable division and imply a 'two Sons' doctrine."[9] The more moderate and learned figures on both sides, Theodoret and Cyril, were moving closer together.

It would be a good time to pause in the historical account to give a bit of an overview of the technical terminology Cyril used, as it would go on to become standard vocabulary in christological orthodoxy. First of all, *ousia* indicates substance or essence. Hans van Loon describes Cyril's use of *hypostasis* thus, "Foundational to the sense of *hypostasis* appears to be real existence. If something is a *hypostasis*, it exists in reality."[10] *Prosopon* means "a 'person,' a rational being, capable of communication with other such beings, capable of a personal relation."[11] This shows a clarification in meaning, since now *prosopon* takes on more weight than just the visible outward form we saw in Theodore from chapter 5. Van Loon continues, "For Cyril, it is important that a person acts as a unity towards the world outside. He is hardly interested in the inner make-up of a person. Therefore, when Christ is called 'one person', this means that all the sayings, acts, and passions, whether divine or human, are to be attributed,

---

6. Tapia, *Theology of Christ*, 108–9.

7. Tapia, *Theology of Christ*, 109.

8. Grillmeier, *From the Apostolic Age*, 488–89 notes that just after the conclusion of the Council of Ephesus, Theodoret accused Cyril of being an Apollinarian.

9. Young and Teal, *From Nicaea to Chalcedon*, 300.

10. Van Loon, *Dyophysite Christology*, 508. This continues the earlier, received meaning of *hypostasis*.

11. Van Loon, *Dyophysite Christology*, 509.

not only to one grammatical person, but also to one ontological person, who is one *hypostasis*, one separate reality."[12] Van Loon adds, "*Physis* usually refers to a substance with its own principle of operation." He continues, "Just as *ousia* may refer either to a common substance or to an individual substance, so *physis* may refer to a common nature or to an individual nature. But beyond this, *physis* may also stand for all the individuals that belong to a particular common nature together."[13] Van Loon concludes that Cyril's Christology, given the way he uses the terminology that is both developing and developed, is substantially dyophysite.[14] Finally, after exhaustively researching all of Cyril's use of the "one nature (*physis*) of the incarnate Word" formula, he concludes that when Cyril utilizes the "one *physis*" formula, he means "the composition of the two individual natures of the Word and his humanity."[15]

One other name deserving mention in the evolution of terminology concerning Christ is Proclus of Cyzicus, who introduced the formula of "one *hypostasis* of the incarnate Word." He clarified Cyril's terminology of "one nature (*physis*) in the Word," even though Cyril meant in his use of "*physis*" here what Proclus meant by "*hypostasis*." Had Proclus's terminology caught on, the Monophysite controversy may have been avoided. Tapia writes, "Thus *hypostasis* concerns 'who'; nature or essence concerns 'what.' By adopting this usage the old ambiguous formula adopted by Cyril, 'the one nature of the God-Logos become flesh,' is changed to 'the one *hypostasis* or person of the God-Logos become flesh'; had this change been made earlier, many of the misunderstandings which had bedeviled the discussions between the rival schools of Alexandria and Antioch might have been removed."[16] A century later, Byzantine Emperor Justinian claimed that when Cyril said the "one nature" of Christ what he really meant was "one person."[17] Precise terminology would have been a great gift to the church at this time, because factious behavior was about to arise.

Dioscorus, Eutyches, and the Robber Synod

Cyril died in 444. He was succeeded by his nephew Dioscorus, who had, in the words of J. F. Bethune-Baker, "in an exaggerated form, all the bad qualities which have been attributed to Cyril, without his undoubted learning."[18] Dioscorus represented the more extreme wing of the Alexandrian world—the one that leaned toward Apollinarius and his Word-flesh Christology all the while wanting to achieve total victory over Antioch. Dioscorus knew his power base and how to work it. It was not very long

---

12. Van Loon, *Dyophysite Christology*, 509–10.
13. Van Loon, *Dyophysite Christology*, 512.
14. Van Loon, *Dyophysite Christology*, 517.
15. Van Loon, *Dyophysite Christology*, 530.
16. Tapia, *Theology of Christ*, 160.
17. Davis, *Councils*, 238.
18. Bethune-Baker, *History*, 281.

before he had the means to go to war on his own, and that means was by the views of a man named Eutyches.

Eutyches was a well-connected monk who was the spiritual confidant for the most trusted advisor of the emperor. He was "devoted to Cyril's theology" and believed Apollinarianism to be orthodox.[19] He taught that after the incarnation, there was only one nature in Christ (one *hypostasis* and one *prosopon*). His thinking was muddled and his teachings were inconsistent.[20] For him, two natures meant two concrete existences, or two *hypostases*. As Davis writes, "The genuine humanity of Christ and the importance of his historical reality were in danger of being swept away by an imprecise terminology and an unbalanced emphasis on Christ's divinity."[21] Eutyches's thinking was so muddled that he even claimed before a panel of bishops that Christ's humanity was not consubstantial with ours.[22] But Eutyches had the backing of Dioscorus and of Emperor Theodosius II, "who considered his best chance of unifying the Empire was by encouraging the Monophysites."[23] With such powerful friends, he was a force to be reckoned with, despite his lopsided and aberrant theology. Both Dioscorus and the emperor wanted a council held that would put an end to the doctrinal and ecclesiastical squabbles. It was planned in Ephesus in 449.

Pope Leo, who was a very formidable theologian in his own right, was called to this council along with the other Christian patriarchs, to rule upon Eutyches and his views. He was significant because he was the first Western theologian to give any sort of significant input to any of the christological questions. He did not attend the Ephesian synod, instead sending a delegation and letters, including his famous *Tome to Flavian*, the bishop of Constantinople, which acknowledged the reality of two natures in Jesus (a strong point of the Antiochenes) and the unity of the person, as the person of Jesus is the Logos (a strong point of Cyril).[24] Leo's *Tome* was never read in 449, though, because the "Robber Synod," as the council came to be known, would not allow it. Under the presumed permission of the emperor, Dioscorus took charge, stacked the council with Egyptians, and restored Eutyches to full priesthood which had been revoked earlier.[25] The Robber Synod was a huge, but short-lived victory for the Alexandrian Patriarch. He succeeded at the synod to depose his theological and political enemies, including all the other sitting Eastern patriarchs, with Flavian of Constantinople eventually dying from the abuse he suffered.[26] The Robber Synod was originally designed to be an ecumenical council, but was not recognized as such, since Pope Leo and the leading

19. Davis, *Councils*, 171.
20. For an example of just how muddled his thinking was, see Wilhite, *Gospel*, 172–76.
21. Davis, *Councils*, 171.
22. Davis, *Councils*, 173.
23. Allison, *Cruelty of Heresy*, 141–42.
24. Davis, *Councils*, 175–76.
25. Davis, *Councils*, 177.
26. Davis, *Councils*, 178.

Antiochene theologian, Theodoret of Cyrus, were not able to attend.[27] At the conclusion of this synod, it looked as if the future of Christian orthodoxy would hold to a "one nature" view of Christ, and be called properly Monophysite. But a huge development was on the horizon politically that would change everything.

The Council of Chalcedon

The emperor Theodosius, who had formally recognized the council of 449 died after a forty-two-year reign in 450 after falling from his horse while riding. Theodosius's sister Pulcheria took the throne, executed the trusted advisor who had been the imperial protector for Eutyches, and proclaimed the faith of Leo. Such a swift turn of events left Eutyches and his patriarch Dioscorus without imperial protection.[28] Without the emperor on their side, Dioscorus's allies from 449 began to swiftly desert him, until before very long only Dioscorus and his most ardent followers—those clinging tightly to the "one nature" formula as the only orthodox way to describe the presence of the divine and the human in Jesus—held to the 449 decision. Pulcheria, anxious to reverse her brother's ecclesiastical policies, demanded, against even Leo's wishes, another council immediately to make a lasting peace, which resulted in the Fourth Ecumenical Council at Chalcedon the next year in 451.[29]

The Council of Chalcedon was the largest ecumenical council yet, with over 600 bishops present.[30] The council opened with the reading of the minutes of the Robber Synod and the Home Council which had originally deposed Eutyches. All of Dioscorus's few remaining supporters deserted him, and he was left alone holding to the single nature in Christ. At Chalcedon, Dioscorus was deposed as he "received Eutyches into communion though he had been condemned by his own bishop; he had not allowed Leo's Tome to be read; he had attempted to excommunicate the pope."[31] The emperor and his wife Pulcheria wanted a doctrinal statement to come from the council, but there was recalcitrance from the East, who wanted to leave Dioscorus's deposition and do no more. The cry went out, "Are you for Leo or Dioscorus?" The obvious answer led to what became the Chalcedonian Creed.[32] The Creed is reproduced here:

> Therefore, following the holy fathers, we all with one accord teach men to acknowledge one and the same Son, our Lord Jesus Christ, at once complete in Godhead and complete in manhood, truly God and truly man, consisting also of a reasonable soul and body; of one substance with the Father as

27. Davis, *Councils*, 178–79.
28. Davis, *Councils*, 180.
29. Davis, *Councils*, 180.
30. Allison, *Cruelty of Heresy*, 142.
31. Davis, *Councils*, 183.
32. Davis, *Councils*, 184–85.

regards his Godhead, and at the same time of one substance with us as regards his manhood; like us in all respects, apart from sin; as regards his Godhead, begotten of the Father before the ages, but yet as regards his manhood begotten, for us men and for our salvation, of Mary the Virgin, the God-bearer; one and the same Christ, Son, Lord, Only-begotten, recognized in two natures, without confusion, without change, without division, without separation; the distinction of natures being in no way annulled by the union, but rather the characteristics of each nature being preserved and coming together to form one person and subsistence, not as parted or separated into two persons, but one and the same Son and Only-begotten God the Word, Lord Jesus Christ; even as the prophets from earliest times spoke of him, and our Lord Jesus Christ himself taught us, and the creed of the fathers has handed down to us.[33]

This is the last creed produced by the Christian church. All other affirmations of faith are now called confessions.[34] Note in the creed the explicit denial of all six sides of the Hexagon of Heresy. "Complete in Godhead" and "truly God" together deny both Ebionism and "Arianism." "Complete in manhood" and "truly man" together deny both Docetism and Apollinarianism. "Begotten . . . of Mary the Virgin, the God-bearer" directly denies Nestorianism, while "recognized in two natures" directly denies the theology of Eutyches. Then follows the four famous Chalcedonian adverbs: without change, without confusion, without division, without separation. The first two oppose Eutyches, while the latter two oppose Nestorianism. Davis writes concerning the use of these adverbs by the Chalcedonian fathers, "They insisted that Christ could not be divided or separated into two persons. By using a series of four Greek negative adverbs—without confusion, without change, without division, without separation—the bishops showed their concern for the mysterious and incomprehensible nature of the subject matter with which they were dealing."[35] He continues, "In their definition the bishops at last clearly distinguished between person and nature; the person of Christ being one, his natures two. They rejected decisively the view that Christ is from two natures and in one by affirming that Christ subsists in two natures. The Apollinarian slogan—One Incarnate Nature of the Incarnate Word—thought by Cyril and his followers to be from Athanasius was opposed."[36] It was the sincere hope of the council that it would end all previous heresies, which proved to be a bit premature.

Even though Dioscorus emerged as the true loser of the council, it was apparent that the church spoke with one voice. There were four documents used as the chief ingredients for the Chalcedonian Creed, each coming from one of the four principal cities of the Christian faith: Cyril's second letter to Nestorius (Alexandria), the Reunion

---

33. Chalcedonian Creed.
34. Allison, *Cruelty of Heresy*, 143.
35. Davis, *Councils*, 187.
36. Davis, *Councils*, 187.

Formula (Antioch), Flavian's *professio fidei* (Constantinople), and Leo's *Tome* (Rome).[37] No major constituency of the church was left without a voice in its last creed.

Regardless of how much the council tried to involve all the major Christian schools of thought, the east was not fully satisfied with the Definition because of "clarity about the hypostatic union, the problems of predication, the single subject of the suffering and death in Christ, and the deification of the human begun in Christ."[38] As Davis notes, many thought "Cyril was a better guide to Christology than the Council of Chalcedon."[39] Meanwhile, the Alexandrians were angry that Dioscorus had been deposed and, after he died in exile, rioted. They became known as the Monophysites, after Cyril's (and Apollinarius's) slogan of "one incarnate nature [*physis*] of the Divine Word."[40] The leaders of the Monophysites, whose eventual leader in Alexandria was named Timothy, believed Chalcedon was Nestorian. Davis writes, "Nature for Timothy and the Cyrillians was almost synonymous with person: 'There is no nature which does not have its *hypostasis* and there is no *hypostasis* which exists without its person (*prosopon*); if then there are two natures, there are of necessity two persons, but if there are two persons, there are two Christs.'"[41] Davis sums up the theology of Monophysitism thus:

> Positively, Timothy and the Cyrillians believed that without change in his divinity the eternal Word, consubstantial with the Father, truly became man in Jesus Christ. The Word was one and the same person before and after the incarnation, for the same person became through a personal, a hypostatic union, incarnate. This is what the Council of Chalcedon had not clearly declared: that the person of the union was the pre-existent person of the Word. The Word was united to flesh consubstantial with ours, consisting of body and rational soul, for we could not have been saved if the Savior were not in all things, sin alone excepted, like to his brethren. Jesus Christ is thus "out of two," out of Godhead and out of manhood, and in their union in his one person, each remains in its reality, inseparable, but perceived as different through intellectual analysis.[42]

Even though the rest of the East was against the Monophysites, their firm belief that the Council of Chalcedon was Nestorian—which can be seen in the language of the creed quoted above, "but rather the characteristics of each nature being preserved and coming together to form one person and subsistence," which could easily be read in a Nestorian light—kept them from surrendering to its definition.[43]

37. Grillmeier, *From the Apostolic Age*, 544.
38. Davis, *Councils*, 188.
39. Davis, *Councils*, 188.
40. Davis, *Councils*, 196.
41. Davis, *Councils*, 196.
42. Davis, *Councils*, 197.
43. Davis, *Councils*, 198. This ambiguity has been clearly shown in McCormack, "Reformed

Severus of Antioch became the new leader of Monophysitism after Chalcedon. He was Cyrillian, holding to a single nature in Christ composed of both divine and human properties. To him, *hypostasis* and *physis* were synonyms. He wrote "One is the agent, one is the activity, but the works are varied."[44] The Monophysites saw the Logos as he had become incarnate, and possessed his humanity and divinity in one new nature that combined both. They could not be separated, for fear of Nestorianism. The orthodox wanted to preserve the real manhood and not one that was a mixture of the two.[45] As time progressed, the Monophysites were beset with factions arguing over the corruptibility of Christ, as should arise from a single-nature view. There is nothing to hold the extremes in check.[46] Today, Monophysitism is still prevalent in North African Christianity including the Coptic Church. As with the Kurdish Nestorians, the Monophysite schism has never been healed.[47]

"Leontius" and the Fifth Council

The century following Chalcedon was the height of the Byzantine Empire. While the government was politically strong, the Eastern half of the church remained divided.

Christology," as he writes, in the context of the Peter Enns controversy at Westminster Theological Seminary, "There is, you see, an ambiguity at the heart of the Chalcedonian Definition where the 'Person' is concerned. On the one hand, the Definition can say that the 'property of both natures is preserved and comes together into a single person and a single subsistent being.' On the other hand, the Definition can say, 'he is not parted or divided into two persons, but is one and the same only-begotten Son, God, Word, Lord Jesus Christ . . .' *On the basis of the first formulation, it would seem that the person is formed out of the coming together of the natures.* On the basis of the second, it would seem that a straightforward and direct equation is being made of the 'person' and the pre-existent Logos as such. It is because of this ambiguity that patristic scholars are, to this day, divided over the question of which party to the controversy actually attained the upper hand at Chalcedon (which already, by itself, would render untenable any simplistic appeal to 'Chalcedonian Christology'). There are those who, leaning heavily on the first of these formulations, say that the Formula grants a certain victory to Nestorius. But there are also those who say that it is Cyril's theology which triumphed at Chalcedon. In the first group is to be found Aloys Grillmeier and Brian Daley; in the second, John McGuckin. *My own view is that a carefully contextualized reading of the Definition will show that it is the second of these opinions which is correct. But here's the thing: classical Reformed theology clearly stood on the side of the first of these options—not the second.*" Italics in original.

44. Davis, *Councils*, 213. The quote of Severus is not referenced by Davis. Like Apollinarius and Theodore before him, Severus was Monoenergist. See Hovorun, *Will, Action and Freedom*, 15–17. Hovorun writes on page 18 that the human in Christ "can be regarded as a vehicle of the dominating divine energies."

45. Davis, *Councils*, 214.

46. Davis, *Councils*, 223–24.

47. The history surrounding the growth of the Monophysite movement in Alexandria, Antioch, and the rest of the east is a complex issue, one intertwined with both religious and political considerations. It is beyond the scope of this chapter to discuss these issues in detail. For a more thorough treatment, see Frend, *Monophysite Movement*; Meyendorff, *Christ in Eastern Christian Thought* (1975); and Grillmeier, *From the Council of Chalcedon*. For a sympathetic treatment of the history of Chalcedon and its aftermath through contemporary Coptic Orthodox eyes, see Ishak, *Christology and Chalcedon*.

The Hexagon of Heresy

The West had no trouble embracing Chalcedon, but the old Apollinarian-Nestorian-Monophysite slurs kept resurfacing in the East, with each faction accusing the other of the appropriate form of heresy. During this time period, an important development in christological terminology occurred, largely through the work of two men both named Leontius, the "*Leontioi*," Leontius of Byzantium and Leontius of Jerusalem—the twin concepts of *anhypostasia* and *enhypostasia*. *Anhypostasia* holds that the Word assumed impersonal human nature. Here is an important distinction between the ever-present metaphysical realities of person and nature: a nature can exist without a person to "actualize" it. *Anhypostasia* denies "the independent, autonomous existence of Christ's human nature."[48] The person of the Word did not take over some already-existing human person, but full and complete human nature that was then actualized, or *enhypostasized*, in the person of the Word. In the *enhypostasia*,

> Leontius distinguishes between nature and *hypostasis*: nature situates a being in a genus; hypostasis denotes individuality. An *hypostasis* always has a nature, but a nature does not always have an *hypostasis*. For things can be united in three ways. An example of the first is the Nestorian juxtaposition of two natures and two *hypostases* in Christ. Secondly, the distinction between two natures may be so merged that a third results as Eutyches argued in his Christology. Thirdly, two natures may subsist in one hypostasis. Thus body and soul are united in a single *hypostasis* called man, and all operations of body and of soul are attributed to this one *hypostasis*. So in Christ, his human nature subsists in the *hypostasis* of the divine nature. Human nature in Christ is an *enhypostaton*, that which subsists in an *hypostasis* of another nature. The single *hypostasis* of Christ is the Eternal Word in which subsist two natures divine and human. All operations of the two natures are attributed to the *hypostasis* of the Divine Word. But in Christ the divinity remains uncircumscribed and unaffected by the human nature, while in humans, the soul is circumscribed and therefore affected by the body. Moreover, Christ is unique, but men are not.[49]

In addition to the critical *an-* and *en-hypostasia* distinction, Leontius (of Byzantium) further clarified the distinction between person and nature, summed up by Demetrios Bathrellos: "essence [nature] denotes a really existing thing, whereas *hypostasis* denotes 'somebody.'"[50] In perhaps his most valuable contribution, Leontius clarified that the *hypostasis* of the Word is the *hypostasis* of Jesus, as he wrote, "the Word is said to have suffered according to the *hypostasis*, for within his *hypostasis* he assumed a passible essence beside his own impassible essence, and what can be asserted of the

---

48. MacLeod, *Person of Christ*, 201.

49. Davis, *Councils*, 234. Whether it was Leontius of Byzantium or of Jerusalem that originated the *an-* and *en-hypostasia* distinction, matters little here. For more information on the two sides of the debate, see the helpful footnote in Wellum, *God the Son Incarnate*, 317n13.

50. Bathrellos, *Byzantine Christ*, 41.

passible essence can be asserted of the *hypostasis*."⁵¹ Thus we see the great advancement in theology of the fifth council, noted most clearly in its fifth canon: "If anyone shall calumniate the holy Council of Chalcedon, pretending that it made use of this expression (one *hypostasis*) in this impious sense, and if he will not recognize rather that the Word of God is united with the flesh hypostatically, and that therefore there is but one *hypostasis* or one only person, and that the holy Council of Chalcedon has professed in this sense the one person of our Lord Jesus Christ: let him be anathema."⁵² This clarification corrects the possibility of a Nestorian misreading of the Chalcedonian Creed, clearly stating that the person of the Word is the person of Christ, and that Christ cannot possibly be the result of the union of the two natures. The fifth council also declared that the *prosopon* was the outward manifestation of the *hypostasis*, and therefore are roughly synonyms.⁵³ One further action by the council was to condemn the works of Origen as well, as the church was beginning to see Origen's speculations at the root of her theological problems.⁵⁴

Unfortunately, this insight was not sufficient to reconcile the Monophysites, even though this was their original theological issue with Chalcedon.⁵⁵ The *enhypostasia* settled some questions but raised others, including, as Frederick McLeod writes,

> While the *enhypostasis* approach provides a reasonable explanation of why Christ can be said to have only one *hypostasis* and a human will that is free, it is vague as to how there is a unity of wills and operations in Christ. Specifically how do Christ's natures relate to each other in regard to how his humanity shares in the Word's knowledge and is able to avoid temptations? Moreover, if the Word's life-giving power vivifies Christ's human nature and enables all of Christ's individual human properties to be actualized and participate in the exercise of divine power, is the Word's life-giving power the same as his operating power? If they are different, how so?⁵⁶

These unanswered questions would lead to a final alternative Christology that would arise a century later that would allow the church, under the guiding genius of Maximus

---

51. Davis, *Councils*, 232. Meyendorff, *Christ in Eastern Christian Thought* (1969), 47–49, argues that Leontius was an Origenist, and what comes down to us is his thought reinterpreted in Chalcedonian language, which both immortalized him for his contributions and kept him from condemnation at the fifth council.

52. *Canons of II Constantinople* 5. The "impious sense" quoted above is that the one *hypostasis* of Christ is in any way a compound of the divine and human.

53. McLeod, "Significance," 380.

54. See the discussion in Meyendorff, *Imperial Unity*, 231–33. The sixth-century disciples of Origen were accused of both Nestorianism and Monophysitism. This should not be surprising, given the Plotinian ambiguity at the heart of his system.

55. Need, *Truly Human and Truly Divine*, 118–19, notes that the fifth council condemned both the writings and the person of Theodore of Mopsuestia, as well as the anti-Cyrillene writings of Ibas of Edessa and Theodoret of Cyrrhus,

56. McLeod, "Significance," 379.

Monothelitism, Monoenergism, and the Sixth Council

As the sixth century turned to the seventh, Eastern Christianity was still divided into three separate parties concerning the union and activity of the divine and human in Christ. The Nestorians, Monophysites, and Orthodox were all existing together uneasily within the boundaries of the Byzantine Empire. With each successive generation, new theological interpretations surfaced, and arising out of the orthodox party was a dispute over the actions and wills in Christ, which became so powerful that the sixth ecumenical council would meet to decide the outcome.

Some members of the orthodox party, in their continuing interpretation of Chalcedon, began to teach that there is one source of action in Christ. As Jaroslav Pelikan helpfully states, "Action [Greek, *energeia*] was a technical term used by Aristotle to refer to operation (as it was translated into Latin), as well as to actuality as distinguished from potentiality."[57] He continues, "In the course of the controversy over 'one action' in Christ, it became necessary to specify the meaning of the term more precisely and to distinguish between 'action', 'activity', which was defined as 'the nature from which action proceeds', 'act' defined as 'the outcome of the action', and 'the agent', defined as 'the one who uses the action, the *hypostasis*.'"[58] Andrew Louth notes that this ambiguity was what allowed the concept of one action to gain traction in the first place—an ambiguity that Maximus the Confessor would later solve with what Louth calls his "Chalcedonian logic."[59] Even though, as Pelikan suggests, the terminology might make it seem as though the action would be the property of the *hypostasis*, the real purpose is to argue for "two actions in Christ."[60]

The metaphysical foundation of Monoenergism (one energy, or one source of action in Christ) was, as Leo Davis writes, "The body is the instrument of the soul, and both are instruments of the Word."[61] As we have seen already, both "Arians" and Apollinarians, as well as the Ebionites and Docetists, were Monoenergist in different ways, leaning toward one side or the other of the Plotinian ambiguity. Ironically, while it would seem that Monoenergism would seem most at home with Monophysitism, the extreme Nestorians were Monoenergist as well, since they held that the

---

57. Pelikan, *Christian Tradition*, 2:63–64. Need, *Truly Divine and Truly Human*, 121, notes that "energy" had a pedigree in Eastern technical theological vocabulary back to the time of Basil, who contrasted the unknowable essence of God with his actions and attributes, which he called energy.

58. Pelikan, *Christian Tradition*, 2:64.

59. Louth, *Maximus the Confessor*, 57.

60. Pelikan, *Christian Tradition*, 2:64.

61. Davis, *Councils*, 264.

"two *hypostases* in Christ concurred in a single action."[62] In a way, Monoenergism was the heresy that tied all of the Christologies beyond the boundary of the Hexagon of Heresy together; none of them could simultaneously account for the human nature in Christ to exist with real integrity hypostatically in the person of the divine Word. It is in this sense that my statement in chapter 1 obtains that Christology is a subset of the larger problem of how creation retains integrity given its status as freely-willed by the creator, and accomplished *ex nihilo*. For such a cosmology and Christology to win the day, both must be disentangled from the two corollaries of definitional simplicity: the identity thesis that confuses person and nature, as well as the Plotinian ambiguity, that places undue emphasis on either the one or the many.

Unfortunately, there was very little help to solve the controversy in either Scripture or the tradition, as the Fathers had not used the careful language to describe the actions that the seventh century demanded. The question was whether the actions of Christ were "hypostatic, belonging to the one *hypostasis*, or natural, belonging to the two natures."[63] One of the earliest protagonists in the dispute, Sophronius, patriarch of Jerusalem, taught, following Gregory of Nyssa's logic in his short treatise to Ablabius, "activity proceeds not from the person of Christ, but from the two natures."[64] Sophronius held a synod proposing two wills in 634, which was in direct opposition to the most powerful patriarch of Orthodoxy, Sergius of Constantinople, who had been working behind the scenes for many years looking for theological and political common ground between the Monophysites and the Orthodox within the empire.[65] In this synod, the teaching was that the duality of operations proceeds from the duality of natures.

> We maintain that all the speech and energy of Christ, whether divine and heavenly, or human and earthly, proceed from one and the same Christ and Son, from the one compound and unique *hypostasis* which is the incarnate Logos of God, who brings forth naturally from himself both energies unseparated and unmixed, according to his natures: according to his divine nature, by which he is consubstantial with the Father, the divine and ineffable energy; according to his human nature, by which he became consubstantial with us men, the human and earthly, the energy being in accordance with the nature to which it belongs.[66]

---

62. Pelikan, *Christian Tradition*, 2:64. See also the discussion in Hovorun, *Will, Action and Freedom*, 11–15.

63. Pelikan, *Christian Tradition*, 2:64–66. For a full overview of the controversy, see Farrell, *Free Choice*, 67–84.

64. Davis, *Councils*, 264.

65. For more on the history of the ecclesiastical and political intrigue involved, see Balthasar, *Cosmic Liturgy*, 75–77, as well as Hovorun, *Will, Action and Freedom*, 53–102.

66. Davis, *Councils*, 265.

The Hexagon of Heresy

In reply, Sergius published an edict, the *Ecthesis* of 636, which concludes, "We confess one will of our Lord Jesus Christ, the true God, for at no time did his rationally quickened flesh, separately and of its own impulse, and in opposition to the suggestion of the hypostatically united Word, exercise its natural activity at the time and in the manner and measure in which the Word of God willed it."[67] Note the presence of definitional simplicity in the principle of distinction as opposition at work in the language of the *Ecthesis*, since distinct wills would imply opposed wills. Pope Honorius agreed with Sergius over Sophronius, preferring to say that there is one actor or one agent, the Lord Jesus, as opposed to two actions within him.[68] Sergius also had the backing of the emperor, Heraclitus, who saw Sergius's answer as an opportunity to keep Monophysites more inclined to both the city of Constantinople and himself. Davis writes, "For what Sergius and the emperor had decreed was that there is in Jesus Christ only one will and one truly free and spontaneous activity, the divine activity and will. Granting the existence of a human nature, its activity is completely subordinate to that of the divine; the humanity in the power of the Word is merely a docile instrument which he uses and which is devoid of any initiative of its own."[69] In such a formulation, Monoenergism collapses into Monophysitism.[70] As Pelikan notes, the conversation gradually turned from the concepts of actions to that of wills, and the Monothelite (one will) controversy was born.[71] As Demetrios Bathrellos notes, "The Monothelites of the seventh century constitute a small team of rather amateur theologians, most of whom were patriarchs, whose interests often lay not in the purity of Christian doctrine but in matters of ecclesial policy."[72] It was a classic case of trying to solve political problems via theological compromise.

---

67. Davis, *Councils*, 267.

68. Pelikan, *Christian Tradition*, 2:67.

69. Davis, *Councils*, 268. It is interesting that Monothelitism is making a comeback among Protestant Evangelicals. See Wessling, "Christology and Conciliar Authority," 151–70. In this essay (on page 152n4), Wessling lists Garrett J. DeWeese, Gordon R. Lewis, Bruce A. Demarest, J. P. Moreland, William Lane Craig, and A. H. Strong as recent or contemporary Monothelites. The usual reason for the acceptance of Monothelitism is that the concept of two wills in Christ cannot be deduced from Scripture. Though it is not a subject of great interest to this work, these contemporary Monothelites have an inverted *ordo theologiae*, prioritizing an energy (Scripture) over person (Christ) in stating the former is the foundation for the latter, which is backwards from the methodology of Athanasius and the Cappadocians (Chapter 3) and Cyril (Chapter 5).

70. If one accepts that there is one will in Christ, then will becomes a property of *hypostasis* and not of nature. This entails a real trinitarian problem, because it would imply three divine wills, with each divine hypostasis possessing his own will. It would also undermine Gregory of Nyssa's argument for one God to Ablabius. He argued that one will implies one nature. If will is hypostatic, then there are three wills in the Godhead which collapses into tritheism quickly. See Meyendorff, *Christ in Eastern Christian Thought* (1975), 145.

71. Pelikan, *Christian Tradition*, 2:68.

72. Bathrellos, *Byzantine Christ*, 60.

Once the point of disagreement became one or two wills in Jesus, the abstractions of terminology disappeared. The will of Jesus was a major theme in the Gospels.[73] As Pelikan notes, the biblical side of the controversy turned on two texts, Luke 22:42 ("not my will, but yours be done") and John 6:38 ("I did not come to do my own will, but the will of him who sent me"). Though Scripture showed two wills, the writings of the Fathers proved inconclusive, because they did not speak with the required precision on the subject.[74] For his part, Pope Honorius taught that these were not two separate wills, that is, the will of the Father and the will of Jesus, but a distinction due to economy.[75] According to Demetrios Bathrellos, Theodore Pharan, a leading Monothelite, taught that "the one energy of Christ was created by God the Logos, whereas his humanity was no more than an instrument" and that "Christ had only one will, the divine."[76] Bathrellos continues that Theodore

> Conceives of Christ's humanity as a mere vehicle through which the acts are accomplished. For Theodore, the humanity of Christ is a more or less passive instrument of his divinity. The active aspect of Christ's soul never enters into the picture. . . . Thus, the active participation of the humanity of Christ in the work of our salvation is jeopardized. The importance of the fact that Christ saved us not merely as God but as *incarnate* God fades away for the sake of an over-asymmetrical emphasis on redemption as exclusively the work of God. Moreover, such is the predominance of the divinity over the humanity—and we should recall here the Apollinarian and Monophysite overtones of this view—that the human qualities of Christ are said to be dispensed with, at least on some occasions, in contrast to what the definition of Chalcedon has stated.[77]

So Monoenergism and Monotheletism were problematic in that they make Christ more God than man in a telltale sign of lurking definitional simplicity, the presence of a zero-sum game; and therefore diminish his humanity in the Docetist/Apollinarian/Monophysite tradition, firmly rooting them in the monist half of the Plotinian ambiguity.

The great champion of the two wills was not Sophronius, but his one-time understudy, the learned monk Maximus the Confessor. Andrew Louth writes, "Maximus owes his title 'Confessor' to his defense of the Orthodox doctrine of the person of Christ against the theological view, emanating from theological circles in Constantinople, and endorsed by imperial authority, that suggested language of one activity,

---

73. Hovorun, *Will, Action and Freedom*, 147–49, notes that in antiquity, the distinction between rationality and volition did not exist. Athanasius was the first to distinguish being and will, and by the early fifth century, the will, at least conceptually, became distinct in both East (Gregory of Nyssa) and West (Augustine).
74. Pelikan, *Christian Tradition*, 2:69–71.
75. Pelikan, *Christian Tradition*, 2:68.
76. Bathrellos, *Byzantine Christ*, 70.
77. Bathrellos, *Byzantine Christ*, 71.

or one will, in Christ, as a compromise with the Monophysites."[78] Before discussing Maximus's articulation of how Jesus possesses two energies and two wills, it would be good to survey his mature understanding of the metaphysics of the incarnation, that is, how person and nature relate in Christ. For this, we will utilize the thought of Demetrios Bathrellos.

Maximus follows the Cappadocian distinction, attributing to *hypostasis* the particular and nature the general, but develops the concept more fully.[79] For Maximus, there is the nature of a being (what it is), the mode of existence (how it is), and person (who it is).[80] *Hypostasis* describes who something is, and indicates an "I."[81] Maximus follows Leontius of Byzantium (and Leontius of Jerusalem) in that

> *Hypostasis* is characterized by subsisting by itself. The humanity of Christ was not a *hypostasis*, Maximus argued, for it never subsisted by itself. Thus the unity of the humanity with the Logos accounts for its not being personally distinct from the Logos. The union between divinity and humanity in Christ is called union according to *hypostasis*, signifies the union of two (different) essences that remain distinct in one *hypostasis*, and is contrasted to the relative union which is the union of two persons through their unity of willed object and their mutual loving disposition.[82]

For Maximus, the "I" in Jesus is the Logos.[83] Moreover, "Maximus follows the tradition of the *Leontioi* [Leontius of Byzantium and Leontius of Jerusalem], according to which it is *hypostasis*, not nature, that subsists by itself *par excellence*."[84] Here we see another instance of the correct *ordo theologiae*.[85] The person is primary, for it is capable of self-subsistence, while nature is not. Bathrellos adds, "The human nature of Christ along with its particular idioms is not a *hypostasis*, for it does not subsist separately (from the Logos and) by itself. . . . So the existence of the Logos' human

---

78. Louth, *Maximus the Confessor*, 48. In both Roman Catholicism and Eastern Orthodoxy, a "confessor" is a person who suffers for their faith but does not die as a martyr. It is well known that Maximus was tortured for his position against Monotheletism, and died shortly thereafter as a result of his brutal treatment.

79. Bathrellos, *Byzantine Christ*, 102. Meyendorff, *Byzantine Theology*, 37, notes that the main thrust of Gregory of Nyssa's argument against Ablabius was that the three divine persons shared the divine essence, which implied there was only one will present. Thus, Maximus had patristic precedent for arguing as he did that will is a property of nature, rather than of person.

80. Bathrellos, *Byzantine Christ*, 103.

81. Bathrellos, *Byzantine Christ*, 104.

82. Bathrellos, *Byzantine Christ*, 104.

83. Bathrellos, *Byzantine Christ*, 105.

84. Bathrellos, *Byzantine Christ*, 110.

85. Meyendorff, *Christ in Eastern Christian Thought*, writes, "Energy is in this way the concrete manifestation of nature; and the hypostasis gives it its quality or manner of being; the triangle—hypostasis, nature, energy—is thus the key to the whole system of Maximus, and in particular to his Christology."

nature is grounded in a person: namely, in the Logos' own person."[86] Again, person has ontological priority over nature. Maximus himself argues "*Hypostasis* is necessarily nature . . . but nature is not necessarily *hypostasis*."[87] Bathrellos continues,

> For Maximus, the Logos is the same before and after the incarnation, namely God, a divine person. . . . Maximus says that the flesh became one with the Logos according to *hypostasis*. However, although the Logos is identical with the human nature according to the *hypostasis*, he is not identical with it according to nature. Maximus draws a distinction between the nature/essence of the flesh and the nature/essence of the Logos, and insists that the flesh differs from the Logos according to essence. He also states his opposition to Apollinarius, who argued that the Logos was identical with the flesh according to nature, as well as to Nestorius, who contended that the Logos and the flesh differed according to *hypostasis*."[88]

Maximus himself drew the distinction from Gen 1:26, as "the scholiast on the polemical writings comments on one of Maximus' ideas: 'Nature is that which was 'created according to the image', the plan of being (*logos*). The *hypostasis* is that which was 'created according to the likeness, historical life (*bios*).'"[89] With this, we see the mature understanding of the ontological distinctions between person and nature, going all the way back to the initial creation of human beings.

Andrew Louth provides a helpful summary of the entirety of the christological controversies, which he argues is the discovery of the definition of person. He notes that the Monothelite question was the last in a series of steps to finally understand the entire concept of *hypostasis*—steps that reached from the apostolic *kerygma* all the way down to the time of Maximus. He writes,

> The great ecumenical councils trace this theological journey, but its starting point is the conviction that in Christ one encounters God as person and its guiding light the growing realization that this entails that the person of the

---

86. Bathrellos, *Byzantine Christ*, 110–11.

87. Bathrellos, *Byzantine Christ*, 111. Here, Bathrellos quotes Maximus the Confessor, *Opuscula*. 23, 264A. Meyendorff, *Christ in Eastern Christian Thought*, also quotes Maximus in the *Opuscula*, as he opposes the Hellenistic concept of nature which is a "'reality in itself necessitating nothing else in order to exist' to that of the fathers who recognize in it 'a natural entity proper to numerous and different hypostases.'"

88. Bathrellos, *Byzantine Christ*, 111–12.

89. Balthasar, *Cosmic Liturgy*, 226. The quote is from Maximus, *Opuscula*, PG 91, 37 BC. Maximus's interpretation addresses an element of the tradition, going back at least to Irenaeus, that the image was retained in the fall, but the likeness was lost. Human nature, therefore, remains after the fall while the personal characteristics of righteousness, life, devotion to God, etc., are lost therein. The distinction between image and likeness, for the Eastern fathers, was therefore the distinction between person and nature, and served as a safeguard against definitional simplicity's identity thesis. Martin Luther, whom we will meet later on, saw image and likeness as an example of Hebrew parallelism, and therefore did not distinguish person and nature. It is not surprising that he was a devoted proponent of definitional simplicity.

incarnate one is the Word, the divine Son, one of the Trinity. The critical issue is: what is a person? And the heresies that litter this theological path—Docetism, Apollinarianism, Eutychianism, Monoenergism, Monotheletism—can be seen as the premature attempts to solve this issue.[90]

Louth has put his finger on the concept of the correct *ordo theologiae*, as well as the development of the explicitly Christian concept of person, though I would add that the process pulled the distinct concept of person out of the confusion of person and nature that definitional simplicity demanded. Louth shows how Maximus answers this question, as he writes, "Person is contrasted to nature: it is concerned with the way we are (the mode, or *tropos*), not what we are (principle or *logos*). When he became incarnate—when he assumed human nature—the Word became everything that we are. But he did it in his own way, because he is a person, just as we are human in our own way, because we are persons."[91] He summarizes Maximus thus:

> Whatever we share with others, we are: it belongs to our nature. But what it is to be a person is not some thing, some quality that we do not share with others—as if there were an irreducible somewhat within each one of us that makes us the unique persons we are. What is unique about each one of us is what we have made of the nature that we have: our own unique mode of existence, which is a matter of our experience in the past, our hopes for the future, the way we live out the nature that we have. What makes the Son of God the unique person he is, is the eternal life of love in the Trinity which he shares in a filial way.[92]

For Maximus, the *hypostasis* of Christ is the eternal Son, who never breaks his union with the Father. This person, or *hypostasis*, takes on real and full human nature, complete with all its properties, and unites it to himself permanently. The human nature of Christ then subsists in the divine person of Christ, so that there is only one person, but two complete natures in him. Jesus is therefore the ultimate example of why person is prioritized over nature.

When the logic of Maximus is applied to the human will, the most basic property of human nature in Maximus's thought, the full import of the hypostatic union may

---

90. Louth, *Maximus the Confessor*, 59. Perceptively, Balthasar, *Cosmic Liturgy*, 262–63, sees that the definition of person is of utmost importance in the controversy, as he writes, "Two ultimate perceptions of the person are on a collision course here. For Pyrrhus [the Monothelite patriarch of Constantinople], person can represent only an irrational dimension, beyond everything natural. He wants to preserve its absolute spontaneity and self-affirmation through negations. Thus, in many respects, Monothelitism is a precursor of the personalistic nominalism of the late Middle ages and modern culture. For Maximus, on the other hand, person is the realization, the concrete living out, of a rational nature; and because every realization points back to a real source, it is the original, functional center of the rational nature itself, the radiant inner expression of its being." He continues to call Monothelitism a new kind of Docetism, a point with which I agree.

91. Louth, *Maximus the Confessor*, 59.

92. Louth, *Maximus the Confessor*, 59.

be realized. His basic concept is that the human will is self-determining, but oriented toward the God in whose image he is made.[93] According to Maximus, God created man self-determining by nature. The will is a property of nature, and a characteristic of all those who share the same nature. Furthermore, the natural will is not a mere characteristic of the rational nature; far more than this, it is its first and foremost idiom. And since Christ is fully human, he therefore must possess a human will.[94] Leo Donald Davis writes,

> In human beings the good of nature is freely reached. As a consequence of the primal sin, humans acquired a gnomic will which chooses, hesitates, ignores the real good. Gnomic will gives to action its moral quality, its mode of existence, and proceeds not from nature but from person. By reason of sin, humans now make free choices of merely relative goods, goods not in accord with the law of their nature. The gnomic will is to be distinguished from the natural will uncontaminated by sin, free will at its highest, liberty which always chooses the real good without the possibility of sin. The Word took to himself a natural will, for according to the age-old rule of the Fathers, what is not assumed is not redeemed. Christ had a fully human natural will. But he could have no gnomic will. Gnomic will is always linked to sin and since Christ is sinless, he can have no will ignorant, hesitant, and in conflict with himself. His human will adheres without doubt or hesitation to its perfect good. He has only natural will, both human and divine, which with sovereign freedom always chooses the appropriate good. Christ therefore has two natures, two operations, two wills really proceeding from the divine and human natures but always in harmony because the single divine person assures their goodness of choice. In human beings salvation and deification consist in bringing the gnomic will, through redemption in Christ, into conformity with the innate drive of our natural will toward God. In the incarnation Christ has revealed the deepest fact about humanity, said Maximus, "as man he accomplishes in all truth the true human destiny that he himself had predetermined as God, and from which man had turned; he unites man to God."[95]

Bathrellos adds, "For Maximus, the denial of Christ's human will has disastrous soteriological implications. If the Logos did not assume the self-determining power of the nature that he had created, he either condemned his own creation as something that is not good . . . or he begrudged us the healing of our will, depriving us of complete salvation and showing himself to be subject to passion, because he either did not want or could not save us completely."[96] Maximus himself writes, "If Adam ate willingly,

---

93. Louth, *Maximus the Confessor*, 60–61.

94. Bathrellos, *Byzantine Christ*, 130. Balthasar, *Cosmic Liturgy*, 261, writes that Pyrrhus and other Monothelites could not be allowed to reason from a unified action to a unified nature, since by this time action revealed nature.

95. Davis, *Councils*, 272–73. The citation of Maximus is again not given.

96. Bathrellos, *Byzantine Christ*, 131. The concept of two energies and wills in Christ goes back at

The Hexagon of Heresy

then the will is the first thing in us that became subject to passion. And since the will is the first thing in us that became subject to passion, if, according to them [the Monothelites], the Word did not assume it along with the nature when he became incarnate, I have not become free from sin. And if I have not become free from sin, I was not saved, since whatever is not assumed is not saved."[97] For Maximus, human will itself does not oppose the divine will; the gnomic will does. "Sin, not nature, is the cause of our rebellion against God."[98] Here is a great step forward in the process of disentanglement. The many do not oppose the one due to being many; the opposition is on account of sin. Sin, and not creation, is identified as the real opposition. It is fully possible, therefore (with Jesus as the prime example), for human nature to be in concord with divine nature. If that is the case, then the removal of one half of the Plotinian ambiguity—distinction as opposition, in that creation (the human nature of Jesus) is not automatically opposed to the divine—will necessitate the collapse of the other half of the ambiguity—the insistence that the one controls the many.[99]

After making the important distinctions in the will, Maximus then moves to the discussion of the human will in Christ, starting with the deification of his humanity. Bathrellos writes,

> A nature that is not assumed remains sinful, and a sinful nature is a nature that is not united with God. Therefore, to say that the human nature of Christ was sinful implies that it did not subsist in the Logos and was not fully united with the divine nature. However, a human nature that does not subsist in the Logos and is not fully united with him and the divine nature subsists separately from him, by itself—namely, as a distinct human *hypostasis*, subject to the sinfulness bequeathed by the fall to all people.[100]

---

least to Athanasius, who made the distinction based on Jesus's agony in Gethsemane. On the other hand, Monothelitism traces itself back to Apollinarius and the Antiochenes Theodore and Nestorius. The union in Monophysitism is natural, while in Nestorianism it is energetic (willful). On this, see Meyendorff, *Christ in Eastern Christian Thought (1975)*, 146.

97. Maximus the Confessor, *Disputatio* 325B, quoted in Bathrellos, *Byzantine Christ*, 131.

98. Bathrellos, *Byzantine Christ*, 132. Meyendorff, *Christ in Eastern Christian Thought* (1975), 148, writes, "Maximus always insisted that nature remained intact in spite of sin, and clearly opposes *physis* to *gnome*. The direct consequence of sin was a sort of contamination of the nature's will, which until then could only will good; the contamination came through the gnome. Man acquired in this way a gnomic will, which chooses, hesitates, ignores the real good, inflicts pain because its decisions are taken blindfolded." Meyendorff continues on page 149, "Sin is always a personal action that does not corrupt nature as such. This explains why the Word could fully assume human nature, *sin excepted*. Sin remains on the level of the *gnome*, of personal choice. Christ possessed a natural human will, but since the subject of this being was the Logos himself, he could have no gnomic will, the only possible source of sin."

99. Hovorun, *Will, Action and Freedom*, 129, writes, "The Monothelites proceeded from the assumption that natural will is identical to the 'fleshly wishes,' hence they refused to accept that Adam had his own will before the fall." They thought that Adam's will was divine and that he moved along with it. In this way, the ideal human state (in both Christ and prelapsarian Adam) is to be passive to the divine movement, and in so remove real integrity from the creation.

100. Bathrellos, *Byzantine Christ*, 153–54.

Maximus denies that Christ has a gnomic will or a *proairesis* (deliberation or searching appetite), because of their connection with ignorance and sinfulness.[101] Again, sin is the root of opposition to God and not created nature as such. Furthermore, Bathrellos argues that Maximus stands firmly in the line of the great tradition, seeing the Logos as the person of Christ, which stretches all the way back through the Alexandrian school. The potential weakness there, seen in Apollinarius and the Monothelites, "was to downplay the integrity of the humanity of Christ and its self-determining and active participation in the work of our salvation. With Maximus, the full humanity of Jesus and his human obedience to the will of the Father, which were among the strongest and healthiest elements of Antiochene Christology, were given a secure place in the theology of the Christian church."[102] Bathrellos adds, "Maximus not only protected the integrity and authenticity of the humanity of Christ, but also made it possible to regard the human history of Jesus as recapitulating and rewriting our history, not as a history of human rebellion against God but as a history of loving obedience to him."[103] For Jesus to truly save, he would need to assume and therefore heal the human will. Moreover, that human will would need to be something authentic and possessing integrity, not a passive thing whose most blessed state is to be moved along by the divine will.

Maximus makes one final distinction between person and nature. Bathrellos writes, "For Maximus, the human will is common to all people and characterizes human *nature*. However, the way in which it is actualized depends upon and characterizes the *person*."[104] He adds, "According to Maximus, human nature and its will are not evil, because they have been created by God. Thus, our human will does not need to be either suppressed by the divine will or absorbed into it. Christ assumed, healed, and deified our will; far from destroying it, he accomplished our salvation through it. In him, it remains distinct from the divine will, as it does in the saints in heaven."[105] In sum, the self-determination of man reflects the self-determination of God.[106] Moreover, Maximus is able to make the person/nature distinction in the human will itself. The will itself is natural, but the way in which it is actualized is personal. This point is well summarized by Joseph Farrell, as he writes, "The will is natural, but it, like the nature, has its own hypostatic mode."[107] The cosmological ramifications to this move will loom large in later chapters.

According to Maximus, Davis writes, "If the natures in Christ are really two, then the operations of those natures must also be two. For activity, operation is essential

---

101. Bathrellos, *Byzantine Christ*, 155, 161.
102. Bathrellos, *Byzantine Christ*, 173.
103. Bathrellos, *Byzantine Christ*, 173.
104. Bathrellos, *Byzantine Christ*, 189.
105. Bathrellos, *Byzantine Christ*, 191.
106. Bathrellos, *Byzantine Christ*, 192.
107. Farrell, *Free Choice*, 164.

to an existent being. Only through operations can natures be discerned and distinguished. Natures and operations are thus necessarily and ineluctably connected. If there are two natures really existent in Christ, there must be as well two really existent operations."[108] This is the result of Maximus's "Chalcedonian logic," mentioned above is this: "So far as activity and will as processes are concerned, they belong to the natural level: activity, and in the case of rational creatures, will—as a process—proceeds from nature, it is bound up with the movement that belongs to nature. But so far as result is concerned, activity and will are an expression of the personal, they express the particular way or mode in which a nature moves in relation to other natures."[109] Pelikan notes that Maximus argued from the doctrine of the Trinity to show that there were two wills in Christ. In the triune Godhead, there are three *hypostases*, yet one divine will. Therefore within the Godhead, will is a property of the one divine nature, rather than of the *hypostases*. In Christ, there is one *hypostasis*, but two natures. To be consistent with the trinitarian understanding of will, will should be a property of nature, and therefore there are two natures, corresponding to the two wills, in the one *hypostasis* of Christ.[110] Such a developed view of the will indeed solidifies what the previous councils were seeking to do.

Recall from chapter 1 that two equivalent ideas obtain from the corollaries of definitional simplicity, one being distinction is opposition (a restatement of the Plotinian ambiguity) and the other is what is natural is compelled (a restatement of the identity thesis, for what God does is what God wills is what God is). These concepts resurface in the Monothelite controversy, showing that Monothelitism itself is the christological end-game of definitional divine simplicity. As Joseph Farrell notes, one of the reasons that Monothelitism seemed plausible, at least in its beginning stages, is the principle of non-contradiction as applied to the wills of Christ.[111] Orthodox and heretics alike (e.g., Gregory of Nazianzus and Arius) agreed that Jesus could not have had opposing wills, and not even a theologian as capable as Gregory was able to fully disentangle the principle of distinction as opposition from theological reflection, which is why he settled on a single will in Christ himself. Such thought is best exemplified in the words of Sergius's successor as patriarch of Constantinople, and main adversary of Maximus, Pyrrhus, who said, "It is impossible for two wills to coexist with each other

---

108. Davis, *Councils*, 272. Lars Thunberg, *Microcosm and Mediator*, 88, writes, "the dynamic potentiality of nature itself is manifest in Maximus' affirmation that a nature is defined through its principle of *energeia*, which is to say that a nature is not made manifest until its potentiality is realized in actuality."

109. Louth, *Maximus the Confessor*, 57.

110. Pelikan, *Christian Tradition*, 2:72–73.

111. Farrell, *Free Choice*, 72–81, see esp. p. 79, in quoting Lethel, *Theologie*, 43, describing the thought process of Sergius, "When the scene of Gethsemane has been described, this mention of the contradiction becomes useless and superfluous, since by definition [that is, the definition of Aristotle] two wills considered at the same time and by relation to one and the same object are not able to be contradictory. If then, they are not contradictory, they cannot be distinguished, rather, one speaks of one sole will."

in one person without opposition."[112] That is, distinction must be opposition—a staple of the Plotinian ambiguity.

It is in the *Disputation with Pyrrhus* that Maximus takes full aim at the corollaries of definitional simplicity lurking in the thought of Pyrrhus. Pyrrhus's claim that "If Christ is one person, then he willed as one person. And if he willed as one person, then doubtless he has one will and not two," is but a restatement of the principle of non-contradiction in rejecting opposition one rejects any distinction.[113] The second issue to be defeated is what is natural is compelled. This language is used by Pyrrhus as well, as Farrell writes, "Responding to St. Maximus' assertion that the will is natural, and that there are thus two natural wills in Christ, Pyrrhus argues that 'if you say that the will is natural, and if what is natural is compelled, and if you say that the wills in Christ are natural, how can you avoid being obliged to take away all his voluntary motion?'"[114] For Pyrrhus, committed as he was to the identity thesis where nature implies compulsion, the *hypostasis* is the seat of freedom to choose, not the nature, which is why he was Monothelite. Maximus opposes the patriarch's reasoning by showing that the principle of what is natural being compelled then directly implies the Origenist Problematic: "If one were to continue in this line of reasoning then God, who is by nature God, by nature good, and by nature creator, must of necessity be not only God and good but also creator. To think, much less to speak, in this manner is extreme blasphemy. For who dares to attribute necessity to God? Consider, my friend, if you will, the blasphemy of such a proposition."[115] So Maximus has shown the flaws of both of the corollaries to divine simplicity—the two on which Monothelitism rests: nature need not imply compulsion and distinction need not imply opposition. That nature does not imply compulsion eliminates the possibility of a cosmology that emanates from the creator; it preserves the freedom of God to create and to thereby create a world distinct from himself that retains its own internal integrity—a point that will be in constant dispute in the upcoming chapters. Second, that distinction need not imply opposition allows for a *descriptional* understanding of divine simplicity that allows for plurality in the Godhead without composition—that the good may be multiple rather than singular. It also puts the real point of contention between God and sin, not between God and the creation itself, for in the sinless one, distinct natures, energies, and wills coexist unopposed. Both of these insights will contain enormous implications for cosmology that will be explored later.

Finally, Farrell addresses the two implications from the idea of distinction as opposition originating in Plotinus's and Origen's definitional divine simplicity. The first, as we have seen, subordinates the human to the divine in Christ, even to the point that

---

112. Farrell, *Free Choice*, 81, Farrell quotes Maximus, *Disputation with Pyrrhus*.
113. Farrell, *Free Choice*, 81. The quote is from Maximus, *Disputation with Pyrrhus*.
114. Farrell, *Free Choice*, 82. Again, the quote is from Maximus, *Disputation with Pyrrhus*.
115. Farrell, *Free Choice*, 82. Farrell quotes Maximus, *Disputation with Pyrrhus*.

The Hexagon of Heresy

the human is "that which is moved by God (*theokinetos*)."[116] Such a belief collapses quickly into Apollinarianism. The second, and subtler implication, is that the presence of two wills in Christ—giving the human nature in him a real action rather than something that is *theokinetos*—destroys the belief that the Origenist *apokatastasis* is a foregone conclusion.[117] All the implications of Origen's definitional simplicity have now been addressed and defeated, and finally Byzantine Christian theology has been completely disentangled from the pagan assumptions he injected into it.

Unfortunately, Maximus died in exile and by wounds suffered at the ill-treatment of Monophysites in 662.[118] But the ramifications of his work are immense. The Origenist concept of defining God as metaphysically simple had disastrous results for Christology. The first corrective step was Athanasius and his distinction between being and energy. The second step was the work of the Cappadocians to give a measured response to Eunomius, working out theologically the intuitions of Athanasius. The third step was the defeat of the Word-flesh model of Christology that could not give sufficient due to the humanity of Christ. The fourth step was Cyril's insistence on the person of the Word as the single subject in the incarnation. Maximus finished the job with his teaching on the will. As John Meyendorff notes, "In Origen's system immobility is one of the essential characteristics of true being; it belongs to God, but also to creatures as long as they remain in conformity with God's will. Diversity and movement come from the fall. For Maximus, however, 'movement,' or 'action,' is a fundamental quality of nature. Each creature possesses its own meaning and purpose, which reflect the eternal and divine Logos 'through whom all things were made.'"[119] The destruction of Origen's definitional simplicity implies that "good" is not one and simple, but many. Free choices need not be dialectical; there are multiple goods, just as there are multiple divine energies (not even attributes, or, more correctly "attributions," or names, for the one simple essence).[120] The Christian Yahweh is not simple in the Platonic sense: he is one in being, three in person, and many in energy, and Maximus's understanding of the Logos being the creative agent to actualize the many *logoi* in space and time—all individual good things in creation—is the final nail in the

---

116. Farrell, *Free Choice*, 83. Farrell quotes Jaroslav Pelikan, *Christian Tradition*, 2:66.

117. Farrell, *Free Choice*, 84. Farrell argues convincingly here that the *apokatastasis* is only possible if the divine and human wills are really one in the eschaton. He writes, "If there was one will of Christ which moved the human nature even in spite of that nature's own innate opposition to God, and if in the eschaton there was to be one will of God and the saints, whose wills were in any case passive before the divine will, then what could logically prevent one from asserting that the Origenistic understanding of the *apokatastasis* was a logical implication of the one hypostatic will?"

118. Davis, *Councils*, 278.

119. Meyendorff, *Byzantine Theology*, 37.

120. See Farrell, *God, History, and Dialectic*, 399. Here Farrell applies the discussion to Aquinas, but it could just as easily be said of Origen's Hellenization.

coffin of Origen's Hellenizing mistake, at least in Eastern theology.[121] Ultimately, God could not be against creation, because he created it.[122]

Constantinople III convened in 680. Those at the council opposed to two wills thought it was Nestorianism, especially Macarius the Patriarch of Antioch.[123] He was later deposed by the council. Davis notes that "All Patriarchs of Constantinople from 610 to 666 were anathematized" as was Pope Honorius.[124] The council used the four Chalcedonian adverbs to describe the wills and operations in Christ, taken directly from the work of Maximus.[125] Even posthumously, the ideas of Maximus lit the way for the conclusion of the christological councils. Unfortunately, the great strides made in Constantinople did not reach the Western church in any lasting way. One of the great names in the Western tradition, Anselm of Canterbury, can write in the early twelfth century that Christ, "came not to do his own will, but that of the Father, because the righteous will that he had did not come from his humanity but from his divinity."[126] Maximus's relative obscurity in Western theology might be a larger hindrance to good Christian theology than had been previously thought.

Conclusion

With the close of the sixth ecumenical council, the christological controversies of the early church have come to an end. The true and full humanity of Jesus has finally been upheld against Monophysitism, Monoenergism, and Monothelitism. Jesus Christ is to be understood as one person, the Logos-made-flesh, possessing two complete natures, divine and human, without change, confusion, division, or separation. The *ordo theologiae* has been finally corrected, as the natures do not and cannot constitute the person. The will has been rightly declared a property of nature, rather than of person, which allows Christ to assume and thus heal the human will, the very first human faculty to fall. This one Jesus, whom we meet both in the pages of Scripture and in our Christian experience, is truly and authentically human, while never ceasing to be truly and authentically God. Finally, and against all of the christological heresies we have

---

121. Meyendorff, *Byzantine Theology* (1975), 132–33, writes, "For Origen, the original, intellectual creation is static. It finds its true logical existence in the contemplation of God's essence, and its first movement is a form of rebellion against God. Change and diversity in creation are consequences of the fall and, therefore, are fundamentally evil. For Maximus, and the entire Byzantine theological tradition, the movement of creatures is the necessary and natural consequence of their creation by God. God therefore, in creating the world, placed outside of himself a system of dynamic beings, which are different from him in that they change and move toward him. The logos of every creature consists, therefore, in being essentially active; there is no nature without 'energy,' or movement." See also Farrell, *Free Choice*, chapter 6. We will visit this more fully later on.

122. See Beeley, *Unity of Christ*, 301.

123. Davis, *Councils*, 280.

124. Davis, *Councils*, 282.

125. Davis, *Councils*, 283.

126. Pelikan, *Christian Tradition*, 3:116–17, cited in Farrell, *Free Choice*, 201.

The Hexagon of Heresy

surveyed, his humanity is seen as possessing its own energy and direction, which all of the deficient Christologies failed to allow.

The providential, anthropological, soteriological, and even bibliological implications of such a well-ordered Christology are immense, because if Christ is so fully human, then his humanity is the prototype of ours. Our humanity, even in its bondage to sin, is not a puppet, completely at the control of outside forces. More importantly for our discussion here, it implies that creation itself possesses its own energy, integrity, and direction. In the Hellenistic cosmologies, the One/Good/Prime Mover is utterly simple, and everything that is not the deity is naturally compelled to be what it is. The many derive their being from the one, are determined by it, and paradoxically determine it. The only real energy is that of the one. Maximus's Christology implies that creation, while dependent on the triune God in its creation out of nothing and in his continuous providential care, possesses its own integrity and self-determination within what we call the doctrines of creation and providence. We know this because the one who recapitulates all of creation possessed his own self-determination free of sin and death. We now move on past the christological controversies to ourselves recapitulate what all of this means, which we do in the following chapter.

7

The Recapitulation of Christology and a Look Ahead

ONCE THE SIXTH COUNCIL concluded in 681, the christological controversies came to an end in the East. The previous five chapters have summarized their history, and in doing so make four distinct observations. First, the chapters trace out the process of a christologically-bounded orthodoxy where the Hexagon of Heresy forms the boundary lines of what can be faithfully believed concerning Jesus. Second is the intellectual defeat of the doctrine of definitional simplicity within Eastern Orthodoxy by taking head-on its two great corollaries, the identity thesis and the Plotinian ambiguity.[1] Third is the recapitulation of pagan metaphysics, as the chapters illustrate the subtle changes of meaning in technical terms like *hypostasis*, *ousia*, *prosopon*, and *physis*.[2] Fourth is the use of "Chalcedonian logic" to draw out the implications of the fourth council to help formulate further needed clarifications. I will discuss the latter and its implications in its own section. Then, this chapter will survey the Western approach to theology, enshrined in the work of Augustine, chiefly in his *On the Trinity*. We will see that Augustine defines the divine essence as simple, just as Origen had done before him. Augustine accepted the very theological model later rejected by the Greek Church, definitional divine simplicity with its attendant identity thesis and dialectical processes.

---

1. One may here appeal to the words of John of Damascus, who famously said that the root of the heresies is the identification of person and nature. Farrell, *God, History, and Dialectic*, 271–77, provides a very helpful summary of the three kinds of heresies: ones that confuse person and a natural property or energy (including Eunomianism, Apollinarianism and Nestorianism), ones that confuse person and nature directly (Sabellianism and Monophysitism), and ones that do both (the Origenist Problematic, "Arianism," and Monothelitism).

2. See Wildberg, "Neoplatonism," for some of the original pagan meanings attached to these technical terms.

The Hexagon of Heresy

A Chalcedonian Logic

Unlike the case of Origen's adoption of definitional simplicity that led to the christological controversies, there was no corrective process for Augustine's move. The christological implications of Origenist simplicity surfaced quickly and required immediate attention. By the time Augustinism was becoming dominant in the West, the councils had put the christological issues to rest. In the West, the symptoms of definitional simplicity manifested themselves in other theological *loci*, and without a christologically grounded methodology to detect and refute them, these symptoms will not be identified as arising from the same source as the "Hexagon of Heresy." In Western Protestant Evangelicalism, my own tradition, there are multiple theological models for each of the *loci* where God and humans interact: the inspiration of Scripture, cosmology, and salvation. It is my contention that a great number of Western cosmological models have the same fundamental axioms (definitional simplicity and its corollaries) as the christological heresies of late antiquity do. I will show that as Origen's injection of a pagan concept into the Christian tradition resulted in aberrant Christology, Augustine's re-injection of the same concept into the Latin Christian tradition resulted in a number of aberrant cosmologies. If a "Hexagon of Heresy" can be constructed for Christology, one can be constructed for cosmology as well, showing models that are out of bounds. Documenting this process is the aim of the rest of the book. But, in the process of writing and researching, I have come to understand that documenting and delineating the boundaries for each of the *loci* are not enough; some diagnosis is in order.

I suggest that the reasoning utilized by the fathers of the first six ecumenical councils must become the process to evaluate the various cosmological, anthropological, and soteriological models that have arisen in Western theology. The orthodox view of Jesus, then, needs to be the measuring stick for the other *loci*, and it becomes apparent as we move along that the same general heresies (used in the etymological sense of "opinions") arise within each of the *loci*. It is my contention that the theological first principle that caused the subtler christological heresies of "Arianism," Apollinarianism, Nestorianism, and Monophysitism is the same first principle that creates the subtler, but exclusively Western, deviations in the other *loci*—defining the essence of God as simple. Let us now "recapitulate" our discussion of the clarification of orthodox Christology

The previous five chapters have given the Christian theologian a blueprint for tackling theological issues consistently and christologically. We saw this at work in the thought of Maximus the Confessor in his battle with Monothelitism. He employed a "Chalcedonian logic" that allowed him to start with the divine-Son-made-flesh to work out the proper interplay among person, energy (will), and nature. Maximus went much further than Monothelitism, working out a cosmology and soteriology based on his Chalcedonian logic, the former of which will be briefly surveyed in the next chapter.

The Recapitulation of Christology and a Look Ahead

As was offered in chapter 1 here, there is, for example, a clearly Arian view of cosmology.[3] At this point, I want to explain a bit. By stating, for example, that a cosmology is "Arian," I mean that it exhibits the characteristics of Arianism in its understanding of the world. That is, such a cosmology, in conjunction with historical, christological "Arianism," denies the fullness of the divine action in the world. I do not mean to imply that such views self-identify as "Arian," or that there is always a clear connection between, say, christological and cosmological Arianism (though there often is). Further, the terminology, as far as I have been able to ascertain, is mine, and does not imply any kind of historical heresy, since the church as a whole has not spoken with a unified voice on such issues. When utilizing christologically heretical terminology to describe non-christological themes, any use of "heresy" reverts to the etymological root of the word meaning "opinion." Given this disclaimer, I have come to realize that just stating what an Arian view of cosmology is does not sufficiently accomplish the task. As we saw in chapter 3, there were real causes for "Arianism"; it did not just pop out of nowhere. Arius saw himself as clearly situated in Christian tradition, and not as some usurper from the outside trying to hijack the faith. The deep-seated Hellenistic assumptions coming from Origen and his problematic theological construction were the real origins of "Arianism." Therefore, to defeat "Arianism" entailed defeating Hellenism at that point. The christological battle continued on for the better part of four centuries until the recapitulation was complete. Now the question must be asked: are there similar deep-seated assumptions and causes that would entail that a large and very influential portion of Western Christianity, including the vast majority of its theologians over several generations, assuming an Arian position on the relationship of God and the world (if not a christological "Arianism" altogether)? All of the christological heresies were entailments of Origen's Hellenistic understanding of divine simplicity—hardwired into the system, so to speak. Does the West have something similar in its theological *loci* that describe divine-creation interaction? The short answer is yes.

Augustine's Divine Simplicity

Augustine is without question the father of Western theology—both Roman Catholic and Protestant.[4] As all who followed Origen were influenced by him, all Western thinkers build upon Augustine. Though his influence in the Greek-speaking East was minimal, he lived at the tipping point of Western civilization, where the linguistic/

---

3. At this point, I will now cease with the "anti-Nicene" terminology, since I am drawing out the broader implications of the anti-Nicene movements into cosmology. "Anti-Nicene" at this point seems clumsy to me, since the Nicenes were interested in Christology. I will return to the more archaic "Arianism" from here on out.

4. Farrell, *God, History, and Dialectic*, 279, states that without Augustine and the specific way he formulated the doctrine of the Trinity, there would be no Western Europe. I think he might be right.

The Hexagon of Heresy

cultural/political/religious break between East and West was beginning. As a result, his writings are the filter through which the West thought for over a millennium after his death. His interpreters are legion, even to the point that Augustinian Studies is a legitimate branch of historical theology and philosophy. No one book can do his thought on any topic justice, and I don't pretend to try to do so here. I do want, however, to focus on one aspect of his theology—definitional divine simplicity.

Contemporary scholars speculate on the amount of influence Origen had on Augustine. Whether or not there is direct influence, one thing is clear: Augustine constructed his doctrine of God on precisely identical principles of definitional divine simplicity and its resulting identity thesis and dialectic of opposition as did Origen. Here we see the same process as followed by Origen, that is, the adoption of the rational process of the Greeks, who demonstrated that their "god" is one simple essence. While the recapitulation of pagan metaphysical terminology was well underway in the East, making meaningful distinctions among person, energy, and nature/essence, Augustine could write, "He is called in respect to himself both God, and great, and good, and just, and anything else of the kind; and just as to Him *to be is the same as to be God, or as to be great, or as to be good, so it is the same thing to Him to be, as to be a person.*"[5] Here we see a crystal clear expression of the identity thesis, identifying person ("to be a person"), energy ("to be great" and "to be good"), and nature ("to be God"). Augustine adds, "And since in the divine simplicity, to be wise is nothing else than to be, therefore wisdom there is the same as essence."[6] R. T. Mullins adds that "Augustine continually argues throughout *The Trinity* that all of God's essential divine attributes are identical to each other."[7] It is Joseph Farrell who coins the phrase that such definitional simplicity works like a great "metaphysical equals sign," where, in reality, nature equals each energy or attribute equals the persons.[8] The presence of the identity thesis is the proof that the understanding of simplicity is the same as that of Plotinus and Origen, though in a more sophisticated form as Augustine does not arrive at the Problematic or *apokatastasis*. We will see how he avoids them in the next chapter.

We should therefore expect similar kinds of theological assertions coming out of Augustine's definitional simplicity as we saw in Origen's. The deviance to orthodoxy in the entailments of Origen's definitional simplicity were limited, historically at least, to Christology, and to a lesser extent cosmology and the *apokatastasis*. As Augustine converts to Christianity in the 380s, the recapitulation of Greek metaphysics is well underway. "Arianism" and Apollinarianism had already been answered. Nestorianism and Monophysitism would be answered within twenty-five years of Augustine's

---

5. Augustine, *Trin.* 7.6.11, quoted in Farrell, *Free Choice*, 209. Italics are Farrell's. See also n79 in chapter 4.

6. Augustine, *Trin.* 7.1.2.

7. Mullins, *Timeless God*, 56. Mullins offers numerous quotes from Augustine, *Trin.*, illustrating the point.

8. See the discussion in Farrell, *Free Choice*, 208–10.

death. By the time Augustine's Hellenization of the doctrine of God takes hold in the West, orthodox Christology would be largely hammered out. No one discovered the potentially-heretical christological entailments of Augustine's system because the recapitulation of metaphysics worked out by the Eastern fathers had become official dogma and no one tried or dared to take Augustine to his logical conclusions in Christology. Where I believe the real destructive tendencies arose as a result of Augustine's definitional simplicity is in the various *loci* that will be discussed later on in this book, specifically cosmology. For example, some of Augustine's theological descendants could not get away with an "Arian" Christology, but they could possess an Arian view of cosmology, because the latter arises from what definitional simplicity entails. What the Eastern fathers fought so hard to overcome simply resurrected itself in the West, a West that either would not or could not correct it before it became too late.[9]

It is very easy to ascribe to Augustine more than what he actually taught. I am doing my best to resist the temptation to do so. That is why I am limiting my discussion of his theology to the embrace of both the identity thesis and the Plotinian ambiguity entailed by a definitional form of divine simplicity. Augustine was a catholic father, committed in his faith and office to teaching the faith as he received it. Although he did introduce some innovations to the tradition, perhaps his most important move was reviving the identity thesis that Athanasius and the Cappadocians worked so hard to defeat. In fairness to both Augustine and Origen, I believe that both of them, in all of their sheer brilliance, could not foresee the trouble the identity thesis of definitional simplicity would cause. Edward Siecienski writes, on the subject of *filioque* specifically, and on Augustine in general,

> While largely unknown in the East (at least until the fourteenth century), Augustine's writings in the West took on the role of a "second canon," with his *De Trinitate* viewed as the criterion *sine qua non* for orthodox trinitarian theology. The *filioque* came to be seen not as a theological opinion but as doctrine, and "the Augustinian version of the trinitarian dogma . . . as the universal faith of the church." While he was not necessarily the point of division between East and West, or the individual responsible for the schism that came to divide the Christian world, it is difficult to escape the conclusion that Augustine himself provided the language and theology that future

---

9. This book is in no way an apologetic for Eastern Orthodoxy over against Roman Catholicism or Protestantism. I write from a firmly Evangelical Protestant tradition, but one cannot deny that there is something amiss somewhere deep in the heart of all the Western traditions. Certainly Eastern Christianity has its own issues, but it has never had to contend with the primacy of the pope, a Dark Age, scholasticism, nominalism, a classical Renaissance, a Reformation, horrible wars of religion, secularism, liberalism, fundamentalism, materialism, atheism, and a whole host of other particularly Western problems front and center. One should stop and ask why all these problems arise in the West and not the East.

The Hexagon of Heresy

generations used to justify that schism. One cannot help but think that the idea would have grieved Augustine greatly.[10]

Now we must move on into the Western theological tradition and a bit of political and military history along the way.

The Medieval Synthesis and Collapse

The fifth century saw various invasions from the Goths and Vandals into the territory of the Western Roman Empire, including Augustine's home city of Hippo in North Africa. By the ninth century, the Franks were in control of most of the West. The Carolingian cathedral schools introduced learning that brought Western Europe out of the Dark Ages. They studied the classics, which brought about a renewed interest in rationalism.[11] Anselm was an early master of the rationalistic method. He stretched the bounds of what reason could show, exemplified in his ontological argument, which "demonstrated" the existence of God without using the Bible. His efforts were to provide a rational foundation for Christianity that unbelievers could accept and follow.[12] Abelard used his famous *Sic et Non* to pose philosophical questions, believing that "the road to belief passes through doubt."[13] By the thirteenth century, scholastic theology was at its zenith. The main thinker of this century was of course Thomas Aquinas. Like his theological father Augustine, Aquinas held to the identity thesis in his understanding of divine simplicity, as he identifies God's essence with his existence, and declares that God is pure act. R. T. Mullins elucidates,

> As Aquinas explains, composite things have potential. They move from potential to actual. But God is simple, so he must lack potentiality and be pure act (*Summa Contra Gentiles* I.16–18). One example of this idea is that God just is his act of existence (*Summa Contra Gentiles* I.22). God is not something that underlies his properties because he does not have any properties. God does not go from potential to actual for he is pure act. God's act is identical to God, and not something distinct. "His action is his being . . . God's action is his substance" (*Summa Contra Gentiles* II.9). "The manifold actions ascribed to God, as intelligence, volition, the production of things, and the like, are not so many different things, since each of these actions in God is his own very being, which is one and the same thing" (*Summa Contra Gentiles* II.10).[14]

---

10. Siecienski, *Filioque*, 63.

11. Lindberg, *Beginnings*, 193.

12. Lindberg, *Beginnings*, 194–95. The early rationalistic method shows the shift of the primary demonstration of the truth of Christianity. In its earlier days, the holy life lived by its adherents showed that Christianity was true. By the days of Anselm, it needed to be rationally demonstrated, which presupposes that God can be subsumed into human rationality.

13. Lindberg, *Beginnings*, 196.

14. Mullins, *Timeless God*, 58.

The Recapitulation of Christology and a Look Ahead

Aquinas offers the most sophisticated exposition of the identity thesis yet, and perhaps in its strongest sense yet as well. We would do well at this point to remember the position played by divine simplicity in Thomas's system. Simplicity was a significant component of his natural theology, which he utilized to form "a rational foundation for a supernatural theology."[15] Here we see in the work of Thomas, as will be present in his scholastic successors as well, a kind of proto-foundationalism, where true knowledge must rest on a universally accessible ("natural") and unassailable ("theology") body of truth. That is, the content of the faith as revealed in Scripture and tradition for Thomas can and should be verified and supported by what can be deduced by universal human reason and observation. It is an attempt to arrive at real knowledge of the one through the assumption that the one and many are united in a monist fashion. The foundation for such an enterprise rested squarely on the shoulders of Greek metaphysics, and the attempt to "baptize" the ultra-rational Prime Mover of Aristotle.[16]

Part of Aquinas's terminology involves the difference between real and conceptual distinctions in the Godhead.[17] A real distinction between two things means that there in an "extra-mental feature in reality that makes them distinct."[18] A conceptual distinction lacks this extra-mental reality. Aquinas believes that there lies only a conceptual distinction between God's essence and his energies, while the Eastern tradition sees the distinction as real. To affirm that any distinctions in God are conceptual and not real is to preserve, for Aquinas, the uniqueness of God over against his creatures.[19] That uniqueness is necessary to preserve the doctrine of the analogy of being, which holds the created universe together.[20] Paul Hinlicky describes its importance as follows:

> The descending doctrine of analogy from the pure actuality of He Who Is to the imperfect actuality of creatures affirms the goodness, truth, and beauty, albeit finite and diversified, of this existing creation composed of many against

15. Hinlicky, *Divine Simplicity*, 61.
16. See Daane, *Freedom*, 172.
17. Such language was previously alluded to in chapter 1.
18. Mullins, *Timeless God,* 52.
19. Mullins, *Timeless God,* 54. The concept is found in Thomas Aquinas, *Summa Theologiae* I.q3.a4.
20. Hinlicky, *Divine Simplicity*, 143–44, writes, "The 'analogy of being' thus emerges as a doctrine from the tradition of Thomism that appeals to the ontological claim of Thomas that all the many creatures, each in its own way, reflect in the mere acts of their beings the sheer act of being that is their creator. Sheer being is, in this context, a perfection; it is better to be than not to be, and to be absolutely is to be perfectly. As the creature exists finitely and so compositely, so analogously the creator exists simply and thus infinitely. As the creature grows into its natural perfection, so analogously the creator is always already its own natural perfection in actuality; correspondingly, the ultimate goal of the creature's desire for perfection is to adhere to God's perfect being. It may achieve this by becoming the similitude of the creator in the perfection of eternal life. Indeed, already now insofar as each creature reflects in some way its creator, it already participates by this analogy in his goodness, albeit partially and imperfectly in its temporal life. As the creator is being itself and goodness itself and truth itself and beauty itself, in him one and the same, so the creature, so far as it exists at all, is in some way good, true, and beautiful, a reflection of God though in diverse ways as the manifold creature in relation to the one who is creator."

the perennial danger in Christianity of gnostic dualism; it identifies the creation as good and the worthy object of divine redemption and fulfillment. The descending analogy of being is, then, a corollary of strong simplicity: since God as God is the perfect identity of essence and existence, imperfect creatures are known as like God in their being so far as they actualize, and as yet imperfectly realize, their essences.[21]

In Aquinas's theology, the created order is a complex and incomplete reflection of the simple divine essence that created it—in other words, monism.[22] There is an order and a rationality—especially among the three clearly distinct (at least for the time) levels of being—God, humanity, and the natural creation—behind all of it, as Michael Allen Gillespie notes, the medieval scholastics "experienced the world as the instantiation of the categories of divine reason."[23] But the strongly-monist Thomistic synthesis, here only briefly summarized, did not last long. Gillespie writes concerning the forces working against the scholastic synthesis:

> For the scholastics, the earthly life mirrored the heavenly. One did not necessarily need Scripture to tell us how to live. It was needed for things beyond this life and this reason. For all of its magnificence, the cathedral of scholastic thought depended on the delicate counterbalancing of Christian belief and pagan rationalism, and it was the instability of this relationship that brought it down. This balance was threatened both by the growing influence of reason and secularism within the church, which fostered a falling away from Christian practices, and by the ever recurring and ever more urgent demands for a more original Christianity, based on revelation and/or an imitation of the life of Christ. The preservation of medieval Christianity depended upon a reconciliation of these two powerful and opposing impulses [belief and rationalism]. Such a synthesis, however, could only be maintained in theory by the creation of an ever more elaborate theology and in practice by the ever-increasing use of papal and princely power.[24]

Thomas did his best to synthesize and harmonize the best of Aristotelian rationalism with the Augustinian Christianity he inherited. However, there was a dark side

21. Hinlicky, *Divine Simplicity*, 144. Hinlicky's "strong simplicity" is what I am calling definitional simplicity.

22. Torrance, *Theological Science*, 66–67, writes, "In the Augustinian tradition, with its powerful ingredient of Neoplatonism, which dominated the Middle Ages, the universe was regarded as a sacramental macrocosm in which the physical and visible creation was held to be the counterpart in time to eternal and heavenly patterns. Thus the world of nature was looked at only sacramentally, i.e. looked through toward God and eternal realities. As such the world had no significance in itself, or only significance in so far as it participated in divine and eternal patterns. It was the longing of the world for the ultimate realities that moved it and directed it and so gave it meaning." In other words, we see the monism of Neoplatonism in full display with "what is natural is compelled" lurking in the background.

23. Gillespie, *Theological Origins*, 12.

24. Gillespie, *Theological Origins*, 20–21.

The Recapitulation of Christology and a Look Ahead

to Aristotle, namely his pagan eternal creation and determinism.[25] Many in the late thirteenth century did not temper Aristotle with the received doctrine, and wanted to allow philosophy to lead them without appeal to church teaching.[26] Aristotle became so dangerous that a mere four years after Aquinas's death in 1273, 219 largely Aristotelian propositions were condemned by first the bishop of Paris and then the pope.

After the "Condemnation of 1277," a shift began to take place in the philosophical theology of Western Europe. Those theologians operative after 1277, in the words of David Lindberg, "while not seeking a total separation between philosophy and theology, diminished their area of overlap by questioning the ability of philosophy to address articles of the faith with demonstrative certainty. Deprived of its ability to achieve certainty, philosophy no longer threatened theology, at least to the same degree; the articles of the faith were not open to philosophical demonstration, but were to be accepted by faith alone."[27] The condemnations and the divorce of philosophy and theology, or more precisely, the rejection of the epistemological validity of the rationalistic, Aristotelian/Thomistic, monist, from-the-one-to-the-many line of argumentation, fueled interest in a return to the basic Augustinian touchstone for human attempts at understanding the divine essence—divine omnipotence.[28] Lindberg writes, "If God is absolutely free and omnipotent, it follows that the physical world is contingent rather than necessary; that is, there is no necessity that it should be what it is, for it is dependent solely on the will of God for its form, its mode of operation, and its very existence. The observed order of cause and effect is not necessary, but freely imposed by divine will."[29] God was still simple in their minds; his essence, will, and reason were still identical. The shift was in how one is to apprehend the divine essence. For Aquinas, divine reason was the key that unlocked every door. The aftermath of the condemnations changed the locks; the new skeleton key is divine volition.

The first criticism of Aquinas's system came from John Duns Scotus. Though Scotus held to the same definition of simplicity as did Aquinas, he detected what he believed to be a problem in Thomism, that is, that Thomas's monist position (God as

---

25. Lindberg, *Beginnings*, 220. Eternal creation is the Aristotelian version of the same hierarchy of being that produced the Origenist Problematic. Because nature is the most basic metaphysical level in Hellenistic metaphysics, and because there what is natural is compelled, determinism follows. It is the "monist half" of the ambiguity discussed in chapter 1.

26. Lindberg, *Beginnings*, 234.

27. Lindberg, *Beginnings*, 242.

28. As should be apparent by now, theologies constructed upon the axiom of definitional simplicity have an obvious dilemma at the beginning of their task: how can one meaningfully describe a God without properties? The Christian theologian committed to definitional simplicity must begin his God-talk with a conceptual distinction that he *a priori* assumes cannot exist. I fail to see how starting one's theological reflection upon something that ultimately must be rejected could ever end well.

29. Lindberg, *Beginnings*, 242. This is the Plotinian ambiguity of the Medieval period. In Thomas, God and creation are held together by the analogy of being: God and creation are one system united in rationality. If God is free and creation is not necessitated to be what it is, then creation is distinct and therefore the dialectical opposite of God. It must rise up against him.

The Hexagon of Heresy

pure act, existence equals essence, and creation rationalistically bound to the essence of God) led to its logical conclusion—what is natural is compelled therefore an eternal creation (the Origenist Problematic all over again!).[30] So he emphasized the will of God as the organizing principle in describing the simple God. In doing so, he attempted to derive simplicity from God's infinity. Paul Hinlicky summarizes, "Between Thomas and Scotus, dare I venture, the medieval tradition of natural theology comes upon the horns of a dilemma under the *shared* axiom of protological [definitional] simplicity. If infinite, the One's freedom is unbounded, a *deus exlex* [arbitrary deity]. If pure actuality, the One's will is necessary, *natura naturans* [what is natural is compelled]."[31] What Thomas and Scotus have accomplished here is to reveal yet another contradiction inherent in the identity thesis. If all of God's energies are truly identical with his essence and with each other, then our reflection upon their differences as they appear to us will lead to contradictory pictures of God. That is, our affirmation of something that is true in God will contradict some other affirmation, which leads us back to Plotinus and his extreme apophaticism as the only way to not get in trouble. If divine reason is our organizing principle, with Thomas, then the result is divine compulsion even to the point of a necessary creation of this universe as the only possible world.[32] If divine freedom is our organizing principle, then God can do whatever he wants, can be arbitrary and capricious, and is only trustworthy because he says so. The latter option is the one chosen by the next great medieval thinker in his rejection of Thomistic universals, the Franciscan William of Ockham.

William of Ockham rejected Thomas's rationalist Christianity. As a Franciscan, he sought a more primitive and pure Christianity over against the corruption of the church and the philosophy of the Dominicans.[33] His answer was a philosophy that came to be known as nominalism, which held that those categories of divine

---

30. Mullins, *Timeless God*, 55, quotes Scotus thus: "There is nothing in the divine that is not the same thing as the divine essence and also the same as anything essential, so that considering such in the abstract, one can say simply 'This is this'" (*God and Creatures* Q5.34). Scotus obviously holds to the identity thesis. Crisp, *Jonathan Edwards*, 61, writes, quoting Thomas in *Summa Contra Gentiles* 1:37, "Thomas argues that God creates in order to diffuse his goodness, saying, 'the good is diffusive of itself and of being. But this diffusion befits God because . . . God is the cause of being for other things.' Since divine goodness is identical to the divine nature and 'diffusive of itself,' as Thomas puts it, it looks like creation is a necessary act. Divine goodness must be diffused; and the only way in which that can happen is by some act of creation, since God himself cannot further diffuse his goodness within his own trinitarian life, if he is a fully realized, pure act." Despite Thomas's protests to the contrary, the entailments of his work lead straight to a necessary creation.

31. Hinlicky, *Divine Simplicity*, 69. Here, what Hinlicky calls "protological" simplicity is the same as what I have referred to as definitional simplicity.

32. See Rogers, "Divine Simplicity," who writes, "The traditional doctrine of divine simplicity does seem to entail that God 'must' create, and that He 'must' create this world." See also Dolezal, *God without Parts*, 207, who writes, "There has never been a temporal or logical moment in the divine life in which God stood volitionally open to other possible worlds."

33. Gillespie, *Theological Origins*, 25. Francis of Assisi, who founded the order, lived his life in a quest to find a purer and more original form of Christianity through the imitation of Christ.

The Recapitulation of Christology and a Look Ahead

reason—universals—were not really real; instead they were "merely signs useful for human understanding."[34] We will address why this move was so important is Western cosmology over the next two chapters. Gillespie writes concerning Ockham, "God could not be understood by human reason but only by biblical revelation or mystical experience."[35] Ockham denied that human reason could be a useful tool in theological endeavors, and denied that the chain of causation so important to Thomas could actually be proven.[36] In nominalism, everything and every person was radically individual, and therefore was its own nature. There was no monist analogy of being that called all things to participate in the God who created them and thereby realize their completion. There was only the inevitable collisions of the simple God and the individual objects he created, which, in the absence of a universal reason, implied that divine and human wills must be in opposition.[37]

The realist-nominalist schism of the medieval world is essentially a reproduction in metaphysics of the Plotinian ambiguity. The Thomistic realists, confident in the monist ordering of God and creation, came ever-so-close to identifying God and the world in the analogy of being. The nominalists, confident in the dichotomist-dualist break between God and creation in claiming "no divine *logos* or reason that can serve as the foundation for a political, cosmopolitan, or theological identity,"[38] came ever-so-close to rejecting the divine Logos in rejecting the divine *logos*. That is, Aquinas and Ockham represent both sides of the Plotinian ambiguity seen in chapter 1. The former is the monist where the one necessarily produces the many who are deterministically dependent on it; the latter is the dichotomist-dualist who insists that the many stand over against the one. Moreover, nominalism was disastrous for the doctrine of God, as Gillespie writes,

> Nominalism sought to tear the rationalistic veil from the face of God in order to found a true Christianity, but in doing so it revealed a capricious God, fearsome in his power, unknowable, unpredictable, unconstrained by nature and reason, and indifferent to good and evil. This vision of God turned the order of nature into a chaos of individual beings and the order of logic into a mere concatenation of names. Man himself was dethroned from his exalted place in the natural order of things and cast adrift in an infinite universe with no natural law to guide him and no certain path to salvation. It is thus not surprising that

---

34. Gillespie, *Theological Origins*, 14.

35. Gillespie, *Theological Origins*, 14. This is a restatement of the famous "Ockham's Razor," found in Gillespie, *Theological Origins*, 300n12, "One should affirm no statement as true or maintain that something exists unless forced to do so by self-evidence, that is, by revelation, experience, or logical deduction from a revealed truth or a proposition verified by observation."

36. Hannam, *God's Philosophers*, 169–70.

37. Gillespie, *Theological Origins*, 134. We saw opposing wills in chapter 6 as the root assumption of the Monothelites.

38. Gillespie, *Theological Origins*, 45.

for all but the most extreme ascetics and mystics, this dark God of nominalism proved to be a profound source of anxiety and insecurity.[39]

Why did nominalism succeed, in a period of about three generations, to dethrone the orderly synthesis of Aquinas and replace it with such uncertainty and angst? As Gillespie writes, nominalism succeeded in large part due to the crises of the fourteenth century: "The Great Schism, the Hundred Years War, the Black Death, the development of gunpowder, the dire economic circumstances brought on throughout Europe by the advent of the Little Ice Age, and the dislocations wrought by urban development, social mobility, and the Crusades, were all of crucial importance to the formation of the anxiety and insecurity that made the nominalist vision of the world believable."[40] We will see this happen again in the seventeenth century as external factors will loom large in driving theological decisions.

The Aftermath of Ockham

Michael Gillespie's thesis is that three movements, each possessing a common ontology but different ontic priority, grew out of the angst caused by the God of nominalism as Europe tried to make some order out of the nominalist chaos. The question of ontic priority concerned the three levels of being that figured prominently in Aquinas's system, God, humanity, and the creation. In the overturning of the Thomist synthesis, the three levels of being were no longer ordered. The Renaissance and later humanists would settle on humanity to have ontic priority over God and nature; the Reformers would prioritize God over humans and nature, and the moderns, as a third way, would emphasize nature over humanity and God.[41] The first two approaches would retain the Franciscan tendency (although neither of them would be Franciscans themselves) to leap backwards into history for better answers than those present in their time, while the moderns would adopt a model that history is progress and that tomorrow is guaranteed to be better than yesterday.[42]

The first attempt at reorganizing ontic priority after the nominalist revolution fell to the humanists, who launched the Renaissance. The humanists, in order to deal with the vision of God and the universe dealt to them by the nominalistic revolution, made humans ontically prior to both God and the creation. The humanist concern was to

---

39. Gillespie, *Theological Origins*, 29.
40. Gillespie, *Theological Origins*, 15.
41. Gillespie, *Theological Origins*, 16–17. Gillespie writes concerning the attempt at a naturalistic third way between God and humanity does not solve the antagonism inherited from medieval scholasticism (and I would argue, from Augustine, Origen, and Platonism as well) between the one, simple God and the many, complex humanity. It remains the contradiction at the heart of modernity, "While this new naturalistic beginning helped to ameliorate the conflict, it could not eliminate the antagonism at its heart without eliminating either God or man. However, one cannot abandon God without turning man into a beast, and one cannot abandon man without falling into theological fanaticism."
42. Gillespie, *Theological Origins*, 281.

create great human lives to overcome the chaos, and the way to do that was to emulate the lives of those in Greco-Roman antiquity.[43] Michael Allen Gillespie writes,

> What lies concealed behind these fabulous examples is the idea that individual human beings and their goals matter, that they have an inherent dignity and worth. This assertion was revolutionary and stood in stark opposition to the regnant doctrine of original sin and the fall, which denied that individuals had either an intrinsic value or a capacity for self-perfection. It was this Petrarchian notion of the ontic priority and value of the individual human being that became the guiding light of the humanist project and that made the Renaissance and the modern world possible.[44]

With their cry of *ad fontes* (to the sources!), they desired to leap over the many centuries of church dominance to allow as much of classical Greece and Rome to guide culture, art, learning, and architecture as possible. Moreover, those same Renaissance men sometimes saw the clear superiority of classical culture to that of their own, and therefore began to become suspicious of the roots of their own culture, which were most often the church and her traditions.[45] The humanists, in prioritizing humanity over both God and nature, would value human freedom and rationalism, self-awareness, morality, and tolerance.[46] The answer proposed by humanism to the uncertainty and angst of the terrible God of Ockham was to elevate human life and will to a place of prominence among all beings. It is the classic case of the creation asserting its independence, in hesitant steps, from the creator, and challenging the thousand year reign of monism in the West. At least in the beginning, most humanists operated within the existing church structures and worked for general reforms from within. But, in the end, the humanists rejected the monist world-order imposed by the Augustinian-Thomist synthesis and the struggle for the real integrity of creation had begun. As the majority of their Catholic counterparts had become dichotomist-dualists (in the Ockhamist sense), the humanists remained allied to Rome, if in name only.

The second attempt at answering the problems posed by nominalism was the Reformation, and especially that of Martin Luther. Luther emphasized the ontic priority of God over humanity and nature, and soon came into open conflict with the

---

43. Hannam, *God's Philosophers*, 216, notes that for the humanists, the older the source the better it is. This allowed them to easily discard medieval ideas for older, classical ones.

44. Gillespie, *Theological Origins*, 70. That the humanists still operated in the identity thesis of definitional simplicity is evident in their embrace of the idea that nature is a form of grace (energy), thereby confusing essence and energy. Gillespie, writes on page 85, "This idea is so important because it provides a foundation for the reconciliation of divine and human will. If nature is ordered by God so that humans naturally are attracted to the good, then humans can freely exercise their wills in a manner that is harmonious with the divine will." Humanists believed in the fall and original sin, but restricted its effects to "a darkening of our reason that was not insuperable even before the redemption and that was even more easily transcended in its aftermath."

45. Sparks, *God's Word*, 30.

46. Reventlow, *Authority of the Bible*, 20.

humanist Erasmus over the concept of human free will. Luther believed God had absolute control over everything, and that Erasmian humanism could never succeed because the focus was on humans and not God. Luther's theistic determinism was a direct result of the identity thesis, as Gillespie writes, "This conclusion in his view was the necessary and unavoidable consequence that under the doctrine of divine simplicity God's foreknowledge and will are one and the same."[47] What God wills, he foreknows, and, if I might add, predestines.[48] The debate between Luther and Erasmus brought the quarrel over freedom and necessity present in the original clash between Thomas and Scotus (and even before them, the inherent Plotinian ambiguity lurking inside definitional simplicity) to the late medieval world. The simple God of Western Christianity that has to be either free or compelled has brought the question into creation, and again we see the identity thesis lurking behind the argument for compulsion. This should not come as a surprise by now. The magisterial Reformers were mostly monist, which is why they ultimately broke with the largely-nominalist Catholic Church, as well as with the humanists. The great difference, as is well known, is that the monism of high medieval and Counter-Reformation Rome was filtered through the tradition and the Magisterium, while the monism of the Reformers came through Scripture.[49]

The Reformation quickly spread across northern Europe in such strength that it demanded an answer from Rome, which they provided in the Council of Trent. Among other things, Trent adopted the philosophy of Thomas as official church doctrine.[50] Their polemics toward the Protestants employed Thomistic logic and arguments, forcing the Lutherans and Reformed to keep step, and they too adopted the same scholastic methods as a defense mechanism. The later Protestant scholastics, as they came to be known, were a curious blend of some humanism, some nominalism, and some Thomism. But in all, the ruling Western understanding of divine simplicity, its attendant identity thesis, and a monist outlook on cosmology, remained.[51] Both groups of monists went to war; after all, only one monist system can truly exist. The

---

47. Gillespie, *Theological Origins*, 145.

48. This was a common theme in all the magisterial Reformers, as they all saw every action as the necessary outcome of the will, foreknowledge, and predestination of God. This view is easily traceable to Augustine, who did not always consistently follow the consequences of the doctrine as rigidly as did the Reformers. We will say more about Augustine's determinism in the next chapter.

49. The magisterial Reformers were not thoroughly monist in their orientation, however. As will be discussed at length later, all of them were determinists and therefore cosmological monists in that sense. They were also monist in their understanding of the inspiration of Scripture. However, all of them had elements of dichotomist-dualism in their cosmology or Christology. They all possessed a dichotomist-dualist system of hermeneutics to counteract the monist process of the Magisterium. In short, the Reformers were a mixture, and one that would ultimately prove unstable within the framework of a theology with definitional simplicity as a first principle.

50. See Cessario, *Short History of Thomism*, 74.

51. See the various historical arguments from the Reformed scholastics surveyed by Dolezal, *God without Parts*.

The Recapitulation of Christology and a Look Ahead

Catholics appealed to the infallibility of their tradition to rationalistically ground their arguments. The Protestants appealed to the infallibility of the Bible.[52]

As a result, the late sixteenth and early seventeenth centuries were a time of political and social upheaval. Areas of Europe that remained staunchly Catholic, in Southern Europe, for example, doubled down on political and ecclesial authority to stop the spread of Protestantism. Northern Europe, where Protestantism was strongest, quickly established Lutheran, Reformed, or Anglican state churches to replace the Catholic state church. These state churches, just like their Catholic counterparts, became the establishment in these territories, and usually demanded the same type of loyalty as their forbears. The Roman Catholics claimed God was on their side. Each Protestant sect claimed God was on its side. The monarchs of Europe, divided over religion, fought numerous lengthy and costly wars to determine which sect would ultimately rule, costing the lives of untold thousands. The polemics between Protestants and Catholics, as well as between Protestants and other Protestants, over who was eternally right continued unabated.[53] The verbal, literary, and military assaults lasted for decades, all in the "name of Christ." The competing truth claims and the resultant carnage were too much. How could one objectively know which side was right, and did it even matter? Before the Reformation and the ensuing century of war and polemics, religious knowledge was mediated through the Roman Catholic Church. Now, there were competing mediators, all claiming to be the one and the true.

Such was the situation in the seventeenth century. The theologians behind the Lutheran and Reformed political powers appealed to the concept—rather than the content—of the Bible as the word of God for their foundation—remember that word, "foundation"—of correct dogmatics. From their entrenched positions of "divinely-granted" certainty, they waged war against others professing Jesus who were equally certain of their own convictions, all the while earning for those religious systems the scorn and mistrust of those who were suspicious of their authoritative claims in the face of their actions which did not mirror those of Jesus. The Protestants, who two generations before had been the revolutionaries breaking free from a corrupt system, were now the reactionaries who suppressed dissidents with zeal that would rival any Catholic. The chaos and havoc wreaked by nominalism was multiplied in a Europe torn by conflict.

Meanwhile, a third way began to emerge from not only the nominalistic revolution, but from the wars of religion in Europe as multiple monist religious visions competed for supremacy washed in each other's blood. Francis Bacon had first posited the ontic priority of the third level of being, creation, and the mastery of it that would

---

52. Harrisville and Sundberg, *Bible in Modern Culture*, 23.

53. Who was right was an important question for all combatants. They were all monists, and therefore believed in an ordered world from God on down. Only one of them could be the representatives of the "true" monism. For them, it was worth dying over.

allow civilization to rise above the chaos. The pendulum swings back to creation's cry for independence, as Gillespie writes,

> Bacon thus offers a new and revolutionary answer to the problem posed by nominalism and the nominalist God. He confronts and accepts the nominalist vision of the world and attempts to find a solution to its fundamental problems. He seeks neither a poetic transfiguration of this world nor a new covenant with its God. Instead, he strives to discover the hidden powers by which nature moves in order to gain mastery over it. For Bacon as for Ockham and Petrarch, man is a willing being who seeks to secure himself in the world. In contrast to both Franciscan asceticism and the humanist notion of godlike individuality, however, Bacon imagines man to be a relatively weak and fearful being who can only succeed by consistently working with his fellow human beings over many years to learn nature's laws and turn this knowledge to human use. Bacon's methodology was considerably expanded and improved upon by Galileo and others, and then the philosophy was added to by Descartes and Hobbes.[54]

The next step in the development of modernism is to turn to Descartes for the philosophy that would make this "third way" of nature a reality, but that will have to wait until chapter 11.

Conclusion and Looking Forward

This chapter has served as an interlude in the main thesis of this book, recapitulating the effects the identity thesis of divine simplicity and its resultant confusion of person and nature exerted on the doctrine of Christ in the East and then setting the stage for how it will wreak havoc on corresponding theological *loci* in the West. It has been demonstrated that Augustine embraced the identity thesis of divine simplicity despite the efforts of Athanasius and the Cappadocians to defeat it due to its disastrous corollaries. I would submit that Augustine believed his carefully constructed and nuanced identity thesis was sufficient to avoid the Origenist Problematic and the resultant Nicene Controversy. Perhaps it was as it was written. But what Augustine did not and could not know was that the "abyss of everything specific" that is definitional simplicity has a voracious appetite.[55] To assert divine simplicity in this way leads to a God who cannot be known. If it is a first principle in theology, every predication to this God becomes anthropomorphic. Even adding special revelation to fill in the gaps of understanding fails, as Hinlicky notes, because "this cut-and-paste job does not survive the vacuity of affirming as divine a timeless self-identity—we know not what. It is betrayed by the ferocious, relentless, 'power of the negative,' as we will see, that

---

54. Gillespie, *Theological Origins*, 39.
55. "The abyss of everything specific" is the description of divine simplicity offered by Paul Tillich.

debunks not only the idols of the nations but also the biblical God, and in the process misconstrues what is at stake in the contest between the God of the gospel and the idols of the nations."[56]

To those who followed the nominalist revolution the simple, willful God of the nominalists was the God of the gospel. The Renaissance humanists, Reformers, and moderns all tried to either de-emphasize or radically embrace this God without abandoning the identity thesis in doing so. In my opinion, the Western tradition did not then possess the conceptual tools to see the inherent dangers in the identity thesis. It is no surprise, then, that humanistic, religious, and scientific attempts at reform could not step outside of the controlling paradigm, so to speak, to solve the problem. It is also ironic that William of Ockham had a contemporary (eleven years younger) in Thessaloniki, Greece, Gregory Palamas, who would solidify the Eastern distinction between essence and energies in God, firmly held since the time of the Cappadocians, making the distinction real rather than conceptual. Palamas did possess the conceptual tools that would have offered a real alternative to the problem posed by nominalism, but history did not turn out that way.

The next chapter will survey two distinct approaches to patristic cosmology, those of Maximus and Augustine. The former, based on what we saw from chapter 6, will avoid the pitfalls of definitional simplicity to construct a christologically based cosmology where there are real distinctions among God's being, person, and energy. The latter, based on the discussion in this chapter above, will utilize definitional simplicity in his ordering of the world, and we will begin to see clear evidence of the divergence between East and West theologically.

---

56. Hinlicky, *Divine Simplicity*, xxi.

8

Patristic Cosmology

THE ARGUMENT OF THIS book so far has been that the doctrine of divine simplicity and its attendant identity thesis—what God does is identical with what God is—has been at the root of the christological controversies. We saw in the previous chapter that Augustine and the Western theological heritage that followed him adopted the same definitional simplicity in theology proper as did Origen in the East. In this and the following three chapters, we turn our focus toward models of cosmology. Because of the pervasive nature of the doctrine of divine simplicity and its attendant identity thesis and Plotinian ambiguity in the Western theological tradition, we should not be surprised to find evidence of it being used to interpret the doctrine of cosmology, how the earth comes to be created and sustained by God. While cosmology obviously contains the theological *loci* of creation and providence, it also assumes the doctrine of anthropology and influences how we view soteriology. In other words, what I am here calling cosmology and what has traditionally been dubbed "the economy" go hand in hand.

I seek to show that, just as in the case of Christology, there exists a similar Hexagon of Heresy for cosmology, where there are similarly deficient understandings of creation and providence, which yield deficiencies in both anthropology and soteriology as well. That is to say, there is a cosmological version of each of the six great christological heresies present in the Western world, and I will attempt to show that these cosmological "heresies" arise from the same root as the christological ones—the doctrine of definitional divine simplicity and its two corollaries, the identity thesis and the Plotinian ambiguity.

With the Hexagon of Heresy of Christology, there exists a neat, linear historical progression from Ebionism to "Arianism" to Nestorianism on the one hand and from Docetism to Apollinarianism to Monophysitism on the other. With cosmology, it is much more difficult to construct the argument in a linear, historical fashion. What I attempt to do in this chapter is lay the groundwork for discussion by offering a historical outline of the doctrine of cosmology in both the East and West, terminating in the great patristic spokesmen in each tradition, Maximus and Augustine. It is similar to what I did in chapter 7. I will argue that Augustine, via his doctrine of definitional simplicity, injects into the cosmological tradition of the West the tendencies of the Plotinian ambiguity—both to separate creator and creation and to confuse them. Recall from Chapter 1 that the ancient Greek philosophers had deconstructed their pantheon to arrive at the One/Good/Prime Mover, who was simple by definition over against all the mutability and composition of the material world. As has been discussed, there was the ambiguity in Hellenistic philosophy between the monist cosmology of emanation and the dualist cosmology of opposition. This ambiguity will finally result, when each side of it is carried to its logical conclusion, in one of two ways to view the world—either the world is god, in a materialistic-pantheistic way, or god is the world, in a monist-panentheistic way. These extremes will need to be avoided by subsequent Christian thinkers who adopt the Platonic simplicity to define the divine essence, and most of the time they will be successful. Of course, we will call these two extremes cosmological Ebionism and cosmological Docetism, respectfully, but that awaits us later. Now we shall survey the various Christian cosmologies of the patristic and medieval eras.

Christian Cosmology through the Fourth Century

This section provides a very brief overview of the Christian understanding of cosmology up through the fourth century. The Judeo-Christian tradition has historically affirmed God as the creator of heaven and earth. The New Testament, specifically in the opening verses of John, Colossians, and Hebrews, places Christ (as God) at the center of creation, going so far as to say that all creation is "in, through, and for him" (Col 1:16).[1] It is not my purpose here to discuss any terminological dependence on Greek philosophy concerning "Logos," but the early Christians co-opted the term to describe Christ and his work of mediation, both of creation and reconciliation. For example, Justin Martyr adopts the *logos spermatikos* from the Stoics, and it is the seed implanted by God in all humans.[2] Christopher Kaiser, in his helpful book, *Creational Theology and the History of Physical Science*, writes, "The idea that human reason is an image of the same Logos that is implanted in all the world was a recurring theme in early Christian writings. We find it, for example, in apostolic fathers like Clement of Rome in the late first century AD. It recurred in Alexandrian writers like Origen and pseudo-Silvanus, as well as in Latin writers like Tertullian and Lactantius. In the fourth century, it was articulated by Athanasius and the two Gregories, as well

---

1. For a fuller treatment of creation and reconciliation in Colossians 1, see Gifford, "Three Levels of the Locative."

2. Kaiser, *Creational Theology*, 15.

by Basil."³ Justin understood, contrary to the Platonic tradition with which he was constantly interacting, that pure thought did not teach us anything about creation; instead biblical revelation does.⁴ For Irenaeus, the fact that the Son took on flesh is an affirmation that the created order is good.⁵ Likewise he is also the first Christian thinker to affirm that God created out of nothing.⁶ Not only this, but his doctrine of creation as being accomplished through the Son and Spirit (his famous "two hands") affirms God creates without any need of emanation, as was common in the Platonic cosmologies.⁷ The first two centuries of Christian reflection formed the foundation for subsequent reflection on the doctrine of creation. While it articulated the received tradition well, it utilized pagan thought structures to describe it, which led to danger in the third century.

Origen's cosmology has already been treated in chapter 2 above. Because of his initial commitment to defining the divine nature as simple, intellectual substance, he could not meaningfully differentiate between the generation of the Son and the creation of the world. In Origen, creation became both eternal and necessary—a teaching I, following Joseph Farrell, have dubbed the "Origenist Problematic." As we shall soon discover, every theologian who commits to such a definitional view of divine simplicity will be susceptible to the Origenist Problematic lurking in the background. In addition to his Problematic, Origen believed that the sun, moon, and stars "were endowed with life and intelligence, a view for which he was later condemned according to the minutes of the Second Council of Constantinople."⁸ As has already been mentioned, Origen was so influential that such doctrines did not die quickly or easily.

As a result of his Problematic, Origen held to, as Colin Gunton writes, a number of "problematic" features in his cosmology, including "a tendency to conceive of a two-stage creation, with the intelligible world prior in both intention and time to the material; the concept of a pre-mundane fall, making the material world a place of reformation and education rather than of value simply for itself; and the stress on unity at the expense of plurality as a desirable feature of reality, leading as it does to an eschatology of return rather than of perfection."⁹ Origen's metaphysical system consists of three parts, *stasis* (immobility), *kinesis* (movement), and *genesis*. The genesis of the first chapters of Scripture is not the true beginning of the universe, for it is only an alteration of the eternal creation that is present at the heart of Origen's Problematic.¹⁰ For Origen, the state of rest in the One is the preferred state of being, which

3. Kaiser, *Creational Theology*, 21.
4. Gunton, *Triune Creator*, 62.
5. Gunton, *Triune Creator*, 52.
6. Gunton, *Triune Creator*, 53.
7. Gunton, *Triune Creator*, 54.
8. Kaiser, *Creational Theology*, 29.
9. Gunton, *Triune Creator*, 68–69.
10. Meyendorff, *Christ in Eastern Christian Thought* (1969), 100.

is ruptured in the fall. This sets the eternal creation in motion dialectically opposed against the *stasis* of the One and allows it to take on matter in its *genesis*. Because, due to his definitional simplicity and the attendant identity thesis, the essence of God is confused with creation in Origen's thought, creation never truly stands on its own. Its *telos* is, following the Greeks, a return to the one who made it.

John Meyendorff describes how the patristic doctrine of creation was hammered out in the polemics against Origenism. He helpfully notes that the biblical account of creation is linear, beginning in the very first verse of the Bible with a creative fiat, over against the pagan Greek concept of the eternal cosmos.[11] The Origenist Problematic, as we saw in chapter 3, was first successfully answered by Athanasius, who first declared that creation is an act of the will of God rather than of his being—making that all-important distinction between the essence of God and his energies. The divine nature and the created order were thus two completely different realms of existence.[12] Meyendoff continues that Athanasius refuses

> To reduce created existence to a mere "phenomenon." God's creative act produced a new "created" order, another "essence" distinct from his own; an "essence" worthy of God, deserving of his love and concern, and fundamentally "very good." That is, as will be referenced many times hereafter, it possesses its own internal integrity. God does not create, as in Origen, simply a collection of equal intellects, which find a meaning of existence only in contemplating the essence of God and which are diversified only as a consequence of their fall.[13]

In this way, the pagan Greek concept of the eternal cosmos could not be compatible with a Christian understanding of creation. For the Platonists, the simple One is the maximal good, while diversity is evil. For Origen, the diversity in creation is only due to the primordial fall and its distance from the simple, undifferentiated God. The diversity of creation, then, is inherently in opposition to the one and simple good.[14] According to Gunton, Origen's cosmology compromises the doctrine of creation out of nothing that was so clearly articulated in Irenaeus, and it will remain compromised until at least William of Ockham.[15] There is a danger in Origen's thinking that will tend to allow the divine Son to mediate in salvation, but not in creation. This tendency will become clarified in Augustine as well.

---

11. Meyendorff, *Byzantine Theology*, 129.
12. Meyendorff, *Byzantine Theology*, 130.
13. Meyendorff, *Byzantine Theology*, 130.
14. Meyendorff, *Byzantine Theology*, 132.
15. Gunton, *Triune Creator*, 60. Ultimately, as Meyendorff, *Christ in Eastern Christian Thought* (1969), 99, notes, Origen's Platonic cosmological axioms ultimately proved to be an unsuitable foundation for a truly Christian metaphysics. Ockham becomes the first major Western thinker to break with the axioms of Platonism, though he failed to loose himself from definitional simplicity and its identity thesis and Plotinian ambiguity.

The Hexagon of Heresy

Perhaps the most important contributions to cosmology in the Eastern tradition between the New Testament and time of Maximus are made by Basil of Caesarea. His *Hexameron* is a treatise on the six days of creation. In it, Basil critiques Aristotle's theory that the creator and creation are co-eternal.[16] For Basil, each created thing has its own *logos*, but this *logos* is not its essence.[17] As in his doctrine of God, where the Logos (person) and the divine essence are distinct, so too in creation the *logos* and essence are distinct. In the *Hexameral* tradition of Basil, the first six days are under the immediate creative activity of God. From the seventh day on, creation operates according to its laws established in its creation.[18] Basil believes that motion is inherently a good part of creation, as Meyendorff writes, "The creatures do not simply receive their form and diversity from God; they possess an energy, certainly also God-given, but authentically their own."[19] Basil advocated the relative autonomy of creation in the *Hexameron*, but not a full autonomy—in more contemporary language, he stressed integrity over autonomy. Kaiser summarizes, "Nature, once created and put in motion, evolves in accordance with the laws assigned to it without interruption or diminishment of energy."[20] Basil, against the Platonic tradition, praises the wonder of the diversity of nature, but at the same time declares that there are no degrees of being. That is, all creation is on the same "ontological plane."[21] Gregory of Nazianzus, according to Meyendorff, "speaks of 'images of the world' as thoughts of God. These 'thoughts' do not limit the freedom of a personal God, since they remain distinct from his nature. Only when he creates in time do they become a 'reality.'"[22] The thoughts themselves are an expression of God's will (energies) and not his nature (essence).[23] By the time the Cappadocians had made their contributions to cosmology, the distinction (but without separation!) of the essence and energies of God was fully established.

Maximus and the *Logoi*

Maximus's cosmology, the key to which is the "mystery of Christ,"[24] is based on the received tradition from Athanasius and the Cappadocians, wherein there is a real distinction between God's essence and God's energies. For Maximus, God's thoughts

---

16. Kaiser, *Creational Theology*, 18. See Basil, *Hex.* 1.8; 4.3.
17. Meyendorff, *Byzantine Theology*, 134.
18. Kaiser, *Creational Theology*, 18. See Basil. *Hex.* 5.16; 9.2.
19. Meyendorff, *Byzantine Theology*, 133.
20. Kaiser, *Creational Theology*, 18. See Basil, *Hex.* 5.16; 9.2.
21. Gunton, *Triune Creator*, 70–71.
22. Meyendorff, *Byzantine Theology*, 131. The quote by Gregory is from Gregory of Nazianzus, *Carm. Theol. IV de mundo*, V, 67–68. The "reality" quote is from John of Damascus, *On the Orthodox Faith* 2.2.
23. Meyendorff, *Byzantine Theology*, 131, again references John of Damascus, *On the Orthodox Faith* 1.9.
24. Tollefsen, *Christocentric Cosmology*, 64.

Patristic Cosmology

are "perfect, eternal thoughts of an eternal God."[25] This implies two levels of eternity in God: the eternity of the divine nature, and the eternal "uncreated expressions of divine life, which represent the unlimited potentiality of divine freedom. God creates the world, not 'out of them,' but out of nothing."[26] For Maximus, cosmology is a function of Christology. His commitment to Chalcedon and its four famous "withouts" (two natures in union without confusion, change, division or separation) shapes his views on creation and anthropology, as he utilizes the same rigorous "Chalcedonian logic" in his cosmological model as he does in refuting Monothelitism (as we saw in chapter 6). Lars Thunberg writes, "This implies that the christological combination of inseparable unity and preserved identity is, in Maximus's view, equally characteristic both of the relationship of God to creation and of the different entities of creation in relation to one another."[27] Therefore one of the key elements in Maximus's cosmology is the doctrine of the Logos. In his thought, the one Logos contains the many *logoi* of creation, and the many *logoi* are the one Logos.

Maximus's concept of the *logoi* in his cosmology is borrowed from both Philo and Origen, but like all other Greek philosophical terms, it undergoes "baptism" into a Christian concept.[28] In Origen, the *logoi* exist in their essential unity with the Logos. But, as Meyendorff writes,

> The great difference between Origen and Maximus is that Maximus rejects Origen's view of visible creation as diversified only through the fall. The "goodness" of creation, according to Maximus, resides in creation itself, and not only in its unity with the divine essence. But creation cannot be truly "good" unless its differentiated *logoi*, which pre-existed as "thoughts" or "wills" of God, are fixed in him and preserve communion with the one "super-essential" divine Logos. Creatures, therefore, do not exist only "as *logoi*," or only by the fact that God eternally "knows them"; they exist "by themselves" from the very moment when God put his foreknowledge into action. In his thought, eternally, creatures exist only potentially, while their actual existence occurs in time. This temporal, actual existence of created beings is not autonomous, but centered in the one Logos and is in communion with him. There is a sense, therefore, in which "the one Logos is many *logoi*, and the many are one."[29]

---

25. Maximus the Confessor, *Scholia*, as quoted and referenced in Meyendorff, *Byzantine Theology*, 131 and 137.

26. Meyendorff, *Byzantine Theology*, 131.

27. Thunberg, *Microcosm and Mediator*, 51.

28. The original use of the concept of *logoi* can be traced back to the Stoics. See the brief discussion in Tollefsen, *Christocentric Cosmology*, 26–27. For Philo and the *logoi*, see Tollefsen, *Christocentric Cosmology*, 33–35.

29. Meyendorff, *Byzantine Theology*, 132. The last quote is from Maximus, *Ambigua* 7; Tollefsen, *Christocentric Cosmology*, 91, writes, to Maximus, "the *logoi* do not really seem to be universals in themselves, but are rather principles of immanent universal arrangements."

Joseph Farrell writes, "The *logoi* are primarily principles and agencies by which God created the world, but they are also the one Logos, a point which gives a unique christological perspective to the doctrine."[30] Nikolaos Loudovikos writes, "These divine *logoi* are assumed in the *hypostasis* of the one Logos/Son of God the Father, and he carries them, since he is the one who brings forth the divine will of the Father in the Spirit *ad extra*," that is, "divine wills moving *ad extra*."[31] Thunberg adds, "If we bear in mind that, according to Maximus, the concrete world in which human beings are living is brought into existence in accordance with preexistent *logoi* which are identical with God's purposes for this world, we realize this statement actualizes, first of all, the relationship between the Logos and these *logoi*, and between Christ and creation."[32] The *logoi* are not the created things themselves, which would confuse creation and creator as Origen had done, for Maximus maintains creation out of nothing.[33] It is the existence of each *logos* of creation which allows that creation to participate in God. Each *logos* is also the *telos* of each of God's creatures, in Meyendorff's words, the "'aim' or 'direction' in conformity with that being."[34] Thunberg adds that the Logos and *logoi* cannot be viewed in terms of a simple identification, for the presence of the Logos in the *logoi* is realized incarnationally, while the presence of the *logoi* in the Logos is ideal and is only realized eschatologically.[35] Therefore the *logoi* are identical neither to the divine essence nor to created things; the *logoi* are decisions of God's will—eternal and uncreated.[36] Such a concept of *logoi* allows for the existence of both immanence in and transcendence over the world.[37]

Rather than implying that creation is an autonomous entity, Maximus sees all creation participating in God, since "natural movement itself requires participation in God. This participation flows from the very notion of *logos*, which is always conceived as an action of the divine Logos."[38] Meyendorff continues, "Created existence as such, in all the stages of its movement, requires God's collaboration and participation, although its movement always remains fully its own: such is its nature, which, far from

---

30. Farrell, *Free Choice*, 136. Italics in original.

31. Loudovikos, "Being and Essence," 119.

32. Thunberg, *Microcosm and Mediator*, 76.

33. Thunberg, *Microcosm and Mediator*, 53. Thunberg writes, "Maximus recognizes in fact a basic gulf between created and uncreated nature, which only the creative will of God can overbridge. Thus not only the economy of salvation, instituted in favor of fallen man, but also the primary act of creation is to be seen as an expression of God's loving-kindness. For in creation God places over against himself a world which is utterly distinct and which he yet intends to bring into union with himself without annihilating the difference. On the one hand, God must always be recognized as a sovereign God, but on the other, the biblical evaluation of creation in its multiplicity as essentially good must not be denied." See also Maximus, *Ambigua* 7.

34. Meyendorff, *Christ in Eastern Christian Thought* (1969), 102.

35. Thunberg, *Microcosm and Mediator*, 81.

36. Thunberg, *Microcosm and Mediator*, 81.

37. Tollefsen, *Christocentric Cosmology*, 50.

38. Meyendorff, *Christ in Eastern Christian Thought* (1969), 103.

being opposed to God's 'grace,' presupposes it."[39] There is a *perichoresis* of the one (Logos) and the many (*logoi*) just as there is a *perichoresis* of nature and grace. In sum, Maximus's doctrine of the *logoi* has them playing a dual role, much like the Logos himself. Just as the Logos is the "man Christ Jesus," the *logoi* are the predetermined individual fulfillments of every individual piece of creation. Additionally, just like the "one who came down from heaven," the *logoi* are the uncreated wills and desires of God for creation that are eternal in their origin.[40] The *logoi* serve as the individual tiles in the overall mediatory mosaic of the Logos between the created and the uncreated. The *logoi* are at home in both worlds, just like the Logos in whom they inhere. It is in this way that Maximus's cosmology is expressly and inherently christological.

Maximus then repeats the Irenaean distinction between the image and likeness of God to the four qualities given to humanity: being, ever-being, goodness, and wisdom. The first two are possessed by humans naturally, and therefore are constitutive of the image; the last two are to be willed by humanity so that they may be by participation what God is essentially: good and wise.[41] That is, God gave Adam both being and ever-being, but also gave him the potential to attain goodness and wisdom in moving toward God. Adam's nature was freely oriented toward this end, and all he had to do was follow it, which of course he did not.[42] Such a construct allows for God to have a real relationship with beings created by him out of nothing without identifying or separating the will/energies and the essence.[43] According to Loudovikos, this essence-energies distinction,

> Partly because of its existential character, cannot be clearly translated into logico-metaphysical terms of an autonomous natural theology with its subsequent metaphysics; . . . this happens not only because uncreated essence and uncreated *logoi*/energies co-exist without any ontological, or typical, or virtual separation, but mainly because it is impossible to see *logoi* "around essence" and essence as two or more logical "forms" of divine being, because they are, in this sense, totally and numerically one.[44]

Here is an important point. The existence of an "autonomous natural theology" is the equivalent of a model of God that is not dependent on special revelation. What else

---

39. Meyendorff, *Christ in Eastern Christian Thought* (1969), 103. According to Blowers, *Maximus*, 111, two images are cited in Maximus that portray this reality are the universe as a wheel with Christ at the center and the *logoi* as spokes, and as a web with Christ at the center and everything connected to him via the *logoi*.

40. See Blowers, *Maximus*, 113.

41. Maximus, *Centuries on Charity* 3.25, as quoted in Meyendorff, *Christ in Eastern Christian Thought* (1969), 103.

42. Meyendorff, *Christ in Eastern Christian Thought* (1969), 104–5.

43. Loudovikos, "Being and Essence," 120.

44. Loudovikos, "Being and Essence," 121.

could this be besides the definitionally-simple God and the identity thesis following as a corollary? Farrell continues,

> The *logoi* thus constitute a genuine *plurality* which are distinct and without confusion with each other, but they are also *one Logos* and *preexist* with him. This is no merely metaphysical conception of the *logoi*, however, for it is intimately bound up with the conception of the recapitulation of the creation in Jesus Christ: they are one with the one *Logos* in virtue of the fact that all things have been offered up to the Father in Christ. It is this christological grounding of the *logoi* in the *Logos* which permits St. Maximus to adapt the Chalcedonian formula of distinction without confusion to the context of the *logoi considered in and of themselves*.[45]

Farrell continues, "This is a patent denial of the Plotinian and Origenist models of simplicity. The *logoi* occupy a 'middle' position between God and the created world, a position which itself is infinite, for 'in God' there is 'an infinite distinction and 'middle' between created things and the uncreate."[46] Maximus's doctrine of the *logoi* inhering in the Logos, the mature expression of the patristic mind as traced out above, allows for Christ to be the one true mediator of both creation and redemption, working out the biblical implications of the openings of John, Colossians, and Hebrews from the New Testament.

The *logoi* are "the means of interpreting the doctrine of providence and foreknowledge in a thoroughly Christocentric way."[47] Maximus writes, "It is in reference to these rational principles that it was said that he knew all things before their genesis, since they already existed in him and with him who is himself the truth of all things," and "The many rational principles are one by being providentially attached, led and offered up, to the one rational principle of the many, as to a source which possesses universal sovereignty."[48] The *logoi*, then, "constitute a plurality, a plurality of energies, energies which are uncreated and divine."[49] Farrell writes,

> It is necessary to distinguish, especially in St. Maximus, between the two models of "simplicity", between the two ways in which the term may be understood. The one is a philosophical and definitional understanding of simplicity, where the term actually functions as a great "metaphysical equals sign" which, far from preserving the real distinctions of the divine energies, *formally identifies them*. The other understanding is a "symbolic" one, where the term simplicity functions rather as a symbol of God's absolute and ineffable unity, and therefore as a means or method whereby to insure that the divine essence, along

---

45. Farrell, *Free Choice*, 137. Italics in original.
46. Farrell, *Free Choice*, 137. Quotations are from Maximus the Confessor, *Amb.* 7. See also the summary of Meyendorff, *Byzantine Theology*, 132.
47. Farrell, *Free Choice*, 137.
48. Maximus the Confessor, *Amb.* 7, as cited in Farrell, *Free Choice*, 137.
49. Farrell, *Free Choice*, 140.

Patristic Cosmology

with each of its energies or *logoi*, is wholly enhypostasized within each person without any partition. For St. Maximus, the term simplicity holds precisely this second significance, not only that the energies are inseparably connected to God and to each other, but also that they are in no way confused with God or each other.... The energies are undivided, and therefore all equally divine and equally good because they are inseparably connected to the divine essence and because God is wholly, and without partition, in each. But they are also unconfused, and therefore they are absolutely unique and distinct, and in no way may they be confused or "identified" with either the divine essence or with each other.[50]

In Origen, the original creation is static and unified in the contemplation of God. Consequently, the fall, as a movement away from the good, simple God, defined movement itself and therefore diversity as rebellious and evil.[51] Meyendorff writes,

> For Maximus, and the entire Byzantine theological tradition, the *movement* of creatures is the necessary and natural consequence of their creation by God. God, therefore, in creating the world, placed outside of himself a system of dynamic beings, which are different from him in that they change and move toward him. The *logos* of every creature consists, therefore, in being essentially *active*; there is no "nature" without "energy" or movement.[52]

Against the pagan, Hellenistic tradition, Maximus sees motion as an inherent and good part of creation.

Now we are able to add some substance to the concept of Monoenergism introduced in chapter 6. Meyendorff writes,

> This dynamic concept of created nature constitutes Maximus' main argument against the "Monoenergists" of the seventh century, whose Christology considered Christ's humanity as having lost its genuinely *human* "energy" or will because of its union with divinity. But, for Maximus, created nature would lose its very existence if it were deprived of its proper energy, its proper purpose, and its proper dynamic identity. This proper movement of nature, however, can be fully itself only if it follows its proper goal, which consists in striving for God, entering into communion with him, and thus fulfilling the *logos*, or divine purpose, through which and for which it is created. The true purpose of creation is, therefore, not contemplation of the divine essence (which is inaccessible), but communion in divine energy, transfiguration, and transparency to divine action in the world.[53]

---

50. Farrell, *Free Choice*, 141.
51. Meyendorff, *Byzantine Theology*, 132–33.
52. Meyendorff, *Byzantine Theology*, 133. Italics in original. Theokritoff, "Creator and Creation," 63–77, states that Maximus understands the fall thus: "It is not the shattering of a golden age, but a failure to take creation forward to its appointed goal."
53. Meyendorff, *Byzantine Theology*, 133. Italics in original.

Maximus summarizes, "God is the principle, the center, and the end insofar as he acts without being passive. . . . He is the principle, as creator; he is the center, as providence; and he is the end, as conclusion, for all things come from him, by him, and toward him [Rom 11:36]."[54] Loudovikos adds, "Let us not forget that one of the most important semantic nuances of the term logos in Greek is *relationship*, and so what we ultimately describe through this word is *a reality of love begging for reciprocity*, and thus unavoidably moving on through proposals and gifts asking for response, or what we have already called syn-energy, something that remains true even in the deepest degree of *perichoresis* of creation by God."[55] This would be a fruitful area of research, and likely a necessary component for a unified, Protestant Evangelical cosmology, but we must move on.

With Maximus, we have the completion of the Eastern patristic conception of cosmology. The creation is "in, by, and for" Christ (Col 1:16) because the *logoi* of creation are eternal divine energies inhering in him. In this way, creation, in its very rational principles, is neither a mere extension of God's will nor is it autonomous. It exists really and distinctly from God, but is not separated from him. Creation cannot be confused with God nor can it, due to the mediation of the Logos, be divided from him. Maximus arrives, using his "Chalcedonian logic" from chapter 6, at a very Chalcedonian expression of creation—God and creation exist together, with the one who is both God and assumed creation standing in both worlds, which prevents change, confusion, division, and separation of creation into, with, and from God. In the days before Maximus, however, the West would take a different track. We turn here next.

Augustine and the Seeds of Separation: The *Rationes Seminales*

Here we come again to the fountainhead of Western theology, Augustine of Hippo. We've met him twice before in this work—in chapter 4 concerning Apollinarianism and in chapter 7 concerning his understanding of divine simplicity. Augustine is famous, in his teaching on creation, for affirming strongly the doctrine of creation out of nothing. He denied the preexistence of matter and in this case departed from the beliefs of his pagan opponents. For this, Augustine is to be commended. The strong affirmation of creation out of nothing has helped to preserve a creator-creature distinction in the Western tradition that has been extremely valuable in battling pagan cosmologies. In what is becoming a familiar refrain, for all the good he did, he injected something into the tradition concerning creation that, as we shall see, has had disastrous consequences when the seed he planted grew, bloomed, and itself went to seed. Let us begin.

As has been demonstrated previously, Augustine held to a definitional version of divine simplicity, which defines God's essence as metaphysically simple, and entails

---

54. Maximus the Confessor, *Cap. gnost.* 1.10, as quoted in Meyendorff, *Byzantine Theology*, 134.
55. Loudovikos, "Being and Essence," 123. Italics in original.

Patristic Cosmology

the identity thesis, which is the idea that what God does is identical with who and what God is. That is, there is no real distinction in person, energy, and nature that we see in the Eastern tradition. Though Augustine saw all of God's actions as identical, he often focused on the divine will as a touchstone for the identical essence/energies. For Augustine, if God is omnipotent will, then it is very difficult to conceive of creation in six "days." Rather, it should happen all at once.[56] Like the tradition he inherited, Augustine held to a concept of the *rationes seminales*, or "seminal rational principles" (They are also called "seeds of creation" or "seminal reasons" elsewhere.) that mediate and govern creation. We saw the same kind of concept in both Justin and Gregory of Nyssa, and as we have seen, will be fully worked out two centuries later in Maximus. Augustine, like all the other patristic thinkers, acknowledges the rational principles "being contained in the divine intelligence."[57] Romero D'Souza adds that these *rationes seminales* explain how Eccl 18:1 ("God created all things together") could be reconciled with the six days of Gen 1.[58]

So far, so good. But here is where Augustine, in his typical subtle fashion, injects something truly novel into the tradition, and though he does not tell us exactly why he does so, I believe we can analyze it. Though all the fathers thought that creation "existed" in the mind or will of God in some way, Augustine departs from that which he received by making the seminal rational principles themselves created things. As we have seen, Maximus will eventually teach that the *logoi* are uncreated divine energies that inhere in the Logos, which maintains a christological focus on the mediation of creation. Augustine, though, decides (without his usual written deliberations, as far as I can tell from his corpus) that the seminal rational principles are created things. The *rationes seminales* were all created at once (Gen 1:1), but then grew, as Bonaventure would later say that a rosebud grows into a rose, into the things we see over time, which allows for the six days of Genesis 1.[59] D'Souza writes,

> St. Augustine's way of reconciling this incoherence [between Eccles 18 and Gen 1] was to say that God did indeed create all things together in the beginning, but he did not create them all in the same condition. In the beginning he created everything—all plants, fishes, birds, animals, and human beings themselves—invisibly, latently, potentially, in germ, in their seminal reasons. In this way God created in the beginning all the vegetation of the earth, for example, before it was actually growing on the earth. Later, prodded by God's plan and activity, they unfold on earth as actual at a time appointed by God.

---

56. Gunton, *Triune Creator*, 77. In Augustine, *Gen. imp.*, 3.7 in Teske, *Augustine on Genesis*, he states that the days are accommodation for weaker souls, which is not unique in the Augustinian corpus, as Gunton shows.

57. Augustine, *Div. quaest.* 83.46.2, in Mosher, *Eighty Three Different Questions*, 80, in Gunton, *Triune Creator*, 78. See a similar discussion in Wolfson, *Philosophy*, 282. See also Augustine, *Civ.* 12.26; 11.29.

58. D'Souza, *Christian Cosmology*, 141–42.

59. D'Souza, *Christian Cosmology*, 141–42.

> St. Augustine would thus solve the apparent contradiction between Ecclesiasticus and Genesis by making a distinction. Ecclesiasticus and Genesis are not speaking of the same thing. Ecclesiasticus is referring to germinal or seminal creation, which takes place all at once, whereas Genesis is speaking of actual formal completion, which takes place in the course of history.[60]

The importance of this move cannot be underestimated. Not only does Augustine depart from the received—through Basil and the Cappadocians—tradition, that the six days of creation were immediately divinely superintended, but he believes that the seminal rational principles of creation were themselves created things, stressing the autonomy of creation to an "unprecedented degree."[61] Kaiser writes,

> As a result of Augustine's interpretation, the seminal causes which had been so closely related to the divine world soul in Stoicism and Neoplatonism and to the Wisdom or Word of God in intertestamental Judaism and early Christianity, could now be regarded as distinct from God's (transcendent) essence. Moreover, the beginning of God's rest and of nature's relative autonomy were pushed back from the first Sabbath (Gen. 2:2) to the very first instant of time. This is, therefore, the first clear indication we have of an autonomous nature that was to prevail in the West after the seventeenth century.[62]

He continues, "Augustine was not a deist in the modern sense, however, for he regarded God's eternal will and power as terminating in time. God's eternal decree functioned as a continuously creative activity by virtue of which seminal causes could produce their respective effects. Still, given the fact of that continuous activity, the inevitability and predictability of cause-effect sequences seemed to follow."[63] Again, we see the seeds, no pun intended, of what would later come to fruition in medieval and modern times in the writings of Augustine.

---

60. D'Souza, *Christian Cosmology*, 142–43. Oliver, "Augustine on Creation," adds, "God's providential establishment of creation is via the *rationes seminales*, a concept of Stoic origin that was deployed by the Neoplatonists. These are 'causal reasons' or 'primal formulae' that are brought to actuality through the motion of time. Within creatures, God provides certain seeds of reason that set limits to their development. Put another way, the *rationes seminales* establish the general direction of a creature's motion towards a particular goal or purpose; by means of its *rationes seminales*, an acorn is set in motion towards the oak tree, the chick towards flight, the child towards learning and knowledge, and so on. Because these seeds are a creature's principle and contain in potential form its *telos*, they are also the basis of creation's intelligible motion in time because they establish a beginning and end. The potentialities within creatures are always defined by their orientation towards an actuality that is eternally established in the Word. So the *rationes seminales* are, in an important sense, the basis of creation's history because they establish the direction of creaturely activity and development."

61. Kaiser, *Creational Theology*, 41. As stated in McMullin, "Darwin," 291–316, Gregory of Nyssa believed something similar in his defense of his brother's *Hexameron*, but never made those principles created things.

62. Kaiser, *Creational Theology*, 42–43.

63. Kaiser, *Creational Theology*, 42–43.

While I do not believe that Augustine could foresee the consequences of his decision, I do think that Augustine made a calculated choice by making the seminal rational principles created things. Why would he separate the rational principles from the Logos? My estimation is that he had to do so because of his commitment to a very Origenist understanding of divine simplicity. Origen, due to his definitional simplicity and its attendant identity thesis that we observed in chapter 2, could not meaningfully differentiate creation from the essence of God. Augustine, to his credit, wanted to maintain creation out of nothing and thereby a strong distinction between creator and creation. To make the seminal reasons uncreated would be the equivalent, given his understanding of simplicity, to making the creation God himself, and reproducing the Origenist Problematic in cosmology. He could not do this and maintain his worthy goals, so he chose, I believe, to make the seminal reasons created things.[64] His simplicity, from my perspective, positioned him between a rock and a hard place. Either he had to succumb to the Origenist problematic and change creation to creator and thereby confuse the two, or he had to make the rational principles created things themselves and thereby separate and divide the Logos from his rational principles. It was, anachronistically, either a kind of cosmological Monophysitism or a kind of cosmological Nestorianism (not to mention the underlying Plotinian ambiguity forcing the choice between a monist or a dichotomist-dualist cosmology), and he chose the latter, at least here. The eternal thoughts in the mind of God and the seminal principles exist contiguously, very much akin to the "two subjects" in Nestorianism. For Maximus, the *logoi* stand in both worlds without contradiction. For Augustine and his commitment to divine simplicity, the divine will and the seminal principles cannot be one without repeating the Origenist Problematic. Nestorius himself would be thrilled with Simon Oliver's description of the seminal principles as written here:

> The *rationes seminales* are created expressions of the eternal reasons that lie in the Word or God's Wisdom. So those formal principles of motion are both intrinsic to creatures and also extrinsic in pointing to the eternal ordering reason of God. The source of cosmic motion and, therefore, life itself lies both within and beyond the creature. The creature truly moves itself, yet cannot move itself without the sustaining motion of God's providential Wisdom that is the motionless motion of the divine life.[65]

---

64. One clue lies in Augustine, *Conf.* 12.7, as he writes, "You created heaven and earth but you did not make them of your own substance. If you had done so, they would have been equal to your only-begotten Son." He sees the Origenist Problematic clearly. He understands that the way out of the Problematic is to maintain a strong distinction between creator and creation, and he evidently feels that making the seminal rational principles created is the way forward.

65. Oliver, "Augustine on Creation." This quotation also notes the very same understanding of Kaiser, *Creational Theology*, 41, that the seminal principles simultaneously separated God and creation while ordering creation in a predetermined sequence of events.

While Augustine retains the idea of creation in the mind of God, the principles that guide creation become created things themselves, separated from the mediator of creation, Christ himself. Other mediators will eventually rush to fill the hole—Mary and the saints. There is another, more insidious connection to christological heresy; these rational principles that mediate creation are the first created things, which sounds a lot like Arius's description of the created Logos who mediates creation in his system. Definitional simplicity creates deep-seated unintended contradictions in theological reflection. Augustine was not "Arian" by any means, and though the Nestorian Controversy was just beginning at the time of his death, I am sure he would have sided with Cyril rather than Nestorius. Yet his cosmology, due to his commitment to definitional simplicity, parallels exactly what we saw as the root causes of all four of the sophisticated christological heresies, and this assertion will become apparent over time. In Augustine's cosmology, only God is truly transcendent and only creation is truly immanent. It requires those operating within the confines of his tradition to eventually waffle back and forth between transcendence and immanence.

The Seeds of Confusion: Grace and Predestination

The previous section has addressed how Augustine, committed as he was to definitional simplicity with its attendant identity thesis and Plotinian ambiguity, was forced to conclude that the seminal rational principles in creation were themselves created. This effectively removed the mediation of creation from the divine side of the economy and placed it within creation itself, replicating the dichotomist-dualism of the Plotinian ambiguity. As I argued above, Augustine, given his doctrine of simplicity, could not conclude that the seminal rational principles were uncreated. For him, there was either the simple God or his creation, and to move the seminal principles fully back into God would then entail that creation and creator were not really distinct after all. To avoid a repeat of the Origenist Problematic while keeping what is essentially Origen's definition of the divine essence, he had to make the move that he did. In this section, I will demonstrate the other side of the coin. Even though his move with the rational principles implied otherwise, Augustine never wanted to separate creator and creation. His Christian tradition obliged him to hold that God is active in the world. But, like in the previous section, his commitment to definitional simplicity, with its attendant *ordo theologiae* beginning in essence and its energies, will again force him into dangerous territory. I will argue that his abstract understanding of divine will and omnipotence and human fall and sinfulness leads to a monist cosmological confusion of God and the world in the doctrines of providence and anthropology that will result in a kind of cosmological Monophysitism.[66]

---

66. Much of this section is a condensation and reworking of Gifford, "Augustine."

Because of Augustine's definitionally simple doctrine of God, each of God's energies is identical to the divine nature and to each other. But even Augustine understood that the energies must be treated as at least what would come to be known as conceptually distinct in order to be able to say anything meaningful about God. It is for this reason that Augustine concentrates on God's omnipotent will as his touchstone expression of what God is.[67] For Augustine, the created order is beautiful, and he wants to avoid opposing God and creation as the Neoplatonists had done.[68] The presence of evil in God's good world was both a philosophical and theological problem for him. Possibly the most vexing question in Augustine's mind was "Why evil?"[69] As Kam-Lun Edwin Lee writes, "Augustine is faced with the challenge of explaining the total goodness of the universe despite the presence of evil in it."[70] Augustine believed he had come to a solution to this challenge by stating that the world remains beautiful and in order as long as sin is punished and the sinner is placed where he cannot disrupt the cosmic order.[71] Augustine's instincts are again correct in seeing sin as the real problem to be addressed, rather than creation itself. To remedy the sin problem, God therefore must be omnipotent in the strongest possible sense (unlimited) to be able to always preserve the cosmic beauty of his creation by punishing sin.[72] Augustine writes, "But, however strong the wills either of angels or of men, whether good or evil, whether they will what God wills or will something else, the will of the Omnipotent is always undefeated."[73] Herein is the decisive move that will cause immense problems: the idea that God's will cannot be defeated minimizes the importance of the human as agent.

---

67. Mozley, *Predestination*, 23, states that the two foundations of determinism are the idea that every event must have a cause and that there is a strong sense of divine omnipotence. Bonner, *Freedom and Necessity*, 5, notes that Augustine's doctrine of creation out of nothing is the clearest expression of the strength of his view of omnipotence. Note also that Augustine assumes that what God wills God necessarily brings to pass, thereby identifying will and power, which is just a restatement of the identity thesis.

68. Kaiser, *Creational Theology*, 41, notes that the seminal principles were ordered in creation to bring about exactly what God predetermines.

69. Rist, *Augustine*, 261.

70. Lee, *Augustine, Manichaeism, and the Good*, 67.

71. Lee, *Augustine, Manichaeism, and the Good*, 69.

72. Augustine, *Enchiridion*, 96. Augustine believed in an unlimited omnipotence (which may foreshadow the theology of his disciples Scotus and Ockham), as he writes, "For if it were not a good that evil should exist, its existence would not be permitted by the omnipotent Good, who without doubt can as easily refuse to permit what He does not wish, as bring about what He does wish.... For He is not truly called Almighty if He cannot do whatsoever He pleases, or if the power of His almighty will is hindered by the will of any creature whatsoever."

73. Augustine, *Enchir.* 102. Karfikova, *Grace and Will*, 119, adds that in Augustine, there are two distinct types of causes in the world: those latent in the seminal rational principles, which are possibilities in creation, and those in the will of God, which, because of the "undefeated" will of the omnipotent God, must necessarily occur. Such a division will manifest itself in medieval terminology as the ordinary and absolute power, respectively, of God. Of course, to say an omnipotent will must occur is to identify will and foreordination, which is to restate the identity thesis.

The Hexagon of Heresy

To preserve the beauty of creation, the will of the creature must be overcome by the divine will in a monist fashion. This is a cosmological form of Monothelitism.

The reason the creaturely (human) will must be overcome, according to Augustine, is because it is fallen and incapable of any good action. Though humans were originally created with freedom and goodness, the fall restricted freedom and all but removed the goodness.[74] Once the fall occurred, thus Augustine reasoned, Adam and Eve became guilty (liable for punishment for their actions) and passed their guilt onto their offspring. He writes, "Now all men are a mass of sin, since as the apostle says 'In Adam all die (1 Cor 15:22)' and to Adam the entire race traces the origin of its sin against God. Sinful humanity must pay a debt of punishment to the supreme divine justice."[75] Notice the confusion of person and nature. Sin is personal, because only persons can commit sin. What all humanity possesses is natural. If "all men are a mass of sin,"[76] the logical conclusion is that sin is natural. Augustine does not draw this conclusion, but his followers increasingly will.[77]

Augustine held to doctrines of both original sin and original guilt. Augustine taught that original sin is all of humanity's participation in the sin of Adam. Original guilt is the liability of punishment for that participation, which includes more sinning and eventual death.[78] All humans are, so to speak, born with the default setting of being damned due to the inherited guilt of Adam's sin, so much so that Augustine regards post-fall human nature itself as but a "metaphor."[79] In other words, the

---

74. It is well known in Augustinian teaching that he believed Adam and Eve had the free will not to sin; but once they sinned, they no longer possessed the freedom not to sin (*non posse non peccare*). This implies that humans are not naturally inclined (that is, as part of our "hard wiring" in creation) to cooperate with God. It is just one possible state that can change given the right circumstances. This further separates the mediation of creation away from the one who always cooperates with God for he is God—Jesus Christ.

75. Augustine, *Simpl.* 1.16. In Augustine's divine simplicity, God's justice is God himself.

76. Farrell, *God, History, and Dialectic*, 877, insightfully notes, the mass is an inert, impersonal substance that only can be (irresistibly) steered by God's grace or left alone to its own destruction. In the case of the former, this is nothing more than the merging of the creation into the creator as the nature of the former is changed into that of the latter. This is both soteriological Monophysitism and Monothelitism at work.

77. Farrell, *God, History, and Dialectic*, 872. Farrell rightly notes that Augustine never explicitly says that human nature is evil, for such an endorsement of natural evil would be a position of Manichaeism. Farrell, on page 885, quotes Augustine in explicit denial that sin is natural and that he does not subscribe to the "sinful human nature" that his followers would embrace (Augustine, *Nat. grat.* 34). He would not go that far, but in time Western theology came to embrace the idea that human nature is sinful.

78. It is also well known that these doctrines, formulated in this way, are original to Augustine. He is the first of the Christian fathers in the East or West to teach naturally transmitted personal guilt, which, as stated above, is a profound confusion of person and nature that is a consequence of definitional simplicity. The received teaching on original sin, as summarized by Ogliari, *Gratia et Certamen*, 274, is that the Eastern tradition (notably Chrysostom) saw original sin as a "simple punishment" which was the "loss of incorruption and immortality as well as that of supernatural knowledge and eternal bliss, and the consequent enslavement to the devil."

79. Augustine, *Retract.* 1.10.3, as noted in Ogliari, *Gratia et Certamen*, 285n458.

Patristic Cosmology

fall renders that which was originally good as something less. Augustine's doctrine of original sin frees God from the blame of evil, while his doctrine of original guilt upholds the beauty of the created order in the punishment of sinners. For Augustine, this guilty participation in Adam nullifies any possibility of good within the human will. He writes, "In one way God presents us with the ability to will and in another way he presents us the thing to be willed. As regards the ability to will, he wills it to be his and ours, his in terms of calling, ours in terms of following. But what we may actually will he alone gives, and that is, to be able to act well and to live happily always."[80] To Augustine, anything that is good within humanity must come from God, because humanity is hopelessly trapped in his own wretched sinfulness.[81] Augustine is only able to uphold the good of created human existence in theory; in practice, it is wretched and opposed to God. Therefore, there can be only one unified will and energy in the "good" creation (the Christian), as the divine will overcomes the human will—an anthropological version of Monothelitism. This dichotomy, that only God is good and all humans are (almost) evil—and one can easily see why some of Augustine's contemporaries accused him of Manichaeism—allowed him to give an answer for why some are not saved.[82] Salvation is dependent on the will of God choosing those whom he will save and by grace taking them out of their damned state. This is Augustine's doctrine of predestination.

Early in his controversy with Pelagius, Augustine's doctrine of predestination was expressly christological, that is, he believed that God predested the elect, but did so through the church and sacraments—that is, through Christ.[83] But, as he progressed in his thought, a more a-historical, abstract view of predestination came to the forefront more and more.[84] Farrell writes, "Now that *death* itself is no longer chiefly in view and *moral culpability* is, Augustine cannot see the effect of Christ's human nature and the resurrection of all men in it. In other words, Christology has begun to take second place to a more fundamental consideration: human nature and culpability in the abstract."[85] Farrell proceeds to quote from one of Augustine's last published works, *On the Predestination of the Saints*, "There is no more eminent instance, I say,

---

80. Augustine, *Simpl.* 1.2.10, quoted in Lee, *Augustine, Manichaeism, and the Good*, 84.

81. Ogliari, *Gratia et Certamen*, 158. Karfíková, *Grace and Will*, 119, observes that the "ordinary" course of created events is set over against the grace that breaks through and is imposed from the outside. In my view, the cosmological Nestorianism that describes the fallen creation must be counterbalanced by the imposition of the efficacious, and therefore cosmologically Monophysite, will of God from the outside.

82. See Lee, *Augustine Manichaeism, and the Good*, 61 and 89, as well as Ogliari, *Gratia et Certamen*, 388, esp. n425

83. Farrell, *God, History, and Dialectic*, 858–59.

84. A move to a-historicity is always a dead giveaway that the monist half of the ambiguity is present.

85. Farrell, *God, History, and Dialectic*, 874. Italics in original.

of predestination than the Mediator himself."[86] Commenting upon this product of Augustine's mature thinking, Farrell says,

> Christ's human will is now being defined in exactly the same categories as Adam's fallen will, i.e., in terms of an opposition of the human will to the divine. And as in individual men, God's will overcomes the human will. Christ is thus the most 'illustrative example,' one example among many examples, of a general phenomenon. In other words, predestination is not considered from the standpoint of Christology, but Christology from the standpoint of predestination: essence, attributes, and finally persons, in this case, Christ.[87]

Farrell further notes the importance of Augustine's *ordo theologiae*, placing energies before persons in the order of theological reflection. He quotes Augustine in *On the Proceedings of Pelagius*, where Augustine speaks of the grace Christ received in his human body and soul. He writes, "The effect of the above considerations now begin to take hold: for in His human nature, Christ is the recipient of graces, just as any other man; His human nature is not the *source* of those graces to other men."[88] This quotation has a decidedly Nestorian tinge to it, but what is important to us now is that Christ the divine person has been made subservient to the divine energy of predestination.[89]

There is a deeper problem in Augustine's cosmology. In discussing what we would call today the possibility of God's knowledge of counterfactuals, things that in a different world could have occurred but did not actually occur in our world (say, had the Cleveland Indians won the 2016 World Series instead of the Chicago Cubs), Augustine intimates that there could have been other ways "God" could have provided salvation outside of the incarnation.[90] He writes, "It is not enough so to refute them as to assert that this way, whereby God designed to liberate us through the

---

86. Augustine, *Praed.* 32–33, quoted in Farrell, *God, History, and Dialectic*, 909.

87. Farrell, *God, History, and Dialectic*, 909. It is interesting to note that Augustine is firmly dyothelite, that is, he sees two distinct wills in Christ. The problem, which will not arise for more than 200 years afterward, is that the wills are naturally in opposition to one another. In order for Christ to remain sinless with his natural, opposed human will, there could only be one operative energy in Christ—the divine—and would thus entail an anachronistic charge of Monoenergism in the thought of Augustine.

88. Farrell, *God, History, and Dialectic*, 906, quoting Augustine, *Gest. Pelag.* 32.

89. Formally, it is anachronistic to say that Augustine was Nestorian in any way, because the Nestorian controversy erupted in his last years and was not settled until after his death. It never explicitly touched his life or thought, as far as I know. But I cannot help but think that if Augustine had made such an argument, that is, that grace is given to the human Jesus as it is to other men, that he would have found himself charged with a version of Nestorianism.

90. One should note here the inherent instability, if not downright absurdity, of discussing counterfactuals in a world where "the will of the omnipotent is always undefeated." In a world where God orders all events, the fact that a particular event does not occur is proof that such an event was never the will of God, and since God is utterly simple, it could not have been a possible deliberation in his mind. Later adherents to absolute simplicity, pushing it to its logical conclusions, will deny the possibility of counterfactuals, because predestination and foreknowledge in God are by definition the same thing. That is, God predestines what he foreknows and vice versa.

mediator between God and men, the man Christ Jesus, was both good and befitting the divine dignity, but we must also show that other possible means were not lacking on God's part, to whose power all things are equally subordinate, and yet that there was no other way more fitting, and no other needed for healing our misery."[91] Here is cosmological Nestorianism at its finest. The created order is not directly mediated by Christ, because the seminal rational principles are themselves created. So then the incarnation becomes the best option among potentially several others to redeem fallen creation, rather than the only way. The incarnation becomes only one choice among many, since all organic connection between the Godhead and creation has been severed. As Farrell writes, "Out of many possibilities available to God at the time, one was actualized."[92] In Augustine's *ordo theologiae*, the incarnate God has been completely surpassed by the doctrine of predestination in both the mediation of creation and the mediation of redemption. Therefore, abstract concepts shorn of any personal content—omnipotence, simplicity, and, at last, predestination—now become the engine that drives the train in the created order, replacing the personal mediation of the Divine Son.

We have arrived at the heart of the confusion. With Christ no longer necessarily mediating the economy in either creation or redemption, predestination and election both become personal, rather than natural. That is, the Son's assumption of our humanity is no longer the interpretive key to the predestination of humanity in the resurrection and ascension of Jesus nor to the election of humanity as the adopted children of the Father in the Son. Christ's unique position as the predestined and elected last Adam gets lost as predestination and election get transferred to the "fixed number" of predestined and elected individuals.[93] Election becomes the act whereby God eternally and unconditionally chooses those whom he wants to save out of the mass of sin. Kam-Lun Edwin Lee writes, "Since the more deeply one is bonded to evil, the less one is able to control one's destiny, the belief in the inevitability of personal evil would then imply a view that the determination is made by the God who orders the cosmos. Expressed in the language of predestination, this view means that God has the power to elect from the *massa damnata* those who receive salvation and to leave the rest in damnation."[94] The elect are then dialectically opposed to the rep-

---

91. Augustine, *Trin.* 13.10.13, quoted in Farrell, *God, History, and Dialectic*, 928–29.

92. Augustine, *Trin.* 13.10.13.

93. See for example, Augustine, *Increp.* 12.36; 13.39–42; *Enchir.* 9.28–29; and *Civ.* 14.26. That the number is fixed and unchangeable is a direct corollary of the immutability contained in definitional simplicity. Ogliari, *Gratia et Certamen*, 351–52, notes that Augustine believed the number of the damned is larger than the number of the saved, which calls into question the love of "the omnipotent whose will is never undefeated." Karfíková, *Grace and Will*, 121, writes "Sticking to God [turning and persevering] actually means (as in Augustine's example of light and air) being penetrated by God, by means of which everything men do is done by God in them." This is simply a kind of soteriological Monoenergism, if not outright soteriological Apollinarianism.

94. Lee, *Augustine, Manichaeism, and the Good*, 91.

robate—those whom God did not choose—who are left to their own devices in the "mass of sin" and receive the damnation their inherited guilt yields. How there could be such an unconditional divided mind in the simple God remains the proverbial elephant in the room that is one of the many contradictions in Augustine's system.[95]

A form of providence, then, becomes the meticulous ordering of personal events in the life of the elect that yield the predestined result: the salvation of the unconditionally-elect. In other words, theological determinism—a very strong form of monism—has taken center stage. It involves the sacraments,[96] the gift of faith, the gift of grace, the subjugation of the human will (that is "naturally" opposed to God since it arises from the sinful mass) to the divine, and all events that possibly influence every decision and occurrence. The divine will creates the play, and the created order, under the stern hand of the definitionally simple playwright/director/set manager, follows the script under an "irresistible" grace.

Here is an example showing why providence becomes determinism. If a certain baby is among those whom God has elected for salvation, then God, in his providence, must work out her life details in space-time in order that she be baptized before death. If she were to die without baptism, she *could not* possibly be saved. Therefore, God must determine temporal events in her life to guarantee her physical baptism and therefore seal her as one of the elect. A baby is unable to arrange the events in order to be baptized. Someone must act on her behalf to bring the act of baptism to pass. Because in Augustine's view there is no ability to will or do the good in humanity apart from divine grace, God must arrange the events so that particular baby is baptized and therefore shows her eternal election to salvation. Therefore meticulous determinism, at least in the lives of the elect, is at work to assure their baptism before death.[97] For Augustine, a person is not saved by eternal decree alone—that decree must be worked out in the administration of the sacrament of baptism before death, as well as all causal events leading up to the physical act of baptism itself.[98] Not only is the initial

---

95. This contradiction will remain as Augustine's original ideas are intensified in those of his followers. Ogliari, *Gratia et Certamen*, 409, writes, "It would be difficult to believe that Augustine did not see a contradiction between the notion of a God who is simple on one side, and the notion of a predestinarian 'discriminating' God on the other." That is, if there is nothing in humans that causes the election of God, it must be some sort of division in God himself that is the basis of choice, and it is impossible to uphold any kind of doctrine of divine simplicity, let alone Augustine's definitional one, in such circumstances. See also Karfikova, *Grace and Will*, 339.

96. Augustine believed that no one could be saved without baptism, thus unbaptized infants, due to their inherited guilt, go to hell. Therefore, anyone who is elect must have events ordered in such a way as to receive baptism at some point in her life. See Bonner, *Freedom and Necessity*, 6, as well as Ogliari, *Gratia et Certamen*, 412.

97. Although I am not able to find this explicit logical deduction in Augustine's corpus, that is, that God must determine any and all events in and around the lives of the elect in order to assure their predestination occurs, I think it is an unavoidable corollary to his system of predestination.

98. Yet baptism does not guarantee salvation. There are those who are baptized who lapse back into a life of sin, and presumably in his opinion, damnation. Therefore, while baptism does not guarantee salvation, the absence of baptism guarantees damnation. Baptism, then, is only valid for the

step of faith in baptism subject to the workings of determinism, so is the work of God in keeping the elect in perseverance. Since perseverance is as much the work of God as the guarantee of baptism in the life of the elect, he again must control all events in order to bring about final perseverance. God's engineering of final perseverance of the saints would require the meticulous determining of their lives to bring about his desired effect.

In such a scenario, there is nothing in a person's life that can provide any sort of conclusive evidence that she is saved. No amount of good works, faithfulness, sacraments, or any other temporal event can give any personal assurance of her salvation, because all of those things originate in this created world,[99] while the *real* decision for salvation is made by God in eternity. Creator and creation remain separated even at this crucial epistemological point. For the soteriological monist Augustine, his greatest fear is the creation being able to assert itself in the other half of the Plotinian ambiguity, that is, opposing the One with its own autonomous integrity. Any good work arising from the human could potentially underlie a claim that salvation is somehow merited, and thus the only way to silence all possible and hypothetical claims of human merit is to set human action and "grace" as dialectical opposites. Therefore, there is nothing in the created world that can possibly give any evidence to the eternal—an eerie foreshadowing of Gotthold Lessing.[100] It is for this reason that the work of Christ, the church, the sacraments, and human obedience mean precious little in Augustine's soteriology. Christ does not truly mediate anything in salvation. He has been completely subordinated to the divine will, an inverted *ordo* of energies over persons. In such a scenario, the created order (at least as far as anything tangentially connected to the elect is concerned) becomes nothing more than an extension of the divine will, which, given definitional simplicity and its attendant identity thesis, is the divine essence itself. Such confusion of the divine and created is cosmological Monophysitism, because it is both Monoenergetic and Monothelite.[101] The only "worker" in Augustine's predestination is God, as he is the only director on the set, so to speak, while creation becomes the passive actor following the script. The only will involved is the

---

elect, and means nothing to the non-elect (except perhaps giving him some false sense of security).

99. This precise point is I believe at the heart of the Western angst over epistemological certainty, for the knowledge of the eternal cannot come from the side of creation within the definitional simplicity paradigm. Western theology would remain agnostic over assurance of salvation until the nominalistic revolution, which then only intensified the soteriological-epistemological anxiety.

100. Daane, *Freedom*, 75–76, writes concerning Lessing, who said that Christianity cannot be both eternal and historical. "An eternal truth, he urged, cannot be contingent on a temporal event; a necessary truth cannot depend on an accidental, that is, historical datum. A necessary truth *is*; it is therefore eternal. Christian truth *became*; it is therefore neither eternal, absolute, nor necessary."

101. Augustine, *Enchir.* 27.103, writes, concerning the will of God, "If he wills, then what he wills must necessarily be." Any opposition to the will of God, which is exactly what the human will is according to Augustine, must be overcome and irresistibly changed by the divine will, which is, in christological terminology, both Monoenergism and Monothelitism, the most visible manifestations of true Monophysitism. Here, it occurs on a cosmological, rather than a christological scale.

will of God, since the human will is silent (as it must be, for it is dialectically opposed to the will of God).

Augustine and His Legacy

The two previous sections have examined the points in Augustine's cosmological thought that entail both the separation and the confusion of creator and creation. I have argued that, similar to the christological separation and confusion of the natures in Jesus (Nestorianism and Monophysitism, respectively), such separation and confusion is unavoidable with absolute divine simplicity and its attendant identity thesis as a first principle. I really believe he did his best to not carry his views to their logical conclusions—that is to stop when his Christian sensibilities told him he was going too far. Augustine himself was a faithful catholic, committed to the ancient Christian faith to which he belonged. As Farrell notes, he personally became a victim of the system he created.[102] As his followers carried his thoughts to their logical conclusions and read his numerous ambiguities in light of those conclusions, Augustine became Augustinized. I have tried very hard to separate what he actually said from how he was interpreted, but, in the end, it is those very interpretations that have guided Western theology and civilization for a millennium and a half. The seeds of all Western theology originated in the Bishop of Hippo, whether or not he intended for them to sprout and grow into what they became.

It is unfortunately no accident that every revival of Augustine's thought has led to an intensification of his cosmologically Monophysite views and a drawing out of his teachings to their logical conclusions. The first such revival was the initial reaction to his teachings culminating in the second Synod of Orange in 529. The second revival was Gottschalk of Orbais and his ninth-century study of Augustine that allowed him to deduce the doctrine for which he was condemned: double predestination. The third revival occurred in the fourteenth century with the determinism of Thomas Bradwardine, Gregory of Rimini, and the heretical John Wycliffe. This revival carried over into the Protestant Reformation, which yielded the most extreme cases of Augustinism, the denial of any sort of created cause, which effectively merges God and the world completely. We will pursue these concepts more fully in subsequent chapters.

It is also unfortunate that Augustine, in addition to his simultaneous cosmological Nestorianism and Monophysitism, actually taught varieties of all four of the sophisticated christological heresies and opened the door to the other four cosmological ones. This should come as no surprise given his commitment to definitional simplicity. I argued in chapter 4 that Augustine's Christology is essentially Apollinarian, and that his created rational principles is an Arian way of understanding the mediation of creation. Footnotes in this chapter allude to his christologically Nestorian

---

102. Farrell, *God, History, and Dialectic*, 306.

and Monophysite language, even though applied anachronistically.[103] His cosmological Nestorianism is the foundation for the growing separation between God and the world that will eventually become cosmological Arianism and Ebionism. His cosmological Monophysitism extended beyond the elect to all creation is the foundation of cosmological Apollinarianism, which in turn, carried to the extreme, becomes cosmological Docetism. Just as in Christology, where Origen's definition of simplicity and its attendant confusion of person and nature produces the four refined heresies concerning the natures of Jesus, Augustine's definitional simplicity and its attendant identity thesis and Plotinian ambiguity produces variant cosmologies that upset the christological balance of creator and creation. Just as in Christology, definitional divine simplicity and the attendant identity thesis end in their own contradiction in the realm of cosmology, providence, and anthropology.

The identification of predestination (confusedly used by Augustine as something personal) and foreknowledge plays out in a choice in eternity that divides the mind of God. In this way, simplicity ends up negating itself. It also forces both a dichotomist-dualist, Nestorian separation of God and human creation of some (with the seminal rational principles created, fallen, and fending on its own toward destruction without any divine interaction) and the monist, Monophysite joining of them in the "gracious" imposition of the will do to good on others. That is, we see the replication of the Plotinian ambiguity in how God deals eternally with individual humans—monist with the elect and dichotomist-dualist with the reprobate. In summarizing all of the difficulties required to hold Augustine's thought together, A. C. McGiffert writes, "The curious combination (in Augustine's doctrine of God and man and sin and grace) of mystical piety, Neoplatonic philosophy, Manichean dualism, Christian tradition, strained exegesis, rigorous logic, and glaring inconsistencies born of religious instincts and moral needs, can hardly be matched anywhere else in human thought."[104] While I fully believe that Augustine never intended any of this, his system, once accepted in the West and enshrined as *the* proper interpretation of the faith, was bound to yield its fruit.

Conclusion

This chapter has been an exercise in contrast between the Eastern and Western views of Christian cosmology. Lurking behind it all, even in Western "Christendom," is that so well said by Colin Gunton, "Once again we meet the problem that has followed us from the beginning. If the creation is to be truly creaturely, it requires its own time and space which are given by God but not continuous with his reality. But can this be done without taking God and the world out of relation with one another? . . . There is a great deal of difference in saying that all things were created in God, *simpliciter*, and

---

103. See previous notes 89 and 87, respectively.
104. McGiffert, *West from Tertullian to Erasmus*, 98–99.

The Hexagon of Heresy

that it happened and happens in Christ."[105] The former has been the story of Western Christianity, while the latter has guided the Eastern interpretation. Maximus's *logoi* neither confuse the creator and creation nor separate them, but constitute a perichoretic middle way—a way that allows for true *theosis* and recapitulation. His way is possible because he sees a real distinction between God's essence and energies. The real distinction, for Maximus, in no way violates the "baptized" understanding of divine simplicity, for in the Eastern patristic tradition, God is really three persons, really many energies, and really one essence and cannot be decomposed from such a "complex simplicity."

The West, on the other hand, following Augustine and his re-adoption of definitional simplicity and its attendant identity thesis and Plotinian ambiguity, cannot admit to real distinctions among person, energy, and essence. To both maintain a healthy distinction between creator and creation, and avoid Origen's problematic, the seminal rational principles in Western theology had to be created entities. This at once injected a cosmologically Nestorian separation between creator and creation into Western thought as well as a cosmologically Arian created mediation. Such a move facilitated the Augustinian interpretation of original sin and original guilt, effectively creating a good/evil dichotomy between God and creation/humanity. For salvation to occur, then, God had to supply the good himself, overcoming and conquering the opposed will of the creature, which entailed a kind of cosmological Monophysitism in the lives of those unconditionally elected. The next chapter will look more closely at the growth of both the cosmological Nestorian and Monophysite tendencies in Western theology, as they grow up together in the medieval world, before blooming into the more pronounced cosmologies concurrent with the other four christological heresies. Finally, Colin Gunton makes the important point that an "apparently orthodox" Christology can exist side-by-side with a deficient and pagan-dependent cosmology, but only at the expense of a displacing Jesus from a proper relation to the Father and the Spirit, which results in the typical Western devaluing of the person and work of the Holy Spirit.[106] We will see much more of this phenomenon in subsequent chapters.

---

105. Gunton, *Triune Creator*, 146–47.
106. Gunton, *Triune Creator*, 169–70.

9

Cosmological Nestorianism and Monophysitism

THIS CHAPTER ADDRESSES THE growth and intertwining of the separation and the confusion of God and creation through the medieval period. In the previous chapter, we looked at two doctrines of Augustine that engendered the separation and the confusion, respectively, the doctrine of the created *rationes seminales* and his doctrine of meticulous determinism within the lives of the elect. I called these two doctrines the beginnings of cosmological Nestorianism and cosmological Monophysitism, respectively. The doctrine of the created seminal rational principles separates God and creation by moving the mediation of creation away from Christ to created entities. As was discussed in the previous chapter, the doctrine of definitional simplicity—one of the first principles in Augustinian theology (if not *the* first)—demands the repeat of the Origenist Problematic if creation is not sharply distinguished from the creator. The identity thesis, the first corollary from definitional simplicity, will not allow for the kind of *logoi*-in-the-Logos doctrine of Maximus that will later come to dominate the East. On the other hand, Augustine's doctrine of predestination, built on the inverted *ordo theologiae* and the identification of the attributes of predestination and foreknowledge—both a result of definitional simplicity—confuse the creation and creator by not giving the elect room to possess their own created integrity. In the life of the elect, we see a single energy at work—the divine will—that ensures what is decreed in eternity will be lived out in time.

I want to reiterate my position, stated repeatedly throughout this book, that I do not believe Augustine saw all of the implications of the novelties he introduced. I am convinced that, as a church father, he was doing his best to explain the faith intelligently in his given context. Unfortunately, however, his adoption of definitional divine simplicity and its attendant identity thesis bequeathed to Western theology its inherent contradictions that could not be made to fit the totality of biblical revelation. As the four sophisticated christological heresies—"Arianism," Apollinarianism,

Nestorianism, and Monophysitism—are byproducts of the contradictions intertwined in the concept of definitional simplicity, we will see those same impulses invade nearly all Western cosmologies, because, lurking behind all of them, is the long shadow of Augustine and his commitment to definitional simplicity. In the West, especially from the eighth century onwards, Augustine became the one father through whom the faith was interpreted. Therefore, his two cosmological innovations became standard fare throughout the Latin-speaking West within a few centuries after his death. All who thus followed him, at least up until the fourteenth century, adopted his created rational principles and predestination. In what follows, I will sketch the growth of these doctrines and their widening into new forms as the centuries pass. While it is tempting to try to isolate the doctrines into two parallel tracks, it seems that, to be less confusing, it would be best to discuss developments in chronological order, noting where the cosmological Nestorianism and Monophysitism occur.

Cosmological Development in the West: Augustine to Aquinas

This initial section of the chapter will reconstruct the history of the development of Augustine's teachings on cosmology from his lifetime up until the time of Aquinas. We will survey several important events, including the first controversy over predestination leading up to the second Synod of Orange in 529, the ascent of the Carolingian Franks and their commitment to Augustinianism, the pivotal ninth century where we first meet the logical conclusions of Augustinian cosmology, and then the further widening of the separation between creator and creation as we reach the high Middle Ages. Augustine and his cosmological doctrines were not devoid of controversy, as we shall see even in his lifetime.

The first Christian to seriously object to Augustine's views on cosmology and predestination was the British monk named Pelagius.[1] He saw in Augustine, based on one of Augustine's famous lines from his *Confessions*, "Give what you command, and command what you will,"[2] the signs of pagan Manichaeism and fatalism. In turn, Augustine opposed Pelagius because he incorrectly believed Pelagius's view of human freedom asserted an independence from God.[3] As Gerald Bonner notes, Pelagius, like Augustine, believed all came from God, while simultaneously holding that God gave

---

1. For over a millennium, Pelagius has been considered the arch-heretic of the West, and he was indeed so committed to his emphasis of human freedom that he departed from the received tradition of orthodoxy. Pelagius, too, was committed to the definitional divine simplicity, and he and Augustine stood at opposite poles of its resulting dialectical dilemma. See the discussion in Farrell, *God, History, and Dialectic*, 856–972.

2. Augustine, *Conf.* 10.29.40.

3. See Bonner, *Freedom and Necessity*, 3. Here is the belief that distinction equals opposition takes a central position in his objection to Pelagius, as any assertion of true freedom within monism implies opposition. It is the same reason Augustine was so afraid of "merit" in salvation, something that still plagues even conservative Evangelical Protestantism to this day.

humans the ability to freely act—an idea Augustine could not accept.[4] In other words, Pelagius seemed to be playing both sides of the Plotinian ambiguity. Western theology has been trying to navigate either with Augustine or between him and Pelagius ever since. Commenting on the Pelagian construction for salvation, Donato Ogliari writes,

> The Pelagians were still attached to the Greek cosmological model according to which grace was communicated and concretely experienced within a pedagogical process through which man, the *imago Dei*, was led toward his prototype. In the eyes of the Pelagians this was made possible because the experience of grace was strictly correlated with human freedom and the historic-salvific situations with which it is confronted, particularly the Christ event. These situations are produced by God from the outside, in order to create the possibilities for human freedom to be exercised, while developing and guiding it to its goal: God. Augustine, on the other hand, detached himself from this cosmological model and built up a theological construction where the doctrine of grace goes hand in hand with that of original sin. In this sense, because of the radical changes of perspective he introduced, Augustine can be regarded as an "innovator."[5]

However, it is not Pelagius who represents the strongest attack upon Augustine's doctrine from his own time. That honor would go to the objections of the Massilian monks from Gaul (incorrectly historically dubbed Semi-Pelagians) and their ablest expositor John Cassian.

Cassian wrote his *Conlatio* (*Conference*) 13 as a direct response to Augustine's *On Rebuke and Grace*.[6] Cassian argued that if goodness only comes from grace, then what importance is goodness?[7] Cassian believed it was within human effort to will the good, but it was only by grace to do the good.[8] He saw his position firmly rooted in the Eastern tradition as well as Scripture.[9] Therefore, good will in humans can come from either God's grace or human will. According to Cassian (and the Pelagians, for that matter), sin does not belong to human nature. For him, man was essentially good, but that the goodness in him needed developing, which could only be done through grace. His will is free to seek the good or the bad. Either will or grace could be the initial action. Thus human good deeds are a result of the work of God, either

---

4. Bonner, *Freedom and Necessity*, 67. Given Augustine's separation of creator and creation through the created seminal rational principles and his overcorrection in grace as the confusion of creator and creation, his mistaken understanding of Pelagius is understandable.

5. Ogliari, *Gratia et Certamen*, 264.

6. Ogliari, *Gratia et Certamen*, 133–39. Augustine understands grace as something imposed upon creation by God.

7. Ogliari, *Gratia et Certamen*, 135.

8. Ogliari, *Gratia et Certamen*, 273. The Gallic monks, in line with the Eastern tradition, believed in the special creation of the human soul, which allowed faith and the desire to do good works to be implanted there directly by God.

9. Ogliari, *Gratia et Certamen*, 139.

directly by an act of grace, or indirectly through the natural will, which is part of the human nature he created.[10] In this way, humans can never be separated from God nor do they need special grace to do good things.

We saw in the last chapter that Augustine's view of human will and sinfulness are very different than that of the tradition he received.[11] For him, even faith itself must be a gift of God, since, as Ogliari writes, "Faith can only be said to belong to human nature inasmuch as the possession of it is believed to belong to the believer who has been graced by God's election. Everything must be attributed to God so that man may not be tempted to glorify himself."[12] Augustine can be seen here standing, due to his monist understanding of grace and human action, in opposition to the tradition he received. Augustine believed that we cannot know why God does what he does, but we can be assured that whatever he does is just,[13] since, by definitional simplicity, God *is* justice. The controversy continued for more than a century beyond Augustine's life, until an uneasy settlement was made at the second Synod of Orange in 529. This local synod—not an ecumenical council—attempted to meet both sides in the middle, affirming Augustine's teachings but rejecting their consequences.[14] As John Fesko writes, Western theology has oscillated between Augustine's predestination and the proclamations of Orange. "As the church moved into the Middle Ages, the legacy of Augustine was carried forward by many because of the foundation of the Augustinian Order, and secondly, because many libraries contained two essential sources: the Bible and the church fathers, namely Augustine."[15] This would not settle the dispute, only prolong it until a later date, as Fesko observes, "In a sense, all Orange did was put off to a later time the issue of Augustine's radical monergism. This virtually ensured that as soon as it was possible to study Patristic texts, such as Augustine, the debate would be reopened."[16] Gottschalk was just that student.

The Carolingian Franks embraced Augustinism as the theology of their kingdom, especially his doctrine of the *filioque* (itself another entailment of definitional divine

---

10. Ogliari, *Gratia et Certamen*, 291, 296. Cassian, relying on Scripture (specifically Prov 16:1; Ps 80:11; Zech 1:3; Luke 19:1–10; Acts 10:4; Matt 7:7) believes that sometimes the person can make the first step toward God, while other times (John 6:44, 65, Eph 2:8) God's grace precedes. As is well-established by now, Cassian lies in the received tradition and claims, in Oligari, *Gratia et Certamen*, 292–96, Clement, Origen, Chrysostom, Cappadocians, Hilary of Poitiers, Ambrosiaster, and Jerome as ancestors.

11. Ogliari, *Gratia et Certamen*, 298. Augustine believed that faith must be a gift from God, because if it were from man, it would be meritorious before God, and God would owe man salvation. The soteriological monist in Augustine recoils at any possibility of the creation asserting anything before God.

12. Ogliari, *Gratia et Certamen*, 158–59. Here is the zero-sum game in action.

13. Ogliari, *Gratia et Certamen*, 160.

14. See Kelly, *Early Christian Doctrines*, 371–72.

15. Fesko, *Diversity*, 20.

16. Fesko, *Diversity*, 33.

Cosmological Nestorianism and Monophysitism

simplicity).[17] The Carolingian kings began to widen the gap between the West and East, as their ambitions of ruling the world grew. It was at this time that the second period of emphasis on Augustine's teachings on predestination surfaced in the monk Gottschalk of Orbais. While at Orbais, "he devoted himself to the study of theology and elaborated an extreme doctrine of divine predestination. Basing himself on the teaching of St. Augustine and St. Fulgentius, he seems to have taught a double predestination, according to which not only are the good predestined to blessedness but the wicked also to damnation."[18] According to his chief opponent, Hincmar of Rheims, he also "denied the universal saving will of God as well as human free will."[19] Though he had many supporters, he was condemned and died unreconciled to the church.[20] He is the first person to really take the implications of Augustine's cosmological Monophysitism and stretch it out to what I would call a cosmological Apollinarianism—a denial of human free will of any kind that makes God the ultimate cause for reprobation as well as for salvation.[21] The corollary to double predestination is the doctrine of limited atonement (particular redemption), which is the belief that Christ died only for the elect. Hincmar stated the position of the first nine centuries of Christianity clearly: "Just as there is not, has not been, and will not be any human being whose nature was not assumed in our Lord Jesus Christ, so there is not, has not been, and will not be any human being for whom he has not suffered."[22] The distinction I draw here is this: as long as one, with Augustine, refuses to draw out the logical implications of his doctrine of predestination, he remains cosmologically Monophysite; but as soon as one moves to the clear implications of those teachings, one moves over into the more serious cosmological Apollinarianism—the denial of the full integrity of creation, which we will survey more deeply in the next chapter. If God decides everything and infallibly brings his will to pass in the created order, then all creation is nothing more than matter under the control of the divine mind, which is how Apollinarius described the humanity of Christ. As Frank James writes,

> How then should one categorize Augustine? It depends on how the question is posed. If one asks whether Augustine unequivocally teaches double predestination, the answer must be no, although on occasion he does make statements which, if taken by themselves, would seem to imply such a doctrine. If one asks, whether double predestination is a logical implication or development of Augustine's doctrine, the answer must be in the affirmative. Augustine had

17. See the discussion in Farrell, *God, History, and Dialectic*, 309–28.
18. Cross, "Gottschalk," 575.
19. Cross, "Gottschalk," 575.
20. Cross, "Gottschalk," 575.
21. It must be noted that the first teacher of double predestination was Isidore of Seville, a seventh-century Spaniard. See Fesko, *Diversity*, 22.
22. Cited without direct reference from Hincmar in Farrell, *Free Choice*, 225n63. Farrell is citing Pelikan, *Christian Tradition*, 3:91.

a talent for subtlety—for communicating ideas and beliefs without stating those ideas specifically. If Augustine advocated double predestination it was by implication.[23]

It is precisely this implication that Gottschalk saw clearly—so clearly, in fact, he took it for what Augustine really meant. The world was not ready for anything quite that radical yet.

Gottschalk's contemporary, John Scotus Eriugena, took Augustine's theology in the other direction. He utilized divine simplicity and an emanation-type of cosmology to argue that God and the world were one, which is the first form of Christian pantheism.[24] For Eriugena, the forms, that is, the seminal principles, were the true reality behind the material creation, and they were all one in the mind of God due to divine simplicity and the attendant identity thesis.[25] He divided all reality, all on the same ontological plane, so to speak, into God, the seminal principles, created things, and nothingness.[26] We will recognize this as an exaggerated form of the Origenist Problematic, except, this time, creation and the One himself are indistinguishable, which is the real outcome of definitional simplicity without the clutter of Christian religious impulse getting in the way. Eriugena continues the Augustinian doctrine that the seminal principles are created things that in turn are able to create, or at least bring to fruition, the rest of the created order.[27] These rational principles will become known as universals. For the Western tradition, while they preexist in the mind of God, they are nevertheless a real creation of God that lie behind and give order to the rest of creation. The nominalists, first in the thought of John Roscelin, will challenge the real existence of these created intermediaries, and argue that they do not have real existence, but are real in "name only."[28] Thus centuries later, we will see why Ockham felt it necessary to use his razor to eliminate them, famously citing that one should not needlessly multiply universals.

Peter Damian (d. 1072) stressed the importance of God's absolute power (*potentia absoluta*) to enter into his creation, overcome its integrity, and act as he sees fit. He was struggling against the natural philosophy of his age.[29] Christopher Kaiser writes,

---

23. James, *Vermigli*. 103.

24. D'Souza, *Christian Cosmology*, 52.

25. Interestingly, Moran, "John Scottus Eriugena," recounts that, in his refutation of Gottschalk's double predestination, Eriugena identified theology and philosophy. Gottschalk was, in effect, doing the same thing from the other side.

26. Moran, "John Scottus Eriugena."

27. Moran, "John Scottus Eriugena."

28. D'Souza, *Christian Cosmology*, 55.

29. Kaiser, *Creational Theology*, 52. Kaiser, on page 53, notes that the twelfth century was a real watershed in the history of the relationship in the West between theology and natural science. Though everyone at this point in time adhered to the doctrine of creation of the world out of nothing by God, there began to be a rift between those that Kaiser labels "left wing" that tended to emphasize science in creation and the "right wing" that stressed theology. Just like those who followed Origen in the

> The scholastics (after Anselm and Peter Lombard) began to make a systematic distinction between the regular [also called "ordinary"] power (*potentia ordinata*) of God, reflected in the normal sequences of cause and effect, and his absolute power (*potentia absoluta*) at any time to suspend or alter those sequences—a distinction that was quite useful in the interpretation of Scripture. But, already in the eleventh and twelfth centuries, the normal sequences of nature were viewed as due to a power delegated to nature by God, and the distinction became an opposition that was quite foreign to the sense of Scripture. In place of a relative autonomy of nature based on the efficacy of God's creative word, one then had an impossible choice: either an autonomous world, created by God but virtually independent of his continued presence and power; or else a world so utterly dependent on God's will moment by moment that all rational, scientific investigation became impossible. In effect, we have the beginning of the dissolution of the creationist tradition itself, even though the total demise of the tradition took seven centuries to complete.[30]

Both of the above alternatives are the good and necessary consequences of Augustinian cosmology, rooted in Augustine himself, but embellished with nearly a millennium of further reflection. God's ordinary power became defined as the way the world "normally" works in the created seminal rational principles, while his absolute power lay in his secret predestination that is brought to pass within creation by the will of God alone. Note the presence of the "distinction equals opposition" corollary to definitional divine simplicity.

By the time of Adelard of Bath (writing in the 1120s) and his contemporary William of Conches, God's only act in creation was upsetting the natural order. God and the world, then, are opposed.[31] This opposition entailed an opposition—even a disjunction—within the realm of epistemology, as the natural world became knowable by reason while the supernatural acts of God were to be articulated by the

---

third and early fourth centuries, the left wing emphasized the dichotomist-dualist half of the Plotinian ambiguity while the right wing emphasized the monist. Kaiser is surely right that the twelfth century was not a conflict between religion and science as such, but rather for the first time a noticeable polarization of emphases within the same tradition. We have already seen this same phenomenon at work in Christology.

30. Kaiser, *Creational Theology*, 53–54. Kaiser, on page 55, helpfully notes that Augustine, anachronistically, believed in something similar to the *potentia ordinata*, but that it was a moment-by-moment ordering of events in a deterministic fashion rather than a creation with its own integrity. By this point in time, grace is seen as the best example of absolute power, and nature the standard for ordinary power. Monism will try to hold them together; dichotomist-dualism will attempt to pull them apart.

31. Kaiser, *Creational Theology*, 54–59. What Adelard accomplished was the elimination of the work of God in everyday affairs and, even though he still held the right to exercise his *potentia absoluta*, the chances of him using it were rare. William of Conches would not allow any act of God in the created order once the original creation was set in motion. This became the impetus for defining a miracle as something contrary to the laws of nature (page 57), upon which David Hume would later capitalize.

church and taken on faith. The two realms for William were mutually exclusive.[32] The creator-creature distinction that Augustine wanted to maintain has morphed into a creator-creature opposition, which the accompanying dialectic inherent in definitional simplicity always accomplishes.[33] Kaiser writes,

> The creationist tradition does not entail a gulf between God and the world, or a deanimation or mechanization of nature in the modern sense. Such an emphasis did begin to enter the tradition with Augustine's separation of the seminal causes from God's consubstantial Word and Spirit, but it was not essential to the tradition itself. The idea of the complete autonomy, or even mechanicity, of nature did not enter until the gulf opened by Augustine widened to the point of suggesting a dichotomy between God's ordering of nature and his absolute power, or even between nature itself and God. This did not happen until the eleventh or twelfth century. In our view then, it was not the original biblical and patristic tradition, but a distortion of it, that tended toward determinism, reductionism and atheism that characterizes so much of modern Western thought.[34]

Similarly, in the medieval West (especially in Fulbert of Chartres in the eleventh century), there was a distinction between natural and supernatural healing, following closely the distinction between God's ordinary and absolute power. The Cappadocians saw God's power in both natural and supernatural works, but now the two are opposed, leading to the two professions, clergy (for the supernatural) and medicine (for the natural).[35] Just as Gottschalk took the implications of Augustine's predestination to its logical conclusions, more and more medieval thinkers were taking created mediation to mean that God and the world were becoming further separated. These are the beginnings of what will become, analogously, cosmological Arianism—God is not fully present in the world.

Another point that will be reinforced and clarified in the next two chapters is that, like their christological counterparts, cosmological Arianism and Apollinarianism have something in common. We saw how both denied the presence of a human soul (and therefore a human will) in Jesus. The cosmological versions of Arianism and Apollinarianism will also deny the presence of created integrity, that is, the absence of

---

32. Kaiser, *Creational Theology*, 58. Kaiser writes, "Finally, we should note the dualism that emerges in William of Conches between two spheres of human existence: (1) the moral and spiritual, now relegated to the jurisdiction of the church; and (2) the technological and natural, based on human art and science." As Kaiser states, the moral and ethical part of humanity is relegated to the world of faith (at that time the Roman Catholic Church) and the world of technological skill is relegated to the world of nature.

33. See the discussion in Farrell, *God, History, and Dialectic*, 93–97, on how in a dialectical construction such as definitional divine simplicity, distinction becomes opposition.

34. Kaiser, *Creational Theology*, 59–60. He adds on page 90, that this conflict occurred within the bounds of Augustine's metaphysics.

35. Kaiser, *Creational Theology*, 78.

free will as normally understood, due to either a mechanistic universe determined by the cause-and-effect "laws of nature" that descend from the ordinary power (cosmological Arianism) or the meticulous divine determinism extended to all creation that results from the absolute power (cosmological Apollinarianism). In either case, the creation has no "soul" or will. Everything that occurs is moved from without, either by "natural" or "divine" causation.

The coming of Aristotle into the West in the thirteenth century was the reinforcement, despite its defeat in Christendom, of the pagan idea that creation is eternal.[36] We now turn to the high medieval thinkers who are the foundation for both Roman Catholicism and Protestantism.

The Cosmological Synthesis of Thomas Aquinas

Thomas Aquinas is the most influential theologian of the medieval period. He was able to bring together the received Western, Augustinian interpretation of the faith with the philosophy of Aristotle, creating a synthesis of utmost brilliance. For Aquinas, once a truth was demonstrable by reason, it ceased to be an object of faith. That which was demonstrable by reason became "a preamble to faith."[37] The goal for medieval thinkers was to recast the biblical faith on a firm foundation of a natural theology, which amounted to what could be deduced from the axiom of God defined as simple essence within the observable world. Joseph Farrell writes concerning the natural theology so prized in the medieval era,

> This "natural theology" assumed the divine simplicity at the outset of all its endeavors, and, thus assuming that God's essence was identical to his existence, assumed moreover that all essences and all existences were somehow inextricably linked. And since God was simple essentially, to prove *that* He exists was also to prove that He was good, just, wise, holy, one ends, in this development, with an abstract God-in-general, who could be the God of the Christian Aquinas, or of the Muslim Averroes, or of the Jew Moses Maimonides."[38]

In the Augustinian-monist tradition of definitional simplicity, the one is to be prized over the many, as unity is greater than plurality. Thomas puts God and creation under the same umbrella—being. The dichotomist-dualist half of the Plotinian ambiguity, then, is deemphasized in favor of the monist half. Colin Gunton writes,

> The world appears to be negated in order that God can be affirmed. Thus the temporal is negated in order to provide the route to the (timeless) eternal, the material treated as the route to the immaterial. Far from being the source of transcendental insight, God appears to be derived from a process of negating

---

36. Kaiser, *Creational Theology*, 89.
37. Kaiser, *Creational Theology*, 93.
38. Farrell, *God, History, and Dialectic*, 379.

> the essential characteristics of the world of time and becoming. This judgement is confirmed when we come to see what Aquinas says explicitly about transcendentality. There are for him four transcendentals, so that "the terms "one", "true", and "good" are, like "being", transcendent of the categories and universally applicable—to God as well as to everything else.[39]

Gunton adds that concepts like plurality and beauty (beauty is only possible in a world of comparison, therefore plurality) become inferior to the four transcendentals, and therefore the only real use of plurality and beauty is to serve as a way into participation in the transcendentals.[40] Plurality, that is, the created order, becomes merely something useful to the one; and the analogy of being holds that what God and creation share is being, or existence. It is a way of merging the divine and created orders, for a person can, so to speak, climb the chain of being up to God. Here lies both sides of the Plotinian (and Origenist) ambiguity in full view. Creation is both dependent upon God and stands in opposition to him.

Aquinas continues the separation of creator and creation inherent in his ancient mentor Augustine. For Thomas, the temporal creation of the world was not demonstrable in natural theology, but only in revealed theology.[41] Dangerously lurking behind Thomas's reflections was the distinct possibility of an eternal creation and the Origenist Problematic that the "chain of being" seems to demand.[42] Colin Gunton writes, "Aquinas' theology of creation is symptomatic of the fact that in general in the Middle Ages, the Platonic forms or the Aristotelian and Stoic *rationes* tend to displace Christ as the framework of creation. The effect is to replace something oriented to materiality with something at best ambivalent about it."[43] He continues, "The chief damage to the doctrine of creation, accordingly, comes from the institutionalization of what we have seen to be the Achilles' heel of theology from Origen to Augustine, the positing of a nearly eternal creation intermediate between God and the material world. The effective quiescence of Christology and pneumatology in the structuring of Western theologies of creation leaves a vacuum which non-biblical ontologies rush to fill."[44] The fruit of Augustine's doctrine of created seminal rational principles is becoming more evident. Creation and creator are now separate, and the mediators of creation are now the created universals (formerly known as the rational principles).

---

39. Gunton, *One, Three, and Many*, 139–40. That the world is to be negated so God can be affirmed is the presence of a zero-sum game, and therefore definitional simplicity.

40. Gunton, *One, Three, and Many*, 139–40.

41. Kaiser, *Creational Theology*, 100.

42. Loudovikos, "Being and Essence," 127, writes, "In Aquinas, the ideas of all created things exist in the mind of God, which, due to divine simplicity, are identical to the essence of God." This is the problem Augustine tried to avoid by making the seminal rational principles created things in the first place.

43. Gunton, *Triune Creator*, 102.

44. Gunton, *Triune Creator*, 102. The last sentence in this quote is extremely profound.

Cosmological Nestorianism and Monophysitism

A further problem exists. For the Eastern tradition, the concept of a reciprocal (though not symmetric) relationship between creator and creation was built into the cosmology exemplified by the *logoi*. The Western medieval construct is very different. Nikolaos Loudovikos writes, "For Thomas any relation between God and creatures can only be created, while for Maximus this relationship is decidedly by grace uncreated, through a *perichoresis* of divine and human logos/energy, in a process of reciprocal exchange of gifts."[45] This allows the relationship between God and creation to be real and permanent, for both God and creation.[46] For Aquinas, the relationship between God and creation is only real to the creature; it does not have reality in God, and is present in him only by reason. With Loudovikos, "therefore we can say that this relation of union is something created."[47] Moreover, Loudovikos adds that Aquinas

> insists that any relation between God and the creature really exists only in the creature, but this does not exist really in God. This indeed reminds us of the Plotinian God/One who 'does not desire us, so as to be around us, but we desire it, so that we are around it', according to the precise translation by A. H. Armstrong of *Enn.* VI.9.8. It is clear that, for the Plotinian God, any relationship with the creatures is *not real*, while any relationship of the creatures with God is absolutely *real*.[48]

Without a reciprocally real relation, the West will turn to more external and juridical explanations for relational concepts, because the reality of the relation ends at the outer limits of the human consciousness. Since God is "unaffected" by us, Western theology will resort to more and more ways to externalize, depersonalize and legalize salvific and cosmological concepts.

On the other hand, Aquinas was just as enthusiastic concerning the doctrine of predestination as was Augustine, though he qualified his views with the concept of primary and secondary causes.[49] Thomas's definition of predestination is the "planned sending of rational creatures to the end which is eternal life." Frank James writes,

---

45. Loudovikos, "Being and Essence," 123. He adds that, on pages 123–25, divine and created energies act together without the former swallowing up the latter. See Thomas Aquinas, *Summa Theologica*, III.2.7 and I.28.1, reply to obj. 3 and Thomas Aquinas, *Summa contra Gentiles*, 2.12.3.

46. Loudovikos, "Being and Essence," 125. For more on gifts and permanence, he writes on page 126, "It is impossible to acquire any sort of divine knowledge unless God becomes a 'God-for-the-world' and man becomes 'a-man-of-God,' primarily in the person of Christ. In this case, man contemplates in Christ, by the Spirit, the deep meaning of created things as a circulation of gifts (divine *logoi* which give existence and life and created *logoi* which are given back and thus become sanctified by getting transformed in the energies expressing the divine *logoi*).

47. Loudovikos, "Being and Essence," 128.

48. Loudovikos, "Being and Essence," 142.

49. Thuesen, *Predestination*, 132, notes that in Aquinas, "consideration of God's normal exercise of providence through second causes led to a replacement of the biblical image of God as cosmic legislator by the idea of God as First Mover." This further led to the separation of God and creation since God's activity was reduced to a cause exercised from without creation. This had already been set up by the aforementioned opposition of the absolute and ordinary power of God from a century before.

"Undoubtedly this definition reflects Thomas' indebtedness to Aristotle. God is the first cause, who moves all secondary causes to a predetermined end. In this case, the end is eternal life."[50] Colin Gunton demonstrates that Aquinas's cosmology has a strong component of divine omnicausality, as he highlights two problems that "threaten to undermine the distinct reality of the creature." He continues, "First is the denial that God acts to achieve a purpose in creating—'he intends only to communicate his own completeness'; and second is the aforementioned denial that creation puts a reality into a creature except as a relation ('[Creation] in God is not a real relation, but only conceptual'). Both of these detract from the creature's value as creature, for they tie the creature too closely to God, and so fail to give it space to be."[51] He summarizes, "It is not that Aquinas does nothing to ensure the reality of the creature; it is rather that the *contingence* of the creature on God (its dependence) is given more adequate weighting than its *contingency*: its freedom to be itself, 'The whole of what is genuinely real and true virtually exists in God though not in creation.'"[52] Again, in his system, God and creation are confused, especially when considering the largely impersonal Aristotelian causes with which Aquinas operates. Aquinas does the very best he can to hold together the omnipotence of God and the freedom of the creature. But even though the creature is free, that freedom is under the control of the predestining providence of God, so that secondary causation is God's means to bring what is predestined to pass. In the end, the creature does not have any true integrity. In this way, Thomas exemplifies how early to high medieval theology is thoroughly monist in orientation.

Christopher Kaiser posits three effects of the scholastic synthesis of faith and reason. First is the order of proceeding from natural revelation to special. As has been stated elsewhere, the natural theology served as a foundation for revealed theology. Second, natural theology moved inductively from observation to first principles while revealed theology moved deductively from first principles. Third is the subdivision of theological studies into *loci*, and the evolution of the specialist.[53] Though I am unable to prove it, I would suspect the epistemological angst that is part of the heritage of Augustine—situated in a world where at least the lives of the elect are preordained by God—where one cannot truly know that one is saved is what lies behind the grounding of the revealed theology of the economy (especially of salvation) in an independent natural theology. It works something like this: man reasons his way to the One, then

---

50. James, *Vermigli*, 118. James notes on page 120 that Thomas utilized human merit in the chain of causation as well, something to which the Reformers would object.

51. Gunton, "End of Causality?," 67–68. Quotations are from Thomas, *Summa Theologica*, I.44.4 and I.45.3 ad 1, respectively.

52. Gunton, "End of Causality?," 67–68. Quotation is from Thomas, *Summa Theologica*, I.19.6. Gunton, in n13, states "Much difference would be made saying 'really exists in the Son,'" rather than "really exists in God." Italics in original. Torrance, *Theological Science*, 62n1, states that medieval thinkers could not fully grasp the concept of contingency, because it could not be expressed logically in the system of causation.

53. Kaiser, *Creational Theology*, 95–97.

identifies the One with the God and Father of our Lord Jesus Christ, which in turn gives some foundation to Christianity's claims of salvation and knowledge of God. That is, believers seeking assurance, firmly situated in the realm of the many, utilize what is observable about the many to reason to the One. The key step is to identify the One and the Father. Then, the faith once delivered from the Father through Christ and the church has a foundation that is circularly applicable to all without the aid of the Spirit or sacrament. Paradoxically, the monist world yields a dualist knowledge of God that exists apart from Christ, since it is the universals who mediate the creation that leads believers to the one. In this paradigm, Jesus's words in John 14:6 are violated, for it is not Christ who reveals the Father, but a distinctly non-christological creation! The process of natural induction to revealed deduction forms a part of the great Thomistic synthesis, but it was not to last long.

Cosmology in the Later Middle Ages: Duns Scotus and Ockham

In the generation after Aquinas, John Duns Scotus became the leading voice of medieval philosophy and theology. Scotus, in attempting to emphasize the will of God over against the rationality of God, asserted that God is the creator both of things and their forms.[54] Scotus also affirmed the univocity of being rather than the analogy of being. This meant, like Basil had taught a thousand years previous, that all creation was on the same "ontological plane" rather than holding a mediating position on a continuum between mind and matter.[55] Gunton summarizes, "Much Western theology has worked with a highly abstract theology of the second person of the Trinity, with the result that the New Testament linking of Jesus Christ and creation ceases to be determinative for the theology of creation."[56] Scotus believed, in disagreement with Aquinas, that the incarnation would have occurred even if the fall had not. Gunton writes, "One of the reasons Aquinas gives for denying the speculation that the incarnation would have happened even if there had been no sin is that creation is naturally ordered to God. Because he had Aristotle, Aquinas did not need a christological mediation of the doctrine of creation. Scotus' opposing view that Christ is definitive for the relation of God to the whole world at least opens up the possibility of a return to a christological mediation of creation."[57] Unfortunately, this was not fully accomplished, as mediation for creation was about to disappear, at least for a while, from the medieval Western tradition.

---

54. Gunton, *Triune Creator*, 118–19. Gunton, on page 169, claims that the one person in the medieval West who gave creation its due in Christ (that is, did not treat creation as a ladder to ascend then discard at the summit) is Francis of Assisi. Both John Duns Scotus and William of Ockham were Franciscans.

55. Gunton, *Triune Creator*, 119–20.

56. Gunton, *Triune Creator*, 121.

57. Gunton, *Triune Creator*, 121.

The Hexagon of Heresy

It took almost nine hundred years, but the seeds of the autonomy of creation planted by Augustine bloomed in William of Ockham. It was the nominalist revolution of Ockham, in which the underlying rationality of creation was transferred from universals or seminal rational principles "operating *above* material being" to "contingencies consisting in *patterning* within it,"[58] that shattered the medieval synthesis of creator and creation—that delicate balance where the many served as a ladder to the one, as the ancient cosmological Nestorianism and Monophysitism were tied together. In other words, absent the real existence of these universals—the seminal rational principles—one must look for a mediating principle within the created things themselves. Moreover, if the mediation of creation is itself created, as had been the claim of Western Christianity for almost a thousand years, then why should there really exist a created, super-material family of "universals" to mediate a creation that seems, at least as far as the nominalists observed, to be so irrational and chaotic? That is, if God is not only radically volitional as we saw in chapter 7, but also a-relational as we saw above in Thomas, then no mediator of creation is necessary.[59] Thus the universals are themselves human constructs that help us make better sense of the chaotic and irrational world in our own mental images. Ockham's razor, then, successfully eliminates the "middle man" from creation, making it directly dependent on the simple, volitional, and a-relational God, and not some created universals that act as real ordering agents for the creation.

We see the shift from Aquinas to Ockham as the shift from cause to will. This shift, it must be remembered, is only "conceptual," for both Aquinas and Ockham held tightly to definitional simplicity and its attendant identity thesis. Reason and will were, after all, the same thing.[60] In Aquinas, given the participation of both God and creation in "being," God could properly be seen as the first cause. The chain of causation, like the chain of being, was rational. In Ockham, "Will has come to predominate over cause, so that causality's tendency to suggest logical links between God and the world is replaced by one suggesting freely willed personal creation."[61] Ockham continues to use the language of causality when describing the act of arbitrary divine will, which will result in a kind of omnicausality, "whose final outcome is an inadequate conception of creaturely reality."[62] The other side of omnicausality is the separation of God and the world, which is another of the entailments of Ockham's philosophy. Moreover, the creation took on the persona of its "creator." As a result of Ockham's

---

58. Gunton, *Triune Creator*, 134. Italics in original.

59. Gunton, *One, Three, and Many*, 57.

60. Duby, *Divine Simplicity*, 16, notes that for Ockham, his nominalism forced him to admit that there existed only one divine perfection, which is an extreme view of the identity thesis. The differentiation into "divine perfections" is only due to our own differentiation.

61. Gunton, "End of Causality?," 69. In n17, Gunton notes that Ockham (*Opera Theologica* 4:663) cannot distinguish between the divine essence and the divine will. It is definitional simplicity with its attendant identity thesis—again!

62. Gunton, "End of Causality?," 70.

Cosmological Nestorianism and Monophysitism

arbitrary God, the human will also became arbitrary. Gunton writes, "Thus Ockham represents a paradox. By cutting the claims of reason down to size, Ockham opened the way not—or not chiefly—for a renewed theology of creation, but for the rationalist reductionism that was to shape the development of modernity."[63] Nominalism, as we saw in chapter 7, paved the way for the three answers to its dilemma—humanism, Reformation, and modernity. Now we can see why this is the case. The universals were the only vestige of God in creation (as they had a counterpart in the divine mind), although they were themselves created. Without the real existence of universals, God is no longer necessary for the ordering and coherence of the world. If God's presence in the world becomes redundant, or, as what will happen later in modernity, is rejected, then "the focus of the unity of things becomes the unifying rational mind."[64] Thus the humanist and modernist turns emerge as replacement cosmologies for the medieval synthesis. They are ultimately unsatisfying from a Christian perspective, because humans become individuals separated from God, bearing the image of God without the mediation of the Image of God.

Pausing for a moment, we must see how far we have come from a patristic understanding of cosmology. The Eastern tradition—beginning in Irenaeus and continuing through Athanasius, the Cappadocians, and reaching a culmination in Maximus—held to the christological mediation of creation and providence. The *logoi* of Maximus, located "in" the Logos, guaranteed that Jesus is the mediator of creation, and therefore its recapitulator, forming an inextricable link between creation and redemption. Augustine's move, in opposition to the Eastern tradition, to make the mediators of creation created things themselves guaranteed a cosmologically Arian overtone that we have and will continue to see repeated throughout Western theology. Nine centuries of construction upon this foundation yielded an unstable structure, one which William of Ockham demolished with his razor and nominalistic revolution, while never damaging the foundation itself—simplicity, identity, and separation between creator and creature. As we have seen, Augustine's decision was all but forced upon him due to his commitment to definitional simplicity. Two implications follow.

First, the Western understanding of the image of God in humanity is exclusively substantive and immaterial. In Platonic forms of dualism, which is the true root of Western definitional simplicity, the material is less real than the immaterial. The Western Christian tradition developed the concept of the image of God as either the possession of something (a rational soul) or the ability to relate to God. The Western picture of the image did not include relating with one another.[65] The God who is one and simple requires an image that is similarly devoid of real relationality or plurality. Second, there is no real doctrine of created otherness. In the Western tradition, the relationship of the person to God is stressed over the relationship of the person

---

63. Gunton, *Triune Creator*, 125.
64. Gunton, *One, Three, and Many*, 28.
65. Gunton, *One, Three, and Many*, 64–65.

The Hexagon of Heresy

to creation.[66] The doctrine of definitional simplicity is unable to provide a robust trinitarian theology of distinct persons in communion, so Western theology tends to emphasize the vertical half of the greatest commandment ("Love the Lord your God") above the horizontal ("Love your neighbor as yourself"). The interweaving of separation and confusion between creator and creation yields a theology where the one is stressed over the many, due to created mediation and divine determinism.[67]

Now, with the coming of nominalism, all creation is immediate, not geared toward a *telos*, and all on the same rational plane. This will not do for the human mind seeking explanation, so the early modern thinkers were forced to see the rationality of creation as something within the creation itself, since, by the time of Kant, God the Logos has been completely evicted from the Western mind as the mediator of creation. Gunton writes,

> The weakness of Ockhamist theology is that it tends to move . . . from what God can do to what he has done, rather than the other way round. The tendency of all theology of creation after Augustine is to move from the abstract to the concrete: from abstract omnipotence or absolute power to the economy of creation and redemption. The deficiencies of the theologies we have traced are shown in part by a concentration on the concept of causality at the expense of a more personally conceived relation between God and the world. Instead of action mediated through Jesus Christ we are presented with abstract considerations which effectively bypass the second and third persons of the Trinity in favor of some immanent continuity between God and the semi-divine ideas, and so between the mind and God. A similar problem returns in the nineteenth century with Schleiermacher, whose conception of the absolute dependence of the world on God, by being conceived for the most part independently of the eternal, let alone the incarnate, Son—in whom that theologian appears not to have believed—is always liable to collapse into pantheism.[68]

The first sentence of the above quote shows the faulty *ordo theologiae* at work. Personal action is only the result of potential power lying in the divine nature. Nature precedes energy and person here, and it has disastrous consequences. Gunton asks, "Is impersonal matter or a personal deity the source of our personal knowledge? It is a repetition at another level of our recurring question: does the world create itself, or is it the product of personal agency?"[69] For Ockham and his successors—the humanists, Reformers, and moderns—creation is unmediated (though the Reformers tried

---

66. Gunton, *One, Three, and Many*, 52n16.

67. The only way to make the concept of "person" work within Augustine's definitionally simple construction of the Trinity is to make persons relations of the essence to itself. If the eternal divine persons are merely relations of the divine essence to itself, the whole concept of a "created other" among humans will likewise suffer. We see it in contemporary Christology where Jesus is said to have assumed "a" human nature rather than human nature itself.

68. Gunton, *Triune Creator*, 147.

69. Gunton, *Triune Creator*, 136.

to correct this, unsuccessfully, in my opinion) and therefore all connection with God, at least as far as we can observe and therefore live, is severed. With created universals, at least there is a superficial connection to the mind of God, though the Thomistic model is far inferior to Maximus's *logoi* in terms of its explanatory power to confirm the biblical account of Christ as mediator of creation. Gunton continues, "Accordingly, some focus of personal mediation there must be if pantheism—too direct a relation between creator and creation—or deism—the lack of real relation—are to be avoided. If some account is to be given of the knowability of the world and the human capacity to know which gives due weight to each, a concept of mediation is essential."[70] Samuel Taylor Coleridge concluded that the only two alternatives to cosmology were a trinitarian theism or an identification of God and the world,[71] or, as we may conclude from what we have been doing, Athanasius or Origen.

The Precursor to Reformation in Cosmology

During the life of William of Ockham, amidst the chaos of European life in the fourteenth century, a third revival of Augustinian predestination arose. It is interesting that the two broad revivals of Augustinian predestination (Gottschalk's revival was a one-man show) occurred in the two most tumultuous eras of pre-Reformation Western history—the fall of Rome (fifth–sixth centuries), and the chaotic fourteenth century. Much the same was the case in sixteenth-century Geneva.[72] This revival of the doctrine of predestination was more widespread. It included those who rejected nominalism (Thomas Bradwardine) and those who embraced it (Gregory of Rimini and John Wycliffe). This fourteenth-century revival was different, however. Both Gregory and Bradwardine did something Augustine, Aquinas, and the rest of the orthodox medieval tradition refused to do—they embraced double predestination. We will speak more of them and their heirs in the next chapter.

The two medieval additions to the creationist tradition received through Augustine from Basil and the East include "the quasi-spatial distancing of God's normal activity under the impact of Aristotelian cosmology in the thirteenth century and the

---

70. Gunton, *Triune Creator*, 136.

71. Gunton, *Triune Creator*, 137. See Gunton's discussion on pages 137–38 of Coleridge, "Promethius," 4:353–55.

72. Thuesen, *Predestination*, 29–30, argues that predestination held an important pastoral meaning for Calvin. Calvin's Geneva was a city made up of a large number of exiles, Calvin among them. The doctrine served as a means of "consolation and survival" in the midst of turbulent times in Geneva much the same way it did for Augustine as the western Roman Empire was crumbling during the Pelagian controversy. He writes, "Predestination and the broader doctrine of providence therefore served the same purpose of convincing a beleaguered community of Christians that God was firmly in control of their destinies. 'We have no other place of refuge than his providence,' Calvin wrote. Commenting on this, the late Reformation historian Heiko Oberman argued that outside of the context of persecuted refugees, 'Calvin's doctrine of election is not only abhorrent but also ungodly. But within this horizon of experience it is a precious experiential asset.'" See Oberman, *Two Reformations*, 165.

emergence of the idea of the clockwork mechanism along with the extensive production of weight-driven clocks in the fourteenth century."[73] Kaiser continues, "From the ancient Near Eastern ideal of kingship to the Neoplatonic and Augustinian concept of transcendent Being, to the Aristotelian First Mover, to the late medieval Clockmaker, the idea of God's normal activity became gradually less immediate to the events of the world, leaving the relatively autonomous cycles of nature to take on the appearance of a completely autonomous mechanism."[74] These events, analogous to the predestination revival of Bradwardine and Gregory, would form a foundation for the humanists and moderns to move toward the complete separation of God and the world, until at last they were fused and God was eliminated. Likewise, more will be devoted to them in chapter 11.

The Reformers believed the created world to be intelligible, as far as human faculties would allow, due to their belief that God created an orderly world and humans in his image.[75] That is, they did not fully subscribe to Ockham's cosmological chaos, but neither did they attempt to emphasize the importance of the mediation of Christ in creation at the level they stressed his mediation in salvation. In this, the Reformers, perhaps unwittingly, maintained the division and separation between Christ and creation while employing the other side of Augustine's cosmological coin, the deterministic understanding of Christ mediating salvation to the elect. Their lack of emphasis on the creation half of the doctrine of the recapitulation of all things in Christ allowed the separation between Christ and creation in general to widen into the opposition between the two we see in much of conservative Evangelicalism today. Christopher Kaiser adds, "In opposition to supporters of papal authority, the Reformers emphasized the divine ordination of Christian laity in secular matters like civil government and the mechanical arts—this was one of the motivations that lay behind their stress on the secular implications of the doctrine of creation."[76] This particular emphasis placed them in the strain of the creation tradition that sought the autonomy of creation rather than its dependence upon God. The Reformers, like the great creationist tradition before them, held to the relative autonomy of creation—that is, the integrity creation possesses. This was a step in the right direction, but without a strong doctrine of recapitulation in the genesis of the Protestant movement, the tide of cosmological Nestorianism could not be turned back toward a truly Christ-mediated creation. One final point of interest, Roman Catholics saw divine revelation as part of God's absolute power, because it could always grow and change. The Protestants, with their concept

---

73. Kaiser, *Creational Theology*, 109.

74. Kaiser, *Creational Theology*, 109.

75. Kaiser, *Creational Theology*, 163.

76. Kaiser, *Creational Theology*, 164. Kaiser describes how the Reformers were actually situated in the left wing of the creationist tradition, that is, the one that emphasized the relative autonomy of creation. This will be discussed further in the next chapter.

of *sola scriptura*, saw revelation as ordinary power.[77] The Protestant foundation for both miracles and personal communion with God as extraordinary was hereby laid, which was a departure from both Orthodoxy and Roman Catholicism.

Effects on Providence, Anthropology, Soteriology, and Life

The effects of the twin maladies of cosmological Nestorianism and Monophysitism on other *loci* in theology are immense. Much of the effects on the doctrines of providence and anthropology in general have already been discussed. I want to specifically outline how cosmological Nestorianism and Monophysitism have specific soteriological and ecclesiological components. Soteriologically, the separation between God and creation is most acutely felt in the saving union between the believer and Christ. Ecclesiologically (not to mention socially or politically), that same separation is most clearly seen in the general ordering of the medieval world where the church effectively becomes the mediator of God to the world, but in a way that does not give "life more abundantly" to her members. On the other hand, soteriological Monophysitism, or, more precisely, soteriological Monoenergism, most clearly identified in the doctrine of monergism, presents its own christological difficulties. We will highlight each of them presently.

I have written on the saving union of the believer and Christ elsewhere, even coining the phrase, to the best of my knowledge, "soteriological Nestorianism."[78] I highlight several dangers that the distinction between creator and creature, in the case of soteriology Jesus and the believer, is being pulled into a separation. One of those dangers is the tendency to overly objectify personal and relational concepts. Doctrines such as justification and atonement tend to become legalistic and impersonal in Western theology. Anselm, the great architect of the objectified atonement, states in the preface of his classic *Cur Deus Homo*, that it is possible to understand both salvation and the *telos* of humanity completely apart from Christ![79]

It is easy to see why this is such a Western problem, since, as we saw above in Thomas, the relation between God and creatures is only real on the side of the creature, which takes us back, again, to definitional simplicity. If God is incapable of real relations with his creation, then all that is left is the impersonal and the a-relational. Removing Christ from the mediation of creation (and salvation too, as the moments

---

77. Kaiser, *Creational Theology*, 176. Additionally, the Roman Catholics saw salvation as a function of God's ordinary power, since the world was already set up to move toward God's pre-determined end via second causes as he is the first mover. On the other hand, salvation for the Reformers was *sola gratia* and brought about as a means of God's exercise of absolute power. It is the distinction as opposition between absolute and ordinary power that forms backdrop to the Reformation *solas*. The later Reformed absolute (hidden) and revealed wills becomes a reinterpretation of absolute and ordinary power.

78. Gifford, *Perichoretic Salvation*, 168.

79. Anselm, *Cur Deus Homo?*, preface.

of the lives of the elect are predetermined from all eternity with no real grounding in the Christ event) in addition to the preexisting lack of relation from the divine side means that the personal and relational content of the great Christian doctrines can be easily lost. Metaphors of bookkeeping or (Western) courtrooms with the statue of the blind lady holding the scales outside replace the covenantal and familial biblical world where these doctrines were first preached. The Western God, for whom the personal is subordinated to the natural and energetic in the *ordo theologiae* of Augustine and his children, is shorn of meaningful personal relations with his creation, so the legalistic and impersonal gloss on personal doctrines come to predominate, and the history of Western theology has proven this to be the case. Paul Hinlicky writes, when this simple God comes into contact with creatures, "God's relation to this world becomes something purely 'accidental' to God." In this way, God stays "above the fray" so that creatures can only imitate him. Jesus shows people "'what God is like' so that they can save themselves from their sins. And the total critique on a world captive to structures of malice and injustice that is the cross of the Son of God goes by the wayside. Jesus becomes the Golden Calf of Christendom."[80] Quite an indictment indeed!

As an aside, it seems to me that this would present a thorny problem for Thomas's Christology. For in such a scenario, how can there be a real relation in the created human nature of Christ toward the divine person who assumes it, but not a real relation from the Son toward his own humanity? In my view, this would entail either a separation between the enhypostasized humanity and the divine person resulting in a kind of Nestorianism where the humanity "stands alone" experiencing no real relation from the person, or the real relation on the human side produces a kind of Monoenergism where the human existence remains passive to the divine action.[81] Again, the West is held captive to the contradictory entailments inherent in its theological first principle—definitional simplicity. Additionally, the ecclesiological dimension of the separation of creator and creation is likewise an issue of mediation. I lack the space to go into a full discussion of the topic here, but I think tracing out the ecclesiological dimensions of Augustine's cosmological novelties would be a worthwhile project indeed. In the church-state that resulted in late antiquity that persisted through the medieval period, the church—true to its Augustinian heritage, a creation—assumed the mediatorial role between God and creation. The church mechanistically dispensed grace from God to the world in an *ex opere operato* fashion, furthering the gulf between God and the world where the separation could worsen over time. Again, Cyril Hovorun's point is important, in that the Christology of Theodore and Nestorius was Monoenergetic.[82] In the paradigm where God and creation are separate, there is an underlying tendency in such a cosmological Nestorianism for there to be only one

---

80. Hinlicky, *Beloved Community*, 823.

81. The latter entailment is seen at least as far back as Anselm, who held that the will to obey in Christ was due to his divine will, rather than his human will.

82. Hovorun, *Will, Action and Freedom*, 13.

energy. The energy and movement of creation itself cannot be denied, which, in the Nestorian paradigm, will leave less and less room for divine energy in the world. I think we have seen this occur in this chapter.

The other side of the cosmological coin is the confusion of creator and creation, something I have been calling cosmological Monophysitism. I believe the best instance of such a phenomenon in the realm of soteriology is in the (mainly) Reformed Protestant doctrine of monergism. From the website bearing the name of the doctrine, monergism is "the doctrine that the Holy Spirit is the only efficient agent in regeneration—that the human will possesses no inclination to holiness until regenerated, and therefore cannot cooperate in regeneration."[83] As the etymology of the word suggests, the "one worker" initiating salvation is God (the Holy Spirit). Such a doctrine follows Augustine very closely. For Augustine, as for the Reformed Protestants, the human will is too badly damaged to will salvation, therefore if salvation is to occur, it must be the work of God, overcoming the sinful human will that is incapable of willing anything truly righteous. As the popular slogan, replete with its zero-sum mentality, reiterates, "it is all of grace and none of man." But does such a doctrine belie problems? I think it does.

First, monergism is clearly a kind of soteriological Monoenergism. The words themselves are almost identical. For monergism to be true, there is only one at work in the act—God himself. The person being regenerated plays no part, for his very will to sin (which, in the dialectical construction of Augustinian simplicity, must be in opposition to God) is being overcome by divine grace. The human will passively bows to the overpowering divine will. But, does soteriological Monoenergism imply its (heretical) christological counterpart? I believe the answer is affirmative. In fact, I will show both kinds of Monoenergism entail one another within an Augustinian framework of predestination.

To show that christological Monoenergism entails its soteriological counterpart, monergism, is fairly straightforward. If the divine overwhelms the human action in Jesus, then it is unthinkable for the human to cooperate on its own with the divine initiative in salvation for two reasons. First, since Jesus is the only man without sin (original or actual), he is the only man who could even be capable of human action that is good on its own. Since the divine energy overcomes even his impeccable human energy in his actions toward both the Father and humanity, it is impossible to think that fallen human energy could attain anything toward salvation. Therefore, the human energy would need to be passive in the face of meticulous divine control, and therefore monergism results. Second, Jesus is the ultimate example for us. If everything in his life is controlled and guided by the divine, how much more us? Again, monergism results.

Conversely, does monergism imply a form of historical Monoenergism? I believe the answer to be yes. Monergism is a soteriological subset of the greater Augustinian/

---

83. Hendryx, "Regeneration," para. 1.

Reformed doctrine of predestination, which holds that all created actions are decreed by God in eternity and rendered certain in time. Both Augustine and the Reformed tradition hold that Jesus is subject to the predestining decree.[84] If so, then he executes the divine will fully and perfectly because his human will is subordinated to the divine. Robin Phillips writes, "The reason we can say that Christ's humanity is reduced to little more than a passive tool is because the human energy of Christ is then subsumed into, overcome by, subordinated to the divine energy, not because the human will genuinely surrenders to the divine in an act of co-operation or synergy, but because such subordination is required by the terms of predestination itself."[85] The Augustinian doctrine of predestination, followed closely by the magisterial Reformers, holds that the human will is opposed to the divine (even in Jesus!) and that the paradigm of the relationship of the two natural wills is one of domination rather than cooperation. Thus, Monoenergism results, primarily because Jesus is subject to predestination in that tradition.[86]

Since, in the context of the Augustinian doctrine of predestination, soteriological monergism and christological Monoenergism imply one another, therefore, within that specific tradition, the two are logically equivalent. It is no great wonder then why my own Evangelical Protestant tradition ignores the Third Council of Constantinople; for to embrace the sixth ecumenical council must logically entail the denial of monergism as a soteriological model. In the same vein, an *a priori* soteriological commitment to an Augustinian-predestinarian kind of monergism will entail a christological Monoenergism. In all fairness to Augustine, his life predated the Monoenergist/Monothelite controversy by more than 200 years, but his novel form of cosmological Monoenergism (predestination) logically entails its christological counterpart. I have argued that the same concept of definitional simplicity that led to Monoenergism likewise brought forth the Augustinian model of predestination. In the end, within that system, the two are logical equivalents. This is further proof that the christological

---

84. Muller, *Christ and the Decree*, 32, shows that Calvin, whom entire Reformed tradition follows on this point, follows Augustine in his doctrine of Jesus's predestination. He writes, "The Son of God is 'appointed . . . to be the overseer of our salvation.' Calvin seems to imply that the Son, like the humanity he assumes, is designated."

85. Phillips, "Why I Stopped," para. 9.

86. Phillips, "Why I Stopped." Phillips notes that if Jesus were not subject to predestination, then he becomes a paradigm for cooperation between God and humanity. It would not be unreasonable to expect that he is not the only instance of such an occurrence, which would defeat the deterministic model of predestination, because, since God is simple, it must be all-encompassing. He writes, "If we say that Christ's human will was exempt from divine predestination, then it is hard to avoid the implication that there must have been true non-monergistic synergy and co-operation between the divine and the human wills of Christ. But if so, then it is equally hard to see why it would be problematic to assert a similar non-monergistic synergy and co-operation between the divine and the human wills when dealing with the rest of humanity, especially since Christ typified the appropriate relation between humanity and divinity. Saying that Christ is exempt from Divine predestination also seems to suggest, at least by implication, that some version of libertarian freedom may not be an intrinsically incoherent concept as Calvinists will frequently assert."

heresies really do possess cosmological counterparts—ones that today we must face due to the historical inability of Western theology to adequately grasp the origins of what we believe.

Conclusion

This chapter has provided an overview of the cosmologically Nestorianizing and Monophysitizing tendencies in Western Christian cosmology, with special attention to how definitional divine simplicity and its attendant identity thesis have shaped the Western tendency to separate Christ and creation, up through the pre-Reformation era. We arrive at the dawn of the modern age, and it is here that the somewhat mild cosmological Nestorianism and Monophysitism we have surveyed will explode into the outright cosmological Arianism, Ebionism, Apollinarianism, and Docetism of the modern world. In the upcoming two chapters, we will see positions harden and polarize. Mediating tendencies accompany them, but seem to fail due to being trapped in the same separation/confusion dilemma that definitional divine simplicity entails. Since they are part of the same paradigm that engenders the problems, they cannot adequately address the full extent of the problems and end up being further points of contention.

In chapter 4, I argued that Augustine holds to a kind of "cosmological Apollinarianism." I have demonstrated here that it is, like Apollinarianism, Monoenergetic, at least as far as Christ and the church are concerned. The import of the full-blown cosmological Apollinarianism comes to the fore in the next chapter, as Augustine's followers take what he believed to its logical conclusions, and, in the case of the cosmological Docetists, even further. Let us turn there now.

10

Cosmological Apollinarianism and Docetism

THIS CHAPTER WILL DISCUSS the concepts of cosmological Apollinarianism and Docetism. In cosmology, the Nestorianizing and Monoenergizing tendencies came into the faith relatively simultaneously in the theology of Augustine. We saw in the previous chapter how those two tendencies matured together throughout the medieval period. I now want to trace the development of each tendency to its more extreme forms a chapter at a time, since there is a logical and temporal progression from cosmological Monophysitism to cosmological Apollinarianism and Docetism, respectively. My aim in this chapter is to discuss how the aforementioned cosmological Monophysitism morphs into a cosmological Apollinarianism in the late medieval and especially the Reformation periods. Then, from within that cosmologically Apollinarian world, a real species of cosmological Docetism appears as an answer to Enlightenment rationalism. We will begin with the move to cosmological Apollinarianism.

Predestination before the Reformation

As we saw in chapter 4, Apollinarianism is the denial of real humanity in Jesus Christ. Apollinarius taught that the divine Logos replaced the human soul in Christ, depriving him of a human will. The soteriological implications of Apollinarius's doctrine are unacceptable, since what is not assumed is not healed. Like its christological counterpart, cosmological Apollinarianism is the denial of the full reality and integrity of the created order, so much so that the christological heresy can be seen as a subset of the larger cosmological model. Augustine, who is the historical innovator responsible for the doctrine of predestination so common in Western theology, was not willing to extend his doctrine to its full logical ramifications. As we discussed in the previous chapter, Augustine's predestination concerned only the elect—those God predetermined to save. The rest of humanity was left to its own devices, so to speak, because

Cosmological Apollinarianism and Docetism

of the radical effects he saw in his doctrine of original sin. He never held to a doctrine of double predestination, where God is just as active in the affairs of the reprobate to guarantee their damnation as he is in the lives of the elect to bring about their salvation. Admittedly, it is not much of a leap to get from Augustine to double predestination, and many of his disciples jumped at the chance. Double predestination serves as a bridge to two doctrines that I believe to be truly cosmologically Apollinarian: the doctrine of the single decree (producing the doctrine of double predestination) and the doctrine of limited atonement.[1]

In the last chapter, we introduced one of the first persons to teach a double predestination and limited atonement, the ninth-century monk Gottschalk of Orbais. He was condemned three times and was generally forgotten. He and his contemporary Florus of Lyons were the only two who professed double predestination and limited atonement in the early medieval era.[2] The next time we see double predestination in church history is during the Augustinian revival of the fourteenth century, in the persons of Thomas Bradwardine and Gregory of Rimini. By the fourteenth century, in the words of Heiko Obermann, "Augustine was no longer presented as only one of the four church fathers, but rather as the authoritative and definitive interpreter of the one *Evangelium* located in the Scriptures."[3] This revival of Augustinian predestination would have great effects on the Protestant Reformation two centuries later.

Thomas Bradwardine was a great scholar in many fields who was elected as Archbishop of Canterbury just before he died of the plague in 1349. He was an Oxford contemporary of William of Ockham, though he rejected his nominalism. He was a fountainhead of the great Augustinian revival of the fourteenth century and acquired the title "doctor *profundus*" in Roman Catholicism. He held to the doctrine of double predestination, holding that human action has nothing to do with election or reprobation.[4] John Fesko writes concerning him, "Nothing happens as the result of luck or chance in Bradwardine's formulation of the doctrine of providence. He believed that God decrees everything that happens in the world past, present, and future."[5] Here we see a noticeable development from Augustine, who believed only the lives of the elect were predestined. Those not saved were not predestined so, but were damned due to the universal condition of original sin and original guilt. For Bradwardine, predestination extended to all of creation, meticulously including the events in the lives of the reprobate. The obvious corollary of such a doctrine seems to make God

---

1. David L. Allen, in his recent monumental investigation of the doctrine of limited atonement, *Extent*, xxi, defines limited atonement (also called particular redemption) as "Christ bore the punishment due for the sins of the elect alone."

2. See Fesko, *Diversity*, 22, as well as Allen, *Extent*, 24–26.

3. Oberman, "Fourteenth-Century Religious Thought," 8, as quoted in Fesko, *Diversity*, 40.

4. Fesko, *Diversity*, 45. In Bradwardine's thought, both election and reprobation are unconditional. This is a departure from Augustine, who believed reprobation to be conditional upon the fallen human condition.

5. Fesko, *Diversity*, 46.

The Hexagon of Heresy

responsible for evil, a charge Augustine was able to avoid. Bradwardine believed he was able to escape the charge of making God responsible for evil, as he "believed in the freedom of the will; he believed that a person can only will what he is most attracted to and not its opposite. He is able to affirm the sovereignty of God and the freedom of man's will by means of divine coefficiency where God 'works supremely, but *in such a way* that the freedom of the will is maintained.'"[6] God foreknows and predestines the good, but "in the case of what is wicked, he brings about only that they exist, not that they are evil."[7] I believe Fesko is understating Bradwardine's case here, because according to the doctor, all actions are determined. Bradwardine is the most deterministic Christian writer up until his time, as he erased some Thomistic distinctions in kinds of necessity.[8] Stephen Lahey writes, "The final effect of Bradwardine's exhaustive catalog of arguments in *De Causa Dei* is to strike down any attempt at compromising the necessity of divine knowing and willing. The correspondent robust predestinarian view regarding human willing struck many of his readers, Wyclif included, as heavy handed."[9] Bradwardine is the last and most influential realist double predestinarian. Simultaneously, he is also the first who insists on a zero-sum game of power and cause between God and humanity, that is, any real integrity on the part of the created order must necessarily rob God of some of his power. Since God causes everything, man has nothing, reminiscent of Apollinarius.

Gregory of Rimini was the other leading figure in the revival of predestination in the fourteenth century. Gregory was a nominalist, as is reflected in the language of Frank James: "The will of God is free, omnipotent, and all its actions are a matter of divine prerogative."[10] For Gregory, as well as for his later Reformed disciple Peter Martyr Vermigli, "the sovereign will of God is the ultimate and exclusive cause of reprobation."[11] Gregory taught that reprobation itself is the cause of human evil, not God. So, God causes reprobation and then reprobation causes evil, since evil is a

---

6. Fesko, *Diversity*, 46. The quote is from Oberman, *Bradwardine*, 85. Italics mine. The "in such a way" phrase will be repeated often in the words of strong monists (generally Calvinists) who want to give place to human freedom for the express purpose of removing from God any accusation of being the cause of sin.

7. Thomas Bradwardine, *De Causa Dei* I.45.421, as quoted in Fesko, *Diversity*, 46. Fesko writes on page 47, "This means that God does not create evil in the hearts of the wicked, he only allows the wicked to exist." While I think Fesko is correct in stating what Bradwardine *wants* to say, I don't think he is successful in *actually* bridging the Plotinian ambiguity between divine determinism and human freedom.

8. Fesko, *Diversity*, 36. Fesko writes concerning Aquinas, representative of medieval thinkers on the subject of predestination, "Aquinas held predestination to be a part of providence. Election was positive, but reprobation was passive and permissive.

9. Lahey, *John Wyclif*, 178. As the identity thesis in the Augustinian tradition will dictate, knowing *is* willing in God.

10. James, *Vermigli*, 134.

11. James, *Vermigli*, 142.

privation.[12] Gregory therefore makes a distinction between reprobation and punishment. "What this means is that Gregory believes reprobation is God's rejection of a person for salvation, whereas eternal condemnation arises from the necessity for God to punish a person for his sin. This may seem like an insignificant distinction, but for Gregory it allows him to maintain a supralapsarian formulation of predestination without indicting God with the culpability for sin."[13] Thus he distinguishes between reprobation and damnation. The Ockhamist emphasis on divine volition as the touchstone for theological reflection enhanced the determinist view, as it created the perfect confluence of absolute sovereignty and absolute freedom. This confluence would produce the deterministic theology of the magisterial Reformers a couple of centuries later.

Predestination in the Reformation

Martin Luther was the first of the magisterial Reformers, and a believer in double predestination. Much of Luther's theology was formulated in reaction against the quasi-humanist, "God helps those who help themselves" theology of Gabriel Biel.[14] In doing so, Luther rejected any notion that human beings do anything to help bring about their salvation. As Michael Gillespie writes, "He held fast to his core doctrine that saw God as everything and man as nothing,"[15] the zero-sum game. This will lead to his battle with Erasmus and would prefigure the numerous wars of religion over the next century-plus. In this we see the same all-or-nothing mentality that exemplifies both cosmological and christological Monoenergism—that the divine and creation compete to control the same space.[16] As could be expected, Luther deeply drew from the well of definitional simplicity. Progressing beyond even the neo-Augustinianism of Bradwardine and Rimini, he asserted that everything occurs of necessity due to the will of God. Gillespie writes, "This is a striking claim not merely because it puts Luther in league with the heretical Wycliffe but because it puts him outside the previous Christian tradition altogether. It has no basis or support in Scripture, the church fathers or scholasticism. Luther in fact was able to support his claim only by citing a fatalistic pagan poet."[17] Gillespie continues, "This conclusion in his view was the

12. James, *Vermigli*, 144–45. See also Gregory of Rimini, *Lectura* 2 Sent. Dist. 34–37 q. 1 art. 3 (vi. 257).

13. Fesko, *Diversity*, 50. He writes on page xxiii "Supralapsarians will discuss election and reprobation apart from any consideration of the fall or original sin," and, ibid., xxv, that supralapsarians will always believe in double predestination.

14. Placher, *Domestication of Transcendence*, 39. This is but another instance of the violent pendulum swing we saw so often in Christology.

15. Gillespie, *Theological Origins*, 128.

16. Phillips, "Why I Stopped."

17. On Wycliffe and predestination, see Pelikan, *Christian Tradition*, 4:32. Wycliffe defined the church as "a congregation of the predestined." Pelikan continues "Behind this definition of the church

necessary and unavoidable consequence that under the doctrine of divine simplicity God's foreknowledge and will are one and the same."[18] In other words, God wills if and only if God (fore)knows. The result is that all things that occur in space/time do so necessarily because God wills them. Simply replace, in the previous sentence, "all things" with "Jesus' actions" and "God wills" with "the Logos directs" and the result is Apollinarianism perfectly stated.

Like his mentor Augustine, whom he stretches to the limit, divine simplicity and its attendant identity thesis lurks at the heart of his doctrine of predestination. I believe he is able to carry Augustine to his logical conclusions with the use of nominalism. Augustine did not see the reprobate as predestined because they were already "left alone" by the ordinary power of God to continue in their sinful ways. The loss of all created mediation in Ockham's revolution necessitated a move (pioneered by Gregory of Rimini) to posit the divine will as the unmediated determination of all created action, something not necessary in Augustine due to the seminal rational principles, which became the universals rejected by Ockham and later Luther.

In the previous chapters, divine determinism was seen as evidence of operating from the monist orientation of the Plotinian ambiguity. Luther, though, was not a thoroughgoing monist. His orientation to theological reflection held to some of the same multivalence as did his ancient mentor Augustine. To put it simply, Luther took the reality of the created world seriously. First, he was committed to Jesus as God-in-flesh. In Luther's theology, for us to see God, we look to Jesus, that is, it is actually God on the cross. Luther's famous attacks against reason are his way of condemning the attempt at a knowledge of God that does not first pass through Jesus as revealed in the flesh. This is a very good thing, and flies in the face of the prevailing (and often his own) philosophical constructions of God.[19] Had he continued on this path, Luther might have been able to work to free the West of its commitment to definitional simplicity. It was not to be, however.

Second, taking the reality of the created world seriously meant for him the realization that real evil existed in the world. Committed as he was to Augustinian definitional simplicity and its attendant identity thesis in his aforementioned belief that all things occur out of necessity by the will of God, the will of God was identical to the divine essence. Therefore, the existence of evil in the world implied the existence

---

lay the insistence that God himself was the first cause and the only cause of predestination to salvation as well as of damnation, with man playing a purely 'passive' part in both. To an extent that appeared to lay his doctrine open to the charge of pagan fatalism, Wycliffe was willing to use the term 'necessity' to describe the involvement of God in everything that happened, although he also asserted that no one could belong to the family of God unless he did so of his own free will." He held to the fact that the fall was necessary because it allowed "for the exaltation of the human race in Christ." Wycliffe's assertion of the "passive" human energy in salvation is very reminiscent of Apollinarius's description of Jesus's humanity, guided and directed necessarily by the Logos.

18. Gillespie, *Theological Origins*, 145. Luther was quoting Virgil, *Aen.* 2.324. The quote from Luther is found in Erasmus, *Works*, 76:306.

19. Placher, *Domestication of Transcendence*, 46.

of evil in God, his *deus absconditus* (hidden God). Even though he insisted we know God through Jesus, the hidden God was another aspect of God—one not revealed in Jesus. For instance, as Placher notes in Luther's thought, God in Christ truly weeps over Jerusalem, but at the same time, God (the hidden one) ordains the apostasy of the Jews and the destruction of their city.[20] Predictably, Luther could not trust God (the *deus absconditus*) to be good because he saw that what has occurred in history is not always good. Luther's answer is to trust Scripture (for it is Scripture that brings the grace that brings the faith that brings salvation in revealing Jesus), but the unknowable, potentially evil *deus absconditus* always lurks in the background.[21]

His *a priori* acceptance of definitional simplicity means that the enormous implications of a divine Jesus cannot be fully worked out in his theology. Luther clearly saw the tension between his commitment to a monistically ordered world and the reality of evil within that world. Jesus is truly God, and truly mediator, but he is unable to stand surety that he is *homoousios* to the *deus absconditus*, which would render him the Son of the Father. Instead, there is God and there is Jesus. As James Daane insightfully notes, Lutheranism took the contradictions posed by divine determinism seriously (that is, both good and evil occur in the visible world, and are therefore ultimately willed by God), and moved the contradiction back into God himself—the hidden and the revealed God, positing a "double decree."[22] To help smooth over this problem, Luther insisted that the Bible is God's word to us, "the method by which God grasps us, possesses us, and enslaves us, folding us into his being, making us one with him."[23] Notice how this language is completely soteriologically, not to mention cosmologically, Monophysite. Then Gillespie asks a pointed question: "But how can this satisfy human beings?"[24] For Luther, there are two truths: one contained in Scripture, and one in which things are the way they really are. If the *deus absconditus* of nominalism stands behind the curtain directing all events necessarily, he is the way things really are, and there is the possibility that the Scriptures cannot be true, because they present a different picture than the *deus absconditus* implies.[25] In sum, as Gillespie writes,

20. Placher, *Domestication of Transcendence*, 48. How such a statement has (presumably) avoided the charge of Arianism is beyond me.

21. Gillespie, *Theological Origins*, 127.

22. Daane, *Freedom*, 47. The "double decree" of Luther is that good is decreed by the revealed God, while evil is decreed by the hidden God. Though, as Hinlicky, *Beloved Community*, 822, notes, Lutheran orthodoxy defined the essence of God as "an independent Spirit—that is, an immaterial, spiritual, or intellectual substance in the metaphysical traditions of Plato and Aristotle." It sounds almost identical to that of Origen.

23. Gillespie, *Theological Origins*, 157. Gillespie draws from *Luther's Works*, 33:139–40.

24. Gillespie, *Theological Origins*, 157.

25. Is it any wonder, then, with the easily verifiable presence of evil in space/time standing as ultimate proof that God might be evil too, that the doubt that the Bible can actually be the word of God rose to prominence in Lutheran Germany in short order? If the presence of evil implies something evil in God, then the Scriptures cannot be his word and would lead to the deconstruction efforts of the early historical-critical school a century or two after Luther's death. The vast majority of them were Lutheran.

"Luther's theology requires the omnipotence of God and the nullity of man in order to relieve man of uncertainty, but this incomprehensible omnipotence itself undermines the very certainty he seeks,"[26] Luther covers over his own contradictions by claiming divine incomprehensibility, just as Augustine did,[27] both seemingly oblivious to the fact that divine simplicity got them here. The *deus absconditus*, in time, would render strict monism unacceptable to much of Lutheranism, and dichotomist-dualist approaches to both Scripture and cosmology would come to rule the day in Germany.[28]

The Reformed tradition suffered from the same double predestination and theological determinism as Luther, but cast through a different prism. Like Ulrich Zwingli in Zurich, John Calvin held to double predestination.[29] Like Luther and Zwingli, Calvin believed that God wills all that occurs.[30] Calvin states explicitly:

> Therefore, we say that his will is the necessity of all things. That does not entail enveloping God in our iniquity—or having the capacity to do anything of the sort. But we must hold to this doctrine, as demonstrated to us in Holy Scripture: God arranges all things in such a way that he does not do any evil on his side, since he is just; but as far as men are concerned, they pervert and turn every good thing into an evil. It is also necessary that the condemnation of all the evil they do remains on their own hands.[31]

Fesko writes, showing Calvin's immense dependence on Augustine, "Calvin makes these important distinctions to dispel the notion that he would implicate God as the author of sin. While Calvin willingly affirms supralapsarianism, he does not construct it in such a way as to say that God works the same way in both the elect and the reprobate. In other words, Calvin does not affirm equal ultimacy. Calvin notes that the salvation of man is entirely a monergistic work of God, whereas the damnation of man is synergistic."[32] Calvin has drawn to the edge of some of the conclusions

---

26. Gillespie, *Theological Origins*, 158. Gillespie then quotes *Luther's Works*, 33:181.

27. Ogliari, *Gratia et Certamen*, 374, writes, "The fact that Augustine ultimately bowed before the unfathomable mystery of God's designs—as if he really wished to leave the last word to him—is a further indication that he could not give an adequate or satisfying answer to the problem of God's attitude and of his way of acting on the two different levels of election and reprobation."

28. Not only would the historical-critical school of biblical interpretation seek to strip away any divine character of the Bible, but German thinkers Immanuel Kant and F. D. E. Schleiermacher would create dichotomist-dualist philosophies and theologies that would rule the Protestant world in the nineteenth and twentieth centuries.

29. It is worth mentioning that Zwingli probably goes further than Luther in his determinism. James, *Vermigli*, 202, notes that providence is all-encompassing in the writings of Zwingli. Every minute detail is a part of it. He goes on to say on page 218, that Zwingli freely admits that God is the cause of sin.

30. Fesko, *Diversity*, 67.

31. Calvin, "Congregation on Eternal Election," 718, quoted in Fesko, *Diversity*, 76. There is that "in such a way" phrase again, though no determinist can adequately describe what that "such a way" is.

32. Fesko, *Diversity*, 97–98. How can a God who is absolutely simple *not* act in equal ultimacy?

that Augustine avoided, and his successors would make the leap. For Calvin, human nature is corrupt, totally depraved, and no longer good. He believes God meticulously controls all events, and, unlike Luther, he fails to note the resultant contradictions[33] of determinism in history. Lutherans, therefore, to uphold the validity of created history put the contradiction in God.[34] The Reformed, to uphold the unity of God, deny that history produces contradictory events.[35] Such is the dilemma in the cosmologically Monophysite world of determinism. One must either, with the Lutherans, make God contradictory or, with the Reformed, make history irrelevant.[36] The Lutheran insistence on the integrity of created history made the Liberal and cosmological Arian/Ebionite turn in Germany, in my opinion, a foregone conclusion. The Reformed stance on the singularity of God is the root of fundamentalism.[37]

The Reformed tradition also varies from the Lutherans in that they see the decree of God itself as singular and simple.[38] If the decree is simple as God is simple, then there is no real distinction between election and reprobation, and created history becomes irrelevant.[39] If the single decree is the simple decree (with its own identity thesis, that all the "decrees" as they appear to us are really and truly one and the same), then three things follow. First, there is the lack of real distinction between reprobation and election that renders all the historical Reformed debates about supra- or

---

It would seem that a denial of equal ultimacy would entail a denial of definitional simplicity as well.

33. By "contradiction," I mean that both good and evil are willed by a completely good God (the proof it is his will, again, is that what he wills and only what he wills necessarily occurs in space/time).

34. That is, Luther held to both a revealed God who is good and a hidden God who may be good, but no one can be absolutely sure. This is the obvious foundation of the Lutheran dichotomy between law and gospel.

35. That is, good and evil lose their distinction in the world because every event is ultimately ordered by a good God, even though these events may appear horribly evil to us. Of course, such thinking is the root of the "greater good" family of theodicies.

36. Daane, *Freedom*, 47–48.

37. The Lutherans, with their insistence on the reality of created history as a vehicle for divine insight, ultimately adopt, within their own monistic structure, a dichotomist-dualist operating procedure, which works from creation toward God. The Reformed, on the other hand, will stay true to their own monist roots and proceed from God and interpret history through the lens of the eternal. They will be the representatives of either side of the Plotinian ambiguity within Protestantism and spawn its two great (and in my opinion unavoidable) theological structures, liberalism and fundamentalism.

38. See Daane, *Freedom*, 47. The Lutherans hold to a double decree because of the existence of both elect and reprobate in the world.

39. Daane, *Freedom*, 46. On page 43, Daane recognizes another problem with regards to creation and predestination. He writes, "Since predestination refers to the final destiny of whatever is predestined, it cannot be defined in terms of 'whatever comes to pass.' One of the things that has come to pass is the act of God by which the world was created. But the creation of the world is not the predestination of the world. God's creative act constitutes the origin of the world, and the origin of the world is not the destiny of the world. To identify the two is to deny the history of the world; indeed, it is to deny that anything other than the creation of the world has come to pass." Denial or de-emphasis of the created order is one of the hallmarks of the monist half of the Plotinian ambiguity in general and Apollinarianism in particular.

infra-lapsarianism, or anything else meaningless.[40] Second, either there is either no real history or there is no single decree. Daane writes, "Either reality is without distinctions because it is determined by a decree that has no distinctions, or the distinctions that differentiate reality in space and time fall outside this single decree." The latter is the Arminian choice (Arminianism holds the single decree to elect all, then the conditional decree to choose some based on foreknowledge). One must affirm either the reality of history with the Lutherans or the single, simple decree of the Reformed (the Plotinian-ambiguity-driven dialectical construction of early Protestantism, the former where creation explains God or the latter where God explains creation). Third, there is no way to distinguish the simple decree from God himself (divine simplicity again). Moreover, by definition, there cannot be two distinct, absolutely and definitionally simple things. It's either God or the decree, or they are identical. And if identical, how does one meaningfully distinguish between God and the world? If that is the case, then one either gets pantheism or occasionalism, as either the world is God or God is the world.[41] And, here we are, right back to an intensified version of the Origenist Problematic. We will see this result obtain later in this chapter as well as the next.

This is only the tip of the iceberg of the problems caused by the single and simple decree. Reformed decretal theology tried to explain "whatever comes to pass in terms of the necessary essence of God, that is, in terms of what this necessary divine essence necessarily required and determined."[42] And, of course, following this Reformed version of the Origenist problematic, what is natural is compelled. Further, Daane notes that Turretin follows Aquinas by being unable to make a clear distinction between God and creation. Even saying that creation "can be called God relatively."[43] What the medieval and Protestant scholastics could not grasp—due to definitonal simplicity and its attendant identity thesis which identifies nature and energy—was that creation was not bound to the essence of God (à la Origen) or to his (in their eyes) equivalent will/reason. It was his free decision that he could just as freely have not chosen. It is energetic, rather than essential.[44] The simple decree also reproduces the Plotinian

---

40. It also entails equal ultimacy between election and reprobation, which is a conclusion still denied by all Reformed except those pejoratively called hyper-Calvinists. That is, the "in such a way" phrase which we have already encountered becomes a meaningless word-game if the assumptions of Reformed theology are taken to their conclusions, as the so-called hyper-Calvinists do.

41. All three entailments of the simple decree are discussed in Daane, *Freedom*, 53–55. Pantheism (a form of cosmological Ebionism) and occasionalism (cosmological Docetism) cannot truly distinguish the two. Once again, here is yet another example of how definitionally-simple-driven monism logically entails a necessary creation, just as in Origen and Aquinas.

42. Daane, *Freedom*, 57.

43. Daane, *Freedom*, 59n13. Daane does not reference the quote of Turretin. For Aquinas, saying creation "never was not" (in "On the Eternality of the World") sounds an awful lot like what was said about Jesus by Athanasius and the rest of the pro-Nicenes. If both Jesus and the world "never was not" then Aquinas is clearly reproducing the Origenist Problematic: Jesus and the world are (eternally) indistinguishable.

44. Daane, *Freedom*, 59n13. In the same footnote, Daane calls for a recognition that the decree

ambiguity perfectly, as the decree separates God from the world (for God never acts in response to the world, but determines everything that happens therein) just as it identifies him with it (in that what occurs is a created extension of the divine decree/will/essence).[45] Daane summarizes the Plotinian ambiguity within such a decretal simplicity well, as he writes, "God bears the marks of Aristotle's unmoved mover. He is regarded as the cause of whatever lies outside of himself, and necessarily so, but he is not free to respond freely in grace to a sinful world; he is not free to respond in Christ with a purpose that is essentially gracious."[46] The ramifications include God as the source of sin, God as not free to respond to man's plight, reprobation grounded in God himself, and the like. "For if the decree is indeed identical to God's essence, the essence of what God decrees is his own essence. Such a decree—and such a decreeing God—cannot get outside of itself. The decree, like God's essence, bears no relation to the world."[47] There is a gap that paradoxically God cannot cross and that simultaneously doesn't exist. It should be clear by now that the single decree is yet another by-product of definitional divine simplicity, as it contains its own version of both the identity thesis and the Plotinian ambiguity. I find it interesting that Daane could argue so well against the simple decree and yet leave the definitional simplicity of God untouched. The problems attendant to the definitionally simple decree have their genesis in the definitionally simple God, but Daane never made the argument.[48]

---

should be recognized as "never was not." Daane does not mention the obvious historical implications of his phrase any further back than Aquinas, but we know this phrase was the rallying cry of the pro-Nicenes to describe the oneness of Jesus and the Father. Maximus's mature cosmology would have seen the differentiated "decrees" as the many *logoi* in the one Logos. And the Logos "never was not." With Daane on this point, I would smile and say, "of course."

45. Daane, *Freedom*, 63. On page 72, he adds, "In the single decree lies the hidden but persistent motif that both [election and reprobation] threatens all human knowledge of God's decree, and at its deepest levels also threatens the actual reality of everything finite and historical. This explains Reformed theology's constant temptation to dissolve the historical character of Christianity in its search for eternal, timeless truth, and its persistent inclination to dismiss scriptural anthropomorphisms as insignificant accommodations to finite minds."

46. Daane, *Freedom*, 160.

47. Daane, *Freedom*, 164. He continues, "Turretin's difficulty is really a problem of 'in' and 'out.' He has an 'in-theology' that cannot become an 'out-theology.' Because he holds that whatever occurs in God is God, Turretin sees God as unable to get out to that which is not-God, that is, to an act of creation and into creation itself. This in-theology has no exit because of its identification of decree and divine essence." The decree is as simple as God is. Moreover, as was discussed earlier, the a-relationality of God invites the replacement of real divine-human relationship with varieties of external legalism. Turretin, through Princeton, is the grandfather of American Fundamentalism with all of its legalistic heritage. This should come as no surprise by now. Moreover, it implies that God is himself determined by his own essence (what is natural is compelled). We will discuss this later in this chapter.

48. I think he was aware of it, though his stated purpose in his book is election. Daane, *Freedom*, 53, states, "Reformed theology has not constructed a theology of the simplicity of God, but it has constructed a theology based on the singularity of the divine decree. Had it attempted to do the former, it would have produced a doctrine of God as empty and abstract as its theology of a single decree turned out to be."

The Hexagon of Heresy

The magisterial Reformers believed all that occurs is due to God's decree.[49] The stream of thought running from Bradwardine up through Calvin is essentially Augustinian, but, with the help of the loss of created mediation via the nominalistic revolution, the Augustinian doctrine expands to include the reprobate (and everything else) in the decree so that double predestination rules the day. However, the nominalistic revolution opened the door for something truly novel in the doctrine of soteriology—Gottschalk and Florus excepted—the doctrine of limited atonement.[50] But how did the doctrine of limited atonement arise in Calvin's successor Theodore Beza and then come to occupy a large segment of Reformed thought thereafter? How did it become so widely held in such a short time? I believe there are four reasons contributing to the "spontaneous" rise of the doctrine of limited atonement, all of them intertwined in the theology of the Reformation period. One I have just finished discussing, which is the single decree leading to double predestination, a doctrine that undoubtedly takes salvation out of space-time and places it in the eternal and unsearchable decree of God, and its necessary soteriological monergism, which, in the framework of late medieval and Reformation thought, implies christological Monoenergism.

A second reason why I believe limited atonement became popular so quickly is due to Reformed Christology itself. Reformed Christology is built on the distinction-as-separation of God and man, greatly exacerbated in the fall. What is needed in such a paradigm is a mediator to bridge the gap. As Richard Muller notes, Calvin develops his understanding of the person of Christ based upon his divinely appointed office of mediator (an *ordo theologiae* privileging energy over person, by the way), rather than beginning his reflection on mediation from the person of the Logos made flesh.[51] Muller states explicitly that Calvin departs from Chalcedon (and its clarifications in Constantinople II and III) at this point because of his "necessity of seeking the person of Christ not in the eternal person of the Son but in the incarnate mediator."[52] It is at this point that Lutherans charge Calvin and his followers with Nestorianism, as his Christology follows closely to that of the school of Diodore in Antioch—to see Christ as a composite of two in an *ordo theologiae* which prioritizes nature and energy rather

---

49. Among the early Reformed thinkers, the very best resource remains Muller, *Christ and the Decree*.

50. Allen, *Extent*, 3–102, painstakingly shows that, with the exception of the two ninth-century figures, the doctrine of limited atonement is nonexistent up through the life of John Calvin.

51. Muller, *Christ and the Decree*, 28, writes, "Having established the principle of mediation as the proper ground of Christology." It is principle (energy) before person for Calvin.

52. Muller, *Christ and the Decree*, 29. Muller continues that Calvin's Christology, "and much of the Reformed Christology after him" is not "a traditional Christology from above," that is, Chalcedonian. Muller is the leading contemporary scholar of sixteenth- and seventeenth-century Reformed theology. His description of "seeking the person of Christ in the incarnate mediator" sounds nearly identical to Nestorius's construction of one *prosopon* out of two *prosopa*. For more, see McCormack, "Reformed Christology," in chapter 6, n43 above. See also the ambiguous language in Reformed confessions of faith, including article 15 in the French Confession, chapter 11 in the Belgic Confession, and chapter 8.2 of the Westminster Confession.

than person. Following the Western Augustinian paradigm, the Reformed separate Christ and creation as a first principle, and therefore confine the mediation of Christ as exclusively soteriological, rather than cosmological. Hence there lies in the mix a strong Nestorianizing tendency in both Reformed Christology and cosmology—the former a tendency, the latter explicit.

A third ingredient in the batter, so to speak, is the reduction of human salvation to a transactional atonement. The patristic understanding of salvation as Christ recapitulating the entire created order was mortally wounded in Augustine's move to make the seminal rational principles created things themselves. The fundamentally Arian concept of creation mediating creation bred, as noted above, a form of cosmological Nestorianism where the Logos no longer mediates the created order. His incarnation then is not to recapitulate all of creation by his permanent assumption of it, but only to save the elect by dying for them. Because he is subservient to predestination he is treated as fundamentally one of us (Think of medieval art, with Jesus haloed like any other saint.), and his incarnate life is reduced to meriting God's favor in active obedience—a necessary but subordinated prelude, if you will, to what *really* saves, his death to pay for sin.[53] The reductionism multiples, as Jesus's death is reduced to a transaction between the Father and the Son, which follows from the Western tradition that the relation of God to creature is not real. Such a model of atonement, one feeling the impersonal and "objective" effects of a millennium of cosmological Nestorianism, can only "wipe away sin, remove God's anger against it, and lay the basis for a new relationship beyond condemnation and death."[54] Once we arrive here, then those for whom Christ died (or, more importantly, for the elect alone) can be considered of utmost importance, for that is why he came. Christ's death, absent any real recapitulation of the entire created order, at the end of the day benefits only the elect.

The fourth reason why I believe limited atonement grew in strength is the collapse of the ancient understanding that the incarnation itself is salvific. As far back as the Council of Constantinople's condemnation of Apollinarianism, Gregory's maxim remained, that is, Jesus fully assumed human nature in order to fully heal human nature. In the nominalism that dominated the succeeding generations of Protestants, however, the lack of created mediation introduced a profound confusion of person and nature, because the concept of nature, as a universal, lost appeal. Therefore, under the increasingly nominalistic Protestants, instead of each human person sharing in human nature, each human was his or her own nature, that is, what had been formerly known as a universal did not really exist—it was a mental construct meant to organize reality as we see it. Thus, while the Logos certainly became human, there was no real universal nature in which he shared with the rest of us. Therefore, human nature could

---

53. Muller, "Arminius," 156, argues that the active obedience of Christ (his obedience to the law as a man) as a prelude to his atoning death originates in Anselm. Christ's active obedience is what is imputed to us forensically in the Reformed doctrine of justification.

54. Wells, *Cross Words*, 139. Note the new relationship itself is not created, just the basis for it.

not be healed. Only those persons who are elect enjoy what the instrumentalized Christ has accomplished. When all four of these ingredients are taken together as presuppositions, here lies the fairly straightforward thinking behind limited atonement: God elects his chosen from all eternity, and then sends the Son to earth to be the mediator in time, who gives his life to atone for the sins of the elect. There is no universal human nature to heal, only sins for which to pay. Because salvation is monergistic and generally identified with the act of atonement in death, and to prevent universalism (or at least the salvation of some of the reprobate), Jesus dies only for the elect.

David Allen shows that is the logic behind the doctrine of limited atonement in Beza, who departs from his teacher. Allen writes,

> For Calvin, the atonement did indeed accomplish the salvation of the elect but not without the necessary faith for the benefit to be applied. Unlike Calvin, Beza said that application is certain for all those for whom Christ died—namely, the elect. For Beza, Christ's death, by necessity, must be effective for all for whom it was performed. Salvation was not made possible in Christ; it was made actual only for the elect. Beza stated that the atonement was limited because Jesus did not die for the damned.[55]

Thus, as Stephen Strehle notes, limited atonement is the logical result of applying predestination to Christ, "as a minister to and for them alone."[56] The cosmological Nestorianism and Monophysitism of Augustine, after a millennium of turbulently cycling through Roman Catholic and then Protestant theology, converge into the perfect storm to create a form of cosmological Apollinarianism, the denial of the full integrity of the creation due to the deterministic decree, in the mother of all soteriological heresies, limited atonement—a doctrine logically deducible from the particulars of the Reformed iteration of the doctrine of predestination, but with no biblical support whatsoever. Due to the lack of scriptural warrant, and it not being something believed "everywhere, always, and by all," the doctrine of limited atonement did not win universal support within the Reformed tradition, as nearly all of Beza's contemporaries, as well as his student Arminius rejected it.[57] Even the Synod of Dort, which rejected the teachings of Arminius's followers, was not unified on limited atonement.[58]

Speaking of Arminius, he is a good example of why corrective attempts within the greater system of Western theology usually fail. Arminius and the Remonstrance rightly saw the good and necessary consequences of Augustinian election and grace as well as Beza's limited atonement; and thus formulated an opposing theological system, one that remains to this day the only real Western, Reformed alternative to moderate

---

55. Allen, *Extent*, 103.

56. Strehle, "Extent," 133. The words in quotation marks are those of Allen, *Extent*, 104, where the reference to Strehle appears.

57. Allen, *Extent*, 106–19, and 135–49.

58. Allen, *Extent*, 149–62.

(four-point) or high (five-point) Calvinism.[59] While Arminius attempted to correct some of the errors that, as I have argued, flow out of the ultimately cosmological entailments of Augustine's definitional simplicity, he is never able to extract himself from the root of the problem, and therefore fails to right the ship.[60] For example, Arminius commits himself to the instrumental view of the person of Christ the mediator, even to the point of subordinating him to the Father.[61] So he attempts to solve the soteriological innovations of his Reformed counterparts (with their attendant christological issues) with a modified Arian Christology that is ultimately unable to restore a proper place to Christ for a robust doctrine of recapitulation. In other words, two wrongs cannot make a right.[62]

To summarize, limited atonement arises from a collection of troublesome ideas, all of which can be traced directly back to Augustine's adoption of definitional divine simplicity for the essence of God and its attendant identity thesis. The combination of cosmologically Nestorian and Monophysite ideas combine to form a cosmological Apollinarianism, which denies that the creation has any real, internal integrity. Concerning christological Apollinarianism (even though he could be referencing its cosmological counterpart as well), Demetrios Bathrellos writes, "Apollinarius and his disciples could not conceive of a coexistence and cooperation between the divine and the human natures and wills in Christ that would respect the particularity and integrity of both. As Norris has rightly noticed, for Apollinarius 'perfect cooperation

---

59. As is well known, the famous five points of Calvinism include total depravity (Augustinian original sin and original guilt, plus a total human inability to initiate any movement toward God apart from grace), (Augustinian) unconditional election, limited atonement, irresistible (I would say Monoenergetic) grace, and Augustinian perseverance of the saints. The famous acrostic "TULIP," taken from the first letters of each of the five points, helps to abbreviate the system. Moderate Calvinists reject limited atonement, and are often called four-point Calvinists. Classical Arminians remove original guilt and total human inability from T, reject U by making election conditional upon God's foreknowledge of who would believe, reject L and I, and are agnostic about P (Wesleyan Arminians reject P altogether, saying one can fall from true faith). As for it being the only alternative within the broadly Reformed tradition, in my judgment a soteriology from that tradition can either be a species of Calvinism or one of Arminianism, since the U and I work as a unit.

60. Though, as Duby, *Divine Simplicity*, 25, writes, the Remonstrance did not formally appeal to definitional simplicity. They nevertheless could not extract themselves from its clutches.

61. Muller, "Arminius," 159, argues that Arminius believed that Christ is subordinate to the Father due to generation, rather than due to the economy. In other words, his Christology is fundamentally "Arian," and he uses a (christologically) "Arian" approach to answer the (cosmological) Apollinarianism of his opponents. We should not be surprised by now, as history repeats itself again and again under definitional simplicity.

62. Muller, "Arminius," 161. Muller writes, "What Arminius seems to have done is to have taken the side of the patristic argument which argues some subordination in order in the Godhead and to have developed it into the basic principle of his view of the Trinity. The subordination of the Son became, in turn, the lynch-pin of his final statement of the doctrine of predestination. There, the Father, as *principium* of the Trinity antecedently wills the election of human beings in Christ and consequently gives to Christ the choice of believers as his own." Luther's hidden-revealed dichotomy in God, Calvin's hidden-revealed dichotomy in will, along with Arminius's antecedent-consequent dichotomy in will, are all examples of the Plotinian ambiguity at work.

between human and divine wills is impossible', which means that the one (the divine) can and must be affirmed only at the expense of the other."[63] In other words, Apollinarius employs a zero-sum game, which the Plotinian ambiguity requires. In such a construction, all actions of the entire creation are determined, and there is a simultaneous separation between God and creation, even to the point where Christ himself is composed. The incarnation is only a means to an end, rather than a recapitulation, and in its end, the Logos does not assume the full creation, just a part of it. Cosmologically, we see the "tape played backwards" of events as they unfolded christologically. In Christology, the Apollinarian Christ was doubly deficient, the Logos living in a human shell. Nestorius returned the fullness of his humanity, but at a cost of a double subject. Monophysitism solved the double subject, but so subordinated the human that there was only one energy at work. The historical progression was one of refinement. Cosmologically, the historical progression is one of worsening. The comparatively mild cosmological Monophysitism of Augustine becomes a much more serious cosmological Apollinarianism of Beza and his followers. What little created integrity Augustine bequeathed to his successors is quickly being eroded.[64] The following quote from Joseph Farrell summarizes the christological entailments of limited atonement.

> *Christ, being truly consubstantial (in his humanity) with all men, truly died for all men, and thus his atoning passion, death, and resurrection are in no way limited (but affect all men irresistibly).* In turn, the doctrine of the limited atonement may be reversed to show its hidden and heretical implications: If not all men rise with the second Adam then not all die with the first Adam. There would consequently be some men who, not being affected by the consubstantiality of Christ's human nature, would not be consubstantial with him. Therefore, they would not be in Adam either. Not being in Adam, they would have no need of Christ. This is a denial of the inheritance of ancestral sin, *and is therefore Pelagianism.* Furthermore, if Christ's human nature is efficacious in salvation only for a limited number of elected individuals, then it would appear that Christ's humanity, insofar as it *is* efficacious for those individuals, is united with them not naturally but only by the object of their wills (i.e., salvation), since his human nature itself is *not* united with them. This union in object of will between God and man in Christ is Nestorianism. (n.b. One might also notice again the effect of Augustine's theory of illumination on his Christology and predestinarian doctrine.) It would also appear that, on this view, the human nature of the elected individuals gives nothing to election,

---

63. Bathrellos, *Byzantine Christ*, 15. Bathrellos cites Norris, *Manhood and Christ*, 139.

64. Recall that, in chapter 4, it was argued that Augustine's Christology was unwittingly Apollinarian in its construction, even though he vehemently condemned the heresy. Now I believe it has become clear that Augustine's Apollinarian bent was due to his larger cosmological views that spring from his doctrine of definitional simplicity. It is not a large leap from Augustine's cosmology to the removal of any integrity within the created order, especially as far as the elect are concerned. If Christ is counted among the elect, then an Apollinarian Christology is sure to follow.

and Christ's human nature certainly does not, as it effects only the elected individuals. Human nature therefore either has no will, which is a kind of "anthropological" Apollinarianism, or it is merely ineffectual in salvation ("soteriological" Apollinarianism). Christ's human decision of salvation at Gethsemane is therefore illusory, and this is Doketism [sic].[65]

The christological and cosmological heresies are multiplying out of control. The christological ramifications of limited atonement are therefore unacceptable, as they lead directly to almost every christological heresy in the hexagon if such a thing as human nature, in the patristic sense, actually exists.[66] Cosmological Apollinarianism, then, is the denial of the full integrity of the created order, to the point where the real control of the many is the one—decretal divine determinism.

Cosmological Docetism: Jonathan Edwards

In Christology, Docetism is the denial of the humanity (or the soteriological importance thereof) of Jesus. It is impossible to have a completely Docetic view of creation, since it is, well, created. As we saw in our discussion of Christology, Monophysitism, Apollinarianism, and Docetism are differences in degree. Cosmologically, we see Monophysitism (or more properly Monoenergism) in the Augustinian doctrine of predestination which renders the acts of the creature (in this case the elect) to be subsumed into the acts of God. A more extreme version of predestination moves through double predestination to a post-Reformation doctrine of limited atonement, which I have dubbed cosmological Apollinarianism. Cosmological Docetism, then, would then, as far as is possible, remove the integrity of the creation altogether.

In other words, cosmological Docetism works in the same way its christological counterpart does. Ancient Docetism, trapped in its Hellenistic assumptions, could not fathom that Jesus could be both God and man with each having integrity. They chose to collapse his being from the divine side, saying that the human was illusory, or at the very least devoid of all soteriological meaning. Cosmological Docetism does the same thing. It so prioritizes the divine over the created in cosmology that the creation can have no integrity of its own. It is therefore little more than an illusion or projection, lacking all of the reality of the divine. In other words, everything is "collapsed" from the divine side so that God is truly all that is. It is a zero-sum game where the divine controls all the resources and the created none. Christological Ebionism had the same problem from the other side. The Ebionites collapsed the divine into the human, so that the human is all there is. We will investigate their cosmological counterparts in the next chapter. The cosmological Docetist, on the other hand, takes the all-or-nothing

---

65. Farrell, *Free Choice*, 224–25. Italics in original.

66. The one thing standing in the way of any possibility of limited atonement is the patristic concept of human nature, which was itself removed in the nominalistic revolution. Once human nature is lost as a universal, limited atonement can rush in to fill the void.

The Hexagon of Heresy

zero-sum game to the extreme in reducing creation as far as can be done. I believe this very scenario occurs in the thought of a very famous American Congregationalist.

We saw the seeds of cosmological Docetism being planted in the last section concerning the doctrine of the single and simple decree. Recall that if, as is standard Reformed orthodoxy, the single decree is identical to God's essence, then God and the world are identified as well. The world is collapsed into God just as christological Docetism collapses the (fullness of or soteriological significance of) humanity of Christ into his divinity. Fortunately, most Reformed do not take their views on the decree to their obvious conclusions, but there is nothing except experience and religious impulse preventing it.

It might seem strange to say, given his almost iconic status in both American and Evangelical theology, but the clearest modern exponent of cosmological Docetism is the eighteenth-century, New England pastor and theologian Jonathan Edwards. Edwards was a prolific writer, pastor, theologian, philosopher, missionary, participant in the Great Awakening, and the first President of Princeton Theological Seminary. He is also likely the greatest American theologian. How could someone so distinguished be guilty of something that seems so far-fetched? Let us examine.

Cosmologically, Edwards is a unique blend of idealism, occasionalism, and continuous creationism. Let us unpack some of these concepts, utilizing the excellent analysis of Oliver Crisp in his study of Edwards's cosmology.[67] First, idealism is the belief that ideas are more real than material things. It is a philosophy rooted in the Hellenism of the Plotinian ambiguity.[68] Second, Crisp defines occasionalism thus: "I take it that occasionalism is the philosophical view according to which God is the only causal agent in the world. I think it is better expressed as: *all creaturely 'acts' are merely the 'occasions' of God's activity*. If occasionalism is true, then there are no causal agents other than God. He creates the world; but all instances of apparently mundane causation that obtain thereafter are actually mere occasions for divine action."[69] Third, Crisp defines continuous creation as "the view according to which God creates the world out of nothing, whereupon it momentarily ceases to exist, to be replaced by a facsimile that has incremental differences built into it to account for what appear to be motion and change across time. This, in turn, is annihilated, or ceases to exist, and is replaced by another facsimile world that has incremental differences built into it to

---

67. Crisp, *Edwards*.

68. The material is but a shadow of the idea in idealism, which ties the two together in a monist fashion, where the idea shapes the material. On the other hand, the material stands over against the ideal, and gives evidence that the ideal exists. It is the immaterial/material version of the Plotinian one/many.

69. Crisp, *Edwards*, 24. Italics in original. Crisp notes that Edwards's occasionalism is "gleaned from a number of places" including his *Some Thoughts Concerning the Revival, Freedom of the Will,* and *Miscellany* 267. Crisp provides the direct quotes from these sources in his text.

Cosmological Apollinarianism and Docetism

account for what appear to be motion and change across time, and so on."[70] Let us now unpack what this means for Edwards's cosmology.

According to Edwards, only God is true substance and real being, and human souls are a kind of created being. The closer one's nature is to God, the more being it has. This is clearly reminiscent of Aquinas and the analogy of being, with echoes back to Plotinus and the chain of emanations. For Edwards, the spiritual world is truly real, and the material world is only a shadow. He is writing in direct response to those whose materialistic pantheism (Baruch Spinoza, for example, whom we will meet in the next chapter) threaten to eliminate the spiritual to emphasize the material.[71] Edwards is surely correct to note the mistakes of Spinoza, but what he does is overcorrect Spinoza's identification of (or really the subsuming into) the divine and the created by doing the same thing in reverse, as we shall see. Let us now take a closer look at some of Edwards's philosophical and theological foundations.

Edwards holds God as pure act as a first principle. In this, Edwards follows the Western scholastic tradition of Aquinas and his Protestant successors, as Crisp writes, "This way of conceiving the divine essence was set forth by those medieval divines who, influenced by the Neoplatonism of theologians like Pseudo-Denys the Areopagite and Boethius, maintained that a perfect being must be one that exists independent of any other thing (*a se*), is a necessary being, and is one whose nature is entirely *realized* without remainder."[72] God as pure act, as we have already seen, is equivalent to the identity thesis corollary of definitional simplicity. Therefore, to define the divine nature as pure act is to define the divine nature as simple, as absence of potency is equivalent to the impossibility of composition. This is nothing new by now, as it is the same path Aquinas trod. That Edwards confesses his belief in definitional simplicity is not surprising, since he believes God to be pure act. Edwards, as quoted by Crisp, defines divine simplicity as "There are no distinctions to be admitted of faculty, habit, and act, between will, inclination, and love: but that it is all one simple act."[73] Crisp notes that if God is pure act, that is, with no unrealized potential, then he cannot have dispositions or inclinations, because dispositions may or may not be realized.[74] So then Edwards concludes that God's "disposition" to create is an essential "part" of his nature, and we are back to the Origenist Problematic all over again. There is no way to differentiate the "emanated" continuous creation from the nature of God himself once religious language is removed as excessive.

---

70. Crisp, *Edwards*, 25.

71. Crisp, *Edwards*, 33. He cites at length Edwards's "Things to Be Full Considered and Written About, Long Series," 44.

72. Crisp, *Edwards*, 38–39. Italics in original.

73. Crisp, *Edwards*, 41, quoting Jonathan Edwards, "Discourse on the Trinity," in Edwards, *Works*, 21:113.

74. Crisp, *Edwards*, 43.

Edwards's problem is not new, as we have seen in numerous examples. The threat of the necessity of creation is always lurking behind definitional simplicity and its attendant identity thesis. Origen capitulated to it. Augustine tried to block it with his seminal rational principles, with disastrous consequences. Aquinas constructed the "theological and philosophical equivalent of a medieval cathedral" to try to mask it.[75] If creation is necessary, then obviously God is not free, in a libertarian sense, concerning the decision to create. Crisp writes,

> Thomas argues that God creates in order to diffuse his goodness, saying, "the good is diffusive of itself and of being. But this diffusion befits God because . . . God is the cause of being for other things." Since divine goodness is identical to the divine nature and "diffusive of itself," as Thomas puts it, it looks like creation is a necessary act. Divine goodness must be diffused; and the only way in which that can happen is by some act of creation, since God himself cannot further diffuse his goodness within his own trinitarian life, if he is a fully realized, pure act.[76]

But Aquinas denies that creation is a necessary act of God. Like the Reformed theologians (including Edwards) who largely copy him, he cannot have it both ways. His assumption of God as pure act (concealing definitional simplicity with its attendant identity thesis) forces him, once he states that the good is diffusive by nature, down a path where the good and necessary consequences entail that creation is necessary, therefore eternal, and thus it is the Origenist Problematic reincarnated.

Edwards, of course, made his home within the Reformed tradition. We have already observed the Origenist Problematic as a necessary consequence of the identification of God and the decree, which is but a restatement of the definitional understanding of divine simplicity at the heart of Reformed theology holding that God's will is identical to God's essence. The Reformed want to emphasize freedom and simplicity simultaneously, which places them in the same sort of logical pickle that the Origenist Problematic does to the Thomists. Crisp writes, "So it seems that at least some of the Reformed were susceptible to a sort of theological doublethink about divine freedom. It looks like God can only be said to will differently if his will is not immutably identical to his essence, as a timeless, simple pure act."[77] Where the Roman and Reformed scholastics want to preserve in God the liberty of indifference ("God is free provided he is able to act or refrain from acting in a particular choice") along with the liberty of spontaneity ("God is free provided he is not constrained or coerced by anything external to choose one thing rather than another"), Edwards removes the liberty of

---

75. See Farrell, *God, History, and Dialectic*, 385–401. I am sure the "medieval cathedral" quotation is from Farrell, though I could not find exactly where he said it.

76. Crisp, *Edwards*, 61. He quotes Thomas Aquinas, *Summa Contra Gentiles*, 1.37.

77. Crisp, *Edwards*, 61.

indifference even from God.⁷⁸ As Crisp argues, because he thought that every action is preceded by a cause of some sort, Edwards is a "global theological determinist," that is, all beings, God included, are determined.⁷⁹ He adds, "For Edwards as a theologian the issue is a simple one: either contingency and liberty of self-determination must be run out of the world, or God will be shut out."⁸⁰ As can be seen, Edwards goes beyond his Reformed forebears. He is willing to remove God's freedom, and is therefore succumbing to that ancient equivalent of the identity thesis: what is natural is compelled. If God's nature is by definition simple, then there cannot be a plurality of choices even in him. Everything is determined, because the simple divine nature compels. It is zero-sum with God controlling all. In his cosmology, Edwards, unlike all of his monist forefathers such as Augustine, Aquinas, and the early Reformed thinkers, consistently applies the logic of monism and its zero-sum methodology to its good and necessary consequences: even God is trapped in the same snare as his creation—his nature compels him to do what he does (*natura naturans*).

What does such a construct do for Edwards's cosmology? While it is glossed in Christian language, the core is Neoplatonist. In Crisp's assessment, Edwards is able to avoid the pitfall of thinking that God somehow needs creation to be what he is, but in that the ultimate end of creation for God is self-glorification, even his relationship to creation is subordinated to that end.⁸¹ But, at the end of the day, Edwards believes that the only real substance is God after all. Creation, then, is just God's tool for his own self-glorification, and he is determined by his own simple nature to create it that way. His idealism thus ends in a world that cannot possess its own created integrity, since it is not truly real and its creator is not truly free. In this, he departs from the Reformed tradition quite noticeably.⁸²

Now we must turn to Edwards's doctrine of continuous creation. It is founded on his idealism and his occasionalism. In his fear that any real integrity in the creature will rob some glory from God, Edwards argues that the creature cannot be the true cause of anything, evidencing the complete inability to conceive of a creation that can do anything. As R. C. DeProspo notes, Edwards argues that the initial creation of the world out of nothing implies that the creation has no power from within itself, but must be completely dependent upon God, moment by moment.⁸³ Only God can be a first cause, and nothing in the created order possesses any kind of self-generating movement. It obviously implies that God does not or cannot create a world with self-generating causation for to do so would give creation at least some kind of minimal

---

78. Crisp, *Edwards*, 63. The definitions are direct quotes, respectively, from pages 59 and 58.
79. Crisp, *Edwards*, 65.
80. Edwards, *Works*, 1:9, quoted in Crisp, *Edwards*, 63.
81. Crisp, *Edwards*, 90.
82. See the Westminster Confession of Faith, 2.1, as well as the discussion in Hinlicky, *Divine Simplicity*, 199.
83. DeProspo, *Theism*, 79.

score in the zero-sum game. In my opinion, this moves beyond the cosmological Monophysitism of Augustine or the cosmological Apollinarianism of the post-Reformation era. They all held to the possibility of secondary causation, even though they may have been sacrificing complete coherence in their theological constructions to uphold such a possibility. Edwards, however, is consistent: there can be no genuine created secondary cause.

Arguing against those convinced of the mechanical closed universe (the cosmological Arians and Ebionites that we will survey in the next chapter), Edwards believed that the interdependence of the created order implied a continuous external cause, rather than a closed internal mechanism.[84] As DeProspo summarizes Edwards's thought on the matter, "Edwards ascribes the form of nature to the fiat of God, this time emphasizing his control of physics. Reason acknowledges not only that 'a thing that begins to be cannot make itself,' but also that nothing that continues to be can itself sustain existence. The complicated economy of the universe depends primarily on the continuous exertion of God's will, secondarily, on natural law."[85] Crisp writes, "Edwards' doctrine of God's relation to the world he creates is rather like that of a projectionist and the motion picture he is responsible for projecting onto the theatrical screen: each world-stage God creates is similar to a discrete photographic still that is one of many such stills in the series, segued together in sequence on a reel that is then projected onto the silver screen of a movie theater, giving the illusion of continuous action across time."[86] That is, God must recreate the world moment by moment, because not only can there not be a cause within creation, creation cannot even sustain its own persistence; God must grant persistence through the doctrine of continuous creation. Occasionalism combined with continuous creation results in the denial of creaturely persistence across time, as well as the elimination of secondary causes and created moral responsibility.[87] Edwards cannot even ascribe moral responsibility to Adam in the transmission of original sin, an Augustinian doctrine Edwards is zealous to uphold. DeProspo writes, "God, not Adam, is properly to be considered the author of man's nature, and to rail against the doctrine of imputation is not . . . to declare one's independence of a wicked earthly parent, but to renounce the heavenly Father."[88] Under the doctrine of continuous creation, then, God is beyond good and evil, because he is now both. He is the Platonic One which emanates all things, both good and evil, but yet is above and beyond both. The logical conclusions of such a doctrine are obvious: God is the author of evil, and he is so for his own glory. Moreover, the cosmological Docetism in such a doctrine is equally obvious. Edwards is a monist in the strongest possible sense.

84. Crisp, *Edwards*, 79–80.
85. Crisp, *Edwards*, 80.
86. Crisp, *Edwards*, 9.
87. Crisp, *Edwards*, 32.
88. DeProspo, *Theism*, 80.

Cosmological Apollinarianism and Docetism

Crisp believes Edwards to be both a Neoplatonist and a panentheist,[89] who looks for a third way between classical (i.e., Western, simplicity-driven) theism and the emerging pantheism of the early modern period, that, in the words of Douglas Elwood, that "would do justice on the one hand to God's all-comprehensiveness, and on the other, to his creative presence in the world."[90] What Edwards as well as all those who followed him have failed to grasp is that there is no third way within the larger system of definitional simplicity and its attendant Plotinian ambiguity. There is no middle ground in which the one and the many can meet. It is either-or, and again, Edwards has cast his lot with the one. The marriage of Neoplatonism and Christianity yielded a world that is "in God" but not identical to God. The only thing that keeps the world from being identical to God is the Christian conviction that there is a distinction. Unfortunately, Edwards cannot ground such a distinction in anything other than assertion, given his cocktail of idealism, occasionalism, and continuous creationism, as the Origenist Problematic resurfaces in colonial America. For Edwards, all reality is in the divine mind, and that is the locus of his panentheism.[91]

There is one more issue with definitional simplicity in Edwards's theology that needs discussed. Edwards believes, according to Crisp, "Necessarily, any created theater of divine glory must be one in which all aspects of that glory are manifested."[92] This means that there must be eternal punishment for some humans because retributive justice is "part" (though only conceptually so due to definitional simplicity) of God's nature and must be demonstrated for God to be fully glorified in creation. In Edwards's doctrine of reprobation and double predestination, which he brings to the table from his Reformed background, there is no account of how the reprobate are linked to Christ, beyond the idea that Christ is creator and sustainer and judge.[93] Again, we should expect this, given the historical and universal Western difficulty in explaining the mediation of creation christologically. Moreover, God cannot save all because reprobation is essential for the full display of his glory.[94] But even Edwards's understanding of eternal reward or punishment is tainted with his doctrine of continuous creation. Because, in Edwards's theology, nothing created persists through time, no one person is ever deified or eternally punished. Also, because of occasionalism, no one merits reward or punishment, for every deed committed arises from God alone as

---

89. DeProspo, *Theism*, 159. He sees Edwards as a panentheist in the mode of Plotinus, that is, a monist.

90. Elwood, *Philosophical Theology*, 21, as quoted in Crisp, *Edwards*, 139.

91. Crisp, *Edwards*, 151.

92. Crisp, *Edwards*, 178.

93. Crisp, *Edwards*, 182–83.

94. Crisp, *Edwards*, 184. It should be obvious by now that "glory" in the thought of Edwards (and just about every other Reformed adherent to definitional simplicity) is a synonym for nature on display. As it should be, for they already identify energy (glory) and essence as a first principle. Such a construction renders the phrase "God's glory" empty, because it can only be *natura naturans*.

sole agent.[95] In the end, Edwards, while using lots of familiar Christian terminology to elucidate his cosmology, has undergirded them with a Neoplatonic substructure that forces us to rethink everything he writes. He has stripped all internal integrity away from creation.

Edwards was widely renowned as a pastor, and by all accounts seems to have been a good one. But the pastoral implications of such a cosmology are immense. If Edwards is correct, then nothing we see is truly real in itself. Even "I" am not real. "I" have disappeared and have been recreated dozens of times while typing this sentence. "I" exist for but a moment, replaced by another "me" who thinks he is the sum total of each and every "I" that has come before. "My" actions, whether good or bad, are not "mine." Both who "I" am and what "I" do are nothing more than occasions in the "simple" mind of God and must necessarily occur. "I" will either enjoy heavenly bliss or tortuous damnation due to what God has determined concerning "me" for eternity, one movie frame at a time. In such a cosmology, everyone and everything is resigned to be what it is and do what it does, with absolutely no hope or no help to be otherwise. Because of Edwards's radical commitment to monism and the zero-sum game it must entail, God must be all and creation must be none. The created order is nothing but a material extension of the mind of a meticulously controlling playwright who himself is determined by his nature to do and think what he does. Such a world cannot even engender the hopelessness and despair it should, because even those, to even exist, must as well be divine occasions. God is the only explanation for absolutely everything.

Edwards's panentheism leads to more theological problems. A necessary creation of this world means that this world is an emanation (in the continuist creation sense) from God. It is, so to speak, his "body." Crisp writes, "If, in some attenuated sense, the world for the panentheistic Edwardsian is akin to the body of God, then it is a body that harbors a cancer that can never be excised and that will generate pain and misery forever."[96] Good and evil lose all their meaning, even in God. In Edwards, we see the full flowering of the Plotinian ambiguity; Edwards's God is Plotinus's One dressed in Christian vocabulary. He monistically emanates the material world which stands in opposition to him, as he wills. The monistic system is both good and evil; both love and hate are equally strong, à la Manichaeism. Everything that is not-God is but an occasion in his mind, showing forth nothing that is meaningful in the end. Everything is collapsed into God from the divine side in the ultimate expression of monism. Crisp writes, "In the final analysis, Edwards is nothing if not a Christian Neoplatonist. The world exists as a divine idea that God 'emanates' moment by moment. But no created thing has the power to persist through time."[97] As christological Docetism was the removal of all the significance, if not the complete removal in fact, of the humanity of Jesus, so Jonathan Edwards succeeded in stripping away all of the significance and

95. Crisp, *Edwards*, 186.
96. Crisp, *Edwards*, 187.
97. Crisp, *Edwards*, 9.

integrity of the created order. It can do nothing of itself. God must move everything, and he must do so by continually creating everything so as to guarantee that nothing created has even the remote possibility for anything self-generating. I do not believe that a clearer case of cosmological Docetism could possibly exist, as Edwards has taken everything from creation, even its ability to persist through time, in order that God may be all in a zero-sum theological construction. At the end of the day, Edwards believes that the only real substance is God after all. Creation, then, is just God's tool for his own self-glorification, and he is determined by his own simple nature to create it that way. It is little wonder, as Perry Robinson points out, that Unitarianism came to dominate Edwards's New England a half century after his death.[98] The Unitarians "simply" removed any plurality from God himself, becoming, literally, the "One."

Conclusion

This chapter has argued that deep in the Reformation tradition lies a view of the world that fundamentally reduces or eliminates the created integrity of everything that is not-God. The fourteenth-century Augustinian revival, led by Bradwardine and Gregory of Rimini, launched a world of theological determinism and double predestination that galvanized into a movement that attempted to make sense of the nominalistic revolution. The magisterial Reformation proved to be a violent swing back to cosmological monism from the dichotomist/dualism of the largely nominalistic Roman Catholic Church of the early sixteenth century. The Reformers, however, in my opinion, failed to diagnose the ultimate cause of all the Western theological angst: the doctrine of definitional simplicity with its attendant identity thesis and Plotinian ambiguity. Their monist determinism, seen in the doctrines of double predestination and limited atonement (the latter in Reformed churches), was a result of the identity thesis in the identification of foreknowledge and predestination, as well as in the inability to distinguish person from nature.[99] In such a cosmology, creation is robbed of its internal integrity, as God must be the ultimate "cause" of all things. This lack of the full integrity in the created order is what I have called cosmological Apollinarianism, paralleling the christological heresy that removes the fullness of creation (humanity) from Jesus. During the intellectually volatile world of the sixteenth through the eighteenth centuries, Bradwardine's successors took his views in a step-by-step fashion to their logical conclusions—the denial of created causes. This endgame is cosmological Docetism.[100]

---

98. See Robinson, "Killing Your Father."

99. Gunton, *Triune Creator*, 182, notes the difficulty involved in the Western tradition to explain providence as anything other than determinism. This problem traces all the way back to Augustine in sowing the seeds of the confusion between predestination and providence. What is needed is a distinction between God's will and God's act, which is impossible in a world dominated by definitional simplicity. Sadly, the Reformers and their successors were unable to disentangle Western Christian theology from the pagan substructure on which it was erected.

100. Gunton, *Triune Creator*, 45.

The Hexagon of Heresy

Within any cosmology where definitional simplicity is a first principle, there is always an extreme tension between the created world and the God who creates it: that is, what I have called the Plotinian ambiguity. The system requires playing one side off of the other. As Luther had a hidden and revealed God, Calvin's God possessed a hidden and revealed will. (Even though Calvin repeatedly stressed that the will of God is one—the distinction is only conceptual—and we have seen this response before.) Both of these positions result from not allowing creation to really exist for itself, and is an immediate vestige of the Plotinian ambiguity lurking behind definitional simplicity.[101] Even within the overarching monist response to the nominalistic revolution, there remains the Plotinian ambiguity. Luther affirms created history within the superstructure of monistic determinism, and this forces him to posit the hidden and revealed God to account for it. On the other hand, Calvin and the later Reformed theologians make created history irrelevant through the adoption of the definitionally simple decree. The former will provide fertile breeding ground for dichotomist-dualism, while the latter will fight tooth and nail to remain purely monist, despite the visible evidence to the contrary. In the next chapter, we will survey the rise of the dichotomist-dualist answers to the Plotinian ambiguity that came out of the nominalistic revolution, those I call cosmological Arianism and Ebionism.

---

101. Placher, *Domestication*, 63.

11

Cosmological Arianism and Ebionism

THIS CHAPTER WILL SURVEY the cosmological models I call Arian and Ebionite. As I will argue, these positions begin with the assumption of definitional divine simplicity inherited from the Western tradition. Unlike the magisterial Protestants and the Augustinian-Thomist Roman Catholic traditions, these models will seek to utilize the data found within the created order to make sense of God and the world. Just as christological "Arianism" denied the fullness of the divinity of Jesus, what I will call cosmological Arianism will deny the fullness of God's action in the world, either by the explanation of "nature," or by a conscious rebellion against more monist cosmological models. Those who take the reality of the created order to the extreme will do so by first unifying God and creation from the side of the world, creating a pantheism, and then take the next step of eliminating God all together in a move to philosophical naturalism. I will call the pantheists and naturalists cosmological Ebionites.

As the seeds of the cosmological Apollinarianism and Docetism were sown in the confusion of God and the world in the Augustinian tradition, so the seeds of the topics of this chapter were likewise firmly planted in the Augustinian separation of creator and creation. Augustine is responsible for the fateful commitment to definitional simplicity as a theological first principle, and, as we have repeatedly seen, it comes with two corollaries: the identity thesis confusing person, nature, and energy, and the Plotinian ambiguity, which holds that cosmology is at the same time one and divided—the simultaneous confusion and division of the one and the many. The Plotinian ambiguity demands a zero-sum game, in that to emphasize either the one or the many (in our case God or the world), demands the decrease of the other. We saw in the last chapter that the exaltation of the one in cosmological Apollinarianism and Docetism forced the reduction of the many. We will see the opposite process occur in this chapter. Let's begin with cosmological Arianism.

The Hexagon of Heresy

Cosmological Arianism: Theological and Historical Background

To begin, I want to very briefly revisit what has already been discussed in chapters 8 and 9. We saw that, due to his adoption of definitional simplicity in the doctrine of God, Augustine was forced to make a major modification in order to avoid the Origenist Problematic. He defined the seminal rational principles as created things through which creation is mediated, thereby separating God and the world in a move that I labeled as cosmologically Nestorian. Chapter 9 then showed how the seeds of separation began to grow throughout the medieval period, especially in the distinction between the ordinary and absolute power of God and the gradual ascendance of the way to view the world as the ordinary power working under natural laws. The great bombshell, precipitated by the volitional turn of Scotus, was the nominalistic revolution of William of Ockham. We noted Michael Gillespie's thesis that there were three great movements following Ockham, each using a different ontic priority to try to make cosmological sense of the God of nominalism—humanism, Reformation, and modernism.

For our purposes, humanism is but a minor player in the controversy once the Reformation is in full swing. Before the Reformation, however, humanism flourished, as it was the first historical (and generally nominalist) revolution against the monist medieval world. Humanism, as was noted above, remained generally loyal to Roman Catholicism, hoping to reform the church from within. The Counter-Reformation return to Thomism and its monistic implications, however, forced the humanists to turn elsewhere, and many became absorbed into the new movement of modernism. It is the modernists that form the largest contingent of what will become the cosmological Arians.

We briefly introduced Francis Bacon as the fountainhead of the modern movement at the end of chapter 7, as he ontically prioritized creation over humans and God, although certainly not to the extent that those who came after him would. Bacon, the father of modern science, thought that previous attempts at doing science were unsuccessful because "they did not use the powers available to them to attain this end, relying instead on mere observation and overhasty generalization." Gillespie continues, "What is needed, he argued, is a total reconstruction of science, the arts, and human knowledge on a proper foundation."[1] Bacon, unlike the scholastics, was more concerned with how things worked than what things are. His concern was practical rather than speculative—that is, focused on this world of the many rather than on the unseen world of the one. Cruelty was the process by which the practicality is obtained. Gillespie writes, "Only as merciless servants who bind and torture their master to learn the source of his power can we win from nature the knowledge of its hidden forces and operation."[2] Thus scientific knowledge comes through experimentation,

---

1. Gillespie, *Theological Origins*, 37.
2. Gillespie, *Theological Origins*, 38–39. Gunton, *Triune Creator*, 126–27, notes concerning the

not through reasoning from monistically-oriented first principles. Christopher Kaiser adds another important contribution by Bacon which is both in continuity with those who came before and a radical departure, as he writes, concerning Bacon's view that "nature and grace were two separate kingdoms or departments of the *potentia Dei ordinate* [ordinary power]."[3] Bacon simultaneously continues the separation of God and the world that he received through the medieval tradition, while moving grace from a transcendent to an immanent reality. Grace is this-worldly, rather than from God directly, which is the first step of widening the received cosmological Nestorianism into something deeper. The next figure in our historical survey leading up to the inception of cosmological Arianism is René Descartes.

Descartes and (Dichotomist-Dualist) Foundationalism

French philosopher René Descartes noticed that things held to be true either by tradition or by perception could be, in reality, completely wrong, such as a belief in a flat earth.[4] His reaction to this possibility was to begin with a methodology of doubt as the beginning of acquiring knowledge. Everything would be doubted until he reached a foundation, a bedrock of sorts, where knowledge was absolutely certain.[5] Then, true and reliable knowledge could be built off of that foundation. His famous quote, "I think, therefore I am," became the bedrock for his method, in that he could legitimately doubt everything but his own capacity to think.[6] All traditions and perceptions were fair game for the doubting process, guided by the one unassailable light, his own reason. Once something was tested and found true after presumed doubt, then it could be confidently proclaimed a "certain truth" and a "first principle" from which

---

tradition, beginning in Bacon, but extending through Galileo to Kant, that if nature will not reveal her secrets, she must be tortured to reveal them. Bacon asserted that real knowledge comes as a result of utilizing a proper method to discover truth. Interestingly, this same process was useful in the higher biblical criticism in the ensuing centuries. We will see this occur in repeatedly in this chapter.

3. Kaiser, *Creational Theology*, 183. This separation will loom large in Descartes as well, as he will build on the idea that matter is passive (Kaiser, *Creational Theology*, 215).

4. Sparks, *God's Word*, 33.

5. Gillespie, *Theological Origins*, 171, writes, "Descartes sought to construct a bastion of reason against this terrifying God of nominalism, a bastion that could provide not only individual certainty and security, and not only mitigate or eliminate the incommodities of nature, but also bring an end to the religious and political strife that were tearing Europe to pieces. Descartes aimed to achieve this and make man master and possessor of nature by developing a mathematical science that could provide a picture of the true world underlying the phenomena."

6. See Gillespie, *Theological Origins*, 196 for the extended discussion and direct quotes as paraphrased here. For Descartes, there were two existing answers to his doubt. One was faith in God, but this could not "alleviate doubt because it is God himself who is the source of the doubts." Atheism is worse than faith, because if atheism is true, then humans are continually deceived about how the world really is, and there is only blind chance. Therefore, neither faith nor atheism is a sufficient foundation for science. He arrives at the personal, thinking subject, "I think, therefore I am" as the only possible foundation, in what Gillespie calls, anachronistically, a "Kantian synthetic *a priori* truth."

other knowledge could be rationally deduced. What both Bacon and Descartes desired was to make humanity the "master and possessor of nature,"[7] and the goal of the latter was a "universal mathematics" that would explain everything.[8]

To accomplish his task, Descartes, like the humanists and Reformers before him (as part of his legacy to nominalism), located the center of human being in the will.[9] Descartes's human was able to divide his mind from his body (Cartesian dualism) to produce a subject that is "abstracted from the historical world, and has no personality, no virtues or vices, no concern with immortal fame. The willing subject, however, is not constrained by the finitude of this world and consequently can imagine becoming its absolute master."[10] In doing so, the will becomes master of not only the self, but also of the world and of God.[11] The recognition of self in the fundamental principle ("I think, therefore I am") is also a recognition of the limitations of the self, so the idea of infinite, or "God," is built in to the system.[12] This is the dichotomist-dualist half of the Plotinian ambiguity clearly on display, as he is emphasizing the creation, in a dichotomist-dualist fashion, by accentuating the divide between it and its creator. Descartes is firmly grounded in definitional simplicity. In an extended quote that goes to the heart of Descartes's ideas, Gillespie writes,

> It thus follows that in the same act that I will myself to be I, I will God to be God. This God that I will, however, is not the omnipotent and potentially

---

7. Gillespie, *Theological Origins*, 190.

8. Buckley, *Origins*, 80. Buckley notes that Descartes wanted a universal mathematics that would consolidate all knowledge, broken down into three general headings: medicine, mechanics, and morals. Buckley writes, "But at what a cost! Descartes has left the world godless" (*Origins*, 97). See chapter 7, n16 for how similar Descartes is to Aquinas at this point.

9. Gillespie, *Theological Origins*, 40–41. Gillespie here discusses how Descartes synthesizes insights from humanism (man the autonomous and self-sufficient being), nominalism (man as infinite will), and Luther (the conjunction of the human and divine will). "It is this potent combination that gives rise to the notion of subjectivity that plays a central role in rationalism, idealism, and later continental thought as well."

10. Gillespie, *Theological Origins*, 199. "I imagine, therefore it is" is but a derivative of the ontological argument of Anselm of Canterbury, which itself rests on definitional simplicity and its attendant identification of essence and energy. Kaiser, *Creational Theology*, 216, shows that Descartes made "geometric extension" the essence of matter. This identification of extension and essence in the material world parallels Aquinas's identification of existence and essence in the divine world. Since the power of the mind has no geometric extension, the Cartesian dualism of mind and matter is therefore established, as well as laying the groundwork for the utter separation of the natural and spiritual.

11. Gillespie, *Theological Origins*, 199. The human will becoming the master of God is possible because of divine simplicity. As Kaiser, *Creational Theology*, 216–17, argues, matter is passive, so all the laws of physics were directly attributable to God. Since God's act and being are identical, what God does is what God is. Therefore, since God is eternal and unchangeable, the laws of physics were likewise eternal and unchangeable. It follows that to master physics is to master God, at least to Descartes.

12. Gillespie, *Theological Origins*, 203. Placher, *Domestication of Transcendence*, 131, notes that Descartes desired univocal language of God that was devoid of all mystery. Buckley, *Origins*, 92–94, notes that in Descartes's philosophy, because God cannot deceive, the sensible universe is derived from the nature of God, which is in turn derived from the self.

malevolent God of nominalism that produced such fear and uncertainty. Nor is he Luther's hidden (or revealed) God. In fact, this God cannot be a deceiver because he is not aware of himself and therefore not aware of the difference between him and I. For Descartes, I come to recognize myself as limited and distinct at the end of the path of doubt. In becoming self-conscious, in positing myself as a finite being, I recognized myself as distinct from other beings, as needy, as imperfect. God, however, comes to no such realization. He is not finite and thus cannot be self-conscious of himself because his will is never impeded, never limited by what it is not. God thus cannot distinguish himself from all that is. As a result, he cannot be a deceiver. And if God is not a deceiver, then Descartes' universal science is secure. Descartes in this way tames the nominalist God by reducing him to pure intellectual substance. . . . He asserts God is pure intelligence. God's intelligence, however, in Descartes' mature thought is equivalent to his will. As pure intelligence, God is pure will. As infinite, God's will is not directed to anything specific; it is causality as such. God is the *causa sui* because he is pure causality, the mechanism at the heart of mechanical nature, a how and not a what.[13]

Descartes's God is totally impersonal, the prime mover, indistinguishable from creation. In other words, he is the Platonic One and we have the Origenist Problematic in full bloom at the heart of this so-called third ontic answer to nominalism. Gillespie adds, "The God that Descartes first imagined and feared was a titanic God, beyond reason and nature, beyond good and evil. Descartes won his struggle with this fearsome God only by taking this God's power upon himself. He thereby opened up the hope and aspiration for human omnipotence, a hope that has manifested itself repeatedly since in monstrous form."[14] Now we see the third answer to nominalism for what it is. It transfers divinity from God to humanity, thereby in time making even the concept of God superfluous. For the thinking and socially conscious European of the seventeenth century, Descartes's philosophy is far more appealing than the oppression

---

13. Gillespie, *Theological Origins*, 204. Cartesian science then aims to master the God of nominalism by "reconstructing the chaos of the world in representation, by transforming the flux of experience into the motion of objects in a mathematically analyzable space. The omnipotent God of nominalism and the Reformation is thus unable to enter into Descartes's rationalized universe unless he gives up his absolute will and lives according to the powers that Descartes ordains. He is dispossessed of his absolute power and his world, which falls increasingly under the hegemony of the scientific ego." The words "pure intellectual substance" should bring to remembrance the initial move of Origen, *Princ.* 1.1.6, in n60 of chapter 2. Descartes's basic understanding of the divine essence is exactly Origen's: pure intellectual substance, and obviously definitionally simple.

14. Gillespie, *Theological Origins*, 206. Gillespie, on page 205, notes that man and God are similar because they are willing beings. The difference does not lie in the power of the will, but in knowledge. For man to become god, he must utilize his will to become master of nature. The human rational will then becomes the image of God in us. Gunton, *One, Three, and Many*, 108, citing Craig, *Mind*, 32, states that Craig "finds to emerge in modern philosophy, beginning with Galileo and Descartes, . . . a tendency to suppose 'quantitative difference by qualitative identity' between divine and human minds." That is, both are part of the great chain of being.

and wars waged by the Catholics and Protestants, each trying to impose or defend its own brand of monism over against the other. The Enlightenment is born.

The implications of Descartes's ideas are immense. What separates Descartes from Bacon, in the words of Gillespie, is that he "grounds all of modern science on an autonomous subject who not only transcends nature but is also able to resist and ultimately challenge (or even replace) God himself. Man for Descartes becomes master and possessor of nature by dispossessing its current owner, that is, by taking it away from God. This is possible because man in some sense already is God, or at least is the same infinite will that constitutes God."[15] If God, as was stated above, is indistinguishable from all that is, then man can claim the throne, so to speak. The Plotinian ambiguity is in full view as Gillespie adds,

> Insofar as Descartes both leaves man within nature as a body in motion and elevates him above it into a quasi-omnipotence, he lays the groundwork for an inevitable and irremediable dissatisfaction that poses tremendous moral and political dangers for modernity. The infinite human will constantly strives to master and transcend the body but is itself at the same time always bodily. In its striving to realize its infinite essence, it must always negate the finite. Such a negation however, is impossible. As idealistic and noble as its aspirations may be, idealism in its practical form thus constantly faces a millenarian temptation to use ever more extreme means of control to achieve its unachievable ends.[16]

Michael Buckley adds, though Descartes has demonstrated the existence of the universe, and has asserted that it depends completely on God, "but the world does not assert or witness the existence of God. Just as the human person became a hazardous unity between the machine that is the body and the thinking that is the ego, so the unity of the sciences became a fragile concatenation of a metaphysics that inquiries into thinking and a physics that examines the mathematical possibilities of extension. Wisdom lay in keeping them together."[17] He summarizes the final outcome: "By elaborating a distinct metaphysics, Descartes had sanctioned off theological enquiry from any evidence in the world studied by the sciences."[18] Therefore, all that is left

---

15. Gillespie, *Theological Origins*, 40.

16. Gillespie, *Theological Origins*, 41. See also Buckley, *Origins*, 203, as control becomes necessary because in Descartes's system, there are no final causes, or *telos* to creation. Descartes's modern man is, unsurprisingly by now, a reproduction of the Plotinian ambiguity in his very self: he is the monist god of his own existence while remaining mortal, created, and opposed to the ideal. On the ever-increasing use of control to keep the fallacy alive, that is what we are seeing played out in the political, economic, financial, educational, and virtually every other institution globally today. Thus, the political ends of both cosmological sides of the Plotinian ambiguity end in total control (high Medieval Catholicism and 21st-century "democracy"), effectively eliminating creaturely freedom in both cases to achieve their ends.

17. Buckley, *Origins*, 98

18. Buckley, *Origins*, 129. Gillespie, *Theological Origins*, 36, notes that because of the chaotic view of creation brought about by nominalism, it is not really important for materialistic science if there is a God or not.

Cosmological Arianism and Ebionism

is the created order on its own, and thus Descartes is the originator of the modern concept of a mechanical world, though the roots of such thought extend well back into medieval times, and in reality all the way back to Augustine's move to make the rational principles created things themselves. Here are the clear beginnings of moving past Augustine into cosmological Arianism: like the cosmological Apollinarianism discussed last chapter, the created order has no integrity (akin to the absence of a human soul in Jesus). If creation is only a machine, then it is determined by its own natural laws, as well as something to be used and exploited, rather than something for which to care. Descartes first framed the "laws of nature" and consistent with his work already discussed, made natural laws immutable and entertained the eternity of creation.[19] His dualism between mind and matter led to Deism.[20] Kaiser summarizes,

> In hindsight we may say that there was no available alternative consistent with the progress of science and human welfare [than the mechanical theory]. Given the theological inheritance of the Middle Ages, in which God's direct action and the normal causal connections of nature were mutually exclusive, the only way to isolate the mechanical aspects of nature was to bracket out the spiritual. The decision in favor of the mechanical philosophy was not made until the mid-seventeenth century, but the theology that required it had been worked out as early as the twelfth.[21]

It should be obvious that Descartes is playing by the same set of philosophical and theological rules (the dialectical construction of the divine essence and the observable world) as his intellectual ancestors: Origen, Augustine, Aquinas, and Ockham. Where he departs from them, in a move of utter genius, is they all used the dialectical construction of definitional simplicity as a way to understand God vis-à-vis the creation. Descartes uses the construction (primarily a variant of Anselm's ontological argument) in an attempt to understand the observable world over against God. This move is "within the rules" because both God and the world are on the same ontological plane, held together by the chain of being. Descartes just reverses the polarity of the discussion, so to speak. His ancestors were all theologians; he was not. For the observant, Descartes's work exposes the "dark side" of the ultimately pagan dialectical construction: it could be used to dethrone and dispose of God just as easily as it could be used to magnify him. No one had ever tried it before.

The early modern period, like the early Reformation era, was torn at its birth by the Plotinian ambiguity. As Luther was a monist who took seriously the saga of created history, so Thomas Hobbes, the dialectical counterpart to Descartes, was a dichotomist-dualist with monist impulses, though his monism was not the one of his philosophical ancestors. To illustrate definitional simplicity at work, Hobbes sees man

---

19. Kaiser, *Creational Theology*, 217.
20. Gunton, *Triune Creator*, 126–27.
21. Kaiser, *Creational Theology*, 234–35. We already discussed this in chapter 9.

as merely a part of nature, with no teleology, but mechanically determined. Man is not moved from within (natural impulses of free will), nor from beyond (by God), but from without, in collision with other natural objects. Humans have no free will and never transcend the natural world in which they live. Hobbes's world is not yearning to break free from the monism of Rome and Geneva; rather it is imprisoned in a fixed determinism that is the glue that binds cosmological Arians and Apollinarians together. On the other hand, Descartes is the purest form of dichotomist-dualism in the early modern period.[22] For Hobbes, the two great dangers are man's desire for glory (humanism) and the belief that this world influences the next (the central idea of the Reformation). For him, a "correct" view of predestination (contra Luther and Calvin) is that since all is predetermined, nothing we do here matters for salvation, because all is already fixed. Paradoxically, following the Plotinian ambiguity, man therefore needs to subdue nature for his own pleasure and well-being.[23]

In the debate between Descartes and Hobbes, it seems as though the two great aims of modernity—"to make man master and possessor of nature and to make human freedom possible"—are mutually incompatible. Although Gillespie sees this as a rehashing of the debate between Erasmus and Luther, we have seen the same dilemma in every chapter of this book. Everywhere the dialectical construction of definitional simplicity has been employed throughout history, it creates the same incompatibility and it is always due to the Plotinian ambiguity: the human dilemma here is identical to the decretal dilemma of the Reformed. Definitional simplicity promises but never delivers that we can have our cake and eat it too. He writes,

> For Descartes as for Erasmus, there is human freedom in addition to the causality through nature. For Hobbes as for Luther there is only the absolute power of God as the ultimate cause behind the motion of all matter. In this way, we see the reemergence at the very heart of modernity of the problematic relationship of the human and the divine that bedeviled Christianity from its beginning. The modern ontic turn away from man and God to nature thus in the end still assumes a continuing metaphysical and structural importance for the very categories it seeks to transcend. The successors to Hobbes and Descartes in the modern tradition struggle with this question. The Enlightenment in particular is characterized by a series of unsuccessful attempts to solve this problem. The centrality of this problem to the modern enterprise becomes apparent in Kant's antinomy doctrine and in the French Revolution. At the end of modernity, we are thus left to confront the question whether there is any

---

22. Recall from chapter 10, although Luther and Calvin were both monists, Luther had some dichotomist-dualist impulses in taking creation seriously. In the dichotomist-dualist world of modernity, it was Thomas Hobbes who had monist leanings. Both the Reformed and Descartes were the "true believers," so to speak, of monism and dichotomist-dualism, respectively.

23. Gillespie, *Theological Origins*, 42. That is, if all is mechanically determined, why does man "need" to do anything? The Plotinian ambiguity forces everyone trapped in it to speak out of "both sides of their mouth," to borrow an Appalachian expression from my youth.

Cosmological Arianism and Ebionism

solution to this problem within the ontological horizon that modernity opens up, and thus whether modernity even in its most secular form can escape from the metaphysical/theological problem from which it began."[24]

To answer Gillespie's question, there is no solution because the great philosophers of the early modern period were held captive by the Plotinian ambiguity and the identity thesis, the two corollaries of definitional simplicity. Modernity attempted to throw off the control of the simple, monist God of both Rome and the Reformers, but could not escape its entailments for their conception of the God they rejected never changed. We now must discuss one more angle to the simplicity problem, epistemological foundationalism.

Both Descartes and the scholastics operated with an epistemological foundationalism as their methodology, that is, the idea that there are the foundational truths off of which to build a body of knowledge. We have seen this operative in both Aquinas with his natural theology and Descartes and his universal mathematics (both "sides" employ it). Christian Smith writes,

> Epistemological foundationalism is a conviction that rational humans can and must identify a common foundation of knowledge directly up from and upon which every reasonable thinker can and ought to build a body of completely reliable knowledge and understanding. Such a foundation upon which all knowledge is to be built must stand indubitably against all challenges, must be universally accessible to all rational people, and must unfailingly produce the kind of reliable knowledge sought after. When such a foundation is secured, then the resultant knowledge that will be built from and upon it will be for all rational people absolutely certain, completely truthful, and universally binding.[25]

Smith continues, "The modern epistemological foundationalist project thus promised and pursued the kind of certainty, universality, and security that people not only often yearn for generally, but also were particularly lacking in the early modern era—as a result of the fracturing of Christendom, religious and civil wars, political instabilities, unsettling new world discoveries, and more."[26] A world in upheaval needs some form of normalcy, which the ontic priority of creation that Bacon and Descartes proposed attempted to provide. The problem is that, just like their religious counterparts in Roman Catholicism and Protestantism, the early moderns were completely devoted to the concept of definitional simplicity and its Plotinian ambiguity that forced a zero-sum game between the one and many, which precipitated epistemological foundationalism.

By the latter decades of the seventeenth century, there were two distinct kinds of foundationalism present in Protestant Europe. One, belonging to the monist Protestant scholastics, started in the supernatural world, with the Bible as the absolute

---

24. Gillespie, *Theological Origins*, 42–43.
25. Smith, *Bible Made Impossible*, 150.
26. Smith, *Bible Made Impossible*, 150.

word of God to humans. The other, the dichotomist-dualist foundationalism of Descartes and the Enlightenment, started in this world, in human reason and what it could know either deductively (rationalism) or inductively (empiricism). The former sought to know the world in terms of God, while the latter, operating in the knowledge gleaned from the world, increasingly saw God as obsolete. Lurking behind the two foundations is the Plotinian ambiguity and definitional simplicity. As Nancey Murphy argues, these two foundations are mutually exclusive;[27] the one and the many stand opposed. The script, as we are coming to realize, is always followed in the same fashion. The dichotomist-dualists wind up asserting creation's independence, while the monists end up in some variation of a necessary creation. For example, at the end of his well-argued case for a Reformed version of the identity thesis, grounded of course in both Aquinas and the Reformed scholastics, James E. Dolezal claims that "There has never been a temporal or logical moment in the divine life in which God stood volitionally open to other possible worlds."[28] The response from Paul Hinlicky is enlightening: "That is to say, there is no third way in the doctrine of God between a libertarian freedom of arbitrary choice and the simple identity in God of intellection and volition. It is either Occam on to Descartes or Thomas on to Dolezal's version of the Westminster Confession. Either/or!"[29] Here are the two foundations that will battle over both cosmology and biblical inspiration for the next 350 years, and both are grounded in the identity thesis of divine simplicity. The great weakness we will continue to see is the inability for foundationalism to adapt to any sort of give-and-take; it is knowledge that progresses in only one direction: from the bedrock to the conclusions. It is the attempt to utilize one side of the Plotinian ambiguity to make sense of the other.[30] With Descartes, though, the modern turn is definitely underway.

---

27. Murphy, *Beyond Liberalism and Fundamentalism*, 79–80. It is the same reason that Lutheran and Reformed versions of Protestantism are mutually exclusive.

28. Dolezal, *God without Parts*, 207, quoted in Hinlicky, *Divine Simplicity*, 198.

29. Hinlicky, *Divine Simplicity*, 198. He further writes on pages 199–200, "One reason for ending up in this false dilemma can be found in Dolezal's rebuke of Occam and his followers for imputing a libertarian freedom of indifference to God as anthropomorphic, without a hint of recognition that intellection (on the model of God as Mind) is just as anthropomorphic (as also is the social model of the Trinity). None of our theological models escape anthropomorphism, especially not by the trick of vicious abstraction, which merely transposes and does not dispose of some myth or narrative telling God to us. These stories and figures of God are in historical fact the starting point of theologies; abstracting from them only succeeds in promoting the false consciousness that reifies the No-Thing."

30. Gillespie, *Theological Origins*, 261, summarizes the use of foundationalism with respect to humanism and the Reformation thus: "Modernity in the broadest sense was a series of attempts to answer the fundamental questions that arose out of the nominalist revolution. These questions were both profound and comprehensive, putting to doubt not merely the knowledge of God, man, and nature, but reason and being as well. The humanist movement and the Reformation were comprehensive attempts to answer these questions. They both accepted the nominalist ontology of radical individualism, but they disagreed ontically about which of the traditional realms of being was foundational. The humanists began their account with man and interpreted the other realms of being anthropomorphically. The Reformers, by contrast, believed that God was primary and interpreted man and nature theologically. As we have seen, however, neither the humanists nor the Reformers were willing to eliminate either

There are two tracks leaving Descartes: those like Baruch Spinoza who took his ideas to their conclusions, and those who were not yet ready to do so. We will discuss the latter first.

The Mechanical World of the Early Enlightenment

The seeds for seeing the world as a self-functioning machine, as has already been noted, began many centuries before in the medieval era. With Descartes, however, the doors were opened to see the world as fully mechanical. The old distinction between absolute and ordinary power has been recast to the miraculous and the laws of nature. Seeing the laws of nature as the ordinary power of God allowed the early moderns to see change as good, and the modern concept of progress was born.[31] Perhaps the clearest expression of such thinking on the miraculous illustrated in that of Robert Boyle. William Placher writes,

> God as first cause set the universe running according to fixed laws, and thereafter intervenes only rarely to perform the occasional miracle. Given such a picture, miracles now had evidentiary value. As long as our mystified wonder defined a miracle, it had no more status as "evidence" for the truth of faith than any other event, properly understood. But if the defining characteristic of a miracle was that it violated the laws of nature, then a properly established miracle constituted good evidence that something existed beyond the (newly discovered) natural order.[32]

Once miracles are questioned or rejected, then the result is a god who creates the world but does not interact with it, which is Deism: one of the clearest examples of what I will call cosmological Arianism, the idea that a transcendent God and creation are mutually exclusive, and further, that the creation explains God.[33] Recall that

---

God or man." The positions were mutually exclusive and rejected the ground of the other.

31. Gillespie, *Theological Origins*, 37. Gillespie writes, "If change is not simply degeneration, then some change may be progressive. Change guided by an enlightened humanity may produce good. Progress in this way is opened up as a human possibility. The ability of the will to master the world was already clear to the Renaissance humanists such as Machiavelli, but their reliance on individual prowess and willing made a thorough mastery of nature inconceivable to them. Human finitude meant that even the greatest individuals would inevitably succumb to all-conquering time. Mastering nature would thus require something more than a merely individual will. Early modern thinkers argued that this problem could be solved only if human beings came to understand that science is not an individual accomplishment but a broadly based social or political enterprise. In this way, it is possible to imagine a human will of unlimited longevity that might finally master the natural world."

32. Placher, *Domesticating Transcendence*, 137. As Farrell, *God, History, and Dialectic*, 653, notes, the distinction between miracle and natural law has widened into opposition.

33. The link between Descartes's philosophy and Deism becomes clear when human willing reason becomes the image of God. As Hinlicky, *Paths Not Taken*, 258, writes, "Descartes's seminal appropriation of the image of God tradition for the new project of deism then prevailed. The modern God becomes infinite, unknowable power who in principle can deceive—the very thing we modern

christological "Arianism" ultimately placed Christ on the side of creation, over against the Father. Such cosmological Arianism, like its christological counterpart, is firmly situated on the dichotomist-dualist side of the Plotinian ambiguity and is an attempt to free creation from the meticulous, unmediated control of the monist, and possibly terrible, God. It must be remembered that both the monists (Roman Catholic and Protestants) and the dichotomist-dualist moderns were completely assured of definitional simplicity, and therefore were both playing a variation of the same zero-sum game. The monists wanted to give God all the pie, while the moderns struggled for as many pieces as they could pry away. Elevating the creation, therefore, required the suppression of God to the same degree, or, more subtly, to identify him more and more with creation. As Colin Gunton has observed, modernity secretly believes that any form of religion is the stress of the one over the many, and therefore will fight to keep some of the pie with creation.[34] Now we will move to survey one of the key figures of the Enlightenment, Isaac Newton and his cosmology.

Michael Gillespie makes the interesting observation that most Ockhamist moderns had great difficulty with the doctrine of the Trinity. The Trinity was a problem for nominalists not just because a divine nature was a universal. "Ontological individualism made the notion of a common essence of the three persons inconceivable. Most nominalists became either tritheists or 'Arians' (or some variation thereof, for example, Socinians or Unitarians)."[35] Though Newton is usually remembered as trying to uphold Christianity during his lifetime, Christopher Kaiser writes, "In his theology, Newton was an 'Arian', that is, he believed that the pre-existent Christ was the first of God's creatures. His views were not widely known during his lifetime and did not influence the teaching of the Church of England in any way. However, they were influential for an important group of his disciples, including Samuel Clarke and William Whiston."[36] Newton is perhaps the best example of those who desired to domesticate the nominalistic God by identifying him more and more (though not fully in Newton's case) with creation. Kaiser continues, "Indeed there was an organic (if not necessary) relation between Newton's natural philosophy and his 'Arianism.' This can be seen by looking again at his concept of the relationship between God, space, and time. For Newton, God was not outside space and time. God's infinity was an infinite extension or spatial infinity, and his eternity was a limitless duration or unending time. God's extension and duration constituted space and time as we know them."[37]

---

people would like to be (if we could, or, so far as we can)."

34. Gunton, *One, Three, and Many*, 26. He also states, on pages 24–25, that "There exists a correspondence between the unitary God and a unitary social structure. Deism, the absolute oneness of God in rejecting the doctrine of the Trinity, became the most ruthless of all thought systems." The global attempt to create a comprehensive unitary social structure is perhaps the most compelling storyline of the twenty-first century's third decade.

35. Gillespie, *Theological Origins*, 250.

36. Kaiser, *Creational Theology*, 247.

37. Kaiser, *Creational Theology*, 247. Kaiser continues, "When challenged on this point by Berkeley

Cosmological Arianism and Ebionism

Newton may have conceived of absolute space and time as a kind of analogy to our relative space and time. But to him they still are created things.[38]

Since space and time have been transferred to God from creation in Newton, God's presence is spatially everywhere and all events in both God and creation are on the same timeline.[39] Newton was therefore unable to qualitatively distinguish between the generation of the Son and the creation of the world, which is the Origenist Problematic all over again, proving that definitional simplicity is lurking in the background. Newton even believed in a prior invisible creation where the Son is a perfect creature just as Origen had. He likewise viewed space as the intermediary between God and creation, but it was both itself a creation and impersonal, so he assigns the biblical and patristic mediatorial role of the Son to a creature, further deepening his "Arianism."[40] Newton wanted to reject the spirit-matter dualism of Descartes's mechanical philosophy. Yet Newton simultaneously wished to avoid pantheism (the full identification of God and creation), disavowing both Deism and atheism. He also saw the historic formulations of Christianity as implausible, and tried to forge ahead, all the while confusing person and nature while operating under the confines of the philosophically simple God and the identity thesis.[41] In the end, Newton's laws removed any need for God in nature.[42] Those who came after him only made things more pronounced. Samuel Clarke, Newton's disciple, rejected the Trinity due to divine simplicity; the simple God cannot be triune. He also limited what God could do in nature and reduced God's actions to those upon which all reasonable people would consent.[43] William Whiston was Newton's successor, and was dismissed from his posi

---

and Leibniz, Newton added a note to the second edition of the *Principia* which differentiated his view from a pantheistic identification of God with space and time but did not alter his essential position" (*Creational Theology*, 183–84). See also Placher, *Domesticating Transcendence*, 141.

38. Gunton, *One, Three, and Many*, 155–56.

39. Kaiser, *Creational Theology*, 248, citing Newton, writes, "He is not eternity and infinity, but eternal and infinite; he is not duration or space, but he endures and is present. He endures forever, and is everywhere present; and by existing always and everywhere, he constitutes duration and space . . . he is omnipresent not virtually only, but also substantially."

40. Kaiser, *Creational Theology*, 248–49.

41. Kaiser, *Creational Theology*, 248. In the end, this led to his "Arian" Christology and cosmology, as Kaiser writes, "Therefore, Newton could not differentiate between God's internal operations (*opera ad intra*), like the generation of the Son and the procession of the Spirit, and his external operations (*opera ad extra*) by appealing to a qualitative difference between eternity and time. Christ was, for Newton, the pre-existent Son of God, begotten before all worlds, but his generation was an event on the same time line as the creation of the world. The only difference was that the former was indivisible and temporarily prior to the latter. Before the creation of this visible world, God exercised his omnipotence by creating an invisible world, as Origen and Basil had led. . . . But, for Newton, this invisible creation included the Son of God as well as the angels. The Son, was, therefore, a perfect creature, the first and greatest of all God's creatures, but neither co-eternal nor consubstantial with the Father. Thus the notion of God's eternity as limitless duration or unending time made Arianism a plausible Christology for Newton."

42. Kaiser, *Creational Theology*, 250–51.

43. Kaiser, *Creational Theology*, 258–59. Buckley, *Origins*, 186 and 193, notes that for Clarke, God

tion at Cambridge due to unorthodoxy as he was Origenist in his understanding of Christ.[44] The stage was set for the rejection of God by the cultured and thinking population of Protestant Europe. Before we go there, however, we must go back in time a bit and discuss some key figures that had already rejected God, those who became, in my terminology, the cosmological Ebionites.

At this point, I want to revisit Augustine briefly. I am aware that it has seemed he has been my whipping boy over the last few chapters, but that is not what I want to convey. In many ways, I feel sorry for him. His great intellect and ambition motivated him into constructing a theology that few could match—one that he thought could be faithful to the received tradition and simultaneously speak deeply to the philosophy of his day. Certainly no one can fault him for his desires to make the faith accessible to all. But in so doing, his uncritical acceptance of definitional simplicity forced him to be self-contradictory. For example, we know from his writings that he was vehemently against both "Arianism" and Apollinarianism. He believed, as a father and a bishop, that Jesus was both fully divine and fully human, and to him those doctrines were unassailable. But what I believe he failed to grasp is that by teaching that creation mediates creation, he was saying exactly the same thing as the anti-Nicenes on a foundational cosmological level. Similarly, by holding to the dialectical opposition of God and creation (humanity) in his doctrine of original sin and guilt that required meticulous divine ordering of all aspects of the lives of the elect, he made the elect passive tools for the overwhelming grace of God, and in so doing was saying exactly the same thing as Apollinarius and the later Monoenergists cosmologically. Tragically, in my opinion, Augustine was driven by his commitment to definitional simplicity to affirm on a broader cosmological level what he expressly denied in Christology, without perceiving that, in this case, the latter is properly a subset of the former. It is such a shame that the great Western father never caught his foundational mistake. Maybe all of this could have been avoided.

Early European Atheism and the Response

There had always been those in Europe who rejected Christianity. They were usually successful in keeping their unbelief hidden from the church and state. We saw a bit of a rise in rationalistic paganism before, with the broad acceptance of Aristotle, and it led to the condemnations of 1277. By the time the Reformation was in full swing, there was another rise in anti-Christian sentiment. The answer to the movement has been brilliantly chronicled by Michael Buckley, in his *At the Origins of Modern Atheism*,

---

is only knowable *a posteriori*, or by what we observe, and that everything in creation points to God.

44. Kaiser, *Creational Theology*, 260. Kaiser writes, "Actually, [Whiston] was more of an Origenist or Eusebian than an Arian; he held that Christ was a 'second god' in the Neoplatonic sense—divine, yet subordinate to the supreme God."

and I will be following his reasoning in this section.[45] He argues that atheism, in its modern variety, is as much a product of the way it was answered in the early modern period as it is a rejection of the prevailing notion of God. He writes that atheism did not begin with the new science, "but with the disintegration of a common religious confession sustained by a teaching Church."[46] He continues, "The first opponents of atheism mistakenly thought that atheism was a simply a revival of ancient paganism, instead of a profound rejection of "the meaning and reality of Jesus Christ."[47] Thus atheism, with its spokesmen as the ancient pagan philosophers, rather than those who were actually rejecting the faith at the time, became a philosophical issue rather than a theological one. This development should come as no surprise by now. The cosmological structures of the early modern period were the identical broad concepts that heretically distorted the Jesus of Bible and history in late antiquity. With no sustained ecclesial challenge to these models (and, as we have noted, often outright acceptance and endorsement of them), it was not much of an intellectual leap to reject the biblical and historical Jesus all over again. As long as the assumptions of definitional simplicity hold sway over cosmological reflection, orthodox Christology is always in danger. Buckley's clearest example of the battle against atheism comes from the thought of the sixteenth-century Jesuit philosopher and apologist, Leonard Lessius, who did not utilize christological arguments in combating atheism. Let us now examine, through Buckley's assessment, Lessius's contributions.

First, all of Lessius's arguments against atheism are variations of the argument from design.[48] In arguing from design, Lessius uses the analogy of being to reason from the created beings to the uncreated being. His two main approaches were arguments from prophecy and miracles, two Stoic lines of thought, rather than anything expressly Christian.[49] Utilizing the principles of natural theology in his book is *De Providentia Numinis*, or *On the Providence of the Deity* (that is, the simple god-in-general, reminiscent of Origen's "it"),[50] Lessius builds his arguments largely from the Stoic

45. See note 8 previously for bibliographical information.

46. Buckley, *Origins*, 47.

47. Buckley, *Origins*, 47. He writes, on page 33, that the theologians who battled the Enlightenment atheists became philosophers first and did not appeal to Jesus or Christian experience.

48. Buckley, *Origins*, 48. Buckley, on page 53, writes that Lessius, like the medieval theologians before him, rejected the possibility of chance as a possible explanation of why the world is the way it is.

49. Buckley, *Origins*, 48–50. Buckley notes that Lessius copies the Stoic arguments against the Epicureans as his arguments for the existence of God. The Stoics identify the divine and the created in their Hellenistic paganism, while Lessius makes them "infinitely distinct." "Infinite distinction" is the language of "Arianism."

50. Lessius, taking advantage of the European exploration going on before and during his lifetime, argues that all the people of the world really worship the god-in-general. Buckley, *Origins*, 47, writes, "If the natural orientation of the mind, which is by nature geared to truth, includes a conviction—however diversified and hazy—about a provident God, then the conviction must be sound." In other words, if all these primitive people groups believe in some kind of God, then God must be. Further, on page 51, assuming the Thomist doctrine *actus purus* (equivalent to the identity thesis), Lessius revives Anselm's ontological argument in a worldwide fashion. To dismiss the existence of God would

argument from design. In doing so, Jesus becomes in effect one more example of how the *numen* (deity) works. On the use of miracles and prophecy to prove Jesus as savior thus to prove the existence of God, Buckley writes, "But this is almost in passing. New facts are subsumed under classical arguments for divine providence. Just as European explorations and the newly-discovered telescope expand the basic arguments from universal consent and from the movement of the heavens, so Jesus and the history of Christianity add more data to the evidence of miracles and prophecy—one more instance, albeit a capital one, among many."[51] Buckley summarizes Lessius's ideas thus:

> All of [Lessius'] arguments receive such a transformation: miracles and prophecy show a knowledge of the designs of nature and the structures of the future. The argument from absurdity becomes a consideration of the disintegration of human order consequent upon a denial of God, and the final arguments show a design or order within the divine governance of human life. Design is everywhere in Lessius' argumentation, but it is not mechanical design, the composition and dissolution of wholes and parts. It is rather the orientation or relationship found within natural bodies and the entire universe. The axiom which underlies this design and the arguments which proceed from it are put in scholastic vocabulary, though its application is continually Stoic: whatever has a final cause to which it is oriented has also an efficient cause by which it has been oriented. The finding of service is the finding of purpose is the finding of efficient cause which has the intelligence and power to set up such a web of connections.[52]

Lessius provides the blueprint for the standard Roman Catholic response to atheism. Buckley writes, "Lessius' problematic methodology separates the question of God from the cognitive claims of Christology in the classic distinction between revelation and reason. The centrality of Christ is relegated to revelation—Christ does not evoke faith in the Father; his intelligibility is consequent upon faith. What Lessius presents is not the person and message of Jesus, but those cosmological and historical experiences which are open to any human being."[53] His solution is inadequate to both the atheist and the Christian. It does not answer why there is anything here in the first place, and it does not satisfy the Christian (or at least should not), as Buckley writes, "The theologian can look at the same procedures and wonder what has happened to Christianity's Christ as the primordial manifestation of the reality of God and the victorious source of the possibility of religious conviction."[54] When the Enlightenment comes, Jesus will not suffice to show God to the world, as he is, with creation,

---

be equivalent to proving he cannot exist.

51. Buckley, *Origins*, 54. That is, Jesus is on the same "ontological plane" as all other created examples of God's work.

52. Buckley, *Origins*, 53–54.

53. Buckley, *Origins*, 54.

54. Buckley, *Origins*, 54–55.

standing against the Father in such a system rooted in definitional simplicity. Buckley writes, "The Enlightenment later takes Jesus as a teacher of morals, but nature and the cosmos teach it about God."[55] The Father and Son are divided in classical Arian fashion.[56] Those who came after him would continue to build on Lessius's work. The summarizing words of Buckley are haunting, as atheism is "the last and inevitable stage of religion become philosophy."[57]

Baruch Spinoza and Immanuel Kant

The next-to-last step of complete cosmological Ebionism is the identification of God and the created order from the side of creation. We already saw this in the ninth-century figure John Scotus Eriugena. Pantheism enters the modern world through the Portuguese Jew Baruch Spinoza, who holds to the necessity of all that is, and if it does not exist then it cannot.[58] He writes, "The eternal and infinite being, whom we call God, or Nature, acts by the same necessity whereby it exists . . . just as he does not exist for an end, so he does not act for an end; just as there is no beginning or end to his existing, so there is no beginning or end to his acting."[59] This quote is the mother-lode of definitional simplicity concepts: action equals being, what is natural is compelled, and essence equals existence. Moreover, Spinoza implies that God can only be known by observation, as he writes. "As everything in Nature involves and expresses the conception of God in proportion to its essence and perfection . . . therefore we acquire a greater and more perfect knowledge of God as we gain more knowledge of natural phenomena."[60] Spinoza continues, "By the light of natural reason, all can clearly understand the power and eternal divinity of God, from which they can know

---

55. Buckley, *Origins*, 55.

56. Buckley, *Origins*, 55. Buckley writes, "Natural theology, then, becomes no longer a part of metaphysics, but derivative by common sense or ordinary philosophic maxims from astronomy, comparative religion, mechanics, and biology. It is a world to which theology itself has very little contribution to make. So it remains in the centuries to come, an effort to provide a preamble to Christian convictions about God which does not include Christ." As such, it continues the objective of Anselm's *Cur Deus Homo?* and Aquinas's *"De Deo Uno"* in the *Summa*: a Christian foundation that is not explicitly Christian.

57. Buckley, *Origins*, 222. Hinlicky concurs, as he writes, "The apparent magnification of God as infinite, unknowable power is in fact the seed of atheism, for it separates physics from ethics and aesthetics" (*Paths Not Taken*, 254). That is, the road from Ockham to Descartes *must* lead on to pantheism, secular humanism, and eventually Western atheism.

58. Hinlicky, *Paths Not Taken*, 75. Mechanical necessity of the material world is the hallmark of cosmological Arianism.

59. Spinoza, *Ethics*, 153, as quoted in Hinlicky, *Paths Not Taken*, 76. Here, according to Gillespie, *Theological Origins*, 275, Spinoza is following Hobbes in the identification of "mechanical causality and divine will." Note how Spinoza makes "Nature" a proper noun. Frampton, *Spinoza*, 225, notes that Spinoza "naturalizes God."

60. Spinoza, *Principles of Cartesian Philosophy*, 11, quoted in Hinlicky, *Paths Not Taken*, 78.

and infer what they should seek and what avoid."[61] Paul Hinlicky continues, "Thus demystified, the final causes traditionally understood as inhering the world's structure and reflecting the divine decree are now understood as human, all-too-human projections of purpose onto God/Nature."[62] Just as we saw in Descartes, final causes (the *telos* of creation) are eliminated and redefined as coming from within the system, rather than from without.[63]

Spinoza, the fervent anti-Christian, has found a way to assert independence from the monist cosmology of both Catholics and Protestants, as well as their God. Hinlicky continues, "The liberating result, for Spinoza, is that human beings alone bear responsibility for the desires they admit and the purposes they undertake. Nothing in the nature of things structures them into organized purposes. There is no longer any recourse to the authority of faith, or of reason according to the anthropomorphic metaphysics of the tradition, to assess and prioritize the divine purposes encoded in cosmic structures into which individual appetites are to be ordered."[64] Nothing transcendent can affect human decisions, because transcendence has been brought completely down to earth in the identification of God and creation. "God," that is nature, is simple. Hinlicky continues, "With the backdrop of nature/god as the great 'empty screen of the Ineffable' (seen best by the relative insignificance of human existence in a universe so vast), humans project meaning onto such a screen in the modern consciousness, only to end in nothing, as in Neitzsche. Individual projections are nothing but that, because god/nature endures always with no beginning and toward no end."[65] Here is where divine simplicity, on the dichotomist-dualist side of the Plotinian ambiguity, finally arrives. If God can only be known by the created order because the identity thesis demands that God is what he creates, then all Spinoza is doing is eliminating the unnecessary middleman (God) from the discussion. But, as we saw earlier in the chapter, there is still the vestige of something that resembles Christianity, though its cosmology is decidedly Arian, in much of Europe. We now must move forward to the figure who will close the period of Enlightenment, Immanuel Kant.

A. T. B. McGowan notes that the genius of Kant was his ability to synthesize the two great schools of Enlightenment thought, empiricism and rationalism, which were themselves the two sides of the Plotinian ambiguity within the Enlightenment. The empiricists argued bottom-up from sense perception to general principles, while the rationalists reasoned top-down from first premises.[66] The most radical empiricist of

61. Hinlicky, *Paths Not Taken*, 59.//
62. Hinlicky, *Paths Not Taken*, 76.//
63. See Spinoza, *Ethics*, in Hinlicky, *Paths Not Taken*, 76.//
64. Hinlicky, *Paths Not Taken*, 76.//
65. Hinlicky, *Paths Not Taken*, 77.//
66. McGowan, *Divine Authenticity*, 51. Even though the Enlightenment was driven by dichotomist-dualism, there was always room for monist impulses within it. We have seen these conflicting pictures before with Martin Luther and Thomas Hobbes, as well as ultimately the two who were intellectually gifted enough to hold all the conflict within themselves—Origen and Augustine.

the eighteenth century was David Hume, who doubted the likelihood of miracles, talk of God, the afterlife, and much more because they could not be empirically demonstrated.[67] To consistent empiricists such as Hume, God could not be demonstrated, so the concept of the divine was either discarded or relegated to the sideline of unimportance. On the other hand, to the rationalists, René Descartes chief among them, empiricist observation was not reliable because it could be deceptive.

Immanuel Kant had a deep respect for both Hume and his skepticism and Newton and his physics.[68] The former doubted we could know things as they are, while the latter seemed to demonstrate real knowledge of the world.[69] Kant's creative solution to this impasse was to reconstruct the Platonic and Origenist concept of two worlds—a noumenal world (objects of thought) which we could not know, and a phenomenal world (what we can observe) which we could.[70] Gunton continues,

> The former world was the cause of the latter; in other words, the metaphysical or higher world—the vanishing remnants of the ideas in the mind of God—was the cause of this one. As Locke had held, our sense experience is caused by something we know not what. But two candidates for who or what this ultimate cause is, God and substance, are now ruled out, at least in the sense of known causes of the way things are. Both concepts are necessary, but only as regulating our thought—enabling it to know this world better. Of what they are in themselves, nothing can be known, because there is no way in which the mind can penetrate beyond appearances into what is really there. Thus Kant combines a Platonic two-world theory of being with complete agnosticism about what the underlying world really is.[71]

Kant, in the *Critique of Pure Reason*, reduces both kinds of natural theology (the rationalist mathematical of Descartes and the empiricist mechanical of Newton) to the work of Descartes and demonstrates that the ontological argument of Descartes cannot work. Physics and mathematics work, but metaphysics cannot move beyond pure reason. "The natural theologies always collapse because their reach exceeds their grasp, because they attempt to employ pure concepts beyond the manifold of

---

67. McGowan, *Divine Authenticity*, 51.

68. Buckley, *Origins*, 327, notes that Kant followed Newton, but "rescued him from the dogmatism of his presuppositions." "Kant insisted that no physics or natural philosophy, no theoretic knowledge of any stamp, could form the basis for any natural theology."

69. Gillespie, *Theological Origins*, 256, notes that Hume's critique of modernity "called into question the idea of a necessary connection between cause and effect that was essential to the modern idea of an apodictic science."

70. Gunton, *Triune Creator*, 131. He adds that the way we can know the phenomenal world, is "only as it is structured in the mind, which itself implies that the mind is structured as a mechanism, further entrenching the mechanistic philosophy of the Enlightenment." God, who belonged to the noumenal world, could not be known and therefore was unnecessary (page 133) for post-Kantian cosmology in understanding how the world worked.

71. Gunton, *Triune Creator*, 131.

experience." That is, the metaphysics of Descartes and Newton "removes its concepts from their necessary connection with sensuous intuition, and it reaches not what can be known but only what can be thought."[72] Kant tried to solve the problem of freedom and necessity by separating the phenomenal world of nature and necessity from the noumenal one of freedom and morality. This ended in failure because science needed freedom to work, but science denied its possibility. As Gillespie writes, "Similarly, if humans were natural beings, they could not be free because they would be subject to the laws governing the motion of all matter, and if they were free they could not be natural beings. Humans were thus either mere matter in motion or they were gods, or to put the matter more clearly they constantly lived the contradiction of being both mere matter in motion and gods."[73] Belief in one (that humans were either gods or just matter) entailed the other, and yet both were mutually contradictory.[74] That is, Kant is faced with the Plotinian ambiguity and cannot solve it. As has been the case throughout this book, definitional simplicity is the problem.

Paul Hinlicky links the work of Kant to that of Cicero. In his own day, Cicero attempted to bridge the problems of multiple representation of the gods in pagan Rome by appealing to a kind of natural theology, one that would get behind all the human representations of the Roman gods to whatever was there. The warring gods of Cicero's day were very much like the warring claims, and the physical wars they produced, of the various Christian denominations. As Cicero turned to a natural theology for a solution, so did Kant. Hinlicky writes,

> As such, natural theology has to be understood historically. The problem natural theology faces is one of social peace. Representations of the divine are notoriously at variance with one another, but social peace seems to depend on mutual toleration in matters of religion. Hence the crucial move of natural theology is *apophatic*: to transcend the "human, all-too-human" representations of the divine by appeal to an essence beyond image, beyond language, beyond thought, beyond being. In the Western, Latin tradition, Cicero's *On the Nature of the Gods* was a foundational text of critical reflection along these lines. Arguably, the great Kant found his agnostic and Pelagian philosophy of religion anticipated in it. Writing in the fateful times of the end of the Roman republic and the transition to dictatorship and imperialism, Cicero undertook natural or philosophical theology as a way out from the situation of polytheistic conflict in and among religions, just as Kant too sought new foundations for culture after the post-Reformation wars of religion.[75]

---

72. Buckley, *Origins*, 327. Both quotes are his.

73. Gillespie, *Theological Origins*, 277. Gillespie, on page 259, notes Kant's third antinomy: Science is unintelligible without a freely acting first cause (e.g., God or man). Freedom is the basis of morality, but it is incompatible with natural necessity. Therefore, freedom is both necessary to causality and incompatible with it.

74. Gillespie, *Theological Origins*, 276.

75. Hinlicky, *Divine Complexity*, 17. Italics in original.

Cosmological Arianism and Ebionism

For Kant, as for Cicero, the way forward was the way of negation. All of the variant, human representations of religions must be stripped away via apophatic theology. The true "god" was everything humans were not. The astute reader will recognize the same methodology in Cicero as was present in all the Greeks down through Plotinus. The problem is, carried to its logical conclusions, the way of negation negates even the existence of God, because once everything is stripped away, there is nothing left. If there is anything utterly transcendent, so the line of thinking goes, it cannot help us, and we cannot know it with any sort of precision. Extreme apophaticism and simplicity are all that are left. The only thing left to know is ourselves, so human reason becomes "god" and human conscience becomes the moral compass.[76]

A key point in Kant's transference of the divine prerogatives into the created order lay in his concept of freedom, which, according to Paul Hinlicky, is "the ability to initiate causal series, motivated only by rational obedience to the moral law of one's own being, without regard to, or rather in defiance of, inclination stemming from the sensual realm, i.e., the causal series to which the self belongs as a feeling body. The ability to conform to the moral law was named the 'kingdom of grace,' i.e., grace now denoting a domain of non-natural, moral, or ideal ends in contrast to the purposeless world of nature."[77] Plainly, here is the mind-matter dualism of his noumenal and phenomenal world at work. The mind as free and noumenal can will apart from the phenomenal body. Colin Gunton adds that in Kant, "It was not that there was a secularization, in the sense of the conceiving of space and time completely or largely non-theologically, so much as a displacement: the locus of the divine ordering of space and time was now the human mind rather than the eternal structures of being."[78] The only God is the god conceived in the individual mind.[79] And this has to be, for in Kant's mind, rational theology must precede revealed theology, for there would be no other way to determine if God had spoken.[80]

The concept of the fully immanent (within the human mind) individual God of one's own construction leads to three modern problems. First, Kant "reduced the idea of God from being constitutive to being merely regulative: merely 'as if.'"[81] In this first problem, Kant is merely restating what has been anticipated since at least Ockham: even if God is there, he is only a moral guide and not absolutely essential to our lives, that is, the mature fruit of the Western, cosmologically Nestorian tendency.

---

76. Hinlicky, *Divine Complexity*, 18.

77. Hinlicky, *Paths Not Taken*, 22.

78. Gunton, *One, Three, and Many*, 156. He adds on page 27 that Kant's philosophy entailed the complete revolt of the many over the one, as seen in the material revolts against church and crown. Gillespie, *Theological Origins*, 275, notes that the Reign of Terror was the first modern example of what could go wrong in ascribing divine attributes to human beings.

79. Gunton, *One Three, and Many*, 26–27. Gunton adds, "It falls to all of the many to dare, individually, to use their own intelligence. Anything else is heteronomous, and a denial of our humanity."

80. Hinlicky, *Paths Not Taken*, 47.

81. Gunton, *One Three, and Many*, 24.

The Hexagon of Heresy

Second, within Kantian philosophy, there is no way to adjudicate among competing truth-claims from the noumenal world. Each person's ideas are equally valid, so long as they are following sound reason. This is the modern problem of moral and spiritual relativism, since one cannot get behind the claims into some kind of objective evaluative criteria. Third, everything is individualized to the extreme, as Robert Solomon writes, "It is worth noting that there is no social element in [Kant's] picture, no community of scientists, public opinions, or pressures from colleagues, employers, or research-granting agencies. Knowledge is purely a relationship between the autonomous individual and the world of nature, and morality is a relationship between the individual and universal law, a product of pure practical reason."[82] The radical individualism of Ockham's nominalist revolution has been fully realized in Kant. But, as we shall see, the tide will turn again, but not before the last great step in cosmological Ebionism has been achieved: atheism.

Once Kant's thought becomes quickly enthroned as the philosophy of the day, the impact on Christianity, with its claims of a knowable transcendent God, are disastrous. As McGowan writes, "In seeking to secure a place for religious experience, he thus stripped Christianity of its supernatural elements, including the idea of faith and of a personal God, and reduced it largely to a religion of self-help. The result is a non-supernatural religion that bears little or no relation to biblical Christianity and that becomes essentially a system of ethics."[83] With the individual as the supreme judge in all matters, there could be neither objectivity nor community. Kant's philosophy took Europe by storm. He gave the intellectual world of Europe something they desperately needed: a way to live that was not hopelessly mired in which an army could prove its religion to be correct. McGowan rightly states, "Few would deny that Kant's work transformed the philosophical world, and therefore one must either come to terms with his conclusions or demonstrate he was mistaken."[84] Those conclusions were clear. If there is a God in the Christian sense, we cannot know him and he cannot help us; it is therefore up to us to fix things. The remnants of a de-supernaturalized, fully immanent Christian faith are useful, however, because of the system of morality and ethics already built into it. For all practical purposes, there is only the here-and-now, because the claims of the representatives of the transcendent world have harmed rather than helped.[85]

---

82. Solomon, *Continental Philosophy*, 40, quoted in Gunton, *One, Three, and Many*, 221. The social and anthropological issues here are obvious. If humans are indeed created for "koinonia" with both God and each other, then post-Kantian impostors will rush in to fill the real void: collectivist ideologies and various forms of critical theory.

83. McGowan, *Divine Authenticity*, 53.

84. McGowan, *Divine Authenticity*, 53.

85. The "Christian" reaction to Kant, of course, is the Protestant Liberalism of F.D.E. Schleiermacher. Rather than fight Kant's philosophy, he embraced it and recast Christianity in light of it. An "Arian" himself, Schleiermacher created a Protestant religious structure that would survive him by over two centuries. In the words of Packer, *Engaging*, 60, "To side-step Kant's critique of the idea of

"Theological" Atheism as the Purest Form of Cosmological Ebionism

Materialistic atheism is the final end of the separation of the divine and created in cosmology. We have traced all the way from Augustine's created rational principles, through William of Ockham and nominalism, to the modern turn, to the cosmological Arianism of making the creator and creation on the same ontological plane, to the pantheism of Spinoza, to the transference of the divine to the created in Kant.[86] The only step left is to dispense with any notion of the divine altogether and declare that, in the end of definitional simplicity, that matter is all there is. Therefore, the fourth solution to the problem of how to answer the nominalist version of God is to simply remove him from public discourse. Michael Gillespie writes, "As a result, knowing ceases to be conceived as metaphysics and is reconceptualized as a universal science that consists of only physics and anthropology. Theology is no longer regarded as a form of knowledge and becomes an expression or interpretation of faith, more akin to rhetoric or poetry than science."[87] In more practical terms, theology becomes an extension of anthropology, called "religious studies" in our universities.

According to Michael Buckley, the French encyclopedist Denis Diderot is the first of the early modern atheists. He stepped beyond Spinoza by declaring "either God or nature."[88] G. W. F. Hegel, along the same lines, said that man, God, and nature were all ontologically the same.[89] It all leads to Feuerbach, who states, "To enrich God, man must become poor; that God may be all, man must be nothing."[90] This is the zero-sum game inherent in divine simplicity. God and creation must fight over the same "space." If God and creation are on the same plane of being, then to elevate one is to debase the other, reminiscent of what we saw in the last chapter from the monist side in Jonathan Edwards. Of course, Feuerbach wound up on the other side of the zero-sum game

---

revealed truth, he [Schleiermacher] abandoned the notion altogether, and argued that Christianity is essentially not knowledge but a feeling of dependence on God through Christ. The Christian faith is simply an infectious historical mysticism, 'caught' (like measles) from contact with others who have it. Doctrine does not create Christian experience, but is created by it. Doctrinal statements are attempts to express in words borrowed from the culture of the day the contents of the corporate Christian consciousness, and theology is the systematic examination of this consciousness as thus expressed. The proper study of theologians is man . . . Schleiermacher's position made the idea of revelation really superfluous, for it actually amounted to a denial that anything is revealed. On his principles, divine revelation must simply be equated with human advance into God-consciousness. Thus, his legacy to the church can be summed up in the axiom that, whatever else revelation may be, it is not a communication of truth from God to man." The Arian thrust here is obvious.

86. See Gillespie, *Theological Origins*, 36.
87. Gillespie, *Theological Origins*, 270.
88. Buckley, *Origins*, 249.
89. Gillespie, *Theological Origins*, 282. See also the "secularized theology" of Laplace in Kaiser, *Creational Theology*, 349–51.
90. Feuerbach, *Essence of Christianity*, 26, as cited in Gunton, *One, Three, and Many*, 26.

from Edwards, reducing God to nothing in the end, and empowering the thought of Karl Marx, the author of the *Communist Manifesto*.[91]

The removal of God, or rather the displacement of him from transcendent to immanent, destroyed human freedom. Freedom requires otherness. That is, "our neighbor either must be feared or dominated."[92] Gunton shows where the end of divine simplicity leads, as he writes, "Just as ancient skepticism developed from a critique of the inadequate theology of the Greek tradition, so modern skepticism and fragmentation derives in part from the justified rejection of the arbitrary [may I say simple?] God and the limited concept of truth associated with that theology."[93] He continues, "Modern relativism and skepticism are, then, in part the outcome of the failure of a doctrine of God, and particularly of a doctrine of God as creator. The modern development begins with a proper rebellion against the authoritarian theological homogenization of truth, and ends with the morally destructive homogenization of culture."[94] In the tradition of definitional simplicity, the one is to be prized over the many, as unity is greater than plurality. Thomas puts God and creation under the same umbrella—being. Gunton writes,

> The negative way, which is so important for the method, means that it is easy for Thomas to become liable to the critique associated with Feuerbach that the concept of God is projected from a negation of the marks of worldly being, so that the world appears to be negated in order that God can be affirmed. Thus the temporal is negated in order to provide the route to the (timeless) eternal, the material treated as the route to the immaterial. Far from being the source of transcendental insight, God appears to be derived from a process of negating the essential characteristics of the world of time and becoming. This judgement is confirmed when we come to see what Aquinas says explicitly about transcendentality. There are for him four transcendentals, so that "the terms 'one', 'true', and 'good' are, like 'being', transcendent of the categories and universally applicable—to God as well as to everything else."[95]

Gunton continues, noting that plurality and beauty become inferior to the four transcendentals, and therefore the only real use of plurality and beauty is to serve as a way

---

91. As Gunton, *One, Three, and Many*, 30–33, notes, Individualism breeds leveling and conformity. Tolerance produces intolerance. Why? When God is displaced as a universal, other universals, false ones such as the public, or the market, rush in to fill the void. But they are false, with no real existence in and of themselves. Moreover, Individualism also breeds instrumentalism, the view that others are only useful for the individual. When the many overthrow the one, there are two dangers. First is fascism, where the many become an aggregate of ones, and the strongest one wins. Second is homogeneity, where the many become "homogenized into the mass." Homogeneity occurs through false universals that are even more oppressive than the old "one."

92. Gunton, *One, Three, and Many*, 36–37.

93. Gunton, *One, Three, and Many*, 122.

94. Gunton, *One, Three, and Many*, 122.

95. Gunton, *One, Three, and Many*, 139–40.

into participation in the transcendentals.[96] The analogy of being holds that what God and creation share is being, or existence. It is a way of merging the divine and created orders, for a person can, so to speak, climb the chain of being up to God.

It is this monist system, most clearly expressed in Aquinas, against which the moderns revolted. But they were not capable of escaping the Plotinian ambiguity buried within the system, for it rested on a theological and philosophical first principle that was never seriously questioned: definitional divine simplicity.[97] The modern atheists represented by Marx and his followers succeeded in bringing down established cultures and religions for a time, but could not deliver on their promised social utopia. To assert that the many wins all the pie in the zero-sun game of the Plotinian ambiguity is to paradoxically destroy the possibility of the real particularity among the many. History shows that communism became "conform-ism." Just as Edwards's occasionalism (giving the one all the pie in the zero-sum game) leads to an identification of God and the world from the divine side, effectively nullifying the integrity of creation, pantheism and atheism collapse both from the side of creation, either merging God into the created order or removing him altogether.

Conclusion and Historical Overview

This brings an end to the discussion of cosmology. I have tried to discuss the seminal thinkers of all the cosmological variants tied to definitional simplicity. In this concluding section, I want to broadly discuss the contours of Western history. At the end of the Medieval period, Ockham's nominalism birthed three ontic responses: Renaissance humanism, the Reformation, and modernism. In the Counter-Reformation, Rome doubled down by adopting the philosophy and theology of Aquinas as the official doctrine of the church. The Reformers who constantly polemicized

---

96. Gunton, *One, Three, and Many*, 139–40.

97. Gunton, *One, Three, and Many*, 194; as Gunton writes, "The modern protest against the idea of God is in part a protest against the kind of notion of divine substance, and particularity of God as a changeless, unitarily conceived will or authority. Much is made of the unrelational character of this God, with some cause, but also with much exaggeration and oversimplification. It could even be argued that because, as a result of the work of Descartes, a similar notion of substance was transferred to human being, modernity has come to be in reaction not only against God, but also against substantialist views of the human person, too." He continues, on page 210, "I argued also that a double movement underlies the problematic. On the one hand, it is possible to understand the ills of modernity as arising from a displacement of God and the replacing of the creator by the creature, with the only superficially paradoxical result that a movement aiming to give central importance to life in time and space has as a matter of fact cramped and distorted that which it claims to preserve. On the other hand, the leading thinkers of the modern world had some cause for the direction they took. The development of theology in the West had been strongly monistic, stressing the oneness and arbitrary will of God in such a way that the reality and importance of the created world appeared to be called into question. Modernity's protest against bad theology is therefore in large measure justified, although its placement of the divine has been catastrophic in its effects." Can a clearer description of the Plotinian ambiguity possibly be stated?

with Rome adopted their own version of scholasticism as an operating procedure. The humanists—Ockhamists within Catholicism—largely became modernists. The armies of the monist scholastics attempted to settle their conflicting truth claims on the battlefield, making both themselves and their claims ever more detestable to the fledgling moderns, who saw identification and exploitation of nature as the only promising way forward.

By the late seventeenth century and into the eighteenth, the monist state churches remained in Europe. Scholasticism was the language of theology. Science was progressing with demonstrable results appealing to the mechanized, Cartesian universe. Modern philosophy was finding ways to domesticate God or to section him off as unimportant in human affairs. The Lutheran axiom that the world explains God was giving rise to the historical-critical method of deconstructing the biblical message. Deism and skepticism grew. As the world became more and more convinced that humans could achieve without or in spite of God, the monist vestiges of church and crown came under increasing suspicion and attack.

The nineteenth century, on the heels of great political revolutions at the end of the eighteenth, saw the floodgates open. The industrial revolution and the resultant shift from an agricultural to a mechanical society made monism even less appealing. Philosophers, always leading the charge, openly rejected the God of their fathers. Science replaced religion with new creation (evolution via natural selection) and redemption (scientific progress) narratives for modernity. Social reforms like abolition, temperance, and compulsory education made it seem like God was not required for human progress. Liberal Protestantism provided a religion that kept the trappings and language of Christianity but replaced the worship of God with the worship of ourselves. By the end of the century, it looked as though utopia without God was possible.

The promise of the nineteenth century was killed by the Great War, the Dust Bowl, Auschwitz, and the Cold War of the twentieth century. The modern project, whereby man would conquer the God of Ockham by becoming master of the universe, was undone by seemingly unlimited human atrocity. It seemed as though man could only prove himself to be master if he exercised the power to destroy. Modernism, it turns out, did not provide a reason or a remedy for human depravity.

At the time of this writing, we are now a couple of decades into the twenty-first century. Western civilization is breathing its last few breaths. We have seemingly succeeding in putting to death the "god" who gave birth to us because we could not endure the ramifications of its contradictory existence. The death of our "god" is the death of our civilization, for the cosmological assumptions that undergird Western civilization are fundamentally contradictory and self-defeating. The time is now for us to recover a Christianity that is not culturally and dialectically constructed from natural theology.

12

Concluding Thoughts

A Brief Recap

THIS BOOK HAS BEEN a case study of the history of a dominant doctrine in Christian theology: definitional divine simplicity. The dialectical construction of the definition of the divine essence seemed innocuous enough at the beginning, and could even be squared with the vast majority of Scripture, church teaching, and Christian experience. The identification of divine essence and divine energy (the identity thesis) quickly produced what this book has called the Origenist Problematic, the inability to meaningfully distinguish between the generation of the Son and the creation of the world. The pagans had no problem with it, because for them matter was eternal anyway. But the Christian, whose Bible's first sentence reads "In the beginning God created the heavens and the earth," cannot (with Origen) hold to the eternality of matter. In quick succession, cosmological models arose to try to hold together both definitional divine simplicity and the distinct (from God) creation of time/space/matter.

The christological distillations of these larger cosmological models were recognized as heretical by some of the greatest theologians in Christian history. Men like Athanasius, the Cappadocians, Cyril, and Maximus saw that these cosmologies produced Christologies that could not be reconciled to what the church believed and taught concerning Jesus. After some prolonged struggles, those Christologies springing from the assumptions of pagan definitional simplicity were finally recognized to be heretical. It should be obvious, utilizing hindsight, that if Jesus is truly and fully divine as well as truly and fully human, it becomes impossible to define God as the simple opposite to the complexity of creation, because in such a definition Jesus could be truly and fully one or the other but not both. And this is the reason why one cannot simultaneously utilize such a natural theology and a christologically centered theology at the same time.

The Hexagon of Heresy

I have argued that Augustine's commitment to definitional simplicity set Western (Roman Catholic and Protestant) theology on a course to replicate the same cosmologies that were defeated in their christological instantiations by the Greek-speaking fathers of late antiquity. What I think has become apparent is that the same apophatic process used to define the divine essence is also responsible for the slow but systematic erosion of the faith itself. To put it another way, in his commitment to definitional simplicity, Augustine sowed the seeds for the ultimate destruction of the church and her voice in the world. The preceding chapters have outlined how, over the span of nearly 1500 years, Augustine's basic (Platonic) cosmological commitments of a two-stage creation (seminal rational principles first) and the dialectical depravity of man over against the goodness of God expanded over time to end in the superfluity of either God or the world. For there exists an ambiguity at the heart of the dialectical construction of the one-and-many problem: simultaneously the one determines the many in a monist system and the many rebel against the one in a dichotomist-dualist system. Both constructs follow immediately from the dialectical construction, but only one can be followed at any given time. The logical conclusion of the monist framework is the subsuming of creation into God in a theistically-determinist fashion so that ultimately the one (God) exerts meticulous control over the many (creation), that, if taken to its extreme, good-and-necessary consequences, ends in an occasionalist panentheism. On the other hand, the dichotomist-dualist frameworks always have creation struggling to distinguish itself over against God, and they ultimately lead to a pantheism where God is the sum total of the material world, and can either be regarded as a divine creation itself (various forms of contemporary paganism or "New Age"), unnecessary (secular humanism) or finally just nonexistent altogether (atheism).

As was hopefully made plain in the first half of the book, the "heretics" promulgating defective Christologies were not pagans attacking the church from without. They were professing and baptized Christians, often bishops, who were operating from within their own received tradition. I have attempted to show that these received traditions were heavily influenced by the doctrine of definitional divine simplicity and its attendant identity thesis and Plotinian ambiguity. It is also the contention of this book that such disastrous cosmologies did not arise from without the church to attack it as an enemy might besiege a fortified city. Instead, like their christological counterparts, they were "built into" the system, so to speak, with definitional simplicity as the underlying axiom. Using the christological controversies as a historical guide, the same commitment to definitional simplicity would yield predictable results for cosmology. Given enough time for the right conditions to materialize, movements like materialistic atheism and secular humanism were guaranteed to occur in a theological culture grounded in the dialectical construction of God and the world. Guaranteed.

The dialectical process of simultaneous confusion and separation can be seen clearly in the thought process of Augustine. His initial confusion of the seminal rational principles and creation resulted in an overreaction to a kind of cosmological

Concluding Thoughts

Nestorianism that drove God and creation apart. His initial separation of God and creation post-fall exacerbated a resultant confusion of God and (part of) the world where God imposed his "grace" on his elect irresistibly in order to guarantee their salvation. A thousand years of both of these undercurrents percolating through the fundamental fabric of Western church-state civilization produced within a couple of generations at the height of the Medieval era the two seminal thinkers of the two great superstructures of Western cosmology: the top-down monist Thomas Aquinas and his rational ordering of God that explains the world and the bottom-up dichotomist-dualist William of Ockham and his chaotic world that revealed a powerful and volitional God. These superstructures would spawn two cosmological "models of explanation" where God and the world would explain one another, holding the common belief that the world was determined, either by God (who explained the world in a cosmological Apollinarianism with an all-encompassing divine determinism) or nature (which explained God in a cosmological Arianism with its mechanistic universe). The lack of a human soul in Jesus in both (christological) "Arianism" and Apollinarianism is therefore directly analogous to the lack of creaturely freedom in their cosmological counterparts, as either a naturalistic or theistic determinism rules the world, respectively. These models of explanation would continue into late modernity either generally untouched or they would occasionally morph into the cosmological "models of identification" (God became the world in occasionalism as cosmological Docetism or the world became God in pantheism as cosmological Ebionism). The latter went one step further and dismissed God altogether in Western materialistic atheism.

We saw in chapter 6 that the one common thread running through all the definitional-simplicity-inspired christological heresies was the concept of Monoenergism. Whether the christological heresy was oriented toward monism or dichotomist-dualism, it always regarded Jesus as Monoenergist: either the Logos moved the passive flesh or the human (or resultant conjunction) acted rather independently. Those heresies, with definitional simplicity as their first principle, could not conceive of a model that did justice to the integrity of both the divinity and humanity of Jesus. It should not surprise that the definitional-simplicity-derived cosmologies also have a "Monoenergist" bent. Either the dialectically constructed God controls the creation or the creation rises in opposition to the dialectically constructed God. The "collective will" (as Monoenergism historically distilled into Monothelitism) is either with the one (God) or the many (creation). As we have repeatedly seen, there is no middle ground. From the monist side, any loss of meticulous determinism creates an unthinkable world where creation is completely independent from its creator. From this perspective, the creation vainly attempts to merit inclusion into the world of the creator all the while being dialectically opposed to him (as the creation possesses little if anything good in itself). The zero-sum game requires an all-or-nothing approach. The same can be said for the dichotomist-dualist side. Any hint of an external authority presuming to rule over or even intermingle among the affairs of the creation is met with hostility or impossibility. For the Anti-Nicene "Arian," Jesus could not possibly be "as God" as the Father. For the Nestorian, two natures could not unite to form one. Jesus has flesh, so he must be on "our" side. The anxiety produced by the presence of the unknowable, dialectically produced "God" drives the dichotomist-dualist impulse to domesticate (Descartes and Newton) or eliminate (Spinoza, Feuerbach, and Marx) him. Depending on which side of the Plotinian ambiguity one chooses to embrace, it is either God or creation with no possibility of meaningful room for the other.

The Historical Implications

While the christological controversies were immensely important in theological and ecclesiological affairs, the broader cultural impact was not as great. Aside from creating some warring political factions, the day-to-day lives of most people in late antiquity were not greatly affected. The cosmological models unleashed on the West by the same implications of divine simplicity, however, impacted everyone. In this section, I want to look at both church and state.

The evolution of the church as an organization within this cosmological framework is an interesting study, to say the least. I can only touch on the high points here. Because it sees itself as the vicar/voice of God on earth, the church has always been most suited to the monist orientation of the dialectically-constructed cosmology. For many centuries after Augustine, both church and society were united in their common monism. The zenith of this phenomenon is the Thomist synthesis. Western civilization came of age in this monist hegemony and became an irrevocably theological culture (remaining just as theological later in the very beliefs it would deny!) grounded in definitional simplicity, with Augustine and Aquinas as its guiding lights. The monists, who in reality see only one principle—God—tend to devalue the creation while elevating creator in a zero-sum fashion. The Thomist monists, due to their rational ordering of everything under the category of being, see the value of creation in the assumption that it is the mirror of the eternal. The more Augustinian monists, due to their belief in divine determinism, see everything in creation as the necessary result of the will of God. Creation is either a means of ascent to the divine or the fallen repository of evil that must be meticulously divinely ordered, respectively. Neither can value creation for creation's own sake. This orientation has led to the (monist) church's mistrust of science, because the latter sees something in creation that is of intrinsic value, conflicting with the basic orientation of monism.

William of Ockham changed everything with the nominalist revolution. Gone was the rational ordering of God and the world. Gone also was the church's perception as the (somewhat) benevolent middleman in such an order. As the dichotomist-dualist ideas of Ockham took hold in society, the church became viewed as the voice of the God that could not be rationally known. Belief and knowledge, as well as faith and reason, were being pulled apart. The humanists tried to fix it by looking to both the self and the past. The Reformers embraced this God and created new monist voices based on his necessary determination of all things. In the Counter-Reformation, Rome reinstated Thomas as the authoritative voice of Catholicism, doubling down in vain to legislate the rational ordering of the universe with an iron fist even though the horse had already left the barn. After a couple of generations, the Protestants, despite differing ideas of who was in charge and why, looked just like the Catholics otherwise. They utilized a scholastic methodology, enforced a monist orientation to society, opposed freedoms of any kind (religious or secular), and, along with the Catholics, attempted to prove their exclusive claims to theological truth by the edge of the sword.

Meanwhile, the moderns, the real heirs of Ockham's orientation to the definitionally simple and dialectically constructed God, were turning to nature to ultimately cut this God down to size. In the early days, most moderns remained nominal Christians if only for fear of execution, as they had no real interest in following such a God. The seventeenth-century wars of religion (and subsequent conflicting truth claims that exist up to the present day) have had the opposite effect of inspiring hope and goodwill among the dichotomist-dualists. Instead, the majority of the world, dialectically opposed to the "one" by definition, yearns to free itself from the potentially pernicious, omnipotent volition of the God of Ockham. Operating from within the same dialectical structure as the monists, they used that system to create cosmologies more to their liking, the "Arian" versions associated with the mechanistic universe and forms of deism, or the full "Ebionite" ones of pantheism and materialistic atheism. Fulfilling the vision of René Descartes, they conquered this "God" by reducing him to creation and ultimately themselves. These same dichotomist-dualists have utilized scientific discovery and technological mastery to create our present technological culture. Modern machines and technological innovations "work" and provide value to all of us, so the monists who object to the value of creation in, of, and by itself are to be all the more rejected. After all, the world explains so much that directly impact lives in thousands of ways, who needs this possibly evil God around, or those numerous groups claiming to be his sole voice?

Like Thomas a few centuries before, the post-Reformation monist churches could not hold their synthesis together. How many times must history repeat itself before we begin to notice that the same assumptions are at work? Recall that, since Luther held everything in creation to be necessary, this belief entailed the existence of evil in God. His answer was to trust Scripture as God's word—*sola scriptura*, the hallmark of the Reformation. But if God is (partly?) evil and Scripture is good, then Scripture cannot give us accurate knowledge of God and therefore cannot be his word. Along comes the (mostly Lutheran in the beginning) higher criticism of Scripture to cut it down to something merely human and not from God. The eighteenth century saw the rise of Deism and the constant shrinking of monist approaches to faith. Kant's philosophy and Schleiermacher's religious answer almost wiped them out. Two Vatican councils and the rise of Protestant fundamentalism (and therefore Evangelicalism) tried to stem the tide with limited success. Of course, "success" is limited because they operate from within the same set of assumptions. As we have seen time and again, any attempt at synthesis from within the system of definitional simplicity will yield a contradiction, because it will always entail the eventual denial of its guiding assumptions.

Likewise, any attempt to correct theological errors from within the system will only take one to the other half of the Plotinian ambiguity. We saw this with the Remonstrants in the early seventeenth century in chapter 10. They rightly saw the errors of the cosmological Apollinarianism of the disciples of Beza. Their counterattack was to adopt an Arian Christology. There have been theological movements that have arisen from outside the scope of the dialectical process, but I do not believe any of them were sufficiently sophisticated to see what they were truly up against. Maybe that will change.

The political upheaval has perhaps been worse. The Thomistic synthesis bequeathed to Western Europe both church and crown, another unstable alliance. It was not long before the state had more power than the church. As the dichotomist-dualist philosophy of men like Descartes would domesticate the unknowable God of nominalism, so too would the revolutionary spirit of the Enlightenment eliminate or domesticate the crowned heads of Europe. Kings and queens were replaced with various republican and democratic forms of government. We know by now that within the dialectical construction, there is always a backlash.

The past century-plus has fundamentally altered the Western mindset. First came a world war, then a worldwide depression, then a second and more terrible world war that introduced a new term: genocide. This was followed by a cold war and the potential of mutually-assured destruction of the two superpowers. The ideological merging that followed the cold war seems to be ushering in a new kind of totalitarianism on a global scale. Weary and tired of incessant evil all around them, Western civilization as a whole has tried to move beyond its dialectical roots, outwardly rejecting both a god who orders the world and a god who can be explained by the world. In the end, most of Western civilization has chosen to just move on into what is now a post-Christian culture. Western civilization, in its post-Christian turn, has done its best to exterminate the "god" who gave birth to it.

Theological Methodology in History

I want to return to my opening discussion in the Introduction. Utilizing the christological controversies as my historical evidence, I have argued that a dialectically-driven natural theology makes arriving at a truly Chalcedonian Christology impossible. Yet the "historical" methodology to studying the *loci* (the methodology of the first few pages of this book) is dependent on such a natural theology. The doctrine of God is near the beginning of the "historical" approach; the doctrine of Christ is much nearer the end. As such, the content of many of the theological *loci* are already decided before one arrives at Christology. Those *loci* thus conceived already shape what the person and work of Christ must necessarily entail. Let us touch a few high points.[1]

I want to start with Christology. The opening chapters of John, Colossians, and Hebrews begin to unpack the concept of a christological creation. In John and Hebrews, it is the Logos/Son who made the world. In Colossians, he is not only its creator, but its sustainer and *telos*. He is both the beginning and the end goal of the creation. The New Testament does not present a creation apart from Christ. Creation is as much the work of Christ as is redemption (recall Athanasius). Yet we do not treat it that way in our theological studies. The study of Western Christology begins with the incarnation, and that is relatively instrumental for taking care of sin and the fall. But seen through the lens of the Eastern Patristic tradition that was able to overcome the intrusion of pagan ideas of divine simplicity into the faith, Christology rightly begins at creation. The incarnation is the beginning of the *telos* of creation, to finally and permanently unite God and man, which has always been God's eternal purpose.

The christological heresies of late antiquity were real challenges to the message of the gospel, because their most foundational assumptions lay outside of the Christian tradition altogether. To rephrase Tertullian of Carthage, they were Athens' limited attempts to explain Jerusalem, describing who Jesus was within foundationally-pagan thought structures. Those attempts were ultimately rejected by the church. If, as this book has shown, that creation (which the Bible describes as christological) is explained utilizing those same pagan structures, we should expect to see the fundamental issues of the christological heresies replicated in cosmological language. I hope I have succeeded in showing that they do.

The doctrine of providence suffers irreparable harm in the dialectically-constructed definition of the divine essence. God and creation are bound together in that divine essence, for nothing else exists. There is no room for freedom on either side. The creation is determined either by the essence/decree of God or by natural laws that are ultimately controlled by God (and eventually nature). In such a world, God cannot uphold creation because he is incapable of having any kind of real relation with it. Because he is defined to be the dialectical opposite of the world, he cannot be influenced by the world. Prayer then becomes a sham, because God is never affected. If prayer is merely the divinely appointed means for the outworking of God's glory, then it is as meaningless as everything else.

The biblical picture of providence is that God is actively involved in moving the world toward his appointed end goal. If every minute occurrence in time is decreed in eternity (or in physics or DNA) and then rendered certain in time, there is no end goal. History—the progression of events in time—is lost in such a construction. The biblical and Christian doctrine of providence requires God's active involvement in

---

1. I truly believe that to discuss the ramifications of definitional simplicity on the *loci* of systematic theology would take several other books the size of this one. I just want to touch on a few key ideas in the upcoming paragraphs.

a sequence of events in time/space/matter toward a *telos*. The dialectical construction renders such a providence impossible. Those who are Christian and uphold both definitional simplicity and providence simply ignore some of the good and necessary consequences of the former to create a syncretistic blend to allow the latter.

Perhaps no doctrine suffers more in the dialectical construction than anthropology. In it, God and humanity are set in opposition from the very beginning. If God is good, then humanity, his dialectical opposite, must be some kind of not-good. We already saw how much the humanity of Jesus became devalued in the heresies. How much more our own in such constructions? The rejection of God is so easy to comprehend once we are under the sway of Ockhamism. One is forced to love either God or creation and despise the other.

The image of God is marred in the dialectical definition as well. The "God" of definitional divine simplicity cannot have real relations outside himself, is all about his own glory (*natura naturans*), and is defined to be the dialectical opposite of everything he created. How then are we as humans his image-bearers? Does Scripture or the Judeo-Christian tradition prohibit us from having real relations with one another, command us to be narcissistic jerks who use others for self-gratification, and live on earth eternally opposed? What I am describing here is the very nature of the definitionally-simple "God." It does not sound like the God and Father of our Lord Jesus Christ, who so loved the world that he gave his only-begotten Son to reconcile and save the world back to himself. If anything, the incarnation is proof of the level of love God has for his creation. Unlike the definitionally-simple god, the God of the Bible and of Christian experience is neither aloof over, hostile toward, nor indifferent to the world which he created.

The doctrine of the Trinity posits three distinct persons in the one divine essence. Augustine "rescues" this doctrine within his construction of divine simplicity by defining the divine persons as relations of the divine essence to itself. Human persons can be no better. If the divine persons are defined by the essence (an inverted *ordo theologiae* prioritizing essence over person), then human persons can be no more than relations of the human essence to itself. The Plotinian ambiguity takes over and we have two extremes within this definition, the radical individualism where each of the "many" fights the pull toward homogenization, or the capitulation to it in a form of collectivism. Both destroy the integrity-within-community of the trinitarian example. The pagan construction is attempting to destroy the Christian discovery of authentic personhood.

In my opinion, the crux of the problem is revealed in the doctrine of sin and evil. If God and the world are eternally co-dependent at the level of essence (for in definitional simplicity, that is all that is), then we are faced with the Protestant (Plotinian) dilemma: either the evil in the world reveals a God that is morally ambiguous and potentially capricious, or what appears to be evil must be explained away as a "greater good." We have already seen Luther's *deus absconditus* and Edwards's occasionalism at work illustrating both sides of the ambiguity. The modern turn dismissed both options but in doing so strayed even further away from the biblical picture.

Missing in all Christian attempts at a dialectical construction of the divine essence is the presence of Satan. His presence is rendered superfluous where the opposites are the one and the many. Our ancient adversary is never truly held accountable within the paradigm of definitional simplicity. In Origen's *apokatastasis*, he is redeemed along with us. In Augustine and his children, it is humanity and not its ancient tempter that incurs the "just" wrath of God. In all forms of theistic determinism, the fall was eternally decreed, so Satan is playing the same pathetic roles as we, being really only occasions in the divine mind once all flowery religious language is finally stripped away. He is a fiction among those who have embraced naturalistic or Kantian forms of Christianity. For those who reject the dialectical construction of definitional simplicity and still believe in the reality of the devil, it is almost as if the dialectical construction itself is one of his many lies. In defining the divine essence in terms of creation, he succeeds in putting "God" (or perhaps himself) on the same ontological plane as creation (he already is a creature, after all) all the while laying the blame for the cause of all pain, suffering, and evil not on himself, but on the true divine essence. As I have stated before, I do not believe Origen or Augustine were capable of seeing the enormous ramifications of their theological decisions. But surely the devil could. He fully understands how fundamentally anti-Christian the root (and therefore the fruit) of the dialectical construction is. He is not omniscient by any means, but he has a much better grasp of the track of history than any human. If this were not his plan, it could have scarcely worked out better for him any other way. The greatest and most productive culture in the history of earth willingly and nearly unilaterally surrendered the Christian faith upon which it was built in very large part due to the enormous implications of one theological decision injected into the tradition by the "right" people at the "right" time(s). If it were not a plan, it is the craziest of coincidences.

The next *locus* of the historical walk through theology is Christology. We have already said plenty there, but note that the doctrines of theology proper, cosmology and providence, anthropology, and sin come before. In the dialectical construction, As said above, Jesus is already pigeon-holed. He does not shape the former doctrines as he should as the one in, for, and by whom all things exist and consist. Rather, the theology worked out in those *loci* shape his person and work. The cart is before the horse.

The rest of the *loci* are likewise damaged. The Holy Spirit is as superfluous as Satan within the structure of definitional simplicity: it is a dialectical system with no room for a third entity, which is why Augustine struggled so much with his understanding of the Spirit. Soteriology is a disaster, starting with the *apokatastasis*. Salvation is reconfigured to be either imposed on the elect few by the monists (Calvinism and really, Arminianism too), or communal human improvement (Protestant liberalism, social gospel and various Liberation theologies) by the dichotomist-dualists. Within Roman Catholicism, Mary and the saints fill the mediatorial void left by Jesus, who, as

God, cannot by definition have meaningful relations with creation, despite the biblical and historical witness. The confusion of person and nature that is the identity thesis causes natural concepts like predestination and election to become personal with their disastrous conclusions.[2] We have already discussed the legalistic and impersonal elements that take precedence once the possibility for any real relation (on the divine side) between God and the creation is removed. Once nominalism is established, the doctrine of union with Christ suffers, because the union of being that engenders *theosis* is replaced by a union of will that replicates Nestorius's "conjunction." Christ and the church (individually or collectively, no matter) can never be joined in union; they can only be at best like two rails of a railroad track: always parallel, never touching. The church itself either becomes the bridge between the eternal and created, dispensing *ex opere operato* grace, or becomes that which seeks to fully conform to the culture around it. Eschatology's great models are a dichotomist-dualist postmillennialism where humanity builds the kingdom for Jesus, a monist premillennial dispensationalism where the elect escape the judgment due the world, or an amillennialism that can be real in either a monist (Roman Catholic) or dichotomist-dualist (Protestant) fashion.

It is not only the *loci* that suffer; so does our witness. Descartes, in a stroke of pure genius, demonstrated that the dialectical construction could be reversed to make us "gods" like the "god" of natural theology. Descartes and later Kant played by the same theological and philosophical rules as those whose methodologies rule Western Christianity. For the Roman Catholic or Magisterial Protestant, Descartes and Kant are unassailable, that is, to truly critique their errors is to pull the house down upon oneself as well. If Descartes uses faulty assumptions, then so do Rome, Augsburg, and Westminster.[3] The only critique available then, is the mutual suspicion and opposing foundations of monism and dichotomist-dualism. That is all that is left. The *real* methodological assumptions are never touched, because, like the Cold War, it is mutually assured destruction. It goes right back to the aftermath of Origen. Because theology is

---

2. Calvinists explicitly accept the assumptions of definitional simplicity. Arminians implicitly do as well, because they are not able to free themselves from Reformed thought-structures. Therefore, to make predestination and election personal is to immediately remove them from their christological basis (by taking them out of space-and-time and placing them into the eternal and immutable decree of God) and to force God to be the one who both saves and condemns from start to finish. The only thing that saves any form of Calvinism from collapsing into an Edwards-style occasionalism is religious impulse. The theological axioms demand it go there.

3. This becomes even more apparent in Christian traditions that have elevated portions of the dialectical construction to dogma. Two obvious examples include Rome's adoption of Aquinas as official church teaching and the Reformed Protestant acceptance of the predestinarian doctrines of Calvin and Beza. Both examples struggle to see the human origin and development of their respective doctrines. Instead, they see their doctrines as quasi-God-breathed, which makes it almost impossible to identify their dialectical obverses for what they really are. When, for example, Roman Catholics rail (rightly, in my opinion) against secular humanism, they fail to see that both Thomas's doctrine of God and secular humanism's apathy toward God have the same dialectical root. That is, to win the battle is to lose it, which we should expect by now.

culturally constructed, it can never critique the culture and thereby fulfill one of the aims of the people of God on earth.

One of the greatest needs of the people of God who "walk by faith and not by sight" is assurance. Assurance is the calming, peaceful knowledge and awareness of ourselves as the recipients of God's love and grace. Assurance is a personal gift from God, accessed by faith rather than by rationality. A dialectical theology of definitional simplicity promises (but as we have seen, fails to deliver) more than assurance—it offers certainty. An *ordo theologiae* that prioritizes nature likewise promises what is natural is compelled, that is, the way it *must* be (and cannot be otherwise). The idolatrous human heart seeks certainty in place of assurance, as it places our knowledge of events above the fray of actual lived experience. But, as we have repeatedly seen, the dialectical construction ultimately fails to deliver on certainty, instead producing a picture of God that is willful, capricious, and ultimately unknowable. The effect is the opposite of certainty. The one man universally revered in the Protestant world—Martin Luther—lived his entire life with his *anfechtung*, his untranslatable terrorizing dread of the absconded God he could not know and could not trust. His deepest theological commitments (and we know what those were) could not fulfill his deep desire for assurance. Perhaps C. S. Lewis said it best in the famous closing lines of his children's classic, *The Lion, the Witch, and the Wardrobe*. Aslan is a good lion (offering assurance), but he is not tame (certainty). There is no certainty with persons.

Conclusion

In the end, we must conclude that a dialectical construction of the divine essence as definitionally simple has had disastrous effects on both the Christian faith and the civilization that came to maturity within it. While definitional simplicity might still look good "on paper," a millennium and a half of Western history says otherwise. The christological heresies of late antiquity were but the tip of an enormous iceberg. The larger cosmological assumptions lurking beneath the surface waters of the ancient heresies forced a dialectical choice among all who have entered therein: because God and the world are dialectically opposed (and co-dependent), a thinking person must choose to embrace and elevate one while despising or diminishing the other. The Thomist Catholics elevate the divine world and diminish the created, seeing the latter as the means of ascent to the former. The more Ockhamist Protestants either embrace the volitional God of nominalism or the humanity which he has determined. The rest, as they say, is history.

Unfortunately, there is no way to reverse this problem. Rome is never going to modify Aquinas's key assumptions. The confessional Protestant churches are not going to repudiate their defining confessions. Augustine, Aquinas, Luther, and Calvin will always be revered as the leading theologians of the Latin tradition, and none are alive to recant. The oldest and most powerful religious bodies on earth cannot free themselves from the problem even if they wanted to do so. They are so trapped in a culturally conditioned theological structure that they are never able to be truly countercultural. The cosmological outworking of the theological commitment to definitional simplicity are deeply and irrevocably rooted in the fabric of Western culture. And, due to the export of both goods and ideas, Western culture is now global culture. Both "Western" capitalism and atheistic communism owe their existence to the definitional-simplicity-shaped ideas of the Enlightenment. The either-or, dialectical construction of everyday choices are all rooted in a dialectical construction of the doctrine of God. To borrow one of Jesus's parables, there is no way to pull up the weeds without simultaneously uprooting the wheat along with it.

What can be done? Unfortunately, at this point, there will be little help from ecclesial or societal institutions. We can only work at the level of individual persons. First, I would recommend a concerted return to Nicene trinitarianism and Chalcedonian Christology at the start of theological reflection. They give us a blueprint for the defeat of pagan ideas. Again, the church is not a great help at present because these two great pillars of the faith have been replaced with more "seeker-sensitive" ideas in a vain attempt to recover the church's voice in culture. In my three-plus decades of church attendance, the only sermons I have heard preached on the Trinity are the ones I did myself. It is very difficult to convert a culture that is steeped in dichotomist-dualist modernism and post-modernism with theological language that sounds monist, as the Plotinian ambiguity demands that the former revolt against the latter. Our present culture is much more concerned with "how" than "why" which works to our disadvantage.

Second, we must recognize the implications of definitional simplicity and reject them. We must reject the fundamental separation of God and the world that was birthed in Augustine's created seminal rational principles and has now grown into the post-Kantian culture where the natural world and supernatural world are inaccessible to one another. In my opinion, Maximus would be a much better cosmological guide than Augustine, because the former refuses to separate or confuse God in the world as the latter has done. Maximus's *logoi* provide a way to see God and the world perichoretically joined together rather than acting as if they were in a zero-sum game. Similarly, we must likewise reject the meticulous divine determinism rooted in both Origen (*apokatastasis*) and Augustine (unconditional individual election and the "gift" of perseverance), both of which are entailments of their definitional simplicity that confuse creator and creation. Ultimately, to separate or confuse God and the world ends up making one or the other irrelevant. To separate God and the world has as its endgame to make God detached, unnecessary, or ultimately nonexistent. To confuse God and the world results in the world itself becoming meaningless, because in the end it is only a created extension of God's will. And that will reveals a God that is beyond good and evil and is ultimately untrustworthy, as everything past, present, and future is as it should be. As Ebionism and Docetism really aren't all that far apart, neither are their pragmatic cosmological counterparts, materialistic or theistic determinism. Unfortunately, when push comes to shove and a choice must be made between the two, the theistic variety seldom survives Ockham's Razor.[4]

Third, we must tell others what we know. That will be painful, as I can attest from personal experience. It will be a lot like the story line portrayed in the popular movie *The Matrix* from a few years ago. We will become like the character Morpheus, who searches for and ultimately finds the character Neo located in the matrix, which is a computer program simulating reality. Neo, to unplug his mind from the alternate reality, must be shown the stark contrast between the way he believes things to be in the program with the way things really are. Once Neo learns the differences between reality and (former) perception, he goes back into the matrix to defeat the forces that have enslaved humanity. Here is where the analogy ends. We cannot undo what has been done. We live in the twenty-first century, rather than the fifth or the fifteenth. We can only "unplug" people by "freeing their minds" to the reality that the pagan weed of definitional simplicity has incredibly weakened the message of the good news of Jesus Christ to the world. Unfortunately, most are so plugged in to the way things are it will be difficult for them to hear. But there is always a chance there is a Neo out there somewhere, who instinctively knows there is something wrong, but can't quite put his finger on it.

Why is it so important to tell people about definitional simplicity? Well, that's a good question. The doctrine itself is pretty technical and frankly quite obscure to most early twenty-first-century Christianity, but its practical outworkings are everywhere, and we who teach about God are being continually bombarded with them. I can only mention them briefly here. First and foremost is probably the most popular answer to the problem of evil, namely that the evil we experience is a part of the plan of God, as he is "teaching us something" in the midst of it. While that may occur, portraying evil as ultimately good makes them indistinguishable. That has a lot more to do with the definitionally simple Plotinian One than the biblical Yahweh. Second, the idea that God is angry with, indifferent about, or generally hostile toward us is directly tied to definitional simplicity. Third, the perverse notion that "God" turned from Jesus on the cross is due to definitional simplicity, as it is fundamentally "Arian." Fourth, so many of us are convinced that human nature is "sinful," an error tied directly to the confusion of person and nature inherent in definitional simplicity. Fifth, the Reformed doctrine of soteriological monergism is nothing more than a repackaging of seventh-century Monoenergism and in turn definitional simplicity in its most advanced christological

---

4. I fear for those who embraced the "Young, Restless, and Reformed" movement within conservative evangelical Protestantism over the past decade and a half. When these young ones become older and the sting of life in this world hits home, they will be faced with a difficult choice of which tenet to surrender: determinism or faith. Many, unfortunately, are so convinced of the truth of determinism they have walked away from faith. I find it incredibly ironic that one of the leading lights of the YRR movement has been Minnesota pastor John Piper, who is a self-proclaimed disciple of Jonathan Edwards, who is perhaps the most consistent and influential cosmological Docetist who ever lived.

form. All of these errors are the result of imposing an alien *hypothesis*[5] on Scripture and its interpretation. Pointing to definitional simplicity as the touchstone of that *hypothesis*, and then showing its pagan origins and its historical atrocities gets down below the surface. Like poison ivy, cutting these errors down at ground level is only a very temporary solution, for the root system remains intact and they quickly grow back. Killing poison ivy means killing the root. We know what the root is by now.

We all remember playing connect-the-dots as children, where we were given a piece of paper with numbered dots on it. We would draw a line from dot one to dot two, then on to dot three, and so on, until we ran out of dots. The dots alone told us nothing, but once we were finished connecting the dots, a picture would emerge. Think of the events of Western civilization as a series of similarly numbered dots. The analysis you just read attempts to connect the dots to make a meaningful picture. If I have been even remotely successful, you should have a picture now, where the dots are the "what" of history and the lines are the "why." The lead in the pencil that makes the lines to connect the dots is made up, at least partly, by definitional simplicity. I say this to reiterate my earlier claim that, now, it matters little that Origen and Augustine did not see the enormous implications of their innovations. We are in the midst of those implications all grown up. How the alligators got into the pond is not as important right now as identifying them and making sure they don't eat us.

I hope you have enjoyed this book. I hope it has enlightened you and convicted you as it has me. I suppose, to complete the analogy from the movie, you now have a red pill and a blue pill in front of you. Swallow the blue pill and you can consign what you just read to the dusty bin of historical speculation. After all, I have presented an alternate reality to many of us in Western Christianity. It might be too much to process. The blue pill will allow you to wake up in your own bed and ignore that what you read might be significant. But, if this book has struck a chord in you, the red pill awaits. And if so, as the movie character Cypher says, "Buckle your seat belt, Dorothy. Because Kansas is going bye-bye."

---

5. *Hypothesis* in the Irenaean sense, where it is the framework through which everything receives meaning.

Bibliography

Adam, Karl. *The Christ of Faith*. Translated by Joyce Clark. New York: Pantheon, 1957.
Allen, David L. *The Extent of the Atonement: A Historical and Critical Review*. Nashville: B & H Academic, 2016.
Allison, C. Fitzsimmons. *The Cruelty of Heresy: An Affirmation of Christian Orthodoxy*. Harrisburg, PA: Morehouse, 1994.
Anatolios, Khaled. *Athanasius: The Coherence of His Thought*. London: Routledge, 1998.
———. *Retrieving Nicaea: The Development and Meaning of Christian Doctrine*. Grand Rapids: Baker Academic, 2011.
Anselm. *Cur Deus Homo?* Scott's Valley, CA: CreateSpace, 2016.
Apollinarius. *De Unione*. In *Apollinaris von Laodicea und seine Schule: Texte und Untersuchungen*, edited by Hans Leitzmann, 204. Tuebingen: Mohr, 1904.
———. *Epistle to Dionysius*. In *Apollinaris von Laodicea und seine Schule: Texte und Untersuchungen*, edited by Hans Leitzmann, 256-62. Tuebingen: Mohr, 1904.
Arius. *Thalia* Fragments. Milwaukee, WI. Fourth Century Christianity, 2022. https://www.fourthcentury.com/arius-thalia-greek/.
Athanasius. *Against the Arians*. In *Nicene and Post-Nicene Fathers, Second Series*, edited by Philip Schaff and Henry Wace, 4:303–447. Peabody, MA: Hendrickson, 1994.
Augustine, *City of God*. In *Nicene and Post-Nicene Fathers, First Series*, edited by Philip Schaff, 2:1–511. Peabody, MA: Hendrickson, 1994.
———. *Confessions*. In *Nicene and Post-Nicene Fathers, First Series*, edited by Philip Schaff, 1:27–207. Peabody, MA: Hendrickson, 1994.
———. *Enchiridion*. In *Nicene and Post-Nicene Fathers, First Series*, edited by Philip Schaff, 3:137–276. Peabody, MA: Hendrickson, 1994.
———. *On Rebuke and Grace*. In *Nicene and Post-Nicene Fathers, First Series*, edited by Philip Schaff, 5:471–92. Peabody, MA: Hendrickson, 1994.
———. *On the Predestination of the Saints*. In *Nicene and Post-Nicene Fathers, First Series*, edited by Philip Schaff, 5:493–520. Peabody, MA: Hendrickson, 1994.
———. *On the Proceedings of Pelagius*. In *Nicene and Post-Nicene Fathers, First Series*, edited by Philip Schaff, 5:183–212. Peabody, MA: Hendrickson, 1994.
———. *On the Trinity*. In *Nicene and Post-Nicene Fathers, First Series*, edited by Philip Schaff, 3:1–228. Peabody, MA: Hendrickson, 1994.

Bibliography

———. *Retractations*. Translated by M. Inez Bogan. Fathers of the Church 60. Washington: Catholic University of America Press, 1968.

———. *To Simplician*. In *Augustine: Earlier Writings*, translated by John H. S. Burleigh, 376–406. Library of Christian Classics. Philadelphia: Westminster, 1953.

Ayres, Lewis. *Nicaea and Its Legacy: An Approach to Fourth-Century Trinitarian Theology*. Oxford: Oxford University Press, 2006.

Balthasar, Hans Urs von. *Cosmic Liturgy: The Universe according to Maximus the Confessor*. Translated by Brian E. Daley. San Francisco: Ignatius, 2003.

Barth, Karl. *Church Dogmatics*. 14 vols. London: T. & T. Clark, 1936–68.

Basil of Caesarea. *The Hexameron*. In *Nicene and Post-Nicene Fathers, Second Series*, edited by Philip Schaff and Henry Wace, 8:51–107. Peabody, MA: Hendrickson, 1994.

———. *Letters*. In *Nicene and Post-Nicene Fathers, Second Series*, edited by Philip Schaff and Henry Wace, 8:109–327. Peabody, MA: Hendrickson, 1994.

Bathrellos, Demetrios. *The Byzantine Christ: Person, Nature, and Will in the Christology of St. Maximus the Confessor*. Oxford: Oxford University Press, 2004.

Beeley, Christopher A. *The Unity of Christ: Continuity and Conflict in Patristic Tradition*. New Haven: Yale University Press, 2012.

Behr, John. *The Nicene Faith*. 2 vols. Formation of Christian Theology 2–3. Crestwood, NY: St. Vladimir's Seminary Press, 2004.

———. *The Way to Nicaea*. Formation of Christian Theology 1. Crestwood, NY: St. Vladimir's Seminary Press, 2001.

Berkhof, Louis. *Systematic Theology*. Grand Rapids: Eerdmans, 1974.

Bethune-Baker, J. F. *An Introduction to the Early History of Christian Doctrine to the Time of the Council of Chalcedon*. 9th ed. London: Methuen, 1951.

Blaising, Craig. "Monarchianism." In *Evangelical Dictionary of Theology*. 2nd edition, edited by Walter A. Elwell, 784–85. Grand Rapids: Baker, 2001.

Blowers, Paul M. *Maximus the Confessor: Jesus Christ and the Transfiguration of the World*. Oxford: Oxford University Press, 2016.

Bonner, Gerald. *Freedom and Necessity: St. Augustine's Teaching on Divine Power and Human Freedom*. Washington: Catholic University Press of America, 2007.

Bradshaw, David. "The Concept of the Divine Energies." *Philosophy and Theology* 18 (2006) 93–120.

Brown, Raymond E. *The Community of the Beloved Disciple: The Life, Loves, and Hates of an Individual Church in New Testament Times*. Mahwah, NJ: Paulist, 1979.

Buckley, Michael J. *At the Origins of Modern Atheism*. New Haven: Yale University Press, 1987.

Bulgakov, Sergius. *The Comforter*. Translated by Boris Jackson. Grand Rapids: Eerdmans, 2004.

Bussanich, John. "Plotinus's Metaphysics of the One." In *The Cambridge Companion to Plotinus*, edited by Lloyd P. Gerson, 38–65. Cambridge: Cambridge University Press, 1996.

Calvin, John. "Congregation on Eternal Election." In *The Bolsec Controversy on Predestination, from 1551 to 1555, The Statements of Jerome Bolsec, and the Responses of John Calvin, Theodore Beza, and Other Reformed Theologians*, vol. 1, pts. 1 & 2, by Philip C. Holtrop, n.p. Lewiston: Edwin Mellon, 1993.

Canons of II Constantinople. In *Nicene and Post-Nicene Fathers, Second Series*, edited by Philip Schaff and Henry Wace, 14:313. Peabody, MA: Hendrickson, 1994.

Bibliography

Cessario, Romanus. *A Short History of Thomism*. Washington: Catholic University Press of America, 2003.

"The Chalcedonian Creed." https://www.apuritansmind.com/creeds-and-confessions/the-chalcedonian-creed-circa-451-a-d/.

Cohen, S. Mark. "Aristotle's Metaphysics." In *Stanford Encyclopedia of Philosophy*, edited by Edward N. Zalta, n.p. http://plato.stanford.edu/entries/aristotle-metaphysics/#WhaSub.

Coleridge, Samuel Taylor. "On the Promethius of Aeschylus." In *Complete Works of Samuel Taylor Coleridge*, edited by W. G. T. Shedd, 4:353–55. New York: Harper, 1853.

Craig, Edward. *The Mind of God and the Works of Man*. Oxford: Clarendon, 1987.

Crisp, Oliver D. *Jonathan Edwards on God and Creation*. Oxford: Oxford University Press, 2016.

Cross, F. L. "Gottschalk." In *The Oxford Dictionary of the Christian Church*, edited by F. L. Cross, 575. London: Oxford University Press, 1958.

Daane, James. *The Freedom of God: A Study of Election and Pulpit*. Grand Rapids: Eerdmans, 1973.

Danielou, Jean. *The Theology of Jewish Christianity*. London: Darton, Longman & Todd, 1964.

Davis, Leo Donald. *The First Seven Ecumenical Councils (325–787): Their History and Theology*. Collegeville, MN: Liturgical, 1983.

DeProspo, R. C. *Theism in the Discourse of Jonathan Edwards*. Newark, DE: University of Delaware Press, 1985.

Dolezal, James E. *God without Parts: Divine Simplicity and the Metaphysics of God's Absoluteness*. Eugene, OR: Pickwick, 2011.

D'Souza, Romero. *Christian Cosmology: A Manual for Philosophy and Theology*. Christian Heritage Rediscovered 7. New Delhi: Christian World Imprints, 2014.

Duby, Steven J. *Divine Simplicity: A Dogmatic Account*. T. & T. Clark Studies in Systematic Theology 30. London: Bloomsbury T. & T. Clark, 2016.

Edwards, Jonathan. *Works of Jonathan Edwards: Yale Edition*. Edited by Paul Ramsey. 26 vols. New Haven: Yale University Press, 1977–2008.

Elwood, Douglas. *The Philosophical Theology of Jonathan Edwards*. New York: Columbia University Press, 1960.

Erasmus. *The Collected Works of Erasmus*. Edited by Charles Trinkaus. 69 vols. Toronto: University of Toronto Press, 1999.

Erickson, Millard J. *The Word Became Flesh: A Contemporary Incarnational Christology*. Grand Rapids: Baker, 1991.

Fairbairn, Donald. *Grace and Christology in the Early Church*. Oxford Early Christian Studies. Oxford: Oxford University Press, 2003.

———. *Life in the Trinity: An Introduction to Theology with the Help of the Church Fathers*. Downers Grove: IVP Academic, 2009.

Farrell, Joseph P. *Free Choice in St. Maximus the Confessor*. South Canaan, PA: St. Tikhon's Seminary Press, 1989.

———. *God, History, and the Dialectic: The Theological Foundation of the Two Europe and their Cultural Consequences*. 2008. https://payhip.com/b/qU4d.

———. *The Mystagogy of the Holy Spirit by St. Photios*. Brookline, MA: Holy Cross Orthodox Press, 1987.

Feinberg, John. *No One Like Him*. Foundations of Evangelical Theology. Wheaton: Crossway, 2001.

Fesko, John V. *Diversity in the Reformed Tradition: Supra- and Infralapsarianism in Calvin, Dort, and Westminster*. Greenville, SC: Reformed Academic, 2001.

Bibliography

Feuerbach, Ludwig. *The Essence of Christianity*. Translated by George Elliot. New York: Harper, 1957.

Frame, John. *The Doctrine of God: A Theology of Lordship Vol. 2*. Phillipsburg, NJ: Prebyterian & Reformed, 2002.

Frampton, Travis L. *Spinoza and the Rise of Historical Criticism of the Bible*. London: T. & T. Clark, 2006.

Frend, W. H. C. *Saints and Sinners in the Early Church: Differing and Conflicting Traditions in the First Six Centuries*. Theology and Life 11. Wilmington, DE: Michael Glazier, 1985.

———. *The Rise of the Monophysite Movement*. Cambridge: Cambridge University Press, 1972.

Gifford, James D., Jr. "Augustine: The Father of 'Christian Determinism.'" Paper presented at the 64th annual meeting of the Evangelical Theological Society, Milwaukee, WI, November 15–17, 2012.

———. *Perichoretic Salvation: The Believer's Union with Christ as a Third Type of Perichoresis*. Eugene, OR: Wipf & Stock, 2011.

———. "Three Levels of the Locative: Union with Christ in Creation, Reconciliation, and Salvation." Paper presented at the 67th annual meeting of the Evangelical Theological Society, November 16–18, 2015, Atlanta, GA.

Gillespie, Michael Allen. *The Theological Origins of Modernity*. Chicago: University of Chicago Press, 2009.

Gonzalez, Justo L. *From the Beginnings to the Council of Chalcedon*. Vol. 1 of *A History of Christian Thought*. Rev. ed. Nashville: Abingdon, 1991.

Goulder, Michael. "Hebrews and the Ebionites." *New Testament Studies* 49 (2003) 393–406.

Greer, Rowan A. *The Captain of Our Salvation: A Study in the Patristic Exegesis of Hebrews*. BGBE 15. Tübingen: Mohr Siebeck, 1973.

———. "The Man from Heaven: Paul's Last Adam and Apollinarius' Christ." In *Paul and the Legacies of Paul*, edited by W. S. Babcock, 165–92. Dallas: Southern Methodist University Press, 1990.

Gregory of Nazianzus. "Carm Theol IV, de Mundo V." In *Patrologia Graeca*, edited by J-P Migne, 37:421. 162 vols. Paris: Garnier, 1857–66.

———. *Epistle 101*. In *Nicene and Post-Nicene Fathers, Second Series*, edited by Philip Schaff and Henry Wace, 7:439–41. Peabody, MA: Hendrickson, 1994.

Gregory of Nyssa. *Against Eunomius*. In *Nicene and Post-Nicene Fathers, Second Series*, edited by Philip Schaff and Henry Wace, 5:33–248. Peabody, MA: Hendrickson, 1994.

———. *To Ablabius*. In *Nicene and Post-Nicene Fathers, Second Series*, edited by Philip Schaff and Henry Wace, 5:529–30. Peabody, MA: Hendrickson, 1994.

Gregory of Rimini. *First and Second Sentences*. St. Bonaventure, NY: Franciscan Institute, 1955.

Grillmeier, Aloys. *From the Apostolic Age to Chalcedon (451)*. Vol. 1 of *Christ in Christian Tradition*. Translated by John Bowden. 2nd ed. Atlanta: John Knox, 1976.

———. *From the Council of Chalcedon (451) to Gregory the Great (590–604)*. Vol. 2 of *Christ in Christian Tradition*. 4 vols. Atlanta: John Knox, 1987–2013.

Gunton, Colin E. "Augustine, the Trinity, and the Theological Crisis of the West." In *The Promise of Trinitarian Theology*, 30–55. London: T. & T. Clark, 1993.

———. "The End of Causality? The Reformers and Their Predecessors." In *The Doctrine of Creation: Essays in Dogmatics, History, and Philosophy*, edited by Colin E. Gunton, 63–82. London: T. & T. Clark, 2004.

Bibliography

———. *The One, the Three, and the Many: God, Creation and the Culture of Modernity: The 1992 Bampton Lectures*. Cambridge: Cambridge University Press, 1993.

———. *The Triune Creator: A Historical and Systematic Study*. Grand Rapids: Eerdmans, 1998.

Häkkinen, Sakari. "Ebionites." In *A Companion to Second Century Christian 'Heretics,'* edited by Antti Marjanen and Petri Luomanen, 247–78. Leiden: Brill, 2008.

Hannam, James. *God's Philosophers: How the Medieval World Laid the Foundations for Modern Science*. London: Icon, 2009.

Hanson, R. P. C. *The Search for the Christian Doctrine of God: The Arian Controversy, 318–381*. Edinburgh: T. & T. Clark, 1988.

Harrisville, Roy A., and Walter Sundberg. *The Bible in Modern Culture: Theology and Historical-Critical Method from Spinoza to Käsemann*. Grand Rapids: Eerdmans, 1995.

Hendryx, John. "Two Views of Regeneration." https://www.monergism.com/thethreshold/articles/onsite/twoviews.html.

Hinlicky, Paul R. *The Beloved Community: Critical Dogmatics after Christendom*. Grand Rapids: Eerdmans, 2015.

———. *Divine Complexity: The Rise of Creedal Christianity*. Minneapolis: Fortress, 2011.

———. *Divine Simplicity: Christ the Crisis of Metaphysics*. Grand Rapids: Baker, 2016.

———. *Paths Not Taken: Fates of Theology from Luther through Leibniz*. Grand Rapids: Eerdmans, 2009.

Hippolytus, *Refutation of All Heresies*. In *Ante-Nicene Fathers*, edited by A. Roberts and J. Donaldson, 5:9–162. Peabody, MA: Hendrickson, 1994.

Hodge, Charles. *Systematic Theology*. 3 vols. Grand Rapids: Eerdmans, 1993.

Hovorun, Cyril. *Will, Action and Freedom: Christological Controversies in the Seventh Century*. Leiden: Brill, 2008.

Hughes, Philip Edgecumbe. *The True Image: The Origin and Destiny of Man in Christ*. Grand Rapids: Eerdmans, 1989.

Hultgren, Arland J., and Steven A. Haggmark, eds. *The Earliest Christian Heretics: Readings from Their Opponents*. Minneapolis: Fortress, 2008.

Irenaeus. *Against Heresies*. In *Ante-Nicene Fathers*, edited by A. Cleveland Coxe, 1:309–67. Peabody, MA: Hendricksen, 1994.

Ishak, Shenouda M. *Christology and the Council of Chalcedon*. Denver: Outskirts, 2013.

James, Frank A., III. *Peter Martyr Vermigli: The Augustinian Inheritance of an Italian Reformer*. Oxford Theological Monographs. Oxford: Clarendon, 2006.

John of Damascus. *On the Orthodox Faith*. Popular Patristics Series. Translated by Norman Russell. Crestwood, NY: St. Vladimir's Seminary Press, 2022.

Justin Martyr. *Dialog with Trypho the Jew*. In *Ante-Nicene Fathers*, edited by W. Robertson Nicoll and A. Cleveland Coxe, 1:194–270. Peabody, MA: Hendrickson, 1994.

Kaiser, Christopher B. *Creational Theology and the History of Physical Science: The Creationist Tradition from Basil to Bohr*. Studies in the History of Christian Thought 78. Leiden: Brill, 1997.

Karfikova, Lenka. *Grace and the Will according to Augustine*. Supplements to *Vigiliae Christianae* 115. Translated by Marketa Janebova. Leiden: Brill, 2012.

Keech, Dominic. *The Anti-Pelagian Christology of Augustine of Hippo, 396–430*. Oxford: Oxford University Press, 2012.

Kelly, J. N. D. *Early Christian Doctrines*. Peabody, MA: Prince, 2007.

Kroeger, C. C. "Origen." In *Evangelical Dictionary of Theology*, edited by Walter A. Elwell, 870. 2nd ed. Grand Rapids: Baker, 2001.

Bibliography

Lahey, Stephen E. *John Wyclif.* Great Medieval Thinkers. Oxford: Oxford University Press, 2009.

Lee, Kam-Lun Edwin. *Augustine, Manichaeism, and the Good.* Patristic Studies 2. New York: Lang, 1999.

Leithart, Peter J. *Athanasius.* Foundations of Theological Exegesis and Christian Spirituality. Grand Rapids: Baker Academic, 2011.

Leitzman, Hans. *A History of the Early Church.* New York: World, 1961.

Letham, Robert. *The Holy Trinity in Scripture, History, Theology and Worship.* Phillipsburg, NJ: Presbyterian and Reformed, 2004.

Lethel, Francois-Marie. *Theologie de L'Agonie du Christ: La Liberte humaine du Fils de dieu et son importance soteriologique mises en Iumere par Saint Maxime le Confesseur.* Paris: Beauchesne, 1988.

Lindberg, David C. *The Beginnings of Western Science: The European Scientific Tradition in Philosophical, Religious, and Institutional Context, 600 B. C. to A. D. 1450.* Chicago: University of Chicago Press, 1992.

Loudovikos, Nikolaos. "Being and Essence Revisited: Reciprocal *Logoi* and Energies in Maximus the Confessor and Thomas Aquinas, and the Genesis of the Self-Referring Subject." *Revista Portuguesa de Filosofia* 72.1 (2016) 117–46.

Louth, Andrew. *Maximus the Confessor.* Early Church Fathers; London: Routledge, 1996.

———. "Why Did the Syrians Reject the Council of Chalcedon?" In *Chalcedon in Context: Church Councils 400–700,* edited by Richard Price and Mary Whitby, 107–16. Liverpool: University of Liverpool Press, 2009.

Luther, Martin. *Luther's Works.* Edited by Jaroslav Pelikan. 79 vols. Minneapolis: Concordia, 1962–2016.

MacLeod, Donald. *The Person of Christ.* Contours of Christian Theology. Downers Grove: InterVarsity, 1998.

Maximus the Confessor. *The Ascetic Life: The Four Centuries on Charity.* Translated by Polycarp Sherwood. Brooklyn: Angelico, 2020.

———. *Capita Gnostica.* Corpus Christianorm Series Graeca 89. Edited by Katrien Levrie. Turnhout: Brepols, 2018.

———. *Disputation with Pyrrhus of Constantinople.* In *Patrologia Graeca,* edited by J-P Migne, 91. 162 vols. Paris: Garnier, 1857–66.

———. *On the Difficulties of the Church Fathers: The Ambigua.* 2 vols. Edited and translated by Nicholas Constans. Cambridge, MA: Harvard University Press, 2014.

McCormack, Bruce. "Reformed Christology and the Westminster HFTC Report." https://docs.google.com/document/pub?id=1W1YMueiPFjozff5bfKJzXuAjheHZTmTtrZVmUC-Ss6I&pli=1.

McCready, Douglas. *He Came Down from Heaven: The Preexistence of Christ and the Christian Faith.* Downers Grove: InterVarsity 2005.

McGiffert, A. C. *The West from Tertullian to Erasmus.* Vol. 2 of *A History of Christian Thought.* New York: Scribner's, 1933.

McGowan, A. T. B. *The Divine Authenticity of Scripture: Retrieving and Evangelical Heritage.* Downers Grove: IVP Academic, 2007.

McGrath, Alister. *Heresy: A History of Defending the Truth.* San Francisco: HarperOne, 2009.

McGuckin, John Anthony. *St. Cyril of Alexandria and the Christological Controversy.* Crestwood, NY: St. Vladimir's Seminary Press, 2004.

McLeod, Frederick G. "The Significance of Constantinople II's Alteration of Chalcedon's Formula about Christ's Natures 'Coinciding in One *Prosopon.*'" *Irish Theological Quarterly* 77.4 (2012) 365–83.

Bibliography

McMullin, Ernan. "Darwin and the Other Christian Tradition." *Zygon* 46.2 (2011) 291–316.
Meyendorff, John. *Byzantine Theology: Historical Trends and Doctrinal Themes*. New York: Fordham University Press, 1983.
———. *Christ in Eastern Christian Thought*. Washington: Corpus, 1969.
———. *Christ in Eastern Christian Thought*. Crestwood, NY: St. Vladimir's Seminary Press, 1975.
———. *Imperial Unity and Christian Divisions: The Church from 450–680 A.D.* The Church in History 2. Crestwood, NY: St. Vladimir's Seminary Press, 1989.
Moran, Dermot. "John Scottus Eriugena." In *The Stanford Encyclopedia of Philosophy*, edited by Edward N. Zalta, n.p. https://plato.stanford.edu/archives/fall2008/entries/scottus-eriugena/.
Mosher, D. L. *St. Augustine: Eighty-Three Different Questions*. Washington: Catholic University Press of America, 1977.
Mozley, J. B. *A Treatise on the Augustinian Doctrine of Predestination*. London: Murray, 1855.
Muller, Richard A. *Christ and the Decree: Christology and Predestination in Reformed Theology from Calvin to Perkins*. Grand Rapids: Baker, 1988.
———. "The Christological Problem in the Thought of Jacobus Arminius." *Dutch Review of Church History* 68.2 (1988) 145–63.
Mullins, R. T. *The End of the Timeless God*. Oxford Studies in Analytic Theology. Oxford: Oxford University Press, 2016.
Murphy, Nancey. *Beyond Liberalism and Fundamentalism: How Modern and Postmodern Philosophy Set the Theological Agenda*. Rockwell Lecture Series 1. Valley Forge, PA: Trinity, 1996.
Need, Stephen W. *Truly Human and Truly Divine: The Story of Christ and the Seven Ecumenical Councils*. Peabody, MA: Hendrickson, 2008.
Norris, R. L. "Christological Models in Cyril of Alexandria." *Studia Patristica* 13 (1975) 255–68.
———. *Manhood and Christ: A Study in the Christology of Theodore of Mopsuestia*. Oxford: Clarendon, 1963.
Novatian. *On the Trinity*. In *Ante-Nicene Fathers*, edited by W. Robertson Nicoll and A. Cleveland Coxe, 5:611–44. Reprint, Peabody, MA: Hendrickson, 1994.
Oberman, Heiko A. *Archbishop Thomas Bradwardine: A Fourteenth Century Augustinian: A Study of his Theology in its Historical Context*. Utrecht: Drukkerijen en Uitgevers-Maatschappij v/h Kemink & Zoon N. V., 1957.
———. "Fourteenth-Century Religious Thought: A Premature Profile." In *The Dawn of the Reformation: Essays in Late Medieval and Early Reformation Thought*. Edinburgh: T. & T. Clark, 1986.
———. *The Two Reformations: The Journey from the Last Days to the New World*. Edited by Donald Weinstein. New Haven: Yale University Press, 2003.
Ogliari, Donato. *Gratia et Certamen: The Relationship between Grace and Free Will in the Discussion of Augustine with the So-Called Semi-Pelagians*. BETL. Louvain: Peeters, 2004.
Oliver, Simon. "Augustine on Creation, Providence, and Motion." *International Journal of Systematic Theology* 18.4 (2016) 379–98.
Origen. *Against Celsus*. In *Ante-Nicene Fathers*, edited by Alexander Roberts and James Donaldson, 4:395–669. Reprint, Peabody, MA: Hendrickson, 2004.
———. *On First Principles*. In *Ante-Nicene Fathers*, edited by Alexander Roberts and James Donaldson, 4:239–384. Reprint, Peabody, MA: Hendrickson, 2004.
Packer, J. I. *Engaging the Written Word of God*. Peabody, MA: Hendrickson, 2012.

Bibliography

Papandrea, James L. *The Earlest Christologies: Five Images of Christ in the Postapostolic Age.* Downers Grove: IVP Academic, 2016.

Pelikan, Jaroslav. *The Christian Tradition: A History of the Development of Doctrine.* 5 vols. Chicago: University of Chicago Press, 1971–89.

Phillips, Robin. "Why I Stopped Being a Calvinist (Part 5): A Deformed Christology." *Orthodoxy and Heterodoxy* (blog), January 23, 2014. https://blogs.ancientfaith.com/orthodoxyandheterodoxy/2014/01/23/why-i-stopped-being-a-calvinist-part-5-a-deformed-christology/.

Placher, William C. *The Domestication of Transcendence: How Modern Thinking about God Went Wrong.* Louisville: Westminster John Knox, 1998.

Prestige, G. L. *Fathers and Heretics.* London: SPCK, 1940.

Plotinus. *The Enneads.* Edited by A. H. Armstrong. Loeb Classical Library 444, 468. Cambridge, MA: Harvard University Press, 1984, 1998.

Radde-Gallwitz, Andrew. *Basil of Caesarea, Gregory of Nyssa, and the Transformation of Divine Simplicity.* Oxford Early Christian Studies. Oxford: Oxford University Press, 2009.

Raven, Charles E. *Apollinarianism: An Essay on the Christology of the Early Church.* Cambridge: Cambridge University Press, 1923.

Reventlow, Henning Graf. *The Authority of the Bible and the Rise of the Modern World.* Translated by John Bowden. Minneapolis: Fortress, 1985.

Richard, M. "L'introduction du mot 'hypostase' dans la theologie de l'incarnation." *Mélanges de Science Religieuse* 2 (1945) 5–32, 243–70.

Rist, John M. *Augustine: Ancient Thought Baptized.* Cambridge: Cambridge University Press, 1994.

Robinson, Perry. "Killing Your Father." *Energetic Procession* (blog), December 3, 2007. https://energeticprocession.wordpress.com/2007/12/03/killing-your-father/.

Rogers, Katherin. "The Traditional Doctrine of Divine Simplicity." *Religious Studies* 32.2 (1996) 165–86.

Russell, Norman. *Cyril of Alexandria.* Early Church Fathers. London: Routledge, 2000.

Schaff, Philip. *Nicene and Post-Nicene Christianity: From Constantine the Great to Gregory the Great, A. D. 311–600.* Vol. 3 of *History of the Christian Church.* Grand Rapids: Eerdmans, 1995.

Siecienski, Edward. *The Filioque: History of a Doctrinal Controversy.* Oxford Studies in Historical Theology. Oxford: Oxford University Press, 2012.

Smalley, Stephen. *1, 2, 3 John.* Word Biblical Commentary 51. Waco: Word, 1984.

Smith, Christian. *The Bible Made Impossible: Why Biblicism Is Not a Truly Evangelical Reading of Scripture.* Grand Rapids: Brazos, 2007.

Socrates. *History of the Church.* In *From Nicaea to Chalcedon: A Guide to the Literature and Its Background,* edited by Frances M. Young and Andrew Teal, 26–30. 2nd ed. Grand Rapids: Baker, 2010.

Solomon, Robert. *Continental Philosophy Since 1750: The Rise and Fall of the Self.* Oxford: Oxford University Press, 1988.

Sparks, Kenton L. *God's Word in Human Words: An Evangelical Appropriation of Critical Biblical Scholarship.* Grand Rapids: Baker Academic, 2008.

Spinoza, Baruch. *Ethics: Treatise on the Emendation of the Intellect and Selected Letters.* Translated by Samuel Shirley. Indianapolis: Hackett, 1992.

———. *Principles of Cartesian Philosophy with Metaphysical Thoughts.* Translated by Samuel Shirley. Indianapolis: Hackett, 1998.

Bibliography

Stead, Christopher. *Philosophy in Christian Antiquity.* Cambridge: Cambridge University Press, 1994.

Strehle, Stephen A. "The Extent of the Atonement within the Theological Systems of the Sixteenth and Seventeenth Centuries." ThD diss., Dallas Theological Seminary, 1980.

Tapia, Ralph J. *The Theology of Christ: Commentary.* Readings in Christology. New York: Bruce, 1971.

Teske, Roland J., ed. *St. Augustine on Genesis.* The Fathers of the Church: A New Translation 84. Washington: Catholic University Press of America, 1991.

Theokritoff, Elizabeth. "Creator and Creation." In *The Cambridge Companion to Orthodox Christian Theology,* edited by Mary B. Cunningham and Elizabeth Theokritoff, 63–77. Cambridge: Cambridge University Press, 2008.

Thomas Aquinas. *Summa Contra Gentiles.* Leopold Classic Library. Victoria, Australia: Leopold, 2017.

———. *Summa Theologica.* Claremont, CA: Coyote Canyon, 2018.

Thomas Bradwardine. *De Causa Dei, Contra Pelagium et de Virtute Causarum ad Suos Mertonenses.* London: ex Officia Nortoniana, 1618.

Thuesen, Peter J. *Predestination: The American Career of a Contentious Doctrine.* Oxford: Oxford University Press, 2009.

Thunberg, Lars. *Microcosm and Mediator: The Theological Anthropology of Maximus the Confessor.* 2nd ed. Peru, IL: Open Court, 1995.

Tollefsen, Torstein Theodor. *The Christocentric Cosmology of St. Maximus the Confessor.* Oxford Early Christian Studies 15. Oxford: Oxford University Press, 2008.

Torrance, Thomas F. *Theological Science.* Edinburgh: T. & T. Clark, 1996.

Tregg, Joseph W. *Origen.* The Early Church Fathers 3. London: Routledge, 1999.

Van Loon, Hans. *The Dyophysite Christology of Cyril of Alexandria.* Supplements to *Vigiliae Christianae* 96. Leiden: Brill, 2009.

Virgil. *The Aeneid.* Translated by Robert Fagles. London: Penguin Classics, 2008.

Walter, V. L. "Apollinarianism." In *Evangelical Dictionary of Theology,* edited by Walter A. Elwell, 81–82. 2nd ed. Grand Rapids: Baker, 2001.

Wells, Paul. *Cross Words: The Biblical Doctrine of the Atonement.* Fearn, Scotland: Christian Focus, 2006.

Wellum, Stephen J. *God the Son Incarnate: The Doctrine of Christ.* Foundations of Evangelical Theology. Wheaton: Crossway, 2016.

Wessling, Jordan. "Christology and Conciliar Authority: On the Viability of Monothelitism for Protestant Theology." In *Christology Ancient and Modern: Explorations in Constructive Dogmatics,* edited by Oliver D. Crisp and Fred Sanders, 151–70. Grand Rapids: Zondervan, 2013.

William of Ockham. *Opera Theologica.* Edited by Gedeon Gal. 10 vols. St. Bonaventure, NY: St. Bonaventure University Press, 1970.

Wildberg, Christian. "Neoplatonism." In *Stanford Encyclopedia of Philosophy,* edited by Edward N. Zalta, n.p. http://plato.stanford.edu/entries/neoplatonism/.

Wilhite, David E. *The Gospel according to Heretics: Discovering Orthodoxy through Early Christological Conflicts.* Grand Rapids: Baker Academic, 2015.

Williams, Rowan. *Arius: Heresy and Tradition.* Rev. ed. Grand Rapids: Eerdmans, 2002.

Wolfson, H. A. *Faith, Trinity, Incarnation.* Vol. 1 of *The Philosophy of the Church Fathers.* 2nd ed. Cambridge, MA: Harvard University Press, 1964.

Young, Frances M., and Andrew Teal. *From Nicaea to Chalcedon: A Guide to the Literature and Its Background.* 2nd ed. Grand Rapids: Baker, 2010.

Index

Abelard, 122
Absolute power, 149, 164–67, 169, 176–77, 208, 211, 214, 217
Adam, Karl, 57, 61, 66
Adelard of Bath, 165
Adoptionism, 15–17, 32, 34, 58
Alexander of Alexandria, 35, 39–41
Alexandria, Council of, 47, 59
Allen, David, 183, 192, 194
Allison, C. Fitzsimmons, 17, 20–21, 32–33, 52, 58, 63, 65, 67, 88–90, 95–97
Ammonius Saccas, 24
Anastasius, 78
Anatolios, Khaled: 22, 29, 35–40, 42–44
Anhypostasia, 100
Anselm of Canterbury, 115, 122, 165, 177–78, 193, 210, 213, 223
Apokatastasis, 26, 29, 54, 114, 120, 241, 244
Apollinarianism (cosmological), 11, 63, 71, 153, 157, 163, 166–67, 181, 182–83, 194–97, 202, 205, 207, 213–14, 235, 238
Apollinarianism (historical), 8, 12, 28, 51, 53–72, 73–75, 78–79, 83, 85, 88, 90, 92, 97, 100, 102, 105, 108, 114, 117–18, 120, 134, 156, 159, 182, 186, 189, 193, 196–97, 220
Apollinarius of Laodicea, 28, 55, 59–67, 68, 71, 76–77, 83, 92, 94–95, 99, 110–11, 163, 184, 186
Aquinas, Thomas, see Thomas
Arianism (cosmological), 11, 32, 119, 121, 157–58, 166–67, 173, 181, 189, 202, 206–20, 223–24, 229, 235, 237
Arianism (historical), 8, 12, 27, 31–33, 34–52, 53, 55, 57–61, 63–66, 68, 73–74, 78, 88–89, 92, 97, 117–20, 121, 134, 148, 156, 159, 193, 195, 218–21, 223, 228, 236, 238, 245

Arius of Alexandria, 28, 31, 34–41, 48, 54–55, 67–68, 71, 76–77, 112
Aristolaus, 91–92
Aristotle, 3, 61, 112, 123, 125, 138, 167, 170–71, 175–76, 187, 191, 220
Arminius, Arminian, 190, 193–95, 238, 241–42
Armstrong, A. H., 169
Asterius, 42
Athanasius of Alexandria, 27, 40–47, 49–50, 54, 56–57, 59, 65, 77, 82–84, 86, 104, 110, 114, 121, 132, 135, 137–38, 173–74, 190, 233, 239
Augustine of Hippo, 2, 7, 9, 10, 11, 41, 68–72, 117–22, 124–25, 132–33, 134–35, 137, 144–58, 159–68, 170, 172–76, 178–81, 182–83, 185–86, 188–89, 192–96, 200–201, 205, 207–8, 213, 220, 224, 229, 234, 236, 240–41, 243–44, 246
Averroes, 167
Ayres, Lewis, 26–27, 31, 34–35, 37, 40–42, 57

Bacon, Francis, 132, 208–10, 212, 215
von Balthasar, Hans Urs, 45, 82, 103, 107–9
Barth, Karl, 1
Basil of Caesarea, 27, 41, 44, 47–50, 59, 65, 136, 138, 146, 166, 171, 175, 219
Bathrellos, Demetrios, 63–64, 100, 104–7, 109–11, 195
Bazaar of Heraclides, 88
Behe, Michae,: 50
Behr, John, 21–23, 27, 35, 41, 45–47, 59–60, 62–64
Beeley, Christopher, 23, 25–26, 28, 36–37, 39, 115
Bethune-Baker, J. F., 31, 37–38, 40, 78–79, 84, 89–90, 94
Beza, Theodore, 192, 194, 238, 242

Index

Biel, Gabriel, 185
Blaising, Craig, 39
Blowers, Paul, 141
Bonaventure, 145
Bonner, Gerald, 149, 154, 160–61
Boyle, Robert, 217
Bradwardine, Thomas, 156, 175–76, 183–85, 192, 205
Bradshaw, David, 4
Brown, Raymond, 20
Buckley, Michael, 210, 212, 219–23, 225–26, 229
Bulgakov, Sergei, 26
Bussanich, Donald, 5–6
Butner, Glenn ,2

Calvin, John, 175, 188–92, 194, 206, 214, 241–43
Cassian, John, 161
Cerinthian Docetism, 19
Cessario, Roman, 130
Chalcedon, Council of, 58, 67, 91, 96–99, 105, 139, 192, 244
Chalcedonian logic, 9–10, 112, 117–18, 139, 144
Christotokos, 79–80
Chrysostom, John, 150, 162
Cicero, 226–27
Clarke, Samuel, 218–19
Clement of Rome, 135
Coleridge, Samuel Taylor, 174
Communication of properties, 28, 60, 76
Conceptual distinction, 5, 123, 125
Condemnation of 1277, 125, 220
Constantine the Great, 39, 41
Constantinople, First Council of, 67–68, 76, 193
Constantinople, Second Council of, 101, 136, 192
Constantinople, Third Council of, 10, 115–16, 117, 180, 192
Continuous creationism, 198–99, 201–4
Counterfactuals, 152
Craig, Edward, 211
Craig, William Lane, 104
Crisp, Oliver, 126, 198–205
Cross, F. L., 163
Cyril of Alexandria, 58, 77–88, 90, 91–94, 97–99, 104, 114, 148, 233

Daane, James, 123, 155, 187, 189–91
Daley, Brian, 99
Damian, Peter, 164
Danielou, Jean, 14
Davis, Leo Donald, 27, 39–41, 46, 51, 67, 75, 78–79, 82–83, 87–88, 94–98, 100–104, 109, 111–12, 114–15
Decree, divine, 189–94, 197–98, 206, 242
Deism, 146, 213, 217–19, 232, 237

Demarest, Bruce, 104
DeProspo, R. C., 201–3
Descartes, Rene, 132, 209–17, 219, 223–25, 232, 236–38, 242
Determinism, 7, 11, 63, 116, 125, 130, 149, 155–56, 166–67, 174, 176, 184, 186–91, 194, 197, 201, 204–6, 213–14, 220, 234–36, 239, 241, 244–45
Deus absconditus, 187–88, 240
DeWeese, Garrett, 104
Dichotomist-dualism, 7, 9, 10, 23, 27–32, 34, 42, 51, 53–54, 58, 60–61, 68–69, 73, 78, 88–90, 127, 129–30, 135, 147–48, 157, 165, 167, 171, 188–89, 205–6, 210, 213, 215–16, 218, 224, 234–38, 241–42, 244
Diderot, Denis, 229
Diodore of Tarsus, 57, 73–74, 79, 83, 192
Dionysius of Alexandria, 30
Dioscorus of Alexandria, 94–98
Docetism (cosmological), 11, 135, 157, 181, 182, 190, 197–206, 207, 235, 245
Docetism (historical), 12, 13, 14, 18–21, 32–33, 53, 55, 58–59, 67, 102, 108, 134, 197, 244
Dolezal, James, 126, 130, 216
D'Souza, Romero, 145–46, 164
Duby, Steven, 172, 195
Duns Scotus, John, 125–26, 130, 149, 171, 208

Ebionism (cosmological), 11, 135, 157, 181, 189–90, 202, 206–7, 220–31, 235, 237
Ebionism (historical), 12, 13, 14–17, 18, 32–33, 34, 53, 55, 58, 73, 89, 97, 102, 134, 197, 244
Ecthesis of 636, 104
Edwards, Jonathan, 27, 197–205, 229–31, 240, 242, 245
Elxaism, 17
Elwood, Douglas, 203
Enhypostasia, 100–101
Enlightenment, 182, 212, 215–16, 221–22, 224, 238, 244
Enns, Peter, 99
Ephesus, Council of, 68, 88–89, 91, 93
Epiphanaus, 30
Erasmus, 130, 185–86, 214
Erickson, Millard, 16, 18–19, 36–39, 53, 56–57, 79
Eriugena, John Scotus, 164, 223
Eunomius of Cyzicus, 42, 47–50, 74, 85, 114, 117
Eusebius of Caesarea, 40–42, 220
Eustathius of Antioch, 43, 57, 73–74, 78, 83
Eutyches, 95–97, 108
Extra calvinisticum, 84

Index

Fairbairn, Donald, 2, 77–78
Farrell, Joseph, 3–4, 5–8, 24–27, 30, 41, 44, 48–51, 64, 68–70, 103, 111–15, 117, 119–20, 136, 140, 142–43, 150–53, 156, 160, 163, 166–67, 196–97, 200, 217
Feinberg, John, 1
Fesko, John, 162, 183–85, 188
Feuerbach, Ludwig, 229–30, 236
Filioque, 121–22, 162
Flavian of Constantinople, 95, 98
Florus of Lyons, 183, 192
Foundationalism, 171, 209–10, 215–16
Frame, John, 1
Frampton, Travis, 223
Francis of Assisi, 171
Frend, W. H. C., 77, 99
Fulbert of Chartres, 166

Galileo, 132, 209, 211
Gifford, James, 135, 148, 177
Gillespie, Michael, 124, 126–30, 132, 185–88, 208–12, 214–18, 223, 225–27, 229
Gnomic will, 109–11
Gonzalez, Justo, 14–17, 19, 22–23, 27–28, 30, 47, 56, 58, 64–66, 73–74, 76, 78, 83, 86
Gottschalk of Orbais. 156, 162–64, 166, 174, 183, 192
Goulder, Michael, 17
Greer, Rowan, 57–58, 64, 74, 80–83
Gregory of Nazianzus, 27, 47, 65, 70, 74, 112, 135, 138, 146, 193
Gregory of Neocaesarea, 30
Gregory of Nyssa, 27, 35, 47, 49–50, 60, 65, 103–5, 135, 145–46
Gregory of Rimini, 156, 175–76, 183–86, 205
Gregory Palamas, 133
Grillmeier, Aloys, 15, 19, 56, 60–62, 65–67, 73–77, 92–93, 98–99
Gunton, Colin, 69, 136–38, 145, 158, 167–68, 170–74, 205, 208, 211, 213, 218–19, 225, 227–31

Haggmark, Steven, 15
Häkkinen, Sakari, 15
Hannam, James, 127, 129
Hanson, R. P. C., 30, 35–38, 43–45
Harrisville, Roy and Walter Sundberg, 131
Von Harnack, Adolf, 32
Hegel, G. W. F., 229
Hendryx, John, 179
Heraclitus, 104
Hincmar of Rheims, 163

Hinlicky, Paul, 18, 20, 22–23, 26–27, 30, 37–38, 40–41, 52, 64, 123–24, 126, 132–33, 178, 187, 201, 216–17, 223–24, 226–27
Hippolytus, 16, 23
Hobbes, Thomas, 132, 213–14, 223–24
Hodge, Charles, 1
Homoousios, 40–41, 43–44, 46, 55, 187
Honorius, 104–5, 115
Hosius of Cordoba, 40
Hovorun, Cyril, 62, 75, 82, 99, 103, 105, 110, 178
Hughes, Philip, 60, 66
Hultgren, Arland, 15
Hume, David, 165, 224–25
Hypostatic union, 85–87, 94, 98–101, 103, 106, 108, 112

Ibas of Edessa, 101
Idealism, 198, 201, 203, 210, 212
Identity thesis, 7, 9, 10, 25, 35, 42, 103, 112–13, 117, 120–21, 123, 130, 132, 134, 137, 142, 145, 147–49, 152, 155, 157–58, 159, 164, 172–73, 181, 184, 186, 190–91, 195, 199–201, 205, 207, 210, 216, 219, 221, 224, 233–34, 242
Irenaeus of Lyons, 15, 84, 136–37, 141, 173, 246
Ishak, Shenouda, 99
Isidore of Seville, 163

James, Frank, 163–64, 169–70, 184
Jerome, 27, 59, 162
John of Antioch, 88, 92
John of Damascus, 3, 31
Julian of Eclanum, 68, 70–71
Justin Martyr, 15, 22, 135–36

Kaiser, Christopher, 135–36, 138, 146–47, 149, 164–68, 170, 175–77, 209–10, 213, 218–20, 229
Kant, Immanuel, 174, 209, 215, 224–29, 237, 241–42, 244
Karfikova, Lenka, 149, 151, 153–54
Keech, Dominic, 68, 70–71
Kelly, J. N. D., 15, 18, 23, 35, 39, 56, 66, 73–74, 76, 162
Kroeger, C. C., 27

Lahey, Stephen, 184
Lee, Kam-Lun Edwin, 149, 151, 153
Leithart, Peter, 44
Leitzman, Hans, 40
Leo I, 68, 95–98
Leontius of Byzantium, 100, 106
Leontius of Jerusalem, 100, 106
Lessing, Gotthold, 155

Index

Lessius, Leonard, 221–22
Letham, Robert, 48
Lethel, Francois-Marie, 112
Lewis, C. S., 243
Lewis, Gordon, 104
Limited atonement, 163, 192–97, 205
Lindberg, David, 122, 125
Locke, John, 225
Logoi, 139–44, 145, 158, 159, 169, 173–74, 244
Lombard, Peter, 165
Loudovikos, Nikolaos, 140–41, 144, 168–69
Louth, Andrew, 57, 86, 102, 105–9, 112
Lucian of Antioch, 30, 35, 39, 54, 74, 83
Luther, Martin, 107, 129–30, 185–90, 195, 206, 210–11, 213–14, 224, 232, 237, 240, 243

Macarius of Antioch, 115
MacLeod, Donald, 18–19, 59, 65, 100
Maimonides, Moses, 167
Malchion, 83
Manichaeism, 150–51, 160
Marcellus of Ancyra, 41, 43, 57
Marcionite Docetism, 19
Marx, Karl, 230–31, 236
Maximus the Confessor, 101–2, 105–16, 118, 133, 135, 138–44, 145, 147, 158, 159, 169, 173–74, 191, 233, 244
McCormack, Bruce, 98–99, 192
McGiffert, A. C., 157
McGowan, A. T. B., 224–25, 228
McGrath, Alister, 16, 19, 34, 37, 52
McGuckin, John, 62, 74, 80–83, 85–86, 99
McLeod, Frederick, 74–75, 101
McMullin, Ernan, 146
Methodius of Olympus, 35, 37
Meyendorff, John, 26, 49, 57, 74–75, 99, 106–7, 110, 114–15, 136–43
Modernism, modernity, 128, 132–33, 173, 208, 212–15, 217–18, 231–32, 235, 237, 244
Monergism, 162, 179–80, 188, 194, 245
Monism, 7, 9, 20, 23, 28–29, 31–32, 42, 51, 53–54, 56, 58, 60–61, 63, 68, 73, 88, 90, 125, 127, 129–30, 135, 147, 154–55, 157, 162, 165, 167, 170–71, 186–89, 198, 201–2, 204–6, 207–8, 212–16, 218, 224, 231–32, 234–37, 241–42, 244
Monoenergism, 62, 75, 99, 102–5, 108, 115, 143, 152–53, 155, 177–80, 185, 192, 220, 235, 245
Monophysitism (cosmological), 10, 11, 147–50, 155–56, 158, 159, 163, 172, 177, 179, 181, 182, 185, 187, 189, 194–96, 202, 235

Monophysitism (historical), 8, 12, 28, 32, 58, 62, 66, 86, 91–15, 117–18, 120, 134, 155–57, 160, 178, 196–97
Monothelitism, 62, 104–5, 107, 111–13, 115, 117–18, 127, 139, 151, 155, 235
Moran, Dermot, 164
Moreland, J. P., 104
Mosher, D. L., 145
Mozley, J. B., 149
Muller, Richard, 180, 192–93
Mullins, R. T., 120, 122–23, 126
Murphy, Nance,: 216

Natura naturans, 6, 126, 201, 203, 240
Need, Stephen, 101–2
Nestorianism (cosmological), 10, 147, 153, 156–58, 159, 172, 176–79, 181, 193–96, 208–9, 227, 235
Nestorianism (historical), 8, 12, 30, 32, 58, 68, 72, 73–90, 91–93, 97–102, 115, 117, 120, 147–48, 152, 156, 160, 178, 192–93, 196, 236
Nestorius, 28, 57, 66, 77–89, 92, 97, 110, 148, 178, 242
Newton, Isaac, 218–20, 225, 236
Nicaea, Council of, 39–42, 51, 53, 58–59
Nietzsche, Friedrich, 224
Nominalism, 10, 126–28, 130–32, 134, 164, 172–74, 184, 186–87, 192–93, 197, 205–6, 208, 210–11, 216, 218, 229, 236, 242
Norris, R. L., 86, 196
Novatian, 23

Obermann, Heiko, 175, 183–84
Occasionalism, 190, 198, 202–4, 231, 240, 242
Ogliari, Donato, 150–51, 153, 154, 161–62, 188
Oliver, Simon, 146–47
Ordinary power, 149, 165, 167, 169, 177, 186, 208–9, 217
Ordo Theologiae, 3, 32, 47, 49, 52, 58, 62, 69, 73, 86, 104, 106, 108, 148, 152–53, 155, 174, 178, 192, 240, 243
Origen of Alexandria, 7, 10, 23–32, 34–38, 42–45, 51, 53–59, 64–65, 68–69, 71, 74, 83, 86, 101, 114–15, 117–21, 128, 134–37, 139, 142–43, 147, 157, 162, 164, 168, 174, 187, 190, 200, 211, 213, 219–21, 224–25, 233, 241–42, 244, 246
Origenism, 31, 35, 83
Origenist Problematic, 25–26, 28–29, 31, 38, 42–43, 45, 113, 117, 125–26, 132, 136–37, 147–48, 159, 164, 168, 190, 199–200, 203, 208, 211, 219, 233
Original guilt, 150–51, 220

Index

Packer, J. I., 228–29
Panentheism, 135, 203–4, 234
Papandrea, James, 15
Pantheism, 135, 164, 174, 190, 199, 203, 207, 212, 219, 223–24, 231, 234, 237
Partitive exegesis, 45–46
Paul of Samosata, 40, 55, 77
Pelagianism, 68, 151, 160–61, 196, 226
Pelikan, Jaroslav, 37, 79–80, 89, 102–5, 112, 114–15, 163, 185–86
Phillips, Robin, 180, 185
Philo of Alexandria, 139
Photinus, 77
Placher, William, 185–87, 210, 217, 219
Plato, Platonism, Neoplatonism, 3, 23–25, 28–29, 54, 69, 114, 117, 128, 136–38, 149, 168, 173, 176, 187, 199, 201–4, 211, 220, 225, 234
Plotinian ambiguity, 7, 9, 10, 20, 25, 27–28, 32, 34–35, 42, 53–54, 56, 58, 61, 78, 103, 110, 112–13, 117, 121, 125, 127, 130, 134–35, 137, 147–48, 155, 157–58, 161, 167–68, 184, 186, 189–91, 195–96, 198, 203–6, 207, 211–16, 218, 224, 226, 231, 236, 238, 240, 244
Plotinus, 5–6, 24, 120, 126, 142, 169, 199, 204, 227, 240, 245
Pulcheria, 96
Preaching of Peter, The, 15
Predestination, doctrine of, 69, 130, 149, 151–57, 159, 163–64, 169–70, 175–76, 178, 180, 182–88, 192–93, 195, 197, 203, 205, 214, 242
Prestige, G. L., 82
Proclus of Cyzicus, 94
Pyrrhus of Constantinople, 108, 113

Radde-Gallwitz, Andrew, 5–6, 26, 47–49
Rationes seminales, 145–49, 153, 157, 159, 164, 166, 168, 172, 186, 208, 213, 234
Raven, Charles, 64
Realism, 127
Reformation, Reformers, 128–31, 133, 173, 175–77, 180, 182, 185–95, 208, 213–14, 216, 220, 231, 237, 245
Renaissance, 128–29, 133, 217, 231
Replacement Docetism, 19
Reunion Formula, 91–93, 97–98
Reventlow, Henning, 129
Richard, M., 62
Rist, John, 149
Robinson, Perry, 46, 205
Robber Synod, 95–96
Rogers, Katherin, 126

Roscelin, John, 164
Russell, Norman, 88–89, 91–92

Sabellianism, 39, 54–55, 117
Schaff, Philip, 51
Schleiermacher, F. D. E., 30, 174, 188, 228–29, 237
Sergius of Constantinople, 103–4, 112
Severus of Antioch, 99
Shepherd of Hermas, 57
Siecienski, Edward, 121–22
Smalley, Stephen, 17
Smith, Christian, 215
Socrates (historian), 77
Solomon, Robert, 228
Sophronius of Jerusalem, 103–4
Sparks, Kenton, 129, 209
Spinoza, Baruch, 199, 217, 223–24, 229, 236
Stead, Christopher, 30
Strehle, Stephen, 194
Strong, A. H., 104
Subordinationism, 21–23, 27, 43, 46, 195
Symmachus, 15
Synod of Orange, 156, 160, 162

Tapia, Ralph, 57, 61, 66, 73, 85, 92–94
Tertullian of Carthage, 58, 135, 239
Theodore of Mopsuestia, 28, 57, 73–80, 82–83, 89, 93, 99, 101, 110, 178
Theodore Pharan, 105
Theodoret of Cyrus, 93, 96, 101
Theodosius II, 95–96
Theophilus of Antioch, 57
Theotokos, 77–78, 84, 87–88
Thomas Aquinas, Thomism: 1, 2, 10, 114, 122–30, 160, 167–72, 174–75, 177–78, 184, 190, 199–201, 207–8, 210, 213, 216, 221, 223, 230–31, 235–38, 242–43
Thuesen, Peter, 169, 175
Thunberg, Lars, 112, 139–40
Tillich, Paul, 132
Timothy the Cyrillian, 98
Tollefson, Torstein, 9, 138–40
Tome to Flavian, 95–96, 98
Torrance, Thomas, 124, 170
Tregg, Joseph, 24
Turretin, Francis, 190–91

Universals, 164, 168, 171–74, 186

Valentinian Docetism, 19
Van Loon, Hans, 93–94
Vermigli, Peter Martyr, 184
Virgil, 185–86

Index

Walter, V. L., 59
Wells, Paul, 193
Wellum, Stephen, 28, 100
Wessling, Jordan, 12, 104
Whiston, William, 218–20
Wildberg, Christian, 117
Wilhite, David, 16, 19, 54–55, 67, 95
William of Conches, 165–66
William of Ockham, 10, 126–29, 132–33, 137, 149, 164, 171–74, 176, 183, 185–86, 208, 213, 216, 223, 227–29, 231–32, 235–37, 240, 243, 245
Williams, Rowan, 26, 30, 34–36, 39

Wolfson, H. A., 145
Word-flesh Christology, 56–66, 73–76, 82, 85, 94, 114
Word-man Christology, 57, 73–74, 76
Wycliffe, John, 156, 175, 184–86

Young, Frances and Andrew Teal, 80–81, 83–84, 86–88, 93

Zero-sum game, 7, 179, 184–85, 196, 198, 201, 207, 215, 218, 229, 231, 235–36
Zwingli, Ulrich, 188

www.ingramcontent.com/pod-product-compliance
Lightning Source LLC
Chambersburg PA
CBHW081348230426
43667CB00017B/2760